Security Markets
Stochastic Models

This is a volume in
ECONOMIC THEORY, ECONOMETRICS,
AND MATHEMATICAL ECONOMICS

Consulting Editor: Karl Shell, *Cornell University*

A complete list of titles in this series is available from the Publishers upon request.

Security Markets
Stochastic Models

Darrell Duffie

Graduate School of Business
Stanford University
Stanford, California

ACADEMIC PRESS, INC.
Harcourt Brace Jovanovich, Publishers
Boston   San Diego   New York   Berkeley
London   Sydney   Tokyo   Toronto

ACADEMIC PRESS, INC.
San Diego, California 92101

United Kingdom Edition published by
ACADEMIC PRESS LIMITED
24-28 Oval Road, London NW1 7DX

Library of Congress Cataloging-in-Publication Data

Duffie, Darrell.
  Security markets / Darrell Duffie.
    p. cm. — (Economic theory, econometrics, and mathematical
  economics)
    Bibliography: p.
    Includes index.
    ISBN 0-12-223345-X
    1. Securities — Mathematical models. I. Title. II. Series.
  HG4515.2.D84 1988
  332.63′2′0724 — dc19   87-28917
                                                              CIP

PRINTED IN THE UNITED STATES OF AMERICA
  90 91 92 93   9 8 7 6 5 4 3

To my parents

CONTENTS

DETAILED CONTENTS

Chapter II. Stochastic Economies   103

Chapter III. Discrete–Time Asset Pricing 169

PREFACE

This work addresses the allocational role and valuation of financial securities in competitive markets with symmetrically informed agents. The intended audience includes researchers and graduate students interested in the economic theory of security markets. Beginning with a review of general equilibrium theory in one period settings under uncertainty, the book then covers equilibrium and arbitrage pricing theory using the classical discrete and continuous time models. Topics include equilibrium with incomplete markets, the Modigliani–Miller Theorem, the Sharpe–Lintner Capital Asset Pricing Model, the Harrison–Kreps theory of martingale representation of security prices, stationary Markov asset pricing à la Lucas, Merton's theory of consumption and asset choice in continuous time (with recent extensions), the Black–Scholes Option Pricing Formula (with various discrete–time and continuous–time proofs and extensions), Breeden's Consumption–Based Capital Asset Pricing Model in continuous time (with Rubinstein's discrete–time antecedents), and the Cox–Ingersoll–Ross theory of the term structure of interest rates. The book also presents the background mathematical techniques, including fixed point theorems, duality theorems of vector spaces, probability theory, the theory of Markov processes, dynamic programming in discrete and continuous–time, stochastic integration, the Ito calculus, stochastic differential equations, and solution methods for elliptic partial differential equations. A more complete list of topics is given in the Table of Contents. This book is the latest version of lecture notes used for the past four years in the doctoral finance program of the Graduate School of Business at Stanford University.

As an empirical domain, finance is aimed at specific answers, such as an appropriate numerical value for a given security, or an optimal number of its shares to hold. As its title suggests, this is a book on finance theory. It adds a new perspective to the excellent books by Fama and Miller (1972), Mossin

(1973), Fama (1976), Ingersoll (1987), Huang and Litzenberger (1988), and Jarrow (1988).

The economic primitives and constructs used here are defined from first principles. A reader who has covered basic microeconomic theory, say at the level of the text by Varian (1984), will have a comfortable preparation in economic theory. The background mathematics have been included, although the reader is presumed to have covered some linear algebra and the basics of undergraduate real analysis, in particular the notion of convergence of a sequence and the classical calculus of several variables. O'Nan (1976) is a useful introduction to linear algebra; Bartle (1976) is a recommended undergraduate survey of real analysis. Although there is no presumption of graduate preparation in measure theory or functional analysis, any familiarity with these subjects will yield a commensurate ability to focus on the central economic principles at play. The book by Royden (1968) is an excellent introduction to functional analysis and measure; Chung (1974) and Billingsley (1986) have prepared standards on probability theory. A knowledge of stochastic processes and control would be of great preparatory value, but not a prerequisite.

Standard point–set–function notation is used. For example, $x \in X$ means that the point x is an element of the set X of points; $X \cap Y$ denotes the set of points that are elements of both X and Y, and so on. A function f mapping a set X into another set Y is denoted $f : X \to Y$. If the *domain* X and *range* Y are implicit, the function is denoted $x \mapsto f(x)$. On the real line, for example, $x \mapsto x^2$ denotes the function mapping any number x to its square. For functions $f : X \to Y$ and $g : Y \to Z$, the *composition* $h : X \to Z$ defined as $x \mapsto g[f(x)]$ is denoted either $g \circ f$ or $g(f)$. The notation $\lim_{\alpha \downarrow \beta} f(\alpha)$ means the limit, when it exists, of $\{f(\alpha_n)\}$, where $\{\alpha_n\}$ is any real sequence converging to β with $\alpha_n > \beta$ for all n. The subset of a set A satisfying a property $\mathcal{P}$ is denoted $\{x \in A : x$ satisfies $\mathcal{P}\}$. *Set subtraction* is defined by $A \setminus B = \{x \in A : x \notin B\}$, not to be confused with the vector difference of sets $A - B$ defined in Section 1. The symbols $\Longrightarrow$ and $\Longleftrightarrow$ mean "implies" and "if and only if", respectively. For notational ease, we denote the real numbers by R.

The chapters are broken into sections by topic, with each section organized in a traditional format of three parts: a body of results and discussion, a set of exercises, and notes to relevant literature. The body of each section is divided into "paragraphs", as we shall call them, lettered $\mathbf{A}, \mathbf{B}, \ldots$. Within each paragraph there is at most one "lemma", one "proposition", one "theorem", and so on. The theorem of Paragraph C of Section 3, for example, is referred to as Theorem 3C. A mathematical relation numbered (6) in Section 9, for example, is called "relation (9.6)" outside of Section

Table 1.   A First Reading

Topics	Paragraphs
Introduction	0 A–K
Vector Spaces*	1 A–G
Preferences*	2 A–G
Market Equilibrium	3 A–F
Portfolios	7 A–E
Probability*	4 A–E
Special Choice Spaces*	6 A–G
The CAPM	11 A–E
Event Tree Economies	12 A–G
Conditional Probability*	9 A–D
Stochastic Processes*	14 A–F
Markov Processes*	18 A–E
Markov Control*	19 A–H
Discrete–Time Pricing	20 A–C
Stochastic Integrals*	15 A–D
Ito Calculus*	21 A–E
Black–Scholes Modeling	22 A–I
Diffusion Control*	23 A
Consumption–Portfolio Control	24 A–E
Continuous–Time Pricing	25 A–M

*Background Concepts

9, and merely "relation (6)" inside Section 9. The end of an example is indicated by ♠.

Although a large number of new results appear here, many are in the way of tying up loose ends. The literature notes at the end of each section are principally for directing attention to proofs and additional results and perspectives. The Notes also attempt, where possible, to point out historical responsibility.

The material has been organized in a more or less logical topic order, first providing background principles or techniques, then applying them. Many sections become more advanced toward the later paragraphs. A reader would be well advised to skip over difficult material on a first pass. A reasonable one semester course or first reading can be organized as indicated in Table 1. The table follows a roughly vertical prerequisite precedence, with background material indicated by an asterisk. The list can be shortened somewhat for a one quarter course by leaving out some of the background material and "waving hands", with the usual risks that entails. A compromise was reached in a one quarter course at Stanford University organized on the above lines, with the background reading assigned for homework along with one problem assignment for each lecture.

I am grateful for the TEX assistance and patience of Andrea Reisman, Teri Bush, Ann Bucher, and Jill Fukuhara. I thank Karl Shell for connecting me with Academic Press, where Bill Sribney, Carolyn Artin, Iris Kramer, and a proofreader were all friendly, patient, and careful. I am also grateful for support from the Graduate School of Business at Stanford University and from the Mathematical Sciences Research Institute at Berkeley, California.

For helpful comments and corrections, I thank Matthew Richardson, Tong–sheng Sun, David Cariño, Susan Cheng, Laurie Simon, Bronwyn Hall, Matheus Mesters, Bob Thomas, Matthew Jackson, Leo Vanderlinden, Jay Muthuswamy, Tom Smith, Alex Triantis, Joe El Masri, Ted Shi, Jay Merves, Elizabeth Olmsted, Teeraboon Intragumtornchai, Pegaret Schuerger, Jonathan Paul, Charles Cuny, Steven Keehn, Peter Wilson, Michael Harrison, Andrew Atkeson, Elchanan Ben Porath, Mark Cronshaw, Peter DeMarzo, Ruth Freedman, Tamim Bayoumi, Michihiro Kandori, Jung-jin Lee, Kjell Nyborg, Ken Judd, Phillipe Artzner, Richard Stanton, Robert Whitelaw, Kobi Boudoukh, Farid Ait Sahlia, Philip Hay, Jerry Feltham, Robert Keeley, Dorothy Koehl, and, especially, Ruth Williams. I am myself responsible for the remaining errors, and offer sincere apologies to anyone whose work has been overlooked or misinterpreted.

Much of my interest and work on this subject originally stems from collaboration with my close friend Chi–fu Huang. By working jointly on related projects, I have also been fortunate to learn from Matthew Jackson, Wayne Shafer, Tong–sheng Sun, John Geanakoplos, Andy McLennan, Bill Zame, Mark Garman, Andreu Mas–Colell, Hugo Sonnenschein, Larry Epstein, Ken Singleton, Philip Protter, and Henry Richardson. David Luenberger's help as a teacher and friend is of special note. There is a great intellectual debt to those who developed this theory. Kenneth Arrow, Michael Harrison, David Kreps, and Andreu Mas–Colell have had a particular influence also by way of their personal guidance or example.

Darrell Duffie

INTRODUCTION

We first introduce several basic principles of security markets. A formal treatment begins with Chapter I. The discussion here is mainly at an informal level, and designed to provide some feeling for the theory of security markets in a unified framework.

A. The theory starts with the notion of competitive market equilibrium. As a special case, consider a vector space L (such as R^n) of marketed choices and a finite set $\{1, \ldots, I\}$ of agents, each defined by an endowment ω_i in L and a utility functional u_i on L. A *feasible allocation* is a collection $x_1, \ldots, x_I$ of choices, with $x_i \in L$ allocated to agent i, satisfying $\sum_{i=1}^{I}(x_i - \omega_i) = 0$. An *equilibrium* is a feasible allocation $x_1, \ldots, x_I$ and a non–zero linear *price functional* p on L satisfying, for each agent i,

$$x_i \quad \text{solves} \quad \max_{z \in L} \quad u_i(z) \quad \text{subject to} \quad p \cdot z \le p \cdot \omega_i. \qquad (*)$$

A feasible allocation $x_1, \ldots, x_I$ is *optimal* if there is no other feasible allocation $y_1, \ldots, y_I$ such that $u_i(y_i) > u_i(x_i)$ for all i. This definition is refined in Section 3. Significantly, an equilibrium allocation is optimal and an optimal allocation is, with regularity conditions and a re–allocation of the total endowment, an equilibrium allocation. For the former implication, we merely note that if $(x_1, \ldots, x_I, p)$ is an equilibrium and if $y_1, \ldots, y_I$ is an allocation with $u_i(y_i) > u_i(x_i)$ for all i, then $p \cdot y_i > p \cdot x_i$ for all i, implying $p \cdot \sum_{i=1}^{I} y_i > p \cdot \sum_{i=1}^{I} \omega_i$, which contradicts $\sum_{i=1}^{I} y_i - \omega_i = 0$. Thus an equilibrium allocation is optimal. We defer the converse result to Section 3. Adding production possibilities to these results is straightforward.

The competitive market model has developed a degree of acceptance as a benchmark for the theory of security markets because of the above optimality property, its simplicity, and the natural decentralized nature of the allocation decision, given prices. It is a heavily simplified model

1

of a market economy. Additional credibility stems from the existence of equilibria under little more than simple continuity, convexity, and non–satiation assumptions, and from the fact that equilibrium allocations can be viewed in different ways as the outcome of strategic bargaining behavior by agents.

B.   In the original concept of competitive markets, the vector choice space L was taken to be the *commodity space* R^C, for some number $C \geq 1$ of commodities, with a typical element $x = (x_1, \ldots, x_C) \in R^C$ representing a claim to x_c units of the c–th commodity, for $1 \leq c \leq C$. Classical examples of commodities are corn and labor. In this context a linear price functional p is represented by a unique vector π in R^C, taking π_c as the unit price of the c–th commodity, and $p \cdot x = \pi^{\top} x \equiv \sum_{c=1}^{C} \pi_c x_c$ for all x in R^C. For this reason, we often use the notation "$\pi \cdot x$" in place of "$\pi^{\top} x$".

Uncertainty can be added to this model as a set $\{1, \ldots, S\}$ of states of the world, one of which will be chosen at random. In this case the vector choice space L can be treated as the space $M^{S,C}$ of $S \times C$ matrices. The (s, c)–element x_{sc} of a typical choice x represents consumption of x_{sc} units of the c–th commodity in state s, as indicated in Figure 1. A given linear price functional p on L can also be represented by an $S \times C$ matrix π, taking π_{sc} as the unit price of consumption of commodity c in state s. That is, writing x_s for the s–th row of any matrix x, there is a unique price matrix π such that $p \cdot x = \sum_{s=1}^{S} \pi_s \cdot x_s$ for all x in L. We can imagine a market for contracts to deliver a particular commodity in a particular state, SC contracts in all. Trading in these contracts occurs before the true state is revealed; then contracted deliveries occur and consumption ensues. There is no change in the definition of an equilibrium, which in this case is called a *contingent commodity market equilibrium*.

C.   Financial security markets are an effective alternative to contingent commodity markets. We take the (S states, C commodities) contingent consumption setting just described. Security markets can be characterized by an $S \times N$ dividend matrix d, where N is the number of securities. The n–th security is defined by the n–th column of d, with d_{sn} representing the number of units of account, say dollars, paid by the n–th security in a given state s. Securities are sold before the true state is resolved, at prices given by a vector $q = (q_1, \ldots, q_N) \in R^N$. Spot markets are opened after the true state is resolved. Spot prices are given by an $S \times C$ matrix ψ, with ψ_{sc} representing the unit price of the c–th commodity in state s. Let $(\omega^1, \ldots, \omega^I)$ denote the endowments of the I agents, taking ω_{sc}^i as the endowment of commodity c to agent i in state s. An *agent's plan* is a pair (θ, x), where the matrix $x \in L$ is a consumption choice and $\theta \in R^N$ is a

COMMODITIES

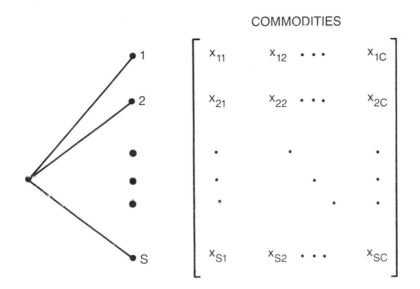

Figure 1.   State–Contingent Consumption

security portfolio. The dollar payoff of portfolio θ in state s is $\theta \cdot d_s$. Given security and spot prices (q, ψ), a plan (θ, x) is *budget feasible* for agent i if

$$q \cdot \theta \leq 0 \tag{1}$$

and

$$\psi_s \cdot x_s \leq \psi_s \cdot \omega_s^i + \theta \cdot d_s, \quad 1 \leq s \leq S. \tag{2}$$

A budget feasible plan (θ, x) is *optimal* for agent i if there is no budget feasible plan (φ, y) such that $u_i(y) > u_i(x)$. A *security–spot market equilibrium* is a collection

$$((\theta^1, x^1), \dots, (\theta^I, x^I), (q, \psi))$$

with the property: for each agent i, the plan (θ^i, x^i) is optimal given the security–spot price pair (q, ψ); and markets clear:

$$\sum_{i=1}^{I} \theta^i = 0 \quad \text{and} \quad \sum_{i=1}^{I} x^i - \omega^i = 0.$$

To see the effectiveness of financial securities in this context, suppose $(x^1, \ldots, x^I, p)$ is a contingent commodity market equilibrium, where p is a price functional represented by the $S \times C$ price matrix π. Take $N = S$ securities and let the security dividend matrix d be the identity matrix, meaning that the n–th security pays one dollar in state n and zero otherwise. Let the security price vector be $q = (1, 1, \ldots, 1) \in R^N$, and take the spot price matrix $\psi = \pi$. For each agent i and state s, let $\theta_s^i = \psi_s \cdot (x_s^i - \omega_s^i)$, equating the number of units of the s–th security held with the spot market cost of the net consumption choice $x_s^i - \omega_s^i$ for state s. Then $\big((\theta^1, x^1), \ldots, (\theta^I, x^I), (q, \psi)\big)$ is a security–spot market equilibrium, as we now verify. Budget feasibility obtains since, for any agent i,

$$\theta^i \cdot q = \sum_{s=1}^{S} \pi_s \cdot (x_s^i - \omega_s^i) = p \cdot x^i - p \cdot \omega^i \leq 0,$$

and

$$\psi_s \cdot x_s^i = \psi_s \cdot \omega_s^i + \theta_s^i = \psi_s \cdot \omega_s^i + \theta^i \cdot d_s, \quad 1 \leq s \leq S.$$

The latter equality is a consequence of the definitions of θ^i and d. Optimality of (θ^i, x^i) is proved as follows. Suppose (φ, y) is a budget feasible plan for agent i and $u_i(y) > u_i(x^i)$. By optimality in the given contingent commodity market equilibrium $(x^1, \ldots, x^I, p)$, we have $p \cdot y > p \cdot x^i$, or

$$\sum_{s=1}^{S} \pi_s \cdot (y_s - \omega_s^i) > \sum_{s=1}^{S} \pi_s \cdot (x_s^i - \omega_s^i) = 0. \tag{3}$$

If (φ, y) is budget feasible for agent i, then (2) implies that $\varphi_s = \varphi \cdot d_s \geq \pi_s \cdot (y_s - \omega_s^i)$, and thus that $q \cdot \varphi \geq \sum_{s=1}^{S} \pi_s \cdot (y_s - \omega_s^i)$ since $q = (1, 1, \ldots, 1)$. But then (3) implies that $q \cdot \varphi > 0$, which contradicts (1). Thus (θ^i, x^i) is indeed optimal for agent i. Spot market clearing follows from the fact that $x^1, \ldots, x^I$ is a feasible allocation. Security market clearing obtains since

$$\sum_{i=1}^{I} \theta_s^i = \sum_{i=1}^{I} \pi_s \cdot (x_s^i - \omega_s^i) = \pi_s \cdot \left(\sum_{i=1}^{I} x_s^i - \omega_s^i \right) = 0, \quad s \in \{1, \ldots, S\},$$

also because $x^1, \ldots, x^I$ is feasible.

These arguments are easily extended to the case of any security dividend matrix d whose column vectors span R^S, or *spanning securities*. One can proceed in the opposite direction to show that a security–spot market equilibrium with spanning securities can be translated into a contingent commodity market equilibrium with the same consumption allocation. Without spanning, other arguments will demonstrate the existence of security–spot market equilibria, but the equilibrium allocation need not be optimal, and thus there will not generally be a complete markets equilibrium with the same allocation.

D. In the general model of Paragraph A, suppose $L = R^N$ for some number N of goods. If u_i is differentiable, the first order necessary condition for optimality of x^i in problem $(*)$ is

$$\frac{\partial u_i(x^i)}{\partial x} - \lambda_i \frac{\partial p \cdot x^i}{\partial x} = 0,$$

where $\lambda_i \geq 0$ is a scalar Lagrange multiplier. The *gradient* $\nabla u_i(x)$ of u_i at a choice x is the linear functional defined by

$$\nabla u_i(x) \cdot y = \sum_{n=1}^{N} \frac{\partial u_i(x)}{\partial r_n} y_n,$$

for any y in R^N. Thus optimality of x^i for agent i implies that $\nabla u_i(x^i) = \lambda_i p$, a fundamental condition. Since $p \cdot x = \pi^\top x$ for some π in R^N, we can also write, for any two goods n and m with $\pi_m > 0$,

$$\frac{\pi_n}{\pi_m} = \frac{\frac{\partial u_i(x^i)}{\partial x_n}}{\frac{\partial u_i(x^i)}{\partial x_m}},$$

a well known identity equating the ratio of prices of two goods to the *marginal rate of substitution* of the two goods for any agent.

For a two period model with one commodity and S different states of nature in the second period, we can take L to be R^{S+1}, where $x = (x_0, x_1, \ldots, x_S) \in L$ represents x_0 units of consumption in the first period and x_s units in state s of the second period, $s \in \{1, \ldots, S\}$. Suppose preferences are given by *expected utility*, or

$$u_i(x) = v_i(x_0) + \sum_{s=1}^{S} \alpha_s v_i(x_s),$$

where $\alpha_s > 0$ denotes the probability of state s occurring, and v_i is a strictly increasing differentiable function. Suppose $(x^1, \ldots, x^I, p)$ is a contingent commodity market equilibrium. We have $p \cdot x = \pi \cdot x$ for some $\pi = (\pi_0, \pi_1, \ldots, \pi_S) \in R^{S+1}$. We can assume that $\pi_0 = 1$ without loss of generality since $(x^1, \ldots, x^I, p/\pi_0)$ is also an equilibrium. For any two states m and n, we have

$$\frac{\pi_n}{\pi_m} = \frac{\frac{\partial u_i(x^i)}{\partial x_n}}{\frac{\partial u_i(x^i)}{\partial x_m}} = \frac{\alpha_n v_i'(x_n^i)}{\alpha_m v_i'(x_m^i)}.$$

The ratio of the prices of state contingent consumption in two different states is the ratio of the marginal utility for consumption in the two states, each weighted by the probability of occurrence of the state. This serves our intuition rather well. We also have

$$\pi_s = \frac{\alpha_s v_i'(x_s^i)}{v_i'(x_0^i)}, \quad 1 \le s \le S. \tag{4}$$

Suppose there are $N \ge S$ securities defined by a full rank $S \times N$ dividend matrix d, whose n–th column $d_n \in R^S$ is the vector of dividends of security n in the S states. Drawing from Paragraph C, we can convert the contingent commodity market equilibrium into a security–spot market equilibrium in which the spot price ψ_s for consumption is one for each $s \in \{0, \dots, S\}$, and in which the market value of the n–th security is

$$q_n = \sum_{s=1}^{S} \pi_s d_{sn}.$$

From (4), for any agent i,

$$q_n = \frac{1}{v_i'(x_0^i)} \sum_{s=1}^{S} \alpha_s v_i'(x_s^i) d_{sn}. \tag{5}$$

In other words, the market value of a security in this setting is the expected value of the product of its future dividend and the future marginal utility for consumption, all divided by the current marginal utility for consumption. Relation (5) is a mainstay of asset pricing models, and will later crop up in various guises.

E.   We have seen that financial securities are a powerful substitute for contingent commodity markets. In general, agents consider themselves limited to those consumption plans that can be realized by some pattern of trades through time on security and spot markets. The more frequently the same securities are traded, the greater is their span. For a dramatic example of spanning, consider an economy in which the state of the world on any given day is *good* or *bad*. A given security, say a *stock*, appreciates in market value by 20 percent on a good day and does not change in value on a bad day. Another security, say a *bond*, has a rate of return of r per day with certainty. Suppose a third security, say a *crown*, will have a market value of C_g if the following day is good and a value of C_b if the following day is bad. We can construct a portfolio of α shares of the stock and β

of the bond whose market value after one day is precisely the value of the crown. The equations determining α and β are:

$$\alpha(1.2S) + \beta(1+r)B = C_g$$

$$\alpha(1.0S) + \beta(1+r)B = C_b,$$

where $S \neq 0$ and $B \neq 0$ are the initial market values of the stock and bond respectively. The solutions are $\alpha = (C_g - C_b)/0.2S$ shares of stock and

$$\beta = \frac{(1.2C_b - C_g)}{0.2(1+r)B}$$

of bond. The initial market value C of the crown must therefore be $C = \alpha S + \beta B$. The supporting argument, one of the most commonly made in finance theory, is that $C = \alpha S + \beta B + k$, with $k \neq 0$, implies the following *arbitrage opportunity*. To make an arbitrage profit of M, one sells M/k units of crown and purchases $M\alpha/k$ shares of stock and $M\beta/k$ of bond. This transaction nets a current value for the investor of

$$\frac{M}{k}C - \frac{M\alpha}{k}S - \frac{M\beta}{k}B = M.$$

The obligations of the investor after one day are nil since the value of the portfolio held will be

$$\frac{M}{k}[\alpha(1.2S) + \beta(1+r)B - C_g] = 0$$

if a good day, and similarly zero if a bad day, since α and β were chosen with this property. The selection of M as a profit is arbitrary. This situation cannot occur in equilibrium, at least if we ignore transactions costs. Indeed then, the absence of arbitrage implies that $C = \alpha S + \beta B$. Given a riskless return r of 10 percent, we calculate from the solutions for α and β that

$$C = \frac{1}{1+r}(0.5C_g + 0.5C_b). \tag{6}$$

This expression could be thought of as the discounted expected value of the crown's market value, taking equal probabilities of good and bad days. Of course no probabilities have been mentioned; the numbers $(0.5, 0.5)$ are constructed entirely from the returns on the stock and the bond. The calculation of these "artificial" probabilities for the general case is shown in Paragraph 22A.

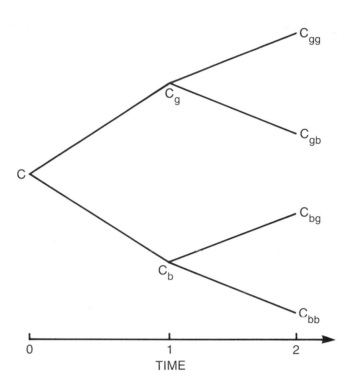

Figure 2.   Recursive Arbitrage Diagram

Now we consider a second day of trade with the same rates of return
on the stock and bond contingent on the outcome of the next day, good or
bad. Let C_{gg} denote the market value of the crown after two good days,
C_{gb} denote its value after a good day followed by a bad day, and so on, as
illustrated in Figure 2.

By the arbitrage reasoning applied earlier,

$$C_g = \frac{1}{1+r}(0.5C_{gg} + 0.5C_{gb}) \tag{6a}$$

$$C_b = \frac{1}{1+r}(0.5C_{bg} + 0.5C_{bb}). \tag{6b}$$

Substituting (6a) and (6b) into (6),

$$C = \frac{1}{(1+r)^2}(0.25C_{gg} + 0.25C_{gb} + 0.25C_{bg} + 0.25C_{bb}).$$

The notion of pricing by taking discounted expected values is preserved, and the recursion can be extended indefinitely. After T days, provided none of the securities pays intermediate dividends, we have

$$C = (1 + r)^{-T} E(C_T), \qquad (7)$$

where C_T denotes the random market value of the crown after T days and E denotes expectation when treating successive days as independently good or bad with equal probability. We are able to price an arbitrary security with random terminal value C_T by relation (7) because there is a strategy for trading the stock and bond through time that requires an initial investment of $(1+r)^{-T} E(C_T)$ and that has a random terminal value of C_T. The argument is easily extended to securities that pay intermediate dividends. There are 2^T different states of the world at time T. Precluding the re–trade of securities, we would thus require 2^T different securities for spanning. With re–trade, as shown, only two securities are sufficient. Any other security, given the stock and bond, is redundant.

The classical example of pricing a redundant security is the *Black–Scholes Option Pricing Formula*. We take the crown to be a call option on a share of the stock at time T with exercise price K. Since the option is exercised only if $S_T \geq K$, and in that case nets an option holder the value $S_T - K$, the terminal value of the option is

$$C_T = (S_T - K)^+ \equiv \max(0, S_T - K),$$

where S_T denotes the random market value of the stock at time T. Given n good days out of T for example, $S_T = 1.2^n S$ and the call option is worth the larger of $1.2^n S - K$ and zero, since the call gives its owner the option to purchase the stock at a cost of K. From (7),

$$C = \frac{1}{(1+r)^T} \sum_{n=0}^{T} \frac{T!}{n!(T-n)!} \frac{1}{2^T} (1.2^n S - K)^+. \qquad (8)$$

This formula evaluates $E(C_T)$ by calculating C_T given n good days out of T, then multiplies this payoff by the binomial formula for the probability of n good days out of T, and finally sums over n. The *Central Limit Theorem* tells us that the normalized sum of independent binomial trials converges to a random variable with a normal distribution as the number of trials goes to infinity. The limit of (8) as the number of trading intervals in $[0, T]$ approaches infinity is not surprisingly, then, an expression involving the cumulative normal distribution function Φ, making appropriate adjustments of the returns per trading interval (as described in Section 22). The limit is the *Black–Scholes Option Pricing Formula*:

$$C = S\Phi(z) - \frac{K}{(1+r)^T}\ \Phi\!\left(z - \sigma\sqrt{T}\right),\tag{9}$$

where

$$z = \frac{1}{\sigma\sqrt{T}}\log\!\left(\frac{S(1+r)^T}{K}\right) + \frac{1}{2}\sigma\sqrt{T}.$$

The scalar σ represents the standard deviation of the rate of return of the stock per day. Details are found in Section 22. The *Black–Scholes Formula* (9) was originally deduced by much different methods, however, using a continuous–time model.

F.   One of the principal applications of security market theory is the explanation of security prices. We will look at a simple static model of security prices and follow this with a multi–period model. The static *Capital Asset Pricing Model*, or *CAPM*, begins with a set Y of random variables with finite variance on some probability space. Each y in Y corresponds to the random payoff of some security. The vector space L of choices for agents is $\text{span}(Y)$, the space of linear combinations of elements of Y, meaning x is in L if and only if $x = \sum_{n=1}^{N}\alpha_n y_n$ for some scalars $\alpha_1, \ldots, \alpha_N$ and some $y_1, \ldots, y_N$ in Y. The elements of L are *portfolios*. Some portfolio in L denoted $\mathbf{1}$ is *riskless*, meaning $\mathbf{1}$ is the random variable whose value is 1 in all states. The utility functional u_i of each agent i is assumed to be *strictly variance averse*, meaning that $u_i(x) > u_i(y)$ whenever $E(x) = E(y)$ and $\text{var}(x) < \text{var}(y)$, where $\text{var}(x) \equiv E(x^2) - [E(x)]^2$ denotes the *variance* of x. This is a special case of "risk aversion", and can be shown to result from different sets of assumptions on the probability distributions of security payoffs and on the utility functional. The total endowment $M = \sum_{i=1}^{I}\omega_i$ of portfolios is the *market portfolio*, and is assumed to have non–zero variance.

Suppose $(x_1, \ldots, x_I, p)$ is a competitive equilibrium for this economy in which $p \cdot \mathbf{1}$ and $p \cdot M$, the market values of the riskless security and the market portfolio, are not zero. Assuming for simplicity that L is finite–dimensional, we can use the fact that the equilibrium price functional p (or any given linear functional on L) is represented by a unique portfolio π in L via the formula:

$$p \cdot x = E(\pi x) \quad \text{for all } x \text{ in } L.\tag{10}$$

For the equilibrium choice x_i of agent i, consider the least squares regression of x_i on π:

$$x_i = A + B\pi + e,$$

where A and B are the regression coefficients and, by the usual least–squares regression theory, the residual term e has zero expectation and zero covariance with π; that is,

$$E(e) = \operatorname{cov}(e, \pi) \equiv E(e\pi) - E(e)E(\pi) = 0.$$

Since both $\mathbf{1}$ and π are available portfolios, agent i could have chosen the portfolio $\widehat{x}_i = A\mathbf{1} + B\pi$. Since $E(\pi e) = E(\pi)E(e) + \operatorname{cov}(\pi, e) = 0$, we have from (10) that

$$p \cdot \widehat{x}_i = E[\pi(A + B\pi)] = E[\pi(A + B\pi + e)] = p \cdot x_i,$$

implying that $\widehat{x}_i$ is budget feasible for agent i. Since $E(e) = 0$ and

$$\operatorname{cov}(\widehat{x}_i, e) = \operatorname{cov}(A + B\pi, e) = 0,$$

strict variance aversion implies that $u_i(\widehat{x}_i) > u_i(x_i)$ unless e is zero. Since x_i is optimal for agent i, it follows that $e = 0$. Thus, for some coefficients A_i and B_i specific to agent i, we have shown that $x_i = A_i + B_i\pi$, implying that

$$M = \sum_{i=1}^{I} \omega_i = \sum_{i=1}^{I} x_i = \sum_{i=1}^{I} (A_i + B_i\pi) = a + b\pi,$$

where $a = \sum_{i=1}^{I} A_i$ and $b = \sum_{i=1}^{I} B_i$. Since the variance of M is non–zero, $b \neq 0$. For any portfolio x, relation (10) implies that

$$p \cdot x = E(\pi x) = E\left[\left(\frac{M - a}{b}\right) x\right] = kE(x) + K \operatorname{cov}(x, M), \qquad (11)$$

where $k = E(M - a)/b$ and $K = 1/b$. Defining the *return* on any portfolio x with non–zero market value to be $\mathcal{R}_x = x/(p \cdot x)$, and denoting the expected return by $\overline{\mathcal{R}}_x \equiv E(\mathcal{R}_x)$, algebraic manipulation of relation (11) leaves

$$\overline{\mathcal{R}}_x - \mathcal{R}_{\mathbf{1}} = \beta_x(\overline{\mathcal{R}}_M - \mathcal{R}_{\mathbf{1}}), \qquad (12)$$

where

$$\beta_x \equiv \frac{\operatorname{cov}(\mathcal{R}_x, \mathcal{R}_M)}{\operatorname{var}(\mathcal{R}_M)},$$

which is known as the *beta* of portfolio x. Relation (12) itself is known as the *Capital Asset Pricing Model*: the expected return on any portfolio in excess of the riskless rate of return is the beta of that portfolio multiplied by the excess expected return of the market portfolio.

For intuition, consider the linear regression of $\mathcal{R}_x - \mathcal{R}_1$ on $\mathcal{R}_y - \mathcal{R}_1$, where y is any portfolio with non–zero variance. The solution is

$$\mathcal{R}_x - \mathcal{R}_1 = \alpha_y + \frac{\operatorname{cov}(\mathcal{R}_x, \mathcal{R}_y)}{\operatorname{var}(\mathcal{R}_y)}(\mathcal{R}_y - \mathcal{R}_1) + \epsilon_y,$$

where α_y is a constant and ϵ_y is of zero mean and uncorrelated with $\mathcal{R}_y$. For the particular case of $y = M$, we have

$$\mathcal{R}_x - \mathcal{R}_1 = \alpha_M + \beta_x(\mathcal{R}_M - \mathcal{R}_1) + \epsilon_M.$$

But taking expectations and comparing with (12) shows that $\alpha_M = 0$. This is a special property distinguishing the market portfolio. We also see that the excess expected return on a portfolio x depends only on that portion of its return, $\beta_x \mathcal{R}_M$, that is correlated with the return on the market portfolio, and not on the residual term ϵ_M that is uncorrelated with the market return. In particular, a portfolio whose return is uncorrelated with the market return has the riskless expected rate of return. The content of the CAPM is not the fact that there exists a portfolio with these properties shown by the market portfolio, for it is easily shown that the portfolio π defined by (10) has these same properties, regardless of risk aversion. The CAPM's contribution is the identification of a particular portfolio, the market portfolio, with the same properties.

G.   For a multiperiod security pricing model, we take the choice space L to be the space of bounded sequences $c = \{c_0, c_1, \ldots\}$ of real–valued random variables on some probability space, with c_t representing consumption at time t. A single agent has a utility function u on L defined by

$$u(c) = E\left[\sum_{t=0}^{\infty} \rho^t v(c_t)\right], \qquad c \in L,$$

where v is a bounded, differentiable, strictly increasing, and concave real–valued function on the real line, and $\rho \in (0, 1)$ is a discount factor. The economy can be in any of S different states at any time, with the state at time t denoted X_t. The transition of states is governed by an $S \times S$ matrix P. The (i, j)–element P_{ij} of P is the probability that X_{t+1} is in state j given that X_t is in state i, for any time t. A security is defined by the consumption dividend sequence in L that a unit shareholder is entitled to receive. For simplicity, we assume that the N available securities are characterized by an $S \times N$ positive matrix d whose i–th row $d(i) \in R^N$ is the payout vector of the N securities in state i. That is, $d(i)_n$ is the payout of the n–th security at any time t when X_t is in state i. The agent is able to purchase or sell any amount of consumption or securities at any time. We will suppose that the prices of the securities, in terms of the consumption numeraire, are given by an $S \times N$ matrix π, whose i–th row, $\pi(i) \in R^N$, denotes the unit prices of the N securities in state i. We take the security prices to be *ex dividend*, so that purchasing a portfolio $\theta \in R^N$ of securities in state i requires an investment of $\theta \cdot \pi(i)$ and promises a market value of $\theta \cdot [\pi(j) + d(j)]$ in the next period with probability P_{ij}, for each state j. An agent's plan is a pair (θ, c), where c is a consumption sequence in L and $\theta = \{\theta_1, \theta_2, \ldots\}$ is an R^N–valued sequence of random variables whose t–th element θ_t is the portfolio of securities purchased at time t. The informational restrictions are that, for any time t, both c_t and θ_t must depend only on observations of $X_0, X_1, \ldots, X_t$, or in technical terms, that there is a function f_t such that

$$(c_t, \theta_t) = f_t(X_0, X_1, \ldots, X_t), \qquad t = 0, 1, 2, \ldots$$

The *wealth process* $W = \{W_0, W_1, \ldots\}$ of the agent, given a plan (θ, c), is defined by $W_0 = w$, where $w \geq 0$ is the scalar for endowed initial wealth, and

$$W_t = \theta_{t-1} \cdot [\pi(X_t) + d(X_t)], \qquad t = 1, 2, \ldots$$

For simplicity, we require positive consumption, $c_t \geq 0$, and no short sales of securities, $\theta_t > 0$, for all t. Such a positive plan (c, θ) is *budget feasible* if, for all $t \geq 0$,

$$W_t \geq c_t + \theta_t \cdot \pi(X_t).$$

A budget feasible plan (c, θ) is *optimal* if there is no budget feasible plan (c', θ') such that $u(c') > u(c)$. The total endowment of securities is one of each, or the vector $\mathbf{1} = (1, \ldots, 1) \in R^N$. The total consumption available in state i is thus $C(i) \equiv \mathbf{1} \cdot d(i)$. A triple (θ, c, π) is an equilibrium if (θ, c) is an optimal plan given prices π, initial state i, and initial wealth $w = \mathbf{1} \cdot [\pi(i) + d(i)]$, and if markets clear:

$$c_t = C(X_t), \quad t = 0, 1, 2, \ldots$$

$$\theta_t = \mathbf{1}, \quad t = 0, 1, 2, \ldots$$

For a given price matrix π, initial wealth w, and initial state i, let (θ, c) be an optimal plan and let $V(i, w) = u(c)$. An unsurprising result of the theory of dynamic programming is that the indirect utility function V defined in this way satisfies the *Bellman Equation*:

$$V(i, w) = \max_{(c_0, \theta_0) \in R_+ \times R_+^N} v(c_0) + \rho E_i \left[V\left(X_1, \theta_0 \cdot [\pi(X_1) + d(X_1)]\right) \right], \quad (13)$$

subject to

$$c_0 \leq w - \theta_0 \cdot \pi(i), \tag{14}$$

where E_i denotes expectation given that $X_0 = i$. The Bellman Equation merely states that the value of starting in state i with wealth w is equal to the utility of current consumption c_0 plus the discounted expected indirect utility of starting in next period's state X_1 with wealth $W_1 = \theta_0 \cdot [\pi(X_1) + d(X_1)]$, where c_0 and θ_0 are chosen to maximize this total utility. Since v is strictly increasing, relation (14) will hold with equality and we can substitute $w - \theta_0 \cdot \pi(i)$ for c_0 in (13). We can then differentiate (13) with respect to w, assuming that $V(i, \cdot)$ is differentiable, to yield

$$\frac{\partial V(i, w)}{\partial w} = v'[w - \theta_0 \cdot \pi(i)].$$

In equilibrium, $w = w(i) \equiv \mathbf{1} \cdot [\pi(i) + d(i)]$ and $c_0 = C(i)$, leaving

$$\frac{\partial V[i, w(i)]}{\partial w} = v'[C(i)] \tag{15}$$

for each state i. Again using $c_0 = w - \theta_0 \cdot \pi(i)$, we can differentiate (13) with respect to the vector θ_0 and, by the first order necessary conditions for optimal choice of θ_0, equate the result to zero. In equilibrium, this calculation yields

$$-v'[C(i)]\pi(i) + \rho E_i \left[\frac{\partial V[X_1, w(X_1)]}{\partial w} [\pi(X_1) + d(X_1)] \right] = 0.$$

Substituting from (15),

$$\pi(i) = \frac{\rho}{v'[C(i)]} E_i \left[v'[C(X_1)][\pi(X_1) + d(X_1)] \right], \quad i \in \{1, \ldots, S\}. \tag{16}$$

This is the so-called *Stochastic Euler Equation* for pricing securities in a multiperiod setting. The equation shows that the current market value, denoted $p_i \cdot x$, of a portfolio of securities that pays off a random amount x in the following period is, in direct analogy with (5), given by

$$p_i \cdot x = \frac{\rho}{v'[C(i)]} E_i \left(v'[C(X_1)]x \right). \tag{17}$$

For each state i, let $\mathcal{R}_C(i) = C(X_1)/C(i)$, and for any portfolio x with non–zero market value, let $\mathcal{R}_x(i) = x/(p_i \cdot x)$. Finally, assuming the variance of $C(X_1)$ is non–zero, let

$$\beta_x(i) = \frac{\mathrm{cov}_i(\mathcal{R}_x, \mathcal{R}_C)}{\mathrm{var}_i(\mathcal{R}_C)} \equiv \frac{E_i[xC(X_1)] - E_i[x]E_i[C(X_1)]}{E_i[C(X_1)^2] - (E_i[C(X_1)])^2} \cdot \frac{C(i)}{p_i(x)}.$$

In other words, $\beta_x(i)$ is the *conditional beta* of x relative to aggregate consumption, in analogy with the static CAPM, where the market portfolio is in fact aggregate consumption since the model is static. Assuming for illustration that v is quadratic in the range of total consumption $C(\cdot)$, manipulation of (17) shows that the expected return $\overline{\mathcal{R}}_x(i) = E_i[\mathcal{R}_x(i)]$ of any portfolio x with non–zero market value satisfies the *Consumption–Based Capital Asset Pricing Model*:

$$\overline{\mathcal{R}}_x(i) - \mathcal{R}_0(i) = k(i)\beta_x(i), \tag{18}$$

where $\mathcal{R}_0(i)$ denotes the return from state i on a riskless portfolio if one exists (or the expected return on a portfolio uncorrelated with aggregate consumption) and $k(i)$ is a constant depending only on the state.

H. We can also simplify (16) to show that the price matrix π is given by a simple equation $\pi = \Pi d$, where the $S \times S$ matrix Π has a useful interpretation. Let A denote the diagonal $S \times S$ matrix whose i th diagonal element is $v'[C(i)]$. Then (16) is equivalent to $\pi = A^{-1}\rho PA(\pi + d)$, using the definition of P. Let $B = A^{-1}\rho PA$, yielding:

$$\pi = Bd + B\pi$$

$$= Bd + B(Bd + B\pi)$$

$$= Bd + B^2 d + B^2 \pi$$

$$\vdots$$

$$= \sum_{t=1}^{T} B^t d + B^T \pi,$$

for any time T. Noting that $B^2 = (A^{-1}\rho PA)(A^{-1}\rho PA) = A^{-1}\rho^2 P^2 A$, and similarly that $B^t = A^{-1}\rho^t P^t A$ for any $t \geq 1$, we see that B^T converges to the zero matrix as T goes to infinity, leaving

$$\pi = \sum_{t=1}^{\infty} B^t d = \Pi d, \tag{19}$$

where $\Pi = \sum_{t=1}^{\infty} B^t$. By a series calculation, $\Pi = A^{-1}(I - \rho P)^{-1}A - I$. Equivalently,

$$\pi(i) = \frac{1}{v'[C(i)]} E_i \left[\sum_{t=1}^{\infty} \rho^t v'[C(X_t)] d(X_t) \right],$$

or the current value of a security is the expected discounted infinite horizon sum of its dividends, discounted by the marginal utility for consumption at the time the dividends occur, all divided by the current marginal utility for consumption. This extends the single period pricing model suggested by relation (5).

This multiperiod pricing model extends easily to the case of state dependent utility for consumption: $u(c) = E[\sum_{t=0}^{\infty} v(c_t, X_t)]$, $c \in L$; to an infinite state–space; and even to continuous–time. In fact, in continuous–time, one can extend the Consumption–Based Capital Asset Pricing Model (18) to non–quadratic utility functions. Under regularity conditions, that is, the increment of a differentiable function can be approximated by the first two terms of its Taylor series expansion, a quadratic function, and this approximation becomes exact in expectation as the time increment shrinks to zero under the uncertainty generated by Brownian Motion. This idea is formalized as Ito's Lemma, as we see in Paragraph I, and leads to many additional results that depend on gradual transitions in time and state.

I. An illustrative model of continuous "perfectly random" fluctuation is a *Standard Brownian Motion*, a stochastic process, that is, a family of random variables,

$$B = \{B_t : t \in [0, \infty)\},$$

on some probability space, with the defining properties:

(a) for any $s \geq 0$ and $t > s$, $B(t) - B(s)$ is normally distributed with zero mean and variance $t - s$,

(b) for any times $0 \leq t_0 < t_1 < \cdots < t_l < \infty$, the increments $B(t_0)$, $B(t_k) - B(t_{k-1})$ for $1 \leq k \leq l$, are independent, and

(c) $B(0) = 0$ almost surely.

We will illustrate the role of Brownian Motion in governing the motion of a Markov state process X. For any times $0 \leq t_0 < t_1 < \cdots$, let $\Delta t_k = t_k - t_{k-1}$, $\Delta X_k = X(t_k) - X(t_{k-1})$, and $\Delta B_k = B(t_k) - B(t_{k-1})$, for $k \geq 1$. A *stochastic difference equation* for the motion of X might be:

$$\Delta X_k = \mu[X(t_{k-1})] \Delta t_k + \sigma[X(t_{k-1})] \Delta B_k, \quad k \geq 1, \tag{20}$$

where μ and σ are given functions. For the moment, we assume that μ and σ are bounded and Lipschitz continuous. (Lipschitz continuity is defined in Section 21; existence of a bounded derivative is sufficient.) Given $X(t_{k-1})$, the properties defining the Brownian Motion B imply that ΔX_k has conditional mean $\mu[X(t_{k-1})]\Delta t_k$ and conditional variance $\sigma[X(t_{k-1})]^2 \Delta t_k$. A continuous–time analogue to (20) is the *stochastic differential equation*

$$dX_t = \mu(X_t)\, dt + \sigma(X_t)\, dB_t, \quad t \geq 0. \tag{21}$$

In this case, X is an example of a *diffusion process*. By analogy with the difference equation, we may heuristically treat $\mu(X_t)\, dt$ and $\sigma(X_t)^2\, dt$ as the "instantaneous mean and variance of dX_t". The stochastic differential equation (21) is merely notation for

$$X_t = X_0 + \int_0^t \mu(X_s)\, ds + \int_0^t \sigma(X_s)\, dB_s, \quad t > 0,$$

for some starting point X_0. By the properties of the (as yet undefined) Ito integral $\int \sigma(X_t)\, dB_t$, we have:

ITO'S LEMMA. *If f is a twice continuously differentiable function, then for any time $T > 0$,*

$$f(X_T) = f(X_0) + \int_0^T \mathcal{D}f(X_t)\, dt + \int_0^T f'(X_t)\sigma(X_t)\, dB_t,$$

where

$$\mathcal{D}f(x) \equiv f'(x)\mu(x) + \frac{1}{2}f''(x)\sigma(x)^2.$$

If f' is bounded, the fact that B has increments of zero expectation implies that

$$E\left[\int_0^T f'(X_t)\sigma(X_t)\, dB_t\right] = 0.$$

It then follows that

$$\lim_{T \to 0} E\left[\frac{f(X_T) - f(X_0)}{T}\right] = \mathcal{D}f(X_0).$$

In other words, Ito's Lemma tells us that the expected rate of change of f at any point x is $\mathcal{D}f(x)$.

J.   We apply Ito's Lemma to the following portfolio control problem. We assume that a risky security has a price process S satisfying the stochastic differential equation

$$dS_t = mS_t\, dt + vS_t\, dB_t, \quad t \geq 0, \tag{22}$$

and pays dividends at the rate of δS_t at any time t, where m, v, and δ are strictly positive scalars. We may think heuristically of $m + \delta$ as the "instantaneous expected rate of return" and v^2 as the "instantaneous variance of the rate of return". A riskless security has a price that is always one, and pays dividends at the constant interest rate r, where $0 \leq r < m + \delta$. Let $X = \{X_t : t \geq 0\}$ denote the stochastic process for the wealth of an agent who may invest in the two given securities and withdraw funds for consumption at the rate c_t at any time $t \geq 0$. If a_t is the fraction of total wealth invested at time t in the risky security, it follows (with mathematical care) that X satisfies the stochastic differential equation:

$$dX_t = a_t X_t(m + \delta)\, dt + a_t X_t v\, dB_t + (1 - a_t)X_t r\, dt - c_t\, dt,$$

which should be easily enough interpreted. Simplifying,

$$dX_t = [a_t X_t(m + \delta - r) + rX_t - c_t]\, dt + a_t X_t v\, dB_t.$$

The positive wealth constraint $X_t \geq 0$ is imposed at all times. We suppose that our investor derives utility from a consumption process $c = \{c_t : t \geq 0\}$ according to

$$U(c) = E\left[\int_0^\infty e^{-\rho t} u(c_t)\, dt\right],$$

where $\rho > 0$ is a discount factor, and u is a strictly increasing, differentiable, and strictly concave function. The problem of optimal choice of portfolio (a_t) and consumption rate (c_t) is solved as follows. Of course, c_t and a_t can only depend on the information available at time t, in a sense to be made precise in Section 24. Because the wealth X_t constitutes all relevant information at any time t, we may limit ourselves without loss of generality to the case $a_t = A(X_t)$ and $c_t = C(X_t)$ for some (measurable) functions A and C. We suppose that A and C are optimal, and note that

$$dX_t = \mu(X_t)\, dt + \sigma(X_t)\, dB_t; \quad X_0 = w,$$

where $\mu(x) \equiv A(x)x(m + \delta - r) + rx - C(x)$, $\sigma(x) \equiv A(x)xv$, and $w > 0$ is the given initial wealth. The indirect utility for wealth w is

$$V(w) = E\left[\int_0^\infty e^{-\rho t} u\left[C(X_t)\right]\, dt\right].$$

For any time $T > 0$, we can break this expression into two parts:

$$V(w) = E\left[\int_0^T e^{-\rho t} u\left[C(X_t)\right] dt\right] + E\left[\int_T^\infty e^{-\rho s} u\left[C(X_s)\right] ds\right].$$

Taking $\tau = s - T$,

$$V(w) = E\left[\int_0^T e^{-\rho t} u\left[C(X_t)\right] dt\right] + e^{-\rho T} E\left[\int_0^\infty e^{-\rho\tau} u\left[C(X_{\tau+T})\right] d\tau\right]$$

$$= E\left[\int_0^T e^{-\rho t} u\left[C(X_t)\right] dt\right] + e^{-\rho T} E[V(X_T)].$$

(The last equality is intuitively appealing, but requires several arguments developed in Section 23.) Adding and subtracting $e^{-\rho T} V(w)$,

$$e^{-\rho T} E\left[V(X_T) - V(w)\right] + (e^{-\rho T} - 1)V(w) + E\left[\int_0^T e^{-\rho t} u\left[C(X_t)\right] dt\right] = 0.$$

We divide each term by T and take limits as T converges to 0, using Ito's Lemma and l'Hôpital's Rule to arrive at

$$\mathcal{D}V(w) - \rho V(w) + u\left[C(w)\right] = 0, \tag{23}$$

where

$$\mathcal{D}V(w) = [A(w)w(m + \delta - r) + rw - C(w)]V'(w) + \frac{1}{2} V''(w)[A(w)wv]^2.$$

(This assumes V is sufficiently differentiable, but that will turn out to be the case.) If A and C are indeed optimal, that is, if they maximize $V(w)$, then they must maximize $E\left[\int_0^T e^{-\rho t} u\left[C(X_t)\right] dt + e^{-\rho T} V(X_T)\right]$ for any time T. By our calculations (and some technical arguments) this is equivalent to the problem:

$$\max_{A(w),C(w)} \mathcal{D}V(w) - \rho V(w) + u\left[C(w)\right]. \tag{24}$$

The first order necessary conditions for (24) are

$$u'\left[C(w)\right] - V'(w) = 0$$

and

$$(m + \delta - r)wV'(w) + V''(w)A(w)w^2v^2 = 0.$$

Solving,

$$A(w) = \frac{-V'(w)\,(m+\delta-r)}{V''(w)\,v^2 w}$$

and

$$C(w) = g\left[V'(w)\right],$$

where g is the function inverting u'. If, for example, $u(c_t) = c_t^\alpha$ for some scalar risk aversion coefficient $\alpha \in (0,1)$, then $g(y) = (y/\alpha)^{1/(\alpha-1)}$. Substituting C and A from these expressions into (23) leaves a second order differential equation for V that has a general solution. For the case $u(c_t) = c_t^\alpha$, $\alpha \in (0,1)$, the solution is $V(w) = kw^\alpha$ for some constant k depending on the parameters. It follows that $A(w) = (m+\delta-r)/v^2(1-\alpha)$ (a constant) and $C(w) = \lambda w$, where

$$\lambda = \frac{(\rho-r\alpha)}{1-\alpha} - \frac{\alpha(m+\delta-r)}{(1-\alpha)^2}.$$

In other words, it is optimal to consume at a rate given by a fixed fraction of wealth and to hold a fixed fraction of wealth in the risky asset. It is a key fact that the objective function (24) is quadratic in $A(w)$. This property carries over to a general continuous–time setting. As the Consumption–Based Capital Asset Pricing Model (CCAPM) holds for quadratic utility functions, we should not then be overly surprised to learn that a version of the CCAPM applies in continuous–time, even for agents whose preferences are not strictly variance averse. This result is developed in Section 25.

K.   The problem solved by the Black–Scholes Option Pricing Formula is a special case of the following continuous–time version of the crown valuation problem, treated in Paragraph E in a binomial random walk setting. We are given the riskless security defined by a constant interest rate r and a risky security whose price process S is described by (22), with dividend rate $\delta = 0$. We are interested in the value of a security, say a crown, that pays a lump sum of $g(S_T)$ at a future time T, where g is sufficiently well behaved to justify the following calculations. (It is certainly enough to know that g is bounded and twice continuously differentiable with a bounded derivative.) In the case of an option on the stock with exercise price K and exercise date T, the payoff function is defined by $g(S_T) = (S_T - K)^+ \equiv \max\left(S_T - K, 0\right)$, which is sufficiently well behaved. We will suppose that the value of the crown at any time $t \in [0,T]$ is $C(S_t, t)$, where C is a function that is twice continuously differentiable for $t \in (0,T)$. In particular, $C(S_T, T) = g(S_T)$. For convenience, we use the notation

$$C_s(s,t) = \frac{\partial C(s,t)}{\partial s}; \qquad C_{ss}(s,t) = \frac{\partial^2 C(s,t)}{\partial s^2}; \qquad C_t(s,t) = \frac{\partial C(s,t)}{\partial t}.$$

We can solve the valuation problem by explicitly determining the function C. For simplicity, we suppose that the riskless security is a discount bond maturing after T, so that its market value β_t at time t is $\beta_0 e^{rt}$. Suppose an investor decides to hold the portfolio (a_t, b_t) of stock and bond at any time t, where $a_t = C_s(S_t, t)$ and $b_t = [C(S_t, t) - C_s(S_t, t)S_t]/\beta_t$. This particular trading strategy has two special properties. First, it is self–financing, meaning that it requires an initial investment of $a_0 S_0 + b_0 \beta_0$, but neither generates nor requires any further funds after time zero. To see this fact, one must only show that

$$a_t S_t + b_t \beta_t = a_0 S_0 + b_0 \beta_0 + \int_0^t a_\tau \, dS_\tau + \int_0^t b_\tau \, d\beta_\tau. \tag{25}$$

The left hand side is the market value of the portfolio at time t; the right hand side is the sum of its initial value and any interim gains or losses from trade. Equation (25) can be verified by an application of Ito's Lemma in the following form, which is slightly more general than that given in Paragraph I.

ITO'S LEMMA. *If* $f : R^2 \to R$ *is twice continuously differentiable and* X *is defined by the stochastic differential equation (21), then for any time* $t \geq 0$,

$$f(X_t, t) = f(X_0, 0) + \int_0^t \mathcal{D}f(X_\tau, \tau) \, d\tau + \int_0^t \frac{\partial f(X_\tau, \tau)}{\partial x} \sigma(X_\tau) \, dB_\tau,$$

where

$$\mathcal{D}f(x, t) \equiv \frac{\partial f(x, t)}{\partial t} + \frac{\partial f(x, t)}{\partial x} \mu(x) + \frac{1}{2} \frac{\partial^2 f(x, t)}{\partial x^2} \sigma(x)^2.$$

The second important property of the trading strategy (a, b) is the equality

$$a_t S_t + b_t \beta_t = C(S_t), \tag{26}$$

which follows immediately from the definitions of a_t and b_t. From Ito's Lemma, (25), and (26), we have

$$\int_0^t \mathcal{D}C(S_\tau, \tau) \, d\tau + \int_0^t C_s(S_\tau, \tau) v S_\tau \, dB_\tau - \int_0^t a_\tau \, dS_\tau - \int_0^t b_\tau \, d\beta_\tau = 0. \tag{27}$$

Using $dS_\tau = mS_\tau \, d\tau + v S_\tau \, dB_\tau$ and $d\beta_\tau = r\beta_\tau \, d\tau$, we can collect the terms in $d\tau$ and dB_τ separately. If (27) holds, the integrals involving $d\tau$ and dB_τ must separately sum to zero. Collecting the terms in $d\tau$ alone,

$$\int_0^t \left[C_t(S_\tau, \tau) + C_s(S_\tau, \tau) r S_\tau + \frac{1}{2} v^2 S_\tau^2 C_{ss}(S_\tau, \tau) - rC(S_\tau, \tau) \right] d\tau = 0, \tag{28}$$

for all $t \in (0, T)$. But then (28) implies that C must satisfy the partial differential equation

$$C_t(s, t) + C_s(s, t) r s + \frac{1}{2} v^2 s^2 C_{ss}(s, t) - r C(s, t) = 0, \qquad (29)$$

for $(s, t) \in (0, \infty) \times (0, T)$. Along with (29) we have the boundary condition

$$C(s, T) = g(s), \qquad s \geq 0. \qquad (30)$$

By applying any of a number of methods, the partial differential equation (29) with boundary condition (30) can be shown to have the solution

$$C(s, t) = E \left[e^{-r(T-t)} g \left(s \, e^Z \right) \right], \qquad (31)$$

where Z is normally distributed with mean $(T - t)(r - v^2/2)$ and variance $v^2(T - t)$. For the case of the call option payoff function, $g(s) = (s - K)^+$, we can quickly check that $C(S, 0)$ given by (31) is precisely the Black–Scholes Option Pricing Formula given by (9). More generally, (31) can be solved numerically by standard Monte Carlo simulation and variance reduction methods.

The point of our analysis is this: If the initial price of the crown were, instead, $V > C(S_0, 0)$ one could sell the crown for V and invest $C(S_0, 0)$ in the above self–financing trading strategy. At time T one may re–purchase the crown with the proceeds $g(S_T)$ of the self–financing strategy, leaving no further obligations. The net effect is an initial risk–free profit of $V - C(S_0, 0)$. Such a profit should not be possible in equilibrium. If $V < C(S_0, 0)$, reversing the strategy yields the same result. Of course, we are ignoring transactions costs.

L. With the choice space $L = R^N$ in the setting of Paragraph D, we saw the first order conditions, for any agent i,

$$\frac{\partial u_i(x^i)}{\partial x} - \lambda_i \frac{\partial p \cdot x^i}{\partial x} = 0. \qquad (32)$$

This gave us a characterization of equilibrium prices: the ratio of the prices of two goods is equal to the ratio of any agent's marginal utilities for the two goods. Of course, if there is only one agent, the first order conditions in fact pinpoint the equilibrium price vector, since the single agent consumes the aggregate available goods. Assuming strictly monotonic utility functions, we would have $p = \nabla u_1(\omega^1)/\lambda_1$, where $\nabla u_1(\omega^1)$ denotes the gradient of the utility function u_1 at the endowment point ω^1, and λ_1 is the Lagrange multiplier for the budget constraint of agent 1. That is, for any choice y in R^N,

$$p \cdot y = \frac{1}{\lambda_1} \sum_{n=1}^{N} \frac{\partial u_1(\omega^1)}{\partial x_n} y_n.$$

This notion extends to a multi–agent economy by the construction of a *representative agent* for a given equilibrium $(x^1, \ldots, x^I, p)$. In this setting, a representative agent is a utility function $u_\gamma : L \to R$ of the form

$$u_\gamma(x) = \max_{y^1, \ldots, y^I} \sum_{i=1}^{I} \gamma_i u_i(y^i) \quad \text{subject to} \quad y^1 + \cdots + y^I \leq x, \quad (33)$$

for some vector $\gamma = (\gamma_1, \ldots, \gamma_I)$ of strictly positive scalars. Of course, the key is the existence of an appropriate vector γ of agent weights such that, for the given equilibrium $(x^1, \ldots, x^I, p)$ we have $p = \nabla u_\gamma(e)$, where $e = \omega^1 + \cdots + \omega^I$, and such that the the given equilibrium allocation $(x^1, \ldots, x^I)$ solves (33). In fact, it can be shown that a suitable choice is $\gamma_i = k/\lambda_i$, where λ_i is the Lagrange multiplier shown above for the wealth constraint of agent i, and k is a constant of normalization.

Suppose we have probabilities $\alpha_1, \ldots, \alpha_S$ of the S states at time 1, and the time–additive expected utility form of Paragraph D:

$$u_i(x) = v_i(x_0) + \sum_{s=1}^{S} \alpha_s v_i(x_s),$$

where v_i is a strictly concave, monotone, differentiable function. We can write $x^i(1)$ for the random variable corresponding to the consumption levels $x_1^i, \ldots, x_S^i$ of agent i in period 1. Likewise, a dividend vector d_n in R^S corresponding to a claim d_{sn} units of consumption in state s, for $1 \leq s \leq S$, can be treated as a random variable. In this way, we can re–write relation (5) to see that the market value q_n of a claim to d_n is

$$q_n = \frac{E\left[v_i'\bigl(x^i(1)\bigr)d_n\right]}{v_i'(x_0^i)}.$$

For the same agent weights $\gamma_1, \ldots, \gamma_I$ defining the equilibrium representative agent u_γ, suppose we define $v_\gamma : R \to R$ by

$$v_\gamma(c) = \max_{(c_1, \ldots, c_I) \in R^I} \sum_{i=1}^{I} \gamma_i v_i(c_i) \quad \text{subject to} \quad \sum_{i=1}^{I} c_i \leq c.$$

It follows that the representative agent function $u_\gamma : R^{S+1} \to R$ takes the form:

$$u_\gamma(x) = v_\gamma(x_0) + \sum_{s=1}^{S} \alpha_s v_\gamma(x_s), \tag{34}$$

and that the market value q_n of the claim to the dividend vector d_n at time 1 is therefore

$$q_n = \frac{E\left[v_\gamma'\big(e(1)\big)d_n\right]}{v_\gamma'(e_0)}. \tag{35}$$

Following the construction in Paragraph C, we could next demonstrate a security–spot market equilibrium in which the market value q_n of a security promising the dividend vector $d_n \in R^S$ at time 1 is given by (35), provided the N available securities $d_1, \ldots, d_N$ span R^S. If the available securities do not span R^S, then representative agent pricing does not apply, except in pathological or extremely special cases. Relation (35) is the basis for all of the available equilibrium asset pricing models, whether in discrete–time or continuous–time settings.

EXERCISES

EXERCISE 0.1   Verify the claim at the end of Paragraph C as follows. Suppose

$$\big((\theta^1, x^1), \ldots, (\theta^I, x^I), (q, \psi)\big)$$

is a security–spot market equilibrium with securities $d_1, \ldots, d_N$ that span R^S. Show the existence of a contingent commodity market equilibrium with the same allocation $(x^1, \ldots, x^I)$. Assume $N = S$.

EXERCISE 0.2   Derive relation (12), the Capital Asset Pricing Model, directly from relation (11) using only the definition of covariance and algebraic manipulation.

EXERCISE 0.3   Show, when the Capital Asset Pricing Model applies, that the expected return on a portfolio uncorrelated with the market portfolio is the riskless return.

EXERCISE 0.4   Verify relation (25) by an application of Ito's Lemma.

EXERCISE 0.5   Verify the calculation $\Pi = A^{-1}(I - \rho P)^{-1} - I$ from relation (19).

EXERCISE 0.6 Derive relation (23) from Ito's Lemma in the form

$$\lim_{T \to 0} \; E\left[\frac{f(X_T) - f(X_0)}{T}\right] = \mathcal{D}f(X_0).$$

EXERCISE 0.7 Solve for the value function V in Paragraph J in the case of the power function $u(c) = c^\alpha$ for $\alpha \in (0,1)$.

EXERCISE 0.8 Verify the self–financing restriction (25) for the proposed trading strategy by applying Ito's Lemma from Paragraph K. Then verify relations (26), (27), and (28).

EXERCISE 0.9 Provide a particular example of a security–spot market equilibrium $\big((\theta^1, x^1), \ldots, (\theta^I, x^I), (q, x)\big)$ in the sense of Paragraph C for which $(x^1, \ldots, x^I)$ is not an efficient allocation. *Hint:* For one possible example, one could try $I = 2$ agents, $N = 1$ security, $s = 2$ states, and

$$u_i(x) = \log(x_0) + \beta_1^i \log(x_1) + \beta_2^i \log(x_2).$$

EXERCISE 0.10 Suppose $L = R^N$ and $u_i : L \to R$ is strictly concave and monotonic for each i (but not necessarily differentiable). Show that $x^1, \ldots, x^I$ is an efficient allocation for $\big((u_i, \omega^i)\big)$ if and only if there exist strictly positive scalars $\gamma_1, \ldots, \gamma_I$ such that

$$(x^1, \ldots, x^I) \text{ solves } \max_{y^1, \ldots, y^I} \; \sum_{i=1}^{I} \gamma_i u_i(y^i) \text{ subject to } \sum_{i=1}^{I} y^i \le \sum_{i=1}^{I} \omega^i.$$

Hint: The "if" portion is easy. For the "only if" portion, one can use the Separating Hyperplane Theorem.

EXERCISE 0.11 Show that the representative agent utility function u_γ is differentiable, and that $p = \nabla u_\gamma$ for suitable γ.

EXERCISE 0.12 Demonstrate relations (34) and (35).

Notes

The notion of competitive equilibrium presented in Paragraph A dates back at least to Walras (1874–77). The proof given for the optimality of an equilibrium allocation is due to Arrow (1951). On the treatment of competitive allocations as the outcome of strategic bargaining, one may consult Gale (1986) as well as McLennan and Sonnenschein (1986). Further references are cited in the Notes of Section 3. The contingent commodity market equilibrium model and the spanning role of securities presented in Paragraphs B and C are due to Arrow (1953). Duffie and Sonnenschein (1988) give further discussion of Arrow (1953). Extensions of this model are discussed in Section 12.

The dynamic spanning idea of Paragraph D is from an early edition of Sharpe (1985). The limiting argument leading to the Black–Scholes (1973) Option Pricing Formula is given by Cox, Ross, and Rubinstein (1979), with further extensions in Section 22. The Capital Asset Pricing Model is credited to Sharpe (1964) and Lintner (1965). The proof given for the CAPM is adapted from Chamberlain (1985). Further results are found in Section 11. A proof of the CAPM based on the representative agent pricing formula (35) is given in Exercise 25.14; there are many other proofs. The dynamic programming asset pricing model of Paragraph G is from Rubinstein (1976) and Lucas (1978), and is extended in Section 20. The overview of Ito calculus of Paragraph I is expanded in Section 21. The continuous–time portfolio–consumption control solution of Paragraph J is due to Merton (1971); more general results are presented in Section 24.

Chapter I
STATIC MARKETS

This chapter outlines a basic theory of agent choice and competitive equilibrium in static linear markets, providing a foundation for the stochastic theory of security markets found in the following three chapters. By a *linear market*, as explained in Section 1, we mean a nexus of economic trading by agents with the properties: (i) any linear combination of two marketed choices forms a third choice also available on the market, and (ii) the market value of a given linear combination of two choices is the same linear combination of the respective market values of the two choices. This, and the assumption that agents express demands taking announced market prices as given, form the cornerstone of competitive market theory as it has developed mainly over the last century. As general equilibrium theory matures, economists increasingly explore other market structures. Competitive linear markets, however, are still the principal focus of financial economic theory. Although this may be due to some degree of conformity of financial markets themselves with the competitive linear markets assumption, one must keep in mind that equilibrium in financial markets is closely entwined with equilibrium in goods markets. We will nevertheless keep a tight grip on our competitive linear market assumption throughout this work. Agents' preferences are added to the story in Section 2. The benchmark theory of competitive equilibrium is then briefly reviewed in Section 3. The first concepts of probability theory are introduced in Section 4. The essential ingredients here are the probability space, random variables, and expectation. This is just in time for an overview of the expected utility representation of preferences in Section 5, along with the usual caveat about its restrictiveness. Section 6 specializes the discussion of vector spaces found in Section 1 to a class of vector spaces of importance for equilibrium under uncertainty and over time. Duality, in particular the Riesz Representation Theorem, is an especially useful concept here. Incomplete markets, the subject of Section 7, is a convenient place to introduce security markets, spanning, and our still unsatisfactory understanding of the firm's behavior in incomplete markets. Section 8 covers the first principles of optimization theory, in particular the role of Lagrange multipliers, which are then connected to equilibrium price vectors. More advanced probability concepts appear in Section 9, where the crucial notion of conditional expectation appears. Section 10 examines a useful definition of risk aversion: x is preferred to $x + y$ if the expectation of y given x is zero. In a setting of static markets under uncertainty, Section 11 characterizes some necessary conditions for market equilibria, principally the Capital Asset Pricing Model, and states sufficient conditions for existence of equilibria in a useful class of choice spaces.

1.   The Geometry of Choices and Prices

This section introduces the vector and topological structures of mathematical models of markets. These supply us with a geometry, allowing us to draw from our Euclidean sense of the physical world for intuition. A third structural aspect, measurability, is added later to model the flow of information in settings of uncertainty. A vector structure for markets arrives from a presumed linearity of market choices: any linear combination of two given choices forms a third choice. If linearity also prevails in market valuation—the market value of the sum of two choices is the sum of their market values—then the vector structures of market choices and market prices are linked through the concept of duality. The geometry of markets is fully established by adding a topology, conveying a sense of "closeness".

A.   In abstract terms, each agent in an economy acts by selecting an element of a *choice set* X, a subset of a *choice space* L common to all agents. Since the choice space L could consist of scalar quantities, Euclidean vectors, random variables, stochastic processes, or even more complicated entities, it is convenient to devise a common terminology and theory for general choice spaces. For many purposes, this turns out to be the theory of topological vector spaces developed in this century. The terms defined in this section should be familiar, if perhaps only in a more specific context.

For our purposes, a "scalar" is merely a real number, although other scalar fields such as the complex numbers also fit the theory of vector spaces. A set L is a *vector space* if: (i) an *addition* function maps any x and y in L to an element in L written $x + y$, (ii) a *scalar multiplication* function maps any scalar α and any $x \in L$ to an element of L denoted αx, and (iii) there is a special element $0 \in L$ variously called "zero", the "origin", or the "null vector", among other suggestive names, such that the following eight properties apply to any x, y, and z in L and any scalars α and β:

(a) $x + y = y + x$,

(b) $x + (y + z) = (x + y) + z$,

(c) $x + 0 = x$,

(d) there exists $w \in L$ such that $w + x = 0$,

(e) $\alpha(x + y) = \alpha x + \alpha y$,

(f) $(\alpha + \beta)x = \alpha x + \beta x$,

(g) $\alpha(\beta x) = (\alpha\beta)x$, and

(h) $1x = x$.

If L is a vector space, also termed a *linear space*, its elements are *vectors*. We write "$-x$" for the vector $-1x$, and "$y - x$" for $y + (-x)$.

B. Most of the specific vector spaces we will see are equipped with a *norm*, defined as a real–valued function $\| \cdot \|$ on a vector space L with the properties: for any x and y in L and any scalar α,

(a) $\| x \| \geq 0$,

(b) $\| \alpha x \| = | \alpha | \| x \|$,

(c) $\| x + y \| \leq \| x \| + \| y \|$, and

(d) $\| x \| = 0 \iff x = 0$.

These properties are easy to appreciate by thinking of the norm of a vector as its "length" or "size", as suggested by the following example.

Example. For any integer $N \geq 1$, *N–dimensional Euclidean space*, denoted R^N, is the set of N–tuples $x = (x_1, \ldots, x_N)$, where x_n is a real number, $1 \leq n \leq N$. Addition is defined by $x + y = (x_1 + y_1, \ldots, x_N + y_N)$, and scalar multiplication by $\alpha x = (\alpha x_1, \ldots, \alpha x_N)$. The *Euclidean norm* on R^N is defined by $\| x \|_{R^N} = \sqrt{x_1^2 + \cdots + x_N^2}$ for all x in R^N. A vector in R^N is classically treated in economics as a commodity bundle of N different goods, such as corn, leisure time, and so on. In a multiperiod setting under uncertainty, each co–ordinate of a Euclidean vector could correspond to a particular good consumed at a particular time provided a particular uncertain event occurs. For example, if there are three different goods consumed at time zero and, contingent on any of four mutually exclusive events, at time one, we would have $N = 3 + 4 \times 3 = 15$. ♠

A *ball* in a vector space L normed by $\| \cdot \|$ is a subset of the form

$$B_{x\rho} = \{y \in L : \| y - x \| \leq \rho\},$$

for some *center* $x \in L$ and scalar *radius* $\rho > 0$. A subset of a normed space is *bounded* if contained by a ball.

C.   A common regularity condition in economics is convexity. A subset X of a vector space is *convex* provided $\alpha x + (1 - \alpha)y \in X$ for any vectors x and y in X and any scalar $\alpha \in [0, 1]$. A *cone* is a subset C of a vector space with the property that $\alpha x \in C$ for all $x \in C$ and all scalars $\alpha \geq 0$. An *ordering* "$\geq$" on a vector space L is induced by a convex cone $C \subset L$ by writing $x \geq y$ whenever $x - y \in C$. In that case, C is called the *positive cone* of L and denoted L_+. Any element of L_+ is labeled *positive*. For instance, the convex cone $R_+^N = \{x \in R^N : x_1 \geq 0, \ldots, x_N \geq 0\}$ defines the usual positive cone or *orthant* of R^N.

D.   A *function space* is a vector space F of real–valued functions on a given set Ω. Vector addition is defined *pointwise*, constructing $f + g$, for any f and g in F, by

$$(f + g)(t) = f(t) + g(t) \quad \text{for all } t \text{ in } \Omega.$$

Scalar multiplication is similarly defined pointwise. The usual positive cone of F is $F_+ = \{f \in F : f(t) \geq 0 \text{ for all } t \in \Omega\}$. If Ω is a convex subset of some vector space, a function $f \in F$ is *convex* provided

$$\alpha f(t) + (1 - \alpha)f(s) \geq f[\alpha t + (1 - \alpha)s]$$

for any t and s in Ω and any scalar $\alpha \in [0, 1]$. A real–valued function on a subset of a vector space is a *functional*. A functional f on Ω is *linear* provided $f(\alpha s + \beta t) = \alpha f(s) + \beta f(t)$ for all s and t in Ω and all scalars α and β such that $\alpha s + \beta t \in \Omega$.

E.   Partly in order to give a general mathematical meaning to "closeness", the concept of topology has been developed. A *topology* for any set Ω is a set of subsets of Ω, called *open sets*, satisfying the conditions:

(a) the intersection of any two open sets is open,

(b) the union of any collection of open sets is open, and

(c) the empty set $\emptyset$ and Ω itself are both open.

Given a particular topology for a set Ω, a subset X is *closed* if its complement, $\Omega \setminus X \equiv \{x \in \Omega : x \notin X\}$, is open. An element x is an *interior point* of a set X if there is an open subset $\mathcal{O}$ of X such that $x \in \mathcal{O}$. The *interior* of a set X, denoted $\text{int}(X)$, is the set of interior points of X. The *closure* of a set X, denoted $\overline{X}$, is the set of all points not in the interior of the complement $\Omega \setminus X$.

We already have a convenient sense of closeness for normed vector spaces by thinking of $\| x - y \|$ as the distance between x and y in a vector space normed by $\| \cdot \|$. This is formalized by defining a subset X of a normed space L to be open if every x in X is the center of some ball contained by X. The resulting family of open sets is the *norm topology*. A *normed space* is a normed vector space endowed with the norm topology. Although normed vector spaces form a sufficiently large class to handle most applications in economics, the bulk of the theory we will develop can be extended to the majority of common *topological vector spaces*, a class of vector spaces that we will not expressly define, but which can be studied in sources cited in the Notes.

We can use the notion of closeness defined by a norm to pose simple versions of the following basic topological concepts. A sequence $\{x_n\}$ of vectors in a normed space L *converges* if there is a unique $x \in L$ such that the sequence of real numbers $\{\| x_n - x \|\}$ converges to zero. We then say $\{x_n\}$ converges to x, write $x_n \to x$, and call x the *limit* of the sequence. If L and M are normed spaces, a function $f : L \to M$ is *continuous* if $\{f(x_n)\}$ converges to $f(x)$ in M whenever $\{x_n\}$ converges to x in L. The case $M = R$ is typical, defining the vector space of continuous functionals on L.

Suppose Ω is a space with a topology. A subset K of Ω is *compact* provided, whenever there exists a collection $\{\mathcal{O}_\lambda : \lambda \in \Lambda\}$ of open sets whose union contains K, there also exists a finite sub–collection $\{\mathcal{O}_{\lambda_1}, \ldots, \mathcal{O}_{\lambda_N}\}$ of these sets whose union contains K. In a Euclidean space a set is compact if and only if the set is closed and bounded, a result known as the *Heine–Borel Theorem*.

F. *Duality*, the relationship between a vector space L and the vector space L' of linear functionals on L, plays a special role in economics because of the usual assumption of *linear markets*. That is, the set of marketed choices is a vector space L, and market values are assigned by some *price functional* p in L', meaning

$$p \cdot (\alpha x + \beta y) = \alpha (p \cdot x) + \beta (p \cdot y)$$

for all x and y in L and scalars α and β. The raised–dot notation "$p \cdot x$" is adopted for the evaluation of linear functionals, and will be maintained throughout as a suggestive signal. The arguments for linear pricing are clear, but also clearly do not apply in many markets, for instance those with volume discounts. The vector space L' is the *algebraic dual* of L. If L is a normed space, then the subset L^* of L' whose elements are continuous is the *topological dual* of L, which is also a vector space.

G.   The *product* of two sets A and B, denoted $A \times B$, is the set of pairs $\{(a, b) : a \in A, \, b \in B\}$. A functional f on the product $L \times M$ of two vector spaces L and M is *bilinear* if both $f(x, \cdot) : M \to R$ and $f(\cdot, y) : L \to R$ are linear functionals for any x in L and y in M. If L is a normed space, L and M are *in duality* if there exists such a bilinear form f with the property: for each p in L^* there is a unique y in M with $p \cdot x = f(x, y)$ for all x in L. If L and M are in duality, each element of L^* is thus identified through a bilinear form with a unique element of M, so we often write $L^* = M$ even though the equal sign is not properly defined here. The duality between certain pairs of vector spaces is important because of our interest in convenient representations for price functionals.

Example.   Any linear functional on R^N is continuous and is identified with a unique vector in R^N through the bilinear form f on $R^N \times R^N$ defined by

$$f(x, y) = x^\top y \equiv x_1 y_1 + \cdots + x_N y_N$$

for all x and y in R^N. Thus R^N is in duality with itself, or *self–dual*. In our informal notation, $(R^N)^* = R^N$. For this reason we often abuse the notation by writing $x \cdot y$ interchangeably with $x^\top y$ for any x and y in R^N. Taking R^N as a choice space and p as a price functional, duality implies the existence of a unique vector $\pi = (\pi_1, \ldots, \pi_N)$ such that $p \cdot x = \pi^\top x$ for all x in R^N. We can think of π_n as the unit price of the n–th co–ordinate good. ♠

In Section 6 we identify the topological duals of other vector spaces. In fact, most of the choice spaces we will use are self–dual. This is indeed convenient, for each price functional p on a vector space L is then identified with a particular market choice π in L. The concept of duality also plays a key role in the theory of optimization, as we see in Section 8.

EXERCISES

EXERCISE 1.1   Show that a ball in a normed vector space is a convex set.

EXERCISE 1.2   Verify that a function space F is indeed a vector space under pointwise addition and scalar multiplication.

EXERCISE 1.3   Show that the Euclidean norm $\| \cdot \|_{R^N}$ satisfies the four properties of a norm on R^N.

EXERCISE 1.4   A functional f is *concave* if $-f$ is convex, and *affine* if both convex and concave. Show that an affine functional can be represented as the sum of a scalar and a linear functional.

EXERCISE 1.5 The *sum* of two subsets X and Y of a vector space L is the subset

$$X + Y = \{z \in L : z = x + y, \quad x \in X, \quad y \in Y\}.$$

Prove that the sum of two convex sets is convex and demonstrate a convex set that is the sum of two sets that are not both convex. Show that the sum of two cones is a cone. Devise the obvious definition of scalar multiplication of subsets of a vector space, and an obvious definition of the "zero set", such that the space of convex subsets of a given vector space satisfies all but one of the eight vector space axioms. Which one?

EXERCISE 1.6 The *recession cone*, denoted $A(X)$, of a convex subset X of a vector space L is defined by $A(X) = \{z \in L : x + z \in X \text{ for all } x \in X\}$. Prove the following properties:

(a) If X is a convex subset of L, then $A(X)$ is a convex cone.
(b) If X is a convex subset of L, then $A(X + \{z\}) = A(X)$ for all z in L.
(c) If X is a convex subset of L and $0 \in X$, then $A(X) \subset X$.
(d) If X and Y are convex subsets of L, then $A(X) \subset A(X + Y)$.

EXERCISE 1.7 Show that a "norm topology", as defined in Paragraph E, is indeed a topology.

EXERCISE 1.8 The *product* of N sets $X_1, \ldots, X_N$, denoted $X_1 \times X_2 \times \cdots \times X_N$, or alternatively $\prod_{n=1}^{N} X_n$, is the set of N–tuples $(x_1, \ldots, x_N)$ where $x_n \in X_n$, $1 \leq n \leq N$. If the sets X_n are all the same set X, the product is denoted X^N (hence the notation R^N). Suppose Y is the product of N convex subsets $X_1, \ldots, X_N$ of a vector space. Show that $A(Y) \subset \prod_{n=1}^{N} A(X_n)$.

EXERCISE 1.9 A *topological space* is a pair $(\Omega, \mathcal{T})$ comprising a set Ω and a topology $\mathcal{T}$ for Ω. Consider the alternative definition of topological space as a pair $(\Omega, \mathcal{A})$ comprising a set Ω and a set $\mathcal{A}$ of subsets of Ω called *closed sets* satisfying: (a) any intersection of closed sets is closed, (b) the union of two closed sets is closed, and (c) Ω and $\emptyset$ are closed. Show that $(\Omega, \mathcal{A})$ is a topological space in this sense (of closed sets) if and only if $(\Omega, \mathcal{T})$ is a topological space in the usual sense (of open sets), where $\mathcal{T} = \{\Omega \setminus A : A \in \mathcal{A}\}$.

EXERCISE 1.10 Suppose L is a normed vector space with a closed convex subset X. Prove that the recession cone $A(X)$ is defined, for any $x \in X$, by

$$A(X) = \{z \in L : x + \alpha z \in X \text{ for all } \alpha \in R_+\}.$$

Suppose $\{X_\lambda : \lambda \in \Lambda\}$ is a family of closed convex subsets of L with non–empty intersection X. Prove $A(X) = \bigcap_{\lambda \in \Lambda} A(X_\lambda)$.

EXERCISE 1.11   Suppose X and Y are closed convex subsets of a normed space L. Prove that if $X \bigcap Y$ is bounded then $A(X) \bigcap A(Y) = \{0\}$. In the case $L = R^N$, prove that the converse is true, or $A(X) \bigcap A(Y) = \{0\}$ implies that $X \bigcap Y$ is bounded.

EXERCISE 1.12   Prove that the algebraic dual of any vector space and the topological dual of any normed vector space are themselves vector spaces under pointwise addition and scalar multiplication.

EXERCISE 1.13   Suppose $L = R^N$. Prove the claims in Example 1G. That is, show that $L' = L^*$, and that $p \in L^*$ if and only if, for some unique $y \in R^N$, $p \cdot x = x^\top y$ for all x in R^N.

EXERCISE 1.14   Suppose the normed spaces $L_1, \ldots, L_N$ are in duality with the vector spaces $M_1, \ldots, M_N$ respectively, through the bilinear forms $f_1, \ldots, f_N$. Show that the product spaces $L = \prod_{n=1}^{N} L_n$ and $M = \prod_{n=1}^{N} M_n$ are in duality through the bilinear form $f : L \times M \to R$ defined by

$$f(x, y) = \sum_{n=1}^{N} f_n(x_n, y_n)$$

for all $x = (x_1, \cdots, x_N) \in L$ and $y = (y_1, \cdots, y_N) \in M$. In other words, the "dual of the product is the product of the duals". Extend this result to the algebraic dual M' of the product $M = \prod_{n=1}^{N} M_n$ of vector spaces $M_1, \ldots, M_N$ by showing that any linear functional p on M can be represented by linear functionals $p_n \in M_n', 1 \leq n \leq N$, in the form $p \cdot x = \sum_{n=1}^{N} p_n \cdot x_n$ for any $x = (x_1, \ldots, x_N)$ in M.

EXERCISE 1.15   For any vector space L normed by $\| \cdot \|$, prove the parallelogram inequality: $\| x + y \|^2 + \| x - y \|^2 \leq 2 \| x \|^2 + 2 \| y \|^2$.

EXERCISE 1.16   The dual norm $\| \cdot \|_*$ on the topological dual L^* of a vector space L normed by $\| \cdot \|$ is defined by

$$\| p \|_* = \sup \{| p \cdot x | : x \in L, \| x \| \leq 1\}, \quad \text{for all } p \in L^*.$$

Verify that $\| \cdot \|_*$ is indeed a norm. A linear functional f on L is bounded if the set of real numbers $\{f(x) : \| x \| \leq 1\}$ is bounded. Show that a given linear functional is continuous if and only if bounded.

EXERCISE 1.17   If X is a closed subset of a topological space, show that $\overline{X} = X$.

Notes

The material in this section is standard. Robertson and Robertson (1973) is an introductory treatment of the topic and highly recommended. At the advanced level, Schaefer (1971) is already a classic. On topology in particular, Jänich (1984) gives a useful overview. Day (1973) is a concise general treatment of normed spaces. Raikov (1965) is definitive on vector spaces. Some of the exercises are original.

2. Preferences

Much of economic theory is based on the premise: given two alternatives, an agent can, and will if able, choose a preferred one. In this section we explore a common interpretation of this statement and outline several convenient analytical properties that preferences may display.

A. Let X be a *choice set*, a collection of alternatives. We model an agent's preferences over these alternatives through a *binary order*, a subset $\succeq$ of $X \times X$. We say x *is preferred to* y if $(x, y) \in \succeq$, which is suggestively denoted $x \succeq y$. Both $x \succeq y$ and $y \succeq x$ may simultaneously be true, in which case we say x is *indifferent* to y, written $x \sim y$. Finally, if $x \succeq y$ but not $y \succeq x$, we say that x is *strictly preferred to* y, and write $x \succ y$. The resulting binary order $\succ \subset X \times X$ is the *strict order* induced by $\succeq$.

A binary order $\succeq$ on X is *complete* if $y \succeq x$ whenever $x \succeq y$ is not the case, meaning that any two choices can be ordered. A binary order is *transitive* if $x \succeq z$ whenever $x \succeq y$ and $y \succeq z$, for any x, y, and z in X. As a convenience, the term *preference relation* is adopted for a complete transitive binary order. Many of the results we will state for preference relations also apply to more general binary orders.

B. For a preference relation $\succeq$ on a set X and any $x \in X$, let G_x denote the "at least as good as x" set $\{y \in X : y \succeq x\}$ and B_x denote the "at least as bad as x" set $\{y \in X : x \succeq y\}$. If X is a subset of a given topological space and both G_x and B_x are closed for all $x \in X$, then $\succeq$ is *continuous*. If X is a subset of a vector space and G_x is convex for all $x \in X$, then $\succeq$ is *convex*.

C. A real–valued function U on a set X is a *utility function* representing the preference relation $\succeq$ on X provided

$$x \succeq y \iff U(x) \geq U(y)$$

for all x and y in X. There are easily stated conditions under which a preference relation is represented by a utility function. First recall that a set is *countable* if its elements are in one–to–one correspondence with a subset of the integers. For example, the rational numbers form a countable set; any finite set is countable; while the real line is not countable. A topological space Z is *separable* if there is a countable subset Y of Z with closure $\overline{Y} = Z$. Any Euclidean space, for example, is separable. The Notes refer to proofs and generalizations of the following two sufficient conditions for utility representations of preference relations.

PROPOSITION. (a) *A preference relation on a countable set is represented by a utility function.* (b) *A continuous preference relation on a convex subset of a separable normed space is represented by a continuous utility function.*

D.   Let g be a *strictly increasing* real–valued function on R, meaning $g(t) > g(s)$ whenever $t > s$. Let $\succeq$ be a preference relation on a set X represented by a utility function U. It should be no surprise that the composition $g \circ U$ also represents $\succeq$. That is

$$g[U(x)] \geq g[U(y)] \iff x \succeq y. \tag{1}$$

The following proposition, whose proof is assigned as an exercise, states slightly more: a utility function representing a preference relation is unique up to a strictly increasing transformation.

PROPOSITION. *Suppose U and V are utility functions representing the same preference relation. Then there exists a strictly increasing function $g : R \to R$ such that $U = g \circ V$.*

E.   A highly developed body of optimization theory can be applied to choice problems provided the choice set is a subset of a vector space and the preference relation is represented by a concave utility function. A utility function representing a convex preference relation need not be concave. A somewhat weaker condition is thus defined. A functional U on a subset X of a vector space L is *quasi–concave* if the set $\{y \in X : U(y) \geq U(x)\}$ is convex for all $x \in X$. By definition, any utility function representing a convex preference relation on X is quasi–concave. A concave utility function represents a convex preference relation (Exercise 2).

F.   A preference relation $\succeq$ on a subset X of a vector space L is z–*monotonic at* x, for $x \in X$ and $z \in L$, if $x + \alpha z \succeq x$ for all $\alpha \in (0,1)$. The notion is that, starting from x, z is a "good" direction to take. The preference relation $\succeq$ is *strictly z–monotonic* at x if $x + \alpha z \succ x$ for all $\alpha \in (0,1)$. The relation $\succeq$ is *z–monotonic* if z–monotonic at all x in X. *Strict z–monotonicity* is similarly defined. It is common, when L is an ordered choice space such as R^n, to suppose that any positive direction is "good". We thus say that $\succeq$ is *monotonic* if $\succeq$ is z–monotonic for all $z \in L_+$, and similarly define strict monotonicity.

G. Several "continuity–like" propositions concerning preferences can actually be stated without reference to a topology by using the following algebraic constructs. For two points x and y in a vector space L, the *segment* (x, y) is defined by

$$(x, y) = \{\alpha x + (1 - \alpha)y : \alpha \in (0,1)\}. \tag{2}$$

The segments $(x, y]$, $[x, y)$, and $[x, y]$ are then defined by substituting $(0, 1]$, $[0, 1)$, and $[0, 1]$ respectively for $(0, 1)$ in relation (2). For two subsets X and Y of a vector space, the *core* of X *relative to* Y is the set

$$\operatorname{core}_Y(X) = \{x \in X : \forall y \in Y \; \exists z \in (x, y) \text{ such that } (x, z) \subset X\}.$$

Roughly speaking, one can move linearly away from any $x \in \operatorname{core}_Y(X)$ toward any element of Y and remain in X. The core of X relative to the entire vector space L is the *core* of X, denoted $\operatorname{core}(X)$.

A preference relation $\succeq$ on a set X is *non–satiated* at x if there exists some $z \in X$ such that $z \succ x$. If X is a subset of a vector space L, then $\succeq$ is *non satiated nearby* $x \in X$ if, for any set Y such that $x \in \operatorname{core}(Y)$, there exists $y \in Y$ such that $y \succ x$. A sufficient (but not necessary) condition is that $\succeq$ is strictly z–monotonic at x for some $z \in L$.

A preference relation $\succeq$ on a subset X of a normed space L is *locally non–satiated* at $x \in X$ provided, for any $Z \subset L$ such that $x \in \operatorname{int}(Z)$, there exists $z \in Z$ such that $z \succ x$. Exercise 9 shows a connection between non–satiation nearby and local non–satiation.

EXERCISES

EXERCISE 2.1 Prove Proposition 2D.

EXERCISE 2.2 Suppose $\succeq$ is a preference relation on a convex subset of a vector space represented by a concave utility function. Prove that $\succeq$ is convex. Thus concavity implies quasi–concavity.

EXERCISE 2.3 Demonstrate a quasi–concave functional that is not concave.

EXERCISE 2.4 Consider the following three convexity conditions on a preference relation $\succeq$ on a convex set X:

(a) $x \succeq y \Rightarrow \alpha x + (1 - \alpha)y \succeq y$

(b) $x \succ y \Rightarrow \alpha x + (1 - \alpha)y \succ y$, and

(c) $x \sim y \Rightarrow \alpha x + (1 - \alpha)y \succ y$,

for any two distinct elements x and y of X and any scalar $\alpha \in (0,1)$. Show that (a) is equivalent to the convexity of $\succeq$. Prove that if X is a subset of a normed separable space and $\succeq$ is continuous, then (c) $\Rightarrow$ (b) $\Rightarrow$ (a). A preference relation $\succeq$ on a convex set satisfying *(b)* is *strongly convex*. A preference relation $\succeq$ satisfying assumption *(c)* is *strictly convex*. (This terminology is not uniformly used.)

EXERCISE 2.5 It is common to treat $\succ$ as the primitive preference order, and then to write $x \succeq y$ if $y \succ x$ does not hold. Formally, $\succ$ is a *strict preference relation* on a choice set X if $\succ$ is a binary order on X satisfying:

(a) *asymmetry*: $x \succ y \Rightarrow$ not $y \succ x$, and

(b) *negative transitivity*: [not $x \succ y$] and [not $y \succ z$] $\Rightarrow$ not $x \succ z$.

Prove that if $\succ$ is a strict preference relation on X, then $\succeq$, as defined above in terms of $\succ$, is a complete transitive binary order and thus a preference relation on X. Conversely, prove that if $\succeq$ is a complete transitive binary order, then the strict preference relation it induces is an asymmetric negatively transitive binary order.

EXERCISE 2.6 Prove the claim made by relation (1).

EXERCISE 2.7 A preference relation $\succeq$ on a subset X of a vector space L is *algebraically continuous* if the sets $\{x \in L : x \succeq y\}$ and $\{x \in L : y \succeq x\}$ are *algebraically closed*. (A set is *algebraically closed* if it includes all of its lineally accessible points. A point $x \in L$ is *lineally accessible* from a set X if there exists $y \in X$ such that the segment $(x, y]$ is contained by X.) Show that a strictly convex algebraically continuous preference relation on a convex set is a convex preference relation. If L is normed and $\succeq$ is continuous, show that $\succeq$ is algebraically continuous.

EXERCISE 2.8 For any x in a vector space L, $p \in L'$, and scalar $\epsilon > 0$, show that
$$x \in \text{core}(\{z \in L : |\, p \cdot z - p \cdot x \,| < \epsilon\}).$$

Suppose $\succeq$ is a preference relation on a subset X of a vector space L and $\succeq$ is non–satiated nearby $x \in X$. For any scalar $\epsilon > 0$ and price functional $p \in L'$, show that there exists $z \in X$ such that $z \succ x$ and $|\, p \cdot z - p \cdot x \,| < \epsilon$. In other words, if $\succeq$ is non–satiated nearby a budget feasible choice x, then, for any budget supplement $\epsilon > 0$, there is a strictly preferred budget feasible choice z.

EXERCISE 2.9 Suppose $\succeq$ is a preference relation on a subset X of a normed space L, and $\succeq$ is non–satiated nearby $x \in X$. Show that $\succeq$ is locally non–satiated at x.

Notes

Most of this material is standard, a good part of it from Debreu (1959). David Kreps' lecture notes (1981b) are recommended reading. The proof of Proposition 2C is given by Kreps (1981b) for assertion (a), and by Debreu (1954) for a generalization of part (b). See Shafer (1984) and Richard (1985) for further such results. Fishburn (1970) is an advanced source. The definition of "non–satiated nearby" seems new.

3. Market Equilibrium

A competitive equilibrium occurs with a system of prices at which firms' profit maximizing production decisions and individuals' preferred affordable consumption choices equate supply and demand in every market. This concept has been formalized in the classic Arrow–Debreu model, the benchmark for our theory of security market behavior. We now look over the basics of that model.

A.   The primitives of our model of an economy are laid out as follows. Let L be a vector space of choices. Each of a finite set $\mathcal{J} = \{1, \ldots, J\}$ of firms is identified with a *production set* $Y_j \subset L$. Each of a finite set $\mathcal{I} = \{1, \ldots, I\}$ of individual agents is identified with the following characteristics: a choice set $X_i \subset L$, a preference relation $\succeq_i$ on X_i, an *endowment* vector $\omega_i \in L$, and a *share* $\theta_{ij} \in [0,1]$ of the production vector $y_j \in Y_j$ chosen by firm j, whatever that choice may be, for each firm $j \in \mathcal{J}$. Because each firm's production choice is completely shared among agents, $\sum_{i=1}^{I} \theta_{ij} = 1$ for all $j \in \mathcal{J}$. The entire collection of these primitives is termed an *economy*, denoted

$$\mathcal{E} = ((X_i, \succeq_i, \omega_i); (Y_j); (\theta_{ij})), \quad i \in \mathcal{I}, j \in \mathcal{J}. \tag{1}$$

B.   For a particular economy $\mathcal{E}$, a *consumption allocation* is an I–tuple $x = (x_1, \ldots, x_I)$ with $x_i \in X_i$ for all $i \in \mathcal{I}$. A *production allocation* is a J–tuple $y = (y_1, \ldots, y_J)$ with $y_j \in Y_j$ for all $j \in \mathcal{J}$. An *allocation* is an $(I + J)$–tuple (x, y), where x is a consumption allocation and y is a production allocation. An allocation (x, y) is *feasible* if

$$\sum_{i=1}^{I}(x_i - \omega_i) = \sum_{j=1}^{J} y_j. \tag{2}$$

An allocation (x, y) is *strictly supported* by a *price vector* (linear functional) $p \in L'$ if $p \neq 0$,

$$z \succ_i x_i \Rightarrow p \cdot z > p \cdot x_i \quad \forall z \in X_i, \quad \forall i \in \mathcal{I}, \tag{3}$$

and

$$p \cdot y_j \geq p \cdot z \quad \forall z \in Y_j, \quad \forall j \in \mathcal{J}. \tag{4}$$

Finally, an allocation (x, y) is *budget–constrained* by a price vector p if, for each $i \in \mathcal{I}$,

$$p \cdot x_i \leq p \cdot \left[\omega_i + \sum_{j=1}^{J} \theta_{ij} y_j \right]. \tag{5}$$

Conditions (3) and (5) are the optimality conditions for agents, given a price vector p. Condition (4) is market value maximization by firms, given p. The reader may prove the following result as a simple exercise.

LEMMA. *If (x, y) is a feasible allocation that is budget constrained by $p \in L'$ then the budget constraint (5) holds with equality for each agent i in $\mathcal{I}$.*

A triple $(x, y, p) \in L^I \times L^J \times L'$ is an *equilibrium* for $\mathcal{E}$ if (x, y) is a feasible allocation that is budget–constrained and strictly supported by p. This fundamental concept, the focal point of these lectures, is variously known as an *Arrow–Debreu equilibrium*, a *competitive equilibrium*, or a *Walrasian equilibrium*, among other terms.

C.   An *exchange economy* is a simpler collection of primitives:

$$\mathcal{E} = (X_i, \succeq_i, \omega_i), \quad i \in \mathcal{I}, \tag{6}$$

where the indicated characteristics for each agent i are as defined in Paragraph A. In order to make a distinction, the original economy (1) may be termed a *production–exchange economy*. The definition of an equilibrium for an exchange economy is clear: $(x, p) \in L^I \times L'$ is an *equilibrium* if x is a feasible consumption allocation that is strictly supported and budget–constrained by p. These terms are applied with the obvious deletions of production choices from relations (2), (3), and (5).

A *net trade exchange economy* is an even simpler collection of primitives:

$$\mathcal{E} = (X_i, \succeq_i), \quad i \in \mathcal{I}.$$

A net trade exchange economy may be treated as an exchange economy with zero endowments, but is more aptly imagined to be an economy in which each agent $i \in \mathcal{I}$ expresses preferences over a choice set X_i of potential additions to endowments. To state the obvious, $(x, p) \in L^I \times L'$ is an equilibrium for a net trade economy provided $p \neq 0$, $\sum_{i=1}^{I} x_i = 0$, and for all $i \in \mathcal{I}$: $p \cdot x_i = 0$, $x \in X_i$, and $z \succ_i x_i \Rightarrow p \cdot z > p \cdot x_i$ for all $z \in X_i$.

Not surprisingly, an exchange economy is equivalent, insofar as market behavior is concerned, to a corresponding net trade economy. From the exchange economy (6), for example, we can define the net trade economy $\mathcal{E}' = (X_i', \succeq_i')$, $i \in \mathcal{I}$, by

$$X_i' = X_i - \{\omega_i\} \tag{7}$$

and

$$s \succeq_i' t \iff s + \omega_i \succeq_i t + \omega_i \tag{8}$$

for all s and t in X_i'. We have simply translated the choice sets and preference relations by the endowment vectors. The relevant equivalence between $\mathcal{E}$ and $\mathcal{E}'$ is stated by the following trivial result.

LEMMA. $(x_1, \ldots, x_I, p)$ *is an equilibrium for an exchange economy* $(X_i, \succeq_i, \omega_i)$, $i \in \mathcal{I}$, *if and only if* $(x_1 - \omega_1, \ldots, x_I - \omega_I, p)$ *is an equilibrium for the associated net trade economy* $(X_i', \succeq_i')$, $i \in \mathcal{I}$, *defined by* (7)–(8).

D. *A production–exchange equilibrium can be treated as an exchange equilibrium in two different senses, via the following two rearrangements.*

Rearrangement 1. If (x, y, p) is an equilibrium for the production–exchange economy (1), then (x, p) is an equilibrium for the exchange economy

$$\mathcal{E}^y = \left(X_i, \succeq_i, \omega_i + \sum_{j=1}^{J} \theta_{ij} y_j \right), \quad i \in \mathcal{I}.$$

Rearrangement 2. (x, y, p) is an equilibrium for the production–exchange economy (1) if and only if $(x_1, \ldots, x_I, -y_1, \ldots, -y_J, p)$ is an equilibrium for the $(I+J)$–agent exchange economy: $\mathcal{E}' = (X_k', \succeq_k', \omega_k')$, $k \in \{1, \ldots, I+J\}$, where

$$(X_k', \succeq_k', \omega_k') = (X_k, \succeq_k, \omega_k + \sum_{j=1}^{J} \theta_{kj} y_j), \quad k \in \mathcal{I},$$

$$= (-Y_j, \succeq_j^P, 0), \quad k = I + j, \quad j \in \mathcal{J},$$

and where the preference relation $\succeq_j^p$ is defined by

$$z \succeq_j^p v \iff p \cdot z \leq p \cdot v$$

for all z and v in $-Y_j$, $j \in \mathcal{J}$.

According to Rearrangement 2, each firm can be treated in equilibrium as though it were an agent "consuming" minus its production vector and minimizing the market value of "consumption", or value maximizing. Both of the above rearrangements will prove useful in later work.

E.   We now turn to the important link between equilibrium and allocational efficiency. A consumption allocation $x \in L^I$ for a given economy *dominates* another consumption allocation x' whenever

$$x_i \succ_i x_i', \quad \forall i \in \mathcal{I}, \tag{9}$$

and *weakly dominates* x' whenever $x_i \succeq_i x_i'$ for all $i \in \mathcal{I}$, with some i in $\mathcal{I}$ satisfying $x_i \succ_i x_i'$. A feasible allocation (x, y) for a production–exchange economy is *efficient* if there is no feasible allocation (x', y') such that x' weakly dominates x. A feasible allocation (x, y) is *weakly efficient* if no other feasible allocation (x', y') exists such that x' dominates x. The term *Pareto optimal* replaces 'efficient' in many vocabularies. The corresponding definitions for exchange economies are the obvious ones. Among the results linking equilibria and efficiency, the following is perhaps the simplest, notably absent of regularity conditions and budget constraints. This is a version of the *First Welfare Theorem*.

PROPOSITION.   *For a given exchange economy, if x is a feasible allocation strictly supported by some price vector, then x is weakly efficient.*

Proofs of the last and the next version of the First Welfare Theorem are left as exercises.

THEOREM.   *Suppose x is a feasible allocation for an exchange economy and x is strictly supported by a price vector. If, for all $i \in \mathcal{I}$, $\succeq_i$ is nonsatiated nearby any choice in X_i, then x is efficient.*

F.   Having claimed that strictly price supported feasible allocations (in particular, equilibria) are efficient under slight conditions, we turn to the converse. A slightly different form of "price support" is defined. A production–exchange economy (1) on a vector choice space L is given. An allocation (x, y) is *supported* by a price vector $p \in L'$ if $p \neq 0$,

$$z \succeq_i x_i \implies p \cdot z \geq p \cdot x_i \quad \forall z \in X_i, \quad \forall i \in \mathcal{I}, \tag{10}$$

and

$$p \cdot y_j \geq p \cdot z \quad \forall z \in Y_j, \quad \forall j \in \mathcal{J}.$$

The distinction between "strict support" (3) and support (10) is dealt with in Exercises 5 and 6. Neither implies the other, but they differ only by weak regularity conditions.

We are about to see that any efficient allocation is supported by some price vector under regularity conditions. For this, we will roll out one of two big mathematical engines driving competitive analysis, the Separating Hyperplane Theorem. (The second, a fixed point theorem, is left parked out of sight for now.) A proof of the following form of the Separating Hyperplane Theorem is cited in the Notes.

PROPOSITION (SEPARATING HYPERPLANE THEOREM). *Let Z be a convex subset with non–empty core of a vector space L. There exists a non–zero $p \subset L'$ such that $p \cdot z \geq 0$ for all z in Z if and only if $0 \notin \mathrm{core}\,(Z)$.*

For a particular economy and consumption allocation $x \in L^I$, let X^x denote the set of vectors z that can be split into I vectors as $z = z_1 + \cdots + z_I$, such that $z_i \succeq_i x_i$ for all i in $\mathcal{I}$. Formally, $X^x = \sum_{i=1}^{I} \{z_i \in X_i : z_i \succeq x_i\}$. The *total production set* for the economy is denoted $Y \equiv \sum_{j=1}^{J} Y_j$. Now we see the promised result, a version of the *Second Welfare Theorem*, happily free of topological considerations.

THEOREM. *Suppose (x, y) is an efficient allocation for an economy satisfying the following conditions:* (a) $X^x - Y$ *is convex and has non–empty core, and* (b) *for some $k \subset \mathcal{I}$, $\succeq_k$ is strictly z monotonic for some $z \in L$. Then (x, y) is supported by some price vector.*

Before proving this theorem, we note that the assumed convexity in (a) follows if $\succeq_i$ is convex for all $i \in \mathcal{I}$ and Y_j is convex for all $j \in \mathcal{J}$. Exercise 9 states an improvement of this theorem, weakening the assumption of non–empty core in (a). Another exercise asks the reader to show that the non–empty core condition can be removed in Euclidean settings.

PROOF: Let $Z = X^x - Y - \{\sum_{i=1}^{I} \omega_i\}$. If $0 \in \mathrm{core}(Z)$ then for some $z \in L$ given by (b) and for some $\alpha \in (0,1)$, $\alpha z \in \mathrm{core}(Z)$. But this implies the existence of an allocation (x', y') such that $x'_i \succeq_i x_i$ for all i and such that

$$(x'_1, \ldots, x'_{k-1}, x'_k + \alpha z, x'_{k+1}, \ldots, x'_I, y'_1, \ldots, y'_J) \quad (11)$$

is feasible, contradicting the efficiency of (x, y), since $x'_k + \alpha z_k \succ_k x'_k \succeq_k x_k$. Thus, $0 \notin \mathrm{core}(Z)$. By (a), $\mathrm{core}(Z)$ is not empty, and by the Separating Hyperplane Theorem (Proposition 3F), there exists a non–zero $p \in L'$ such that $p \cdot z \geq 0$ for all $z \in Z$.

Suppose $v \succeq_h x_h$ for some $h \in \mathcal{I}$. Since $\sum_{i=1}^{I} x_i - \omega_i \in Y$ and $v + \sum_{i \neq h} x_i \in X^x$, we have $v - x_h \in Z$ and $p \cdot v \geq p \cdot x_h$. This is true for all $h \in \mathcal{I}$. By a similar argument, $p \cdot v \leq p \cdot y_j$ for all $v \in Y_j$ and for all $j \in \mathcal{J}$. ∎

G.   We turn now to conditions ensuring the existence of equilibria. Proofs are omitted, but cited in the Notes. The proof of a simple case is outlined in an exercise. We fix the economy $\mathcal{E}$ of (1). If $(x, y) \in L^I \times L^J$ is a feasible allocation that is supported and budget–constrained by $p \in L'$, then (x, y, p) is a *compensated equilibrium*. Because conditions ensuring strict price support are cumbersome to state in generality, it is common to establish general sufficient conditions for compensated equilibria, and then to bridge the gap to an equilibrium with assumptions particularly suited to the situation. We have, for example, the following result, a trivial consequence of Exercise 5.

PROPOSITION.   *Suppose* (x, y, p) *is a compensated equilibrium such that for all* i, X_i *is convex,* $\succeq_i$ *is algebraically continuous, and there exists* $\underline{x}_i \in X_i$ *such that* $p \cdot \underline{x}_i < p \cdot x_i$. *Then* (x, y, p) *is an equilibrium.*

(For normed choice spaces, algebraic continuity of preferences is implied by continuity, as stated by Exercise 2.7.) As in Paragraph B, translation of choice sets and preference relations allows us to work in the net trade case, assuming without loss of generality that $\omega_i = 0$ for all $i \in \mathcal{I}$. Let $X = \sum_{i=1}^{I} X_i$ denote the *total consumption set*, analogous to the total production set Y. A set $\ddot{Y} \subset L$ is an *augmented production set* for the economy if $Y \subset \ddot{Y}$ and $\ddot{Y} \cap X = Y \cap X$. In other words, $\ddot{Y}$ and Y produce the same feasible allocations, in fact, the same equilibria (Exercise 3.7). A choice $z \in X_i$ is *feasible for agent* i if there exists a feasible allocation (x, y) such that $z = x_i$. Let $\widehat{X}_i$ denote the set of feasible choices for agent $i \in \mathcal{I}$. Let $\mathcal{D}$ denote the subset of L whose elements are of the form $z = z_1 + \cdots + z_I$, with

$$z_i \succ_i x_i \quad \forall x_i \in \widehat{X}_i \quad \forall i \in \mathcal{I}.$$

That is, $\mathcal{D}$ is the set of choices that can be shared among agents making each better off than possible in any feasible allocation. Let D denote the *cone generated* by $\mathcal{D}$, that is, the intersection of all cones containing $\mathcal{D}$. For example, if L is an ordered vector space, the economy has no positive production, and all preference relations are strictly monotonic, then $L_+ \subset D$. The following conditions ensure the existence of compensated equilibria for Euclidean choice spaces.

The Debreu Conditions

(a) $X \cap (-X)$ is bounded,

(b) X_i is closed and convex for all $i \in \mathcal{I}$,

(c) D is not empty,

(d) $\succeq_i$ is continuous and convex for all $i \in \mathcal{I}$,

(e) $Y \cap X$ is bounded and not empty,

(f) $0 \in Y_j$ for all $j \in \mathcal{J}$, and

(g) there exists a closed convex augmented production set $\ddot{Y}$ such that

$$0 \in A\left(\ddot{Y}\right) - D - X_i \quad \forall i \in \mathcal{I}.$$

For an economy with non–zero endowments, these conditions apply to the translates of X_i and $\succeq_i$ according to relations (7) and (8).

THEOREM. *If $\mathcal{E}$ is an economy on a Euclidean choice space L satisfying the Debreu conditions, then $\mathcal{E}$ has a compensated equilibrium (x, y, p). Furthermore, p may be chosen to satisfy $p \cdot z \leq 0$ for all z in $A\left(Y\right) - D$.*

With slight additional conditions, the Debreu conditions ensure the existence of equilibria in a class of non–Euclidean choice spaces, as indicated in the Notes. An approach to the existence of equilibria under simple conditions is given in an exercise.

EXERCISES

EXERCISE 3.1 Prove Lemma 3B.

EXERCISE 3.2 Prove Proposition 3E.

EXERCISE 3.3 Prove Theorem 3E. *Hint:* Use Exercise 2.8.

EXERCISE 3.4 Extend Theorem 3E to production–exchange economies by proving the following result. Suppose (x, y) is a feasible allocation that is strictly supported by $p \in L'$. Assume X_i is convex and $\succeq_i$ is strongly convex and non–satiated at x_i for all $i \in \mathcal{I}$. Then (x, y) is an efficient allocation.

EXERCISE 3.5 Let $\succeq$ be a preference relation on a convex subset X of a vector space L, and p be a non–zero element of L'. Consider the alternative support properties:

(a) $x \succ y \Rightarrow p \cdot x > p \cdot y \quad \forall x \in X$,

(b) $x \succeq y \Rightarrow p \cdot x \geq p \cdot y \quad \forall x \in X$, and

(c) $x \succ y \Rightarrow p \cdot x \geq p \cdot y \quad \forall x \in X$,

where y is a given element of X. Prove the following implications. First, if $\succeq$ is algebraically continuous and there exists $\underline{x} \in X$ such that $p \cdot \underline{x} < p \cdot y$, then (c) $\Leftarrow$ (b) $\Rightarrow$ (a) $\Longleftrightarrow$ (c). Second, if $\succeq$ is non–satiated nearby y, then (c) $\Leftarrow$ (a) $\Rightarrow$ (b) $\Rightarrow$ (c). Thus, under all of the above conditions, (a), (b), and (c) are equivalent. Now prove Proposition 3G.

EXERCISE 3.6 Under the setup of the previous exercise, let L be a normed space and $p \in L^*$. Show that the conclusions of Exercise 5 follow if "continuous" is substituted for "algebraically continuous" and "locally non–satiated at" is substituted for "non–satiated nearby". Thus we see a relationship between algebraic and topological considerations.

EXERCISE 3.7 Let $\mathcal{E}$ be an economy with total production set $Y = \sum_{i=1}^{J} Y_j$ and let $\ddot{Y}$ be an augmented production set for Y. Let $\mathcal{E}\left(\ddot{Y}\right)$ denote the same economy with the single firm $\ddot{Y}$ substituted for the original J firms. Prove that if $(x, \ddot{y}, p)$ is an equilibrium for $\mathcal{E}\left(\ddot{Y}\right)$, then there exists a production allocation $y = (y_1, \ldots, y_J)$ for $\mathcal{E}$ such that (x, y, p) is an equilibrium for $\mathcal{E}$ and $\ddot{y} = y_1 + \cdots + y_J$. Thus the existence of equilibria does not depend on $Y_1, \ldots, Y_J$ given any augmented total production set.

EXERCISE 3.8 Suppose the total production set for an economy is a cone. If $0 \in Y_j$ for all $j \in \mathcal{J}$ (zero production is feasible), and (x, y, p) is an equilibrium, show that $p \cdot y_j = 0$ for all $j \in \mathcal{J}$.

EXERCISE 3.9 Theorem 3F is improved as follows. The *intrinsic core* of a convex set Z, denoted icr(Z), is the set of points $z \in Z$ such that for all $x \in Z$ there exists $\alpha \in (0, 1)$ with $(1 + \alpha)z - \alpha x \in Z$. That is, $z \in$ icr (Z) if and only if it is possible to move linearly from any other point in Z past z and remain in Z. If icr(Z) $\neq \emptyset$ and $0 \notin$ icr(Z), then there exists a non–zero $p \in L'$ such that $p \cdot z \geq 0$ for all z in Z, a simple consequence of the Separating Hyperplane Theorem. Prove Theorem 3F after substituting "intrinsic core" for "core" in its statement. The core of a convex set may be empty while its intrinsic core is not. Give an example of this.

EXERCISE 3.10 Show in the context of the proof of Theorem 3F that the allocation shown in (11) is indeed feasible.

EXERCISE 3.11 Prove the following corollary to the Separating Hyperplane Theorem. Suppose Z is a convex subset of a normed space L, Z has non–empty interior, and $0 \notin$ int(Z). Then there exists a non–zero continuous linear functional p on L such that $p \cdot z \geq 0$ for all $z \in Z$.

EXERCISE 3.12 We have the following improved version of the

SEPARATING HYPERPLANE THEOREM FOR EUCLIDEAN SPACES. *Suppose X is a convex subset of a Euclidean space L and 0 is not in X. Then there is a non–zero linear functional p on L such that $p \cdot x \geq 0$ for all x in X.*

Prove the following.

WEAK SECOND WELFARE THEOREM. *Suppose $(X_i, \succeq_i, \omega_i)$, $i \in \mathcal{I}$, is an exchange economy on a Euclidean choice space, with convex choice sets and continuous strongly convex preference relations. Suppose further that $x = (x_1, \ldots, x_I)$ is an efficient allocation at which every agent is non–satiated. Then there exists a price vector p supporting x.*

EXERCISE 3.13 A hyperplane in a vector space L is a set of points of the form $[p; \alpha] = \{x \in L : p \cdot x = \alpha\}$ for some non–zero linear functional p on L and scalar α. Two subsets A and B of L can be separated by a hyperplane if there exists a hyperplane $[p; \alpha]$ such that $p \cdot x \geq \alpha$ for all x in A and $p \cdot x \leq \alpha$ for all x in B. Prove the following corollary to the separating hyperplane theorem. Suppose A and B are non empty convex subsets of L, and one of them, say A, has a non–empty core. Then A and B can be separated by a hyperplane if and only if $\text{core}(A) \bigcap B$ is empty. Furthermore, if $[p; \alpha]$ is such a separating hyperplane and $x \in \text{core}(A)$, then $p \cdot x > 0$.

EXERCISE 3.14 Suppose L is a normed vector space. Show that a hyperplane $[p, \alpha]$ is closed if and only if the associated linear functional p is continuous. Suppose A and B are convex subsets of L and A has a non–empty interior. Prove that A and B can be separated by a closed hyperplane if and only if $\text{int}(A) \bigcap B$ is empty.

EXERCISE 3.15 Suppose X is a closed convex subset of a normed space L and $x \notin X$. Demonstrate the existence of a continuous linear functional p on L such that
$$p \cdot x < \inf\{p \cdot y : y \in X\}.$$

EXERCISE 3.16 Write a more detailed proof of Theorem 3F, filling in all missing arguments.

EXERCISE 3.17 Suppose $\mathcal{E} = (X_i, \succeq_i, \omega_i)$, $i \in \mathcal{I}$, is an exchange economy on a Euclidean choice space L such that, for all i in $\mathcal{I}$, $\omega_i \in \text{int}(L_+)$, $X_i = L_+$, and $\succeq_i$ is continuous, convex, and strictly monotonic. Prove the existence of an equilibrium. *Hint:* Apply Theorem 3G and Proposition 3G.

EXERCISE 3.18   Verify the existence of an equilibrium for an economy satisfying the conditions of the previous exercise by applying the following fixed point theorem. Do not use Theorem 3G.

THEOREM (KAKUTANI'S FIXED POINT THEOREM). *Suppose Z is a non–empty convex compact subset of a Euclidean space L, and for each x in Z, $\varphi(x)$ denotes some non–empty convex compact subset of Z. Suppose also that $\{(x,y) \in Z \times Z : x \in \varphi(y)\}$ is a closed set. Then there exists some x^* in Z such that $x^* \in \varphi(x^*)$.*

A point $x \in \varphi(x)$ is a *fixed point* of φ. For the benefit of readers familiar with the terminology, the same fixed point theorem applies even when the words "Hausdorff locally convex topological vector" are substituted for the word "Euclidean". In this generality, the result is known as the *Fan–Glicksberg–Kakutani Fixed Point Theorem*.

Steps:

(A)   Let $\mathbf{1} = (1, 1, \ldots, 1) \in L$ and let $\Delta = \{\pi \in L_+ : \pi \cdot \mathbf{1} = 1\}$. For each $\pi \in L_+$, let $\beta_i(\pi) = \{x \in L_+ : \pi \cdot (x - \omega_i) \leq 0\}$ and let

$$\xi_i(\pi) = \{x \in \beta_i(\pi) : \{y \in L_+ : y \succ_i x\} \cap \beta_i(\pi) = \emptyset\}.$$

Let $\xi(\pi) = \sum_i \xi_i(\pi) - \{\omega_i\}$ for each $\pi \in L_+$.

(B)   Show that $\xi_i(\pi)$ is convex and compact for any $\pi \in \mathrm{int}(\Delta)$, and that $\pi_n \to \pi \in \mathrm{int}(\Delta)$ with $x_n \in \xi_i(\pi_n)$ for all n implies that $\{x_n\}$ has a subsequence with a limit point in $\xi_i(\pi)$. (This requires care and patience, but is not difficult.)

(C)   For each positive integer n, let $\Delta_n = \{\pi \in \Delta : \pi \geq 1/n\}$, and for each $x \in L$, let

$$\psi_n(x) = \{\pi \in \Delta_n : \pi \cdot x \geq \pi' \cdot x \quad \forall \pi' \in \Delta_n\}.$$

Show the existence of a set $X_n \subset L$ such that the set $Z_n \equiv X_n \times \Delta_n$ and the sets

$$\varphi_n(x, \pi) = \{(x', \pi') \in Z_n : x' \in \xi(\pi), \ \pi' \in \psi_n(\pi)\}, \qquad (x, \pi) \in Z_n,$$

satisfy the conditions of Kakutani's Fixed Point Theorem.

(D)   Let $n \to \infty$ and show that any sequence $\{(x_n, \pi_n)\}$ of fixed points of φ_n has a subsequence $\{(x_m, \pi_m)\}$ with a limit point, say (x^*, π^*). Prove that $\pi^* \in \mathrm{int}(\Delta)$.

Hint: For the latter, show that otherwise we must have the contradiction: $\parallel x_m \parallel \rightarrow \infty$. Then show that $x^* = 0$.

(E)   Using the definition of ξ, we have the existence of $x_i \in \xi_i(\pi^*)$, $1 \leq i \leq I$, such that $\sum_i x_i - \omega_i = 0$. Let p be the linear functional on L represented by π^*. Complete the proof.

(F)   Weaken the endowment assumption from $\omega_i \in \text{int}(L_+)$ to: $\omega_i \in L_+$, $\omega_i \neq 0$, and $\sum_i \omega_i \in \text{int}(L_+)$. *Hint:* Only step (D) is affected.

Notes

This section does not do justice to the breadth and depth of General Equilibrium Theory; it merely relates a few of the main ideas. "Competitive equilibrium" is the conception of Leon Walras (1874–77). Early mathematical treatments of existence are those of Wald (1936) and von Neumann (1937). Finally, Arrow and Debreu (1954) generated a complete existence proof. McKenzie (1954) simultaneously achieved an existence proof for a similar model. Theorem 3G, due to Debreu (1962), is among the most general available for Euclidean choice spaces and preferences given by complete transitive binary orders. Shafer and Sonnenschein (1975) extend existence to agents with general (possibly incomplete or non-transitive) preferences. Aumann (1966) extended the model to a continuum of agents. This allows one to relax the convexity condition for the existence of equilibria. The important concept of a *core allocation* for an economy, not covered here, is not to be confused with the core of a subset of a vector space. Hildenbrand (1974) is a comprehensive treatment of general equilibrium, core allocations, and economies with an infinite number of agents.

Bewley (1972) provided the first proof of existence of equilibrium in infinite–dimensional choice spaces. Extensions of Bewley's result, along the lines of Theorem 3G, are reported in Duffie (1986a). The "quasi–equilibrium" concept of Debreu (1962) is equivalent to a "compensated equilibrium" (a term found in Arrow and Hahn (1971)) under convex choice sets and algebraically continuous preferences. Mas–Colell (1986a) found compensated equilibrium existence conditions for economies with choice spaces especially suited to the theory of security markets. An example of this is found in Section 11, where further references are given.

The Separating Hyperplane Theorem (Proposition 3F) is equivalent to one stated by Holmes (1975). The result applies in Euclidean spaces without the non–empty core condition (Exercise 3.12). Theorem 3F and its extension in Exercise 9 are found in Duffie (1986a); both are algebraic simplifications of a 1953 Theorem of Debreu (1983, Chapter 6). The essence of Proposition 3G may be found in Arrow (1951). Some of the exercises are original. Kakutani's Fixed Point Theorem, along with extensions and related results, is found in Klein and Thompson (1984). Kakutani's (1941) Fixed Point Theorem is extended to infinite–dimensional spaces by Fan (1952) and Glicksberg (1952).

Background reading on General Equilibrium Theory may be found in the collected papers of Arrow (1983) and Debreu (1983). Debreu (1982) reviews proofs of existence of general equilibrium and their historical development. Introductory treatments are given by Debreu (1959), Varian (1984), and Hildenbrand and Kirman (1976).

4. First Probability Concepts

Assigning a "probability" to an "event" is a simple concept requiring only a few definitions to formalize. Much of this section will merely transpose those definitions from measure theory to a terminology suitable for discussing uncertainty. A lack of familiarity with measure theory is not a major disadvantage when accompanied by some faith that the concepts are natural extensions from the finite to the infinite.

A.   We start by outlining the primitives of any discussion of measure or probability. Let Ω be a set. A *tribe* on Ω is a collection $\mathcal{F}$ of subsets of Ω that includes the *empty set* $\emptyset$ and satisfies the two conditions:

(a) if $B \in \mathcal{F}$ then its *complement* $\Omega \setminus B \equiv \{\omega \in \Omega : \omega \notin B\}$ is also in $\mathcal{F}$, and

(b) if $\{B_1, B_2, \ldots\}$ is a sequence of elements of $\mathcal{F}$, then

$$\bigcup_{n=1}^{\infty} B_n \in \mathcal{F} \quad \text{and} \quad \bigcap_{n=1}^{\infty} B_n \in \mathcal{F}.$$

Other terms such as σ–*algebra* are often used for "tribe". The definition requires of course that Ω is itself an element of any tribe on Ω.

A pair $(\Omega, \mathcal{F})$ consisting of a set Ω and a tribe $\mathcal{F}$ on Ω is a *measurable space*. The elements of $\mathcal{F}$ are *measurable subsets* of Ω. A *measure* on a measurable space $(\Omega, \mathcal{F})$ is a function $\mu : \mathcal{F} \to [0, \infty]$ satisfying $\mu(\emptyset) = 0$ and, for any sequence $\{B_1, B_2, \ldots\}$ of disjoint measurable sets,

$$\mu\left(\bigcup_{n=1}^{\infty} B_n\right) = \sum_{n=1}^{\infty} \mu(B_n).$$

A *measure space* is a triple $(\Omega, \mathcal{F}, \mu)$ consisting of a measurable space $(\Omega, \mathcal{F})$ and a measure μ on $(\Omega, \mathcal{F})$. If $\mu(\Omega) = 1$, the measure space $(\Omega, \mathcal{F}, \mu)$ is a *probability space*, and μ is a *probability measure*. For a probability space $(\Omega, \mathcal{F}, P)$, it is natural to think of Ω as the set of "possible states of the world". The elements of $\mathcal{F}$ are those subsets of Ω that are *events*, capable of being assigned a probability. The *probability of an event* B is $P(B) \in [0, 1]$. An *atom* is an event $B \in \mathcal{F}$ such that $P(B) > 0$ and, for any event $C \subset B$, $P(C) = 0$ or $P(C) = P(B)$. The measure P is *atomless* if it has no atoms.

B.   To speak of *random variables*, more definitions are required. First, let Z describe an *outcome space*. Quite often $Z = R$, in economics typically representing "wealth", "consumption", or some other scalar good. The outcome space Z is also given its own tribe $\mathcal{Z}$ of measurable subsets. For given measurable spaces $(\Omega, \mathcal{F})$ and $(Z, \mathcal{Z})$, a function $x : \Omega \to Z$ is *measurable*, or equivalently a *random variable*, if, for any set A in $\mathcal{Z}$, the set

$$x^{-1}(A) \equiv \{\omega \in \Omega : x(\omega) \in A\}$$

is in $\mathcal{F}$. To repeat this vital definition, x is not a random variable unless, for any measurable subset A of outcomes, the set of states $\{\omega \in \Omega$ such that $x(\omega) \in A\}$ is an event. The *distribution* of a random variable x on a probability space $(\Omega, \mathcal{F}, P)$ into a measurable space $(Z, \mathcal{Z})$ is the probability measure μ on $(Z, \mathcal{Z})$ defined by

$$\mu(A) = P\left[x^{-1}(A)\right] \text{ for all } A \in \mathcal{Z}.$$

The terms *law* and *image law* commonly interchange with "distribution". Two random variables are *equivalent in distribution* if they have the same distribution.

Example.   Consider the *fair coin toss space* $(\Omega, \mathcal{F}, P)$, where $\Omega = \{H, T\}$, $\mathcal{F}$ is the set of all subsets, $\{\emptyset, \{H\}, \{T\}, \Omega\}$, and $P(\{H\}) = P(\{T\}) = 1/2$. Consider the random variables x and y into $Z = \{0, 1\}$, with tribe $\mathcal{Z} = \{\emptyset, \{0\}, \{1\}, Z\}$, defined by

$$x(H) = y(T) = 1$$

$$x(T) = y(H) = 0.$$

These different random variables x and y are equivalent in distribution. ♠

C.   Given any collection $\mathcal{A}$ of subsets of a set Ω, there exists a tribe on Ω that contains $\mathcal{A}$. An obvious choice is the tribe consisting of all subsets of

Ω, the *power set*, denoted 2^Ω. The smallest tribe containing $\mathcal{A}$, that is, the intersection of all tribes containing $\mathcal{A}$, is the tribe *generated* by $\mathcal{A}$, denoted $\sigma(\mathcal{A})$. Usually an outcome space Z for random variables is endowed with a topology $\mathcal{T}$. In that case we often take the tribe on Z to be the *Borel tribe* $\sigma(\mathcal{T})$, that tribe generated by $\mathcal{T}$. In fact, if an outcome space Z has been given a topology, we will always assume the Borel tribe is the relevant tribe for discussion unless otherwise cautioned, and refer simply to Z–*valued random variables*, dropping the "$(Z, \mathcal{Z})$" notation. If Ω and Z are both topological spaces with respective Borel tribes $\mathcal{F}$ and $\mathcal{Z}$, then a measurable function from $(\Omega, \mathcal{F})$ into $(Z, \mathcal{Z})$ is termed *Borel measurable*.

A *partition* of a set Ω is a finite collection $\mathcal{A} = \{A_1, \ldots, A_N\}$ of disjoint subsets of Ω whose union is Ω. In a sense, the tribe $\sigma(\mathcal{A})$ generated by the partition $\mathcal{A}$ includes all possible events whose outcomes, true or false, can be determined by observing the outcomes of $A_1, \ldots, A_N$.

Example.   Suppose $\Omega = \{1, \ldots, 10\}$ and $\mathcal{A}$ is the partition $\{A_1, A_2, A_3\}$, where $A_1 = \{1, 2, 3\}$, $A_2 = \{4, 5, 6\}$, and $A_3 = \{7, 8, 9, 10\}$. Then $\sigma(\mathcal{A})$ is the tribe

$$\{\Omega, \emptyset, A_1, A_2, A_3, A_1 \cup A_2, A_1 \cup A_3, A_2 \cup A_3\}.$$

For instance, if A_1 is known to be true in some state of the world, for example state 3, then $A_2 \bigcup A_3$ must be known to be false, explaining its presence in $\sigma(\mathcal{A})$. With information received according to the partition $\mathcal{A}$, one will never know the precise state of the world chosen randomly from Ω, but one does learn whether any given event in $\sigma(\mathcal{A})$ is true or false. ♠

We also define the smallest tribe $\mathcal{G}$ on Ω for which each function in a given collection $\mathcal{C}$ of functions on Ω (valued in some respective outcome spaces) is measurable. Again, $\mathcal{G}$ is termed the tribe *generated* by $\mathcal{C}$, and denoted $\sigma(\mathcal{C})$. A real–valued function S on Ω, for example, could be interpreted as a *signal*, and the tribe $\sigma(S)$ as the set of all events whose occurrence or non–occurrence can be determined by observing the outcome of S. Suppose, returning to the previous example for illustration, that $\Omega = \{1, \ldots, 10\}$ and that S is the function taking values 1 on A_1, 2 on A_2, and 0 on A_3. Then $\sigma(S)$ is the tribe $\sigma(\mathcal{A})$ described in the example.

D.   Given a probability space $(\Omega, \mathcal{F}, P)$, an event B is "sure" if $B = \Omega$, and *almost sure* if $P(B) = 1$; there is a difference. Any event of zero probability is *negligible*. In probability treatments one often sees the notation $x = y$ almost surely (or a.s.) for two random variables x and y into the same outcome space that are equal with probability one. We might also write $P(x = y) = 1$, which is merely a short informal notation for:

$$P(\{\omega \in \Omega : x(\omega) = y(\omega)\}) = 1.$$

In this case, x and y are *versions* of one another. The expression "almost surely" appears in the same way that one sees *almost everywhere* (or a.e.) in measure theory; they are identical in meaning.

E. Expectation and integration are identical concepts. The idea behind integration is easy to explain. Let Z be an arbitrary vector space of outcomes. A random variable x on a probability space $(\Omega, \mathcal{F}, P)$ with values in Z is *simple* if there exists a partition $B_1, \ldots, B_N$ of Ω and corresponding elements $z_1, \ldots, z_N$ of Z such that:

$$x(\omega) = z_n \text{ for all } \omega \in B_n, \quad 1 \leq n \leq N. \tag{1}$$

In other words, a random variable is simple if it takes only a finite number of different values. The expected value of a simple random variable x of the form (1), denoted $E(x)$, also denoted $\int_\Omega x \, dP$, is merely the average of the outcomes of x weighted by the probabilities with which these outcomes occur, or

$$E(x) \equiv \int_\Omega x \, dP \equiv \sum_{n=1}^{N} P(B_n) z_n.$$

We extend this definition to arbitrary random variables by various methods, depending on the nature of the outcome space Z. For the important case $Z = R$, the extension is as follows. On $(\Omega, \mathcal{F}, P)$, let $\mathcal{S}$ denote the collection of all simple real–valued random variables and let x be any positive real–valued random variable. Now define

$$E(x) \equiv \sup\{E(y) : y \in \mathcal{S}, y \leq x\}.$$

That is, $E(x)$ is defined as the least upper bound on the expectations of simple random variables that are less than x. If $E(x)$ is finite, we say x is *integrable*. For the final extension, let x be any real–valued random variable, which can always be written as $x = x^+ - x^-$, where $x^+(\omega) = \max\{x(\omega), 0\}$ and $x^-(\omega) = \max\{-x(\omega), 0\}$. Both x^+ and x^- are positive random variables, termed the *positive* and *negative parts* of x respectively. If both x^+ and x^- are integrable, then x is also said to be *integrable*, and the expectation of x is defined as

$$E(x) \equiv \int_\Omega x \, dP = E(x^+) - E(x^-).$$

If $(\Omega, \mathcal{F}, P)$ is a measure space but not a probability space, we drop the use of "$E(x)$", and call the expression $\int_\Omega x \, dP$ "the integral of the (measurable) function x with respect to the measure P". Similar extensions of integration have been devised for a general class of outcome spaces, with references given in Section 9. To be explicit, we sometimes write $\int x(\omega)\, dP(\omega)$ for $\int x\, dP$.

F. The notation $\int_\Omega x\, dP$ conveys the sense that an expected value is a weighted sum, with weights (or probabilities) corresponding to events. A secondary definition of expected value comes from applying weights instead to the outcomes of the random variable in question. The *cumulative distribution function* $F : R \to [0, 1]$ of a real–valued random variable x on a probability space $(\Omega, \mathcal{F}, P)$ is defined by

$$F(t) = P(\{x \le t\}) \quad \text{for all } t \text{ in } R.$$

Let us suppose that x is an integrable random variable and F is a differentiable function, whose derivative f is then termed the *density* of x. It follows that

$$E(x) = \int_\Omega x\, dP = \int_R tf(t)\, dt. \tag{2}$$

The first integral sums over states ω in Ω; the second sums over outcomes t in R. Most readers will be familiar with the notation of the second integral, which integrates the function $t \mapsto tf(t)$ with respect to *Lebesgue measure* on the real line, the unique measure on the Borel subsets of R with the property that the measure of any interval is the length of the interval. This second integral is convenient for calculation purposes, for if g is a measurable real–valued function on R such that the *composition* $g \circ x$ (the function $\omega \mapsto g[x(\omega)]$) is integrable, then $E[g \circ x] = \int_R g(t)f(t)\, dt$. The exercises provide practice in such calculations. Whether or not F is differentiable, we can express $E(x)$ as the *Stieltjes integral*, denoted $\int_R t\, dF(t)$, whose definition may be found in a cited reference. If x is an R^n–valued random variable with a density $f : R^n \to R$, and $g : R^n \to R$ is such that $g \circ x$ is integrable, we can also write $E[g \circ x] = \int_{R^n} g(t)f(t)\, dt$, in which case "$dt$" denotes integration with respect to Lebesgue measure on R^n, the unique measure on the Borel subsets of R^n with the property that the measure of a box (a product of intervals) is the "volume" of the box (the product of the lengths of the respective intervals).

EXERCISES

EXERCISE 4.1   Let $(\Omega, \mathcal{F})$ be a measurable space. If $B \in \mathcal{F}$, the *indicator function* for B is the real–valued random variable, 1_B defined by

$$1_B(\omega) = 1 \quad \forall \omega \in B,$$

$$1_B(\omega) = 0 \quad \text{otherwise.}$$

If P is a probability measure on $(\Omega, \mathcal{F})$, show that $P(B) = E(1_B)$ for any $B \in \mathcal{F}$. (The notation "$\int_B x \, dP$" for $E(1_B x)$ is useful and commonly used.)

EXERCISE 4.2 A positive integer–valued random variable x has a *Poisson distribution* with parameter λ if the distribution μ of x is of the form

$$\mu(\{n\}) = \frac{e^{-\lambda}\lambda^n}{n!}, \quad n = 0, 1, 2, \ldots$$

Calculate $E(x)$.

EXERCISE 4.3 If an R^N–valued random variable $x = (x_1, \ldots, x_N)$ is *normally distributed* with mean vector $\mu \in R^N$ and $N \times N$ positive definite covariance matrix Σ, then it has the density function $f : R^N \to R$ defined by

$$f(t) = 2\pi^{-N/2}[\det(\Sigma)]^{-1/2} \exp\left[-\frac{1}{2}(t - \mu)^T \Sigma^{-1}(t - \mu)\right], \quad t \in R^N,$$

where $\det(\Sigma)$ denotes the determinant of Σ. For a given scalar $\gamma > 0$, let $u : R \to R$ be the function $t \mapsto -e^{-\gamma t}$, and let y be the random variable $\alpha_1 x_1 + \cdots + \alpha_N x_N$, for arbitrary scalars $\alpha_1, \ldots, \alpha_N$. Calculate $E(u \circ y)$, which is often denoted $E[u(y)]$.

EXERCISE 4.4 For the set $\Omega = \{1, \ldots, 10\}$ and the partition $\mathcal{A}$ of Ω given in Example 4C, suppose Y is the real–valued function on Ω defined by $Y(\omega) = 1$ for $1 \leq \omega \leq 6$ and $Y(\omega) = 0$ for $7 \leq \omega \leq 10$. Is Y measurable with respect to the tribe $\sigma(\mathcal{A})$ generated by $\mathcal{A}$? State the tribe generated by Y. Now suppose X is the real–valued function on Ω defined by $X(1) = 0, X(\omega) = 2$ for $\omega \geq 2$. Is X measurable with respect to $\sigma(\mathcal{A})$?

Notes

This material is ubiquitous. Standard references on probability theory include Chung (1974). A simpler text is Ross (1980). Chow and Teicher (1978) and Billingsley (1986) are also recommended. The Stieltjes integral is defined in Bartle (1976) and Royden (1968), with an example in Paragraph 15C.

5. Expected Utility

Although the conditions on a decision–maker's preferences implied by the use of the expected utility maximization criterion are generally agreed to be severe, the concept is intuitively appealing to some, and certainly allows one to illustrate many basic economic notions and to generate solutions to many concrete problems. We will examine sufficient conditions for the use of expected utility in the simplest possible setting.

A.   For the entire section we suppose that the decision–maker's choice set X is a subset of the random variables on some measurable space $(\Omega, \mathcal{F})$ into some measurable outcome space $(Z, \mathcal{Z})$. A major portion of economic theory is built on the assumption that a preference relation $\succeq$ on X can be given an "expected utility" representation. In this section we will barely touch on the meaning of this statement and on conditions on $\succeq$ and X that validate it. The full theory is quite involved, as can be seen by perusing some of the sources suggested in the Notes.

There are several major axiomatic lines of construction for expected value representation. The simplest is the *von Neumann–Morgenstern* theory, which will be cast here in a slightly different mold than the "objective probability" framework in which it is usually found. In the von Neumann–Morgenstern theory the decision–maker's probability measure P on $(\Omega, \mathcal{F})$ is given by assumption, playing a major role in determining his or her preference relation $\succeq$ on X. In the alternative *Savage* model, the preference relation $\succeq$ is primitive. Under certain conditions, the decision–maker's probability assessments can nevertheless be deduced from $\succeq$ within an elegant axiomatic framework.

B.   Given a probability measure P on $(\Omega, \mathcal{F})$, a function $u : Z \to R$ is an *expected utility representation* for a preference relation $\succeq$ on X provided $u \circ x \equiv u(x)$ is an integrable random variable for all $x \in X$ and

$$x \succeq y \iff E[u(x)] \geq E[u(y)] \tag{1}$$

for all x and y in X. The measure P enters the definition through the operation of expectation.

For contrast, consider the somewhat deeper concept: A pair (P, u) consisting of a probability measure P on $(\Omega, \mathcal{F})$ and a function $u : Z \to R$ is a *Savage model of beliefs and preferences* for $\succeq$ on X provided u is an expected utility representation of $\succeq$ given P. Axiomatic justifications

of the Savage model are not simple. For brevity, we take the decision–
maker's probability measure P on $(\Omega, \mathcal{F})$ as given. Our task is to find a
simple axiomatic justification for expected utility representations.

It is immediate from (1) that a preference relation with an expected
utility representation is "state–independent" in the sense that $E[u(x)]$ depends on x only through the distribution of x. Formally, a preference
relation $\succeq$ on X is *state–independent* provided $x \sim y$ (indifference) whenever x and y in X have the same distribution. Suppose, for example, that
$(\Omega, \mathcal{F}, P)$ is the *fair coin toss space* of Example 4B, while x and y are the
random variables:

$$x(H) = 1 \qquad\qquad y(H) = 0$$
$$x(T) = 0 \qquad\qquad y(T) = 1.$$

Interpreting the outcome space Z as "dollars", some decision–makers might
well have state–independent preferences and thus be indifferent between x
and y. Suppose, however, that it rains if and only if the coin lands Heads,
and one unit in the outcome space is a claim to one umbrella. Decision–
makers could then strictly prefer x to y.

C. For the remainder of this section we take a probability measure P
on $(\Omega, \mathcal{F})$ as given. Let Π denote the set of probability measures on the
outcome space Z, and let $\mu_x \in \Pi$ denote the distribution of a given $x \in X$.
If $\succeq$ is a state–independent preference relation on X, a preference relation
$\succeq_d$ is induced on Π by

$$\mu_x \succeq_d \mu_y \iff x \succeq y$$

for any x and y in X.

D. We interrupt the main story for a useful but abstract looking concept.
A set $\mathcal{M}$ is a *mixture space* if, for any $\alpha \in [0,1]$ and any x and y in the $\mathcal{M}$
there is a unique element of $\mathcal{M}$ denoted $x\alpha y$, where the following properties
hold for all x and y in $\mathcal{M}$ and α and β in $[0,1]$:
  (a) $x1y = x$,
  (b) $x\alpha y = y(1 - \alpha)x$, and
  (c) $(x\beta y)\alpha y = x(\alpha\beta)y$.

As one reads this definition one could think of "$x\alpha y$" as the convex combination "$\alpha x + (1 - \alpha)y$", although the definition has more general implications than that would suggest. Indeed, we see that the set of probability
measures on any measurable space is a mixture space with this interpretation. We state a couple of axioms applying to a preference relation $\succeq$ on a
mixture space $\mathcal{M}$.

THE ARCHIMEDEAN AXIOM. *For all x, y, and z in $\mathcal{M}$, if $x \succ y$ and $y \succ z$, then there are α and β in $(0,1)$ such that $x\alpha z \succ y$ and $y \succ x\beta z$.*

The idea of the axiom is: No matter how "bad" z is, we can modify x with "just a dash" of z with the result that $x\alpha z$ is still preferred to y. One can interpret the second part of the axiom similarly. The Archimedean Axiom[1] is not so controversial as the following.

THE INDEPENDENCE AXIOM. *For all x, y, and z in $\mathcal{M}$ and α in $[0,1]$, if $x \succeq y$ then $x\alpha z \succeq y\alpha z$.*

This has also been called a *substitution axiom* or *cancellation axiom*. The usual argument for its reasonableness goes something like the following. Suppose John prefers x to y. Mary has a coin that lands Heads with probability α. Mary offers John one of the *lotteries* A and B defined by:

   A: Heads you get x; tails you get something else, say z.

   B: Heads you get y; tails you get z.

"If the coin lands Tails," John thinks, "I'm going to get z no matter which lottery I choose, so I'll pick lottery A. Then, at least I get my favorite when the coin lands Heads." The axiom might be read again to verify its interpretation in this scenario, treating $x\alpha z$ as "x with probability α, z with probability $(1-\alpha)$". John's reaction in this scenario may seem reasonable, but the Independence Axiom is a major point of contention. Empirical work shows that many decision–makers faced with the choice between lotteries A and B, with certain values of α and interpretations for x, y and z, will pick B. There is certainly no logical contradiction in this type of choice behavior. For better or worse, however, the Independence Axiom is crucial in establishing expected utility representations. The following theorem goes much of the way toward showing this. The statement is actually somewhat less than the classical "Mixture Space Theorem", which may be found along with a proof through the Notes.

MIXTURE SPACE THEOREM. *Suppose $\succeq$ is a preference relation on a mixture space $\mathcal{M}$. Then $\succeq$ obeys the Archimdean and Independence Axioms if and only if the preference relation has a linear functional representation U.*

By "linear", of course, we mean that the functional U in the statement of the theorem satisfies $U(x\alpha y) = \alpha U(x) + (1-\alpha)U(y)$ for all x and y in $\mathcal{M}$ and any scalar $\alpha \in [0,1]$.

---

   [1] The terminology is from a vague resemblance with Archimedes' Principle: for any strictly positive real numbers x and y, no matter how small x is, there is some integer n large enough that $nx > y$.

E. We now give one axiomatic basis for expected utility representations, at least in a simple case. Let X° denote the set of simple Z–valued random variables on $(\Omega, \mathcal{F}, P)$ and Π° denote the set of distributions of the elements of X°. We suppose, for any $\alpha \in (0, 1)$, there exists $A \in \mathcal{F}$ with $P(A) = \alpha$.

PROPOSITION. *Suppose $\succeq$ is a state–independent preference relation on X°. Let $\succeq'$ denote the preference relation induced by $\succeq$ on Π°. Then $\succeq'$ obeys the Archimedean and Independence Axioms if and only if $\succeq$ has an expected utility representation.*

PROOF: (Only if) It is trivial that Π° is a mixture space. Then the Mixture Space Theorem implies the existence of a linear functional U on Π° such that

$$x \succeq y \iff U(\mu_x) \geq U(\mu_y) \tag{2}$$

for any x and y in X°. The support of the distribution μ_x of a simple random variable x is the finite set $\text{supp}(\mu_x) = \{z_1, \dots, z_N\} \subset Z$ of outcomes that x takes with strictly positive probability, meaning $\mu_x(\{z_n\}) > 0$ for all n and $\mu_x(\text{supp}(\mu_x)) = 1$. The number of elements in the support of μ_x is denoted $\#(\mu_x)$. For any $z \in Z$, the notation "$\mu_x(z)$" for "$\mu_x(\{z\})$" is adopted for simplicity. For any $z \in Z$, let $\mu^z \in \Pi$ denote the distribution with support $\{z\}$, a "sure thing". Define $u : Z \to R$ by $u(z) = U(\mu^z)$ for all $z \in Z$. It remains to show that u is an expected utility representation for $\succeq$ given P. By virtue of (2), this is true provided

$$U(\mu_x) = \sum_{z \,\in\, \text{supp}(\mu_x)} u(z)\mu_x(z) = E[u(x)], \tag{3}$$

for all $x \in X^\circ$. We complete the proof by induction on the number of elements in the support of μ_x for any $x \in X^\circ$. Suppose $\#(\mu_x) = 1$, or $\mu_x = \mu^z$ for some $z \in Z$. Then (3) is true by the definition of u. Next suppose (3) holds for $\#(\mu_x) \leq n - 1$, for some integer $n \geq 2$. Take $\mu_x = \nu \in \Pi^\circ$ with $\#(\nu) = n$, and let $w \in \text{supp}(\nu)$. Define $\lambda \in \Pi^\circ$ by $\lambda(w) = 0$ and $\lambda(z) = \nu(z)/[1 - \nu(w)]$ for $z \neq w$. Then $\#(\lambda) = n - 1$ and $\nu = \nu(w)\mu^w + [1 - \nu(w)]\lambda$. Since U is linear,

$$U(\nu) = \nu(w)U(\mu^w) + [1 - \nu(w)]U(\lambda)$$

$$= \nu(w)u(w) + [1 - \nu(w)] \sum_{z \,\in\, \text{supp}(\lambda)} \frac{\nu(z)u(z)}{1 - \nu(w)}$$

$$= \sum_{z \,\in\, \text{supp}(\nu)} \nu(z)\, u(z) = E[u(x)].$$

This verifies (3), completing the induction proof. The "if" part of the proof is left as an exercise. ∎

This proposition can be extended to more general cases at the expense of messier axiomatic foundations. The "if" part, however, is true in general: whenever one uses an expected utility representation one has accepted the controversial Independence Axiom.

EXERCISES

EXERCISE 5.1   Show that the set of all probability measures on a given measurable space is a mixture space, where $P\alpha Q$ denotes the mixture $\alpha P + (1-\alpha)Q$ of measures P and Q.

EXERCISE 5.2   Show that an affine functional representation U for a preference relation $\succeq$ on a convex set X is unique up to an affine transformation. That is, if U and V are both affine functional representations of $\succeq$, then there exist scalars $\beta > 0$ and α such that $U(\cdot) = \alpha + \beta V(\cdot)$.

EXERCISE 5.3   Prove that an expected utility representation for a preference relation is unique up to an affine transformation. That is, if u and v are expected utility representations of the same preference relation, then for some scalars $\beta > 0$ and α, $u(\cdot) = \alpha + \beta v(\cdot)$.

EXERCISE 5.4   Show that expected utility is linear in distributions by attacking the case of two simple random variables x and y, with distributions μ_x and μ_y. If u is an expected utility representation for a preference relation, and the random variable z has distribution $\alpha \mu_x + (1-\alpha)\mu_y$, show that $E[u(z)] = \alpha E[u(x)] + (1-\alpha)E[u(y)]$.

EXERCISE 5.5   Prove the (if) part of Proposition 5E.

Notes

Kreps (1981b) and Fishburn (1970) are excellent sources on this material; the former enjoyable reading, the latter including more esoteric details. Machina (1982) has prepared a new overview of the implications of expected utility, citing a large number of references, and showing that much of the economic analysis typically associated with expected utility representations of preferences is actually possible without the independence axiom. Fishburn (1982) is an advanced treatment of expected utility theory, including the Mixture Space Theorem and an axiomatic basis for a Savage model of preferences. Dekel (1986, 1987) has done recent work on the independence axiom.

6. Special Choice Spaces

Certain choice spaces are particularly well suited to the theory of markets under uncertainty. This section introduces some of these spaces and a few of their properties. Proofs of the claims in this section are easily found in sources cited in the Notes.

A.   A sequence $\{x_n\}$ in a normed space L is *Cauchy* if, for any scalar $\epsilon > 0$ there is an integer N so large that $\| x_n - x_m \| \leq \epsilon$ for all n and m larger than N. A *Banach space* is a normed space L with the property that every Cauchy sequence in L converges. All of the vector choice spaces to appear in this work are Banach spaces. Of special interest is the class of "L^q" spaces, to be defined shortly. Conveniently, any finite product of Banach spaces is a Banach space, as are closed vector subspaces of a Banach space, and (topological) duals of Banach spaces.

B.   Let $\mathcal{L}$ denote the vector space of real–valued measurable functions on a given measure space $(M, \mathcal{M}, \mu)$. That is, a vector $x \in \mathcal{L}$ is a measurable function taking the value $x(m)$ at $m \in M$. Depending on the nature and interpretation of the measure space, x could be a random variable, a function of "time", or perhaps a stochastic process (as defined in Section 14), among other examples. To each $x \in \mathcal{L}$ there corresponds the *equivalence class* $(x) \subset \mathcal{L}$ of versions of x (those elements of $\mathcal{L}$ that are equal to x almost everywhere). It is common and convenient to identify all such versions with x. We therefore construct a new vector space L whose elements are these equivalence classes of $\mathcal{L}$. The scalar multiplication and vector addition operations on L are defined in the obvious way: for α a scalar, $\alpha(x) \equiv (\alpha x)$; and $(x) + (y) \equiv (x + y)$. It simplifies matters to abuse the notation by dropping the parentheses, simply writing "x" in place of "(x)", and we usually do so.

C.   Now we select vector subspaces of L with pleasant geometric properties. For any $x \in L$ and any $q \in [1, \infty)$, let

$$\| x \|_q \equiv \left(\int_M | x(m) |^q \, d\mu(m) \right)^{1/q},$$

which may take the value $+\infty$. This integral is precisely as defined in Section 4. For example, if x is a positive random variable then $\| x \|_1 = E(x)$. For any $q \in [1, \infty)$, let $L^q(\mu) \equiv \{x \in L : \| x \|_q < \infty\}$. It has been shown that $\| \cdot \|_q$ is a norm on $L^q(\mu)$ and that $L^q(\mu)$ is a Banach space under this norm.

D.   We now construct the Banach space $L^\infty(\mu)$ of *essentially bounded* elements of L. That is, $x \in L^\infty(\mu)$ if and only if there is a version of x whose absolute value has an upper bound. Let $\| x \|_\infty$ denote the infimum of all such bounds. Indeed, $L^\infty(\mu)$ is a Banach space under $\| \cdot \|_\infty$, finishing off the family $\{ L^q(\mu) : q \in [1, \infty] \}$ of Banach spaces. We commonly refer to this class of vector spaces as "the L^q spaces".

E.   For any two elements x and y of $\mathcal{L}$, define the *product xy* pointwise, or

$$[xy](m) = x(m)y(m), \qquad m \in M.$$

For any $q \in (1, \infty)$, the *conjugate* of q is the scalar $q* \in (1, \infty)$ defined by $1/q + 1/q* = 1$. We define $1*$ to be ∞.

PROPOSITION (HÖLDER'S INEQUALITY). *For any $q \in [1, \infty)$, if $x \in L^q(\mu)$ and $y \in L^{q*}(\mu)$, then $xy \in L^1(\mu)$, and*

$$\| xy \|_1 \le \| x \|_q \| y \|_{q*} . \tag{1}$$

For the case $q = q* = 2$, relation (1) is the *Cauchy–Schwarz Inequality*. Hölder's Inequality paves the way for the following important identification of the topological duals of L^q spaces.

RIESZ REPRESENTATION THEOREM. *For $q \in (1, \infty)$, let p be a continuous linear functional on $L^q(\mu)$. Then there exists a unique $\pi \in L^{q*}(\mu)$ such that*

$$p \cdot x = \int_M x(m)\pi(m) \, d\mu(m) \qquad \forall x \in L^q(\mu).$$

The case $q = 2$ is special since $2* = 2$ shows $L^2(\mu)$ to be self–dual. We will rely on this fact relentlessly. Provided μ is σ–finite, meaning M is the union of a countable collection of measurable sets, each of finite measure, then the same result applies for $q = 1$ and $q* = \infty$. Of course, a probability measure is trivially σ–finite. In the terminology of Paragraph 1G, $L^q(\mu)$ and $L^{q*}(\mu)$ are in duality through the bilinear form $(x, y) \mapsto \int_M xy \, d\mu$.

Example.   Let $(\Omega, \mathcal{F}, P)$ be a probability space. We take $L^2(P)$ as the choice space for some economy, treating a vector x in $L^2(P)$ as a random variable describing the amount $x(\omega)$ of "consumption" received in state of the world $\omega \in \Omega$. Sometimes $L^2(P)$ is denoted $L^2(\Omega, \mathcal{F}, P)$. A vector $x \in L^2(P)$ is called an *asset* in this context. The integrability condition $\int_\Omega x^2 \, dP < \infty$ means simply that the variance of x, defined below, is finite. The Cauchy–Schwarz inequality implies that the expected value of any x in $L^2(P)$ is finite, an assigned exercise. Suppose p is a continuous price functional on $L^2(P)$. By the Riesz Representation Theorem, there exists a unique random variable π in $L^2(P)$ such that $p \cdot x = E(\pi x)$ for all x in $L^2(P)$. The *covariance* of two elements x and y of $L^2(P)$, denoted $\text{cov}(x, y)$, is the scalar

$$\text{cov}(x, y) = E(xy) - E(x)E(y).$$

The *variance* of any x in $L^2(P)$, denoted $\text{var}(x)$, is $\text{cov}(x, x)$. The above representation π of the price functional p implies that

$$p \cdot x = E(\pi)E(x) + \text{cov}(x, \pi), \quad x \in L^2(P).$$

The market value of any asset x is thus the covariance of x and a fixed asset π, plus a fixed multiple of $E(x)$. This is the starting point for "asset pricing models", which aim to identify π. An example is the Capital Asset Pricing Model, found in Section 11. ♠

F. For any ordered vector space L with positive cone L_+, consider

$$L'_+ = \{p \in L' : p \cdot x \geq 0, \quad x \in L_+\},$$

the *positive dual cone* of L. Let L^*_+ denote the subset of L'_+ whose elements are continuous. The elements of L'_+ and L^*_+ have special significance in economics because positive choice vectors are typically assigned positive market values in equilibrium. This is the case, for example, with free disposal or monotonic preferences by any agent. Then any equilibrium price vector p must be in L'_+. Since continuity is a useful property and $L^q(\mu)$ is a typical choice space, we quote the following result.

PROPOSITION. *For $q \in [1, \infty]$, $L^q(\mu)'_+ = L^q(\mu)^*_+$.*

In words, any positive linear functional on an L^q space is continuous.

G. A *Hilbert space* is a Banach space H under a norm $\| \cdot \|$ for which the parallelogram inequality holds with equality, or

$$\| x + y \|^2 + \| x - y \|^2 = 2 \| x \|^2 + 2 \| y \|^2 \tag{2}$$

for all x and y in H. A Hilbert space H has many intuitively Euclidean properties. For example, H is self–dual in the following way. Let $(\cdot \mid \cdot)$ denote the bilinear form:

$$(x \mid y) \equiv \frac{\| x + y \|^2 - \| x \|^2 - \| y \|^2}{2} \tag{3}$$

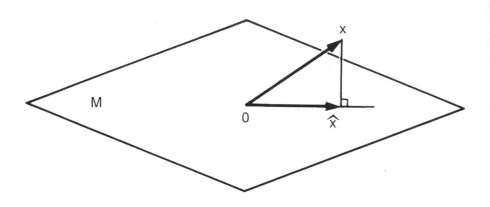

Figure 6.1   Orthogonal Projection

for all x and y in H. Then any $p \in H^*$ is identified with a unique $\pi \in H$ satisfying $p \cdot x = (\pi \mid x)$ for all $x \in H$. The bilinear form $(\cdot \mid \cdot)$ is the *inner product* for H.

Example. We have already remarked that $L^2(\mu)$ is self–dual. Indeed, $L^2(\mu)$ is a Hilbert space. In particular, if $(M, \mathcal{M}, \mu)$ is a probability space, then $(x \mid y) \equiv E(xy)$ for all x and y in $L^2(\mu)$. ♠

Other Hilbert spaces are illustrated in exercises. As with Banach spaces: any closed vector subspace of a Hilbert space is a Hilbert space under the same norm; any finite product of Hilbert spaces is a Hilbert space under the product norm.

In a Hilbert space H with inner product $(\cdot \mid \cdot)$, two vectors x and y are *orthogonal* if $(x \mid y) = 0$, denoted $x \perp y$. A vector y is orthogonal to a subset X of H, denoted $y \in X^\perp$, if $y \perp x$ for all x in X. The term *perpendicular* is sometimes used synonymously with orthogonal. The following result, illustrated in Figure 6.1, is the basis for a wide range of applications.

THE HILBERT SPACE PROJECTION THEOREM. *Suppose M is a closed vector subspace of a Hilbert space H normed by $\|\cdot\|$, and $x \in H$. There exists a unique vector $\hat{x}$ in M such that $x - \hat{x} \in M^\perp$. Furthermore, $\hat{x}$ is the unique vector in M satisfying $\| x - \hat{x} \| \leq \| x - m \|$ for all m in M.*

The proof is actually quite straightforward and assigned as an exercise. The projection theorem states that one can apply to Hilbert spaces the conventional Euclidean notion of minimizing the distance from a point to a plane by "dropping a perpendicular" from the point to the plane. The unique point $\hat{x}$ in a closed subspace M of a Hilbert space for which $x - \hat{x}$ is orthogonal to M is the *orthogonal projection* of the given vector x onto the subspace M.

EXERCISES

EXERCISE 6.1   Suppose L is a vector space. A *vector subspace* of L is a subset of L that is a vector space under the same addition and scalar multiplication operations. Show that any closed vector subspace of a Banach space is a Banach space under the same norm.

EXERCISE 6.2   Suppose L is the product of the Banach spaces $L_1, \ldots, L_N$ and is given the product norm. Prove that L is a Banach space.

EXERCISE 6.3   Prove that any convergent sequence in a normed space is Cauchy.

EXERCISE 6.4   Prove that a Euclidean space is a Hilbert space, and identify the inner product.

EXERCISE 6.5   Let $(\Omega, \mathcal{F}, P)$ be a probability space. Prove that the expectation of any element of $L^2(P)$ is finite. *Hint:* Use the Cauchy–Schwarz inequality.

EXERCISE 6.6   Let $(\Omega, \mathcal{F}, P)$ be a probability space and let H be a closed vector subspace of $L^2(P)$ such that the indicator function 1_Ω is not an element of H. Show that H is a Hilbert space under the norm

$$\| x \| = \sqrt{\operatorname{var}(x)}, \qquad x \in H,$$

where $\operatorname{var}(x)$ denotes the variance of x. Also show that the inner product $(\cdot \mid \cdot)$ for this Hilbert space is covariance: or $(x \mid y) = \operatorname{cov}(x, y)$ for all x and y in H.

EXERCISE 6.7   Prove *Minkowski's Inequality*: that the norm $\| \cdot \|_q$ on $L^q(\mu)$, $q \in [1, \infty]$, indeed obeys the triangle inequality: $\| x + y \|_q \leq \| x \|_q + \| y \|_q$.

EXERCISE 6.8   Prove that $L^2(\mu)$ is a Hilbert space. (The fact that $L^2(\mu)$ is a Banach space may be assumed.)

EXERCISE 6.9   In this section the primitive geometry for a Hilbert space is given by its norm. It is common however to define a (real) *inner product space* (L, f) to be a vector space L together with a scalar–valued bilinear form f on $L \times L$ satisfying, in addition to its bilinearity, the properties: $f(x, y) = f(y, x)$ for all x and y in L; $f(x, x) \geq 0$ for all $x \in L$; and $f(x, x) = 0 \iff x = 0$. Such a bilinear form is an *inner product*. Show that the form $(\cdot \mid \cdot)$ constructed for a Hilbert space in relation (3) is indeed an inner product in this sense. Show that the functional $\| x \|_f \equiv \sqrt{f(x, x)}$, $x \in L$, defines a norm on any inner product space (L, f). An inner product space is also called a *pre–Hilbert space*. Give an example of an inner product space that is not a Hilbert space. Prove that $\| \cdot \|_f$ satisfies the *parallelogram law* (2).

EXERCISE 6.10   Suppose L is an inner product space under the norm $\| \cdot \|$ and prove the following relationships, for any x and y in L:
  (a) If $\| x \| = \| y \|$, then for any scalars α and β, $\| \alpha x + \beta y \| = \| \beta x + \alpha y \|$.
  (b) If $\| x + y \| = \| x - y \|$, then for any scalar α, $\| x + \alpha y \| = \| x - \alpha y \|$.
  (c) If $\| x \| = \| y \| = 1$, then $\| x + y \|^2 + \| x - y \|^2 = 4$.
  (d) If $\| x \| = \| y \|$, then for any non–zero scalar α, $\| \alpha x + \frac{1}{\alpha} y \| \geq \| x + y \|$.

EXERCISE 6.11   Prove the Hilbert Space Projection Theorem. As a hint, it may help to first prove the

PYTHAGOREAN THEOREM.   *Suppose H is a Hilbert space normed by $\| \cdot \|$ and x and y are vectors in H. Then $x \perp y$ if and only if $\| x + y \|^2 = \| x \|^2 + \| y \|^2$.*

EXERCISE 6.12   (Regression is Orthogonal Projection in $L^2(P)$).   Let $H = L^2(P)$ for some probability space $(\Omega, \mathcal{F}, P)$, and for some fixed finite subset $\{y_1, \ldots, y_N\}$ of H, let M denote the set of all linear combinations of the form $\beta^\top y \equiv \sum_{n=1}^N \beta_n y_n$, for some $\beta \in R^N$. Show that M is a closed vector subspace of H. Let $x \in L^2(P)$ be any random variable with the property that $\alpha x + \beta^\top y = 1_\Omega$ is impossible. (No linear combination of x and $y_1, \ldots, y_N$ is a non–zero constant, a non–degeneracy condition.) Let $\operatorname{cov}(y, y)$ denote the $N \times N$ matrix whose (i, j)–element is $\operatorname{cov}(y_i, y_j)$, and let $\text{cov}(x, y) \in R^N$ denote the vector whose i-th element is $\text{cov}(x, y_i)$. Assuming that $\text{cov}(y, y)$ is non–singular, show that the orthogonal projection of x onto M is $\widehat{x} = \widehat{\beta}^\top y$, where $\widehat{\beta} = [\text{cov}(y, y)]^{-1}\text{cov}(x, y)$. *Hint:* Use Exercise 6.6. Interpret the result as a minimum variance regression equation. Is it true that $\widehat{x}$ is an *unbiased* estimate of x, meaning $E(\widehat{x}) = E(x)$? If not, explain, and modify this application of the projection theorem to get an unbiased minimum variance approximation of x as a linear combination of 1_Ω and $y_1, \ldots, y_N$.

Notes

This material is standard fare in functional analysis. The L^q space theory may be found in Royden (1968). On Hilbert space theory, Luenberger (1969) and Reed and Simon (1980) complement one another with many applications. The problem book by Halmos (1982) is a source of more advanced Hilbert space concepts. Proposition 6F and extensions may be found in Schaefer (1974). Exercise 6.10 is from Day (1973). Other versions of the Hilbert space projection theorem are found in Luenberger (1969).

7.   Portfolios

In the classical general equilibrium theory of Section 3, we implicitly assume that any choice is available "at a price", or *complete markets*. Now we consider an economy in which the set of available choices is the span of the available set of securities. This is a prelude to the "incomplete markets" theory that is surveyed in Section 12. In the exercises, we consider the problem of extending a price functional from an incomplete markets subspace to the entire choice space. This is related to the arbitrage–free pricing of securities, and ties together a number of results: the Separating Hyperplane Theorem, Farkas' Lemma, and the Hahn–Banach Extension Theorem.

A.   For any subset A of a vector space L, the *span* of A, denoted span(A), is the set of finite linear combinations of elements of A. That is, $m \in$ span(A) if and only if

$$m = \sum_{n=1}^{N} \beta_n a_n, \tag{1}$$

for some finite subset $\{a_1, \ldots, a_N\}$ of A and scalars $\beta_1, \ldots, \beta_N$.

A *security* for an economy on a vector space L is identified with a particular vector in L, and is treated as the exclusive property rights corresponding to that vector. The *security set* is the set of all securities available for trade. With *complete markets*, the security set is L itself. The *marketed space* corresponding to a security set $A \subset L$ is the span of A. The elements of span(A) are *marketed choices*. This presumes that an agent can hold any "portfolio", or finite linear combination, of securities. Any marketed space is *vector subspace*, also known as a *linear subspace*, that is, a subset of L that is a vector space under the addition and scalar multiplication operations of L.

B. A subset B of a vector space L is *linearly independent* if no element b of B is in the span of $B \backslash \{b\}$, meaning that no element of B is a linear combination of other elements of B. For any vector subspace M of L, a *Hamel basis* for M is a linearly independent subset B of M whose span is M. For example, the usual Euclidean basis vectors $e_1 = (1, 0, \ldots, 0)$, $e_2 = (0, 1, 0, \ldots, 0), \ldots, e_N = (0, 0, \ldots, 0, 1)$ form a Hamel basis for R^N. If a security set A is not a Hamel basis for the marketed space $M = \text{span}(A)$, then some proper subset $\widehat{A} \subset A$ forms a Hamel basis for M. In that case, the remaining securities $A \backslash \widehat{A}$ are *redundant* given $\widehat{A}$, in the sense that $\text{span}\left(\widehat{A}\right) = \text{span}(A) = M$. It is a fact, cited in the Notes, that every vector space has a Hamel basis. A vector space is *finite–dimensional* if it has a finite Hamel basis, and otherwise *infinite–dimensional*. The number of elements in a Hamel basis of a finite–dimensional vector space is unique, and defined as the *dimension* of the vector space.

With linear pricing, the market value of every security, indeed every marketed choice, is determined by the market values of any Hamel basis $\widehat{A}$ for the marketed space M. Specifically, for a price vector $p \in M'$ and any $m \in M$, we have $m = \sum_{n=1}^{N} \beta_n a_n$ and

$$
p \cdot m = p \cdot \left(\sum_{n=1}^{N} \beta_n a_n \right) = \sum_{n=1}^{N} \beta_n (p \cdot a_n),
$$

for unique $a_1, \ldots, a_N$ in $\widehat{A}$ and unique scalars $\beta_1, \ldots, \beta_N$. This is one sense of the expression: "A redundant security is priced by arbitrage considerations." To be specific, we say m is *redundant* given $A = \{a_1, \ldots, a_n\}$, in this static setting, if $m \in \text{span}(A)$. In this context, "no arbitrage" is a trivial consequence of linear pricing.

C. Given a fixed exogenously specified marketed space M, agents restrict their net trades to M. It is then a simple matter to formulate equilibrium for an exchange economy:

$$\mathcal{E} = (X_i, \succeq_i, \omega_i), \qquad i \in \mathcal{I} = \{1, \ldots, I\},$$

restricted to the marketed space M. For each $i \in \mathcal{I}$, let $X_i^M = (X_i - \{\omega_i\}) \cap M$, and define the preference relation $\succeq_i^M$ on X_i^M by

$$m \succeq_i^M n \quad \Longleftrightarrow \quad m + \omega_i \succeq_i n + \omega_i$$

for all m and n in X_i^M. We have simply re–expressed an agent's preferences over the set of marketed additions to endowments. An *equilibrium for $\mathcal{E}$ restricted to M* is simply an equilibrium (in the original, complete markets, sense) for the net trade economy

$$\mathcal{E}^M = (X_i^M, \succeq_i^M), \qquad i \in \mathcal{I}, \tag{2}$$

on the choice space M. This definition bypasses the role of market structure, the main object at hand, to which we now turn.

D. Let $A \subset L$ denote a security set. A *portfolio* on A is a real–valued function φ on A; for each security a in A, $\varphi(a)$ denotes the number of units of a held. Since we currently assume agents hold only a finite number of different securities (or $\varphi(a) = 0$ except for a in a finite subset of A), the L–valued "integral" $\int_A a\varphi(a)$ is trivially defined as the sum of $a\varphi(a)$ over all a in A. (We extend the definition of a portfolio to a non finite sum of securities in the exercises of Section 9.) An $(I + 1)$–tuple $(\varphi_1, \ldots, \varphi_I, p)$ consisting of a linear functional p on $M \equiv \mathrm{span}(A)$ and a portfolio φ_i on A for each i in $\mathcal{I}$ is an *equilibrium for the security market exchange economy* $(\mathcal{E}, A)$ provided $(\int_A a\varphi_1(a), \ldots, \int_A a\varphi_I(a), p)$ is an equilibrium for the net trade economy $\mathcal{E}^M$ constructed earlier, and in addition,

$$\sum_{i=1}^{I} \varphi_i(a) = 0, \quad a \in A. \tag{3}$$

Relation (3) expresses market clearing in individual security markets. As a suggestive but unnecessary frill, one could replace the price vector p in the last definition by a real–valued function π on A specifying the market value of each security, with π having a linear extension to M. If A is a linearly independent set, condition (3) is superfluous (Exercise 7.2). Otherwise, given an equilibrium $(x_1, \ldots, x_I, p)$ for $\mathcal{E}^M$, we can demonstrate portfolios $\varphi_1, \ldots, \varphi_I$ such that $(\varphi_1, \ldots, \varphi_I, p)$ is an equilibrium for $(\mathcal{E}, A)$. Simply let

$\varphi_2, \ldots, \varphi_I$ satisfy $\int_A a\varphi_i(a) = x_i$; this is possible by the definition of M. Then let $\varphi_1 = -\sum_{i=2}^{I} \varphi_i$. It follows that

$$\int_A a\varphi_1(a) = -\sum_{i=2}^{I} \int_A a\varphi_i(a) = -\sum_{i=2}^{I} x_i = x_1.$$

E.   For a given vector subspace M of the choice space L, an alloca-tion $(x_1, \ldots, x_I)$ for the economy $\mathcal{E}$ is M–*constrained efficient* provided $(x_1 - \omega_1, \ldots, x_I - \omega_I)$ is an efficient allocation for the net trade economy $\mathcal{E}^M$ formed by restricting $\mathcal{E}$ to M. Under regularity conditions stated in Exercise 7.3, a security market equilibrium allocation is M–constrained efficient, where M is the marketed space. The implication is that there exists no feasible allocation for $\mathcal{E}$ that can be obtained by trading on avail-able security markets and that dominates a security market equilibrium allocation.

EXERCISES

EXERCISE 7.1   Suppose A is a Hamel basis for a vector space M. Show that any element m of M has a representation of the form $m = \sum_{n=1}^{N} \beta_n a_n$ for unique scalars $\beta_1, \ldots, \beta_N$ and unique vectors $a_1, \ldots, a_N$ in A.

EXERCISE 7.2   Suppose A is a linearly independent subset of the choice space L. Show that condition (3) is superfluous in the definition in Para-graph D of an equilibrium for the security market exchange economy $(\mathcal{E}, A)$. That is, if $(\varphi_1, \ldots, \varphi_I)$ are portfolios on A such that

$$\left(\int_A a\varphi_1(a), \ldots, \int_A a\varphi_I(a) \right)$$

is a feasible allocation for $\mathcal{E}^M$, then relation (3) must hold.

EXERCISE 7.3   Let $(\mathcal{E}, A)$ be a security market exchange economy with an equilibrium $(\varphi_1, \ldots, \varphi_I, p)$. Suppose the preference relation $\succeq_i$ is strictly z_i–monotonic for some $z_i \in M \equiv \text{span}(A)$, for all $i \in \mathcal{I}$. Show that the equilibrium is M–constrained Pareto efficient, meaning that the allocation $(\int_A a\varphi_1(a), \ldots, \int_A a\varphi_I(a))$ is efficient for the net trade economy $\mathcal{E}^M$ defined by (2) on the choice space M.

EXERCISE 7.4   Show that the number of elements of a Hamel basis for a finite dimensional vector space is uniquely determined.

EXERCISE 7.5 A linearly independent subset of a vector space is a *repère*. Show that any repère with n elements in an n–dimensional vector space L is a Hamel basis for L.

EXERCISE 7.6 It is a consequence of the axiom of choice that every repère for a vector space is contained by a Hamel basis. Show that every Hamel basis for a vector subspace M of a vector space L is contained by a Hamel basis for L.

EXERCISE 7.7 Prove the following form of *Farkas' Lemma* with an application of the Separating Hyperplane Theorem. (See Exercise 3.12.)

FARKA'S LEMMA. *Let D be a real $m \times n$ matrix. Then a vector $\pi \in R^n$ satisfies $\pi^\top x \geq 0$ for all x in R^n with $Dx \geq 0$ if and only if there exists a positive vector $\lambda \in R^m$ such that $\pi^\top = \lambda^\top D$.*

EXERCISE 7.8 Suppose there are m states of the world in a model with an $m \times n$ security dividend matrix D, where D_{ij} is the payoff of security j in state i. Let $\pi \in R^n$ denote the vector of prices of the n securities. The securities' price–dividend pair (π, D) is *weakly arbitrage–free*, by definition, if any portfolio $\theta \in R^n$ of securities has positive market value $\pi^\top \theta \geq 0$ whenever it has positive payoffs in every state, or $D\theta \geq 0$. Prove the securities are weakly arbitrage–free if and only if there exists a *state–price vector*, some $\lambda \in R_+^m$ satisfying $\pi^\top = \lambda^\top D$.

EXERCISE 7.9 Continuing with the notation of the last problem, we define the securities with price–dividend pair (π, D) to be *arbitrage free* (in a strict sense) if, for any portfolio $\theta \in R^n$ satisfying $D\theta > 0$, or positive non–zero dividends, we have $\pi^\top \theta > 0$. Show that (π, D) is strictly arbitrage–free if and only if there exists a state–price vector $\lambda \gg 0$, meaning $\lambda \in \mathrm{int}(R_+^m)$. *Hint:* You may wish to use the following strict version of Farkas' Lemma, which is sometimes known as *Stiemke's Lemma*. For an ordered normed space L, our inequality sign conventions are $x \in L_+ \Leftrightarrow x \geq 0$; $x \in L_+ \setminus \{0\} \Leftrightarrow x > 0$; $x \in \mathrm{int}(L_+) \Leftrightarrow x \gg 0$.

STIEMKE'S LEMMA. *Suppose A is an $m \times n$ real matrix. Then one and only one of the following statements is correct:*
(a) *There exists a solution $x \gg 0$ in R^n to the equation $Ax = 0$.*
(b) *There exists a solution $y \in R^m$ to the inequality $y^\top A > 0$.*

A proof is cited in the Notes.

EXERCISE 7.10 A *zero–sum game* is defined by an $m \times n$ matrix G. A *strategy* for player $\mathcal{R}$ is a vector $r \in \Delta^{m-1} \equiv \{x \in R_+^m : \sum_{i=1}^m x_i =$

1}, with r_i representing the probability with which $\mathcal{R}$ "plays" row i of G. Similarly, a strategy for $\mathcal{C}$ is a vector $c \in \Delta^{n-1}$, with c_j representing the probability that player $\mathcal{C}$ chooses column j of G. The value for $\mathcal{R}$ of strategy pair $(r, c) \in \Delta^{m-1} \times \Delta^{n-1}$ is $-r^\top Gc$. Player $\mathcal{C}$ receives the value $r^\top Gc$. (Hence: "zero sum".) The following result, proved originally by more difficult methods, is a consequence of Farkas' Lemma.

MINMAX THEOREM. *Suppose G is a zero sum game with the property: for any strategy r for $\mathcal{R}$ there exists a strategy c for $\mathcal{C}$ such that $r^\top Gc \geq 0$. Then there exists a strategy $\bar{c}$ for $\mathcal{C}$ such that $r^\top G\bar{c} \geq 0$ for any strategy r of $\mathcal{R}$.*

(A)   Prove the MinMax Theorem.

(B)   Using the MinMax Theorem, derive the conclusion of Exercise 7.8 on the existence of "state prices." *Hint:* Let G be a $2n \times m$ matrix, and let $\mathcal{R}$ be thought of as an investor who, rather than choosing probabilities, chooses portfolio weights $r = (r_1, \ldots, r_n, r_{n+1}, \ldots, r_{2n})$ that assign the fraction r_i of $\mathcal{R}$'s wealth to security i and fraction r_{n+i} to short sales of security i.

EXERCISE 7.11   Suppose p is a linear functional on a vector subspace M of a vector space L. A *linear extension* of p is a linear functional q on L such that $q \cdot x = p \cdot x$ for any x in M. As indicated in the Notes, any linear functional on any vector subspace of any vector space has a linear extension. Prove the following special case of the *Hahn–Banach Extension Theorem*: A continuous linear functional p on a vector subspace M of a normed space L has a continuous linear extension. (The subspace is given the norm of the vector space.) *Hint:* Use the Separating Hyperplane Theorem and corollaries reported in the exercises to Section 3, as well as the definition of a continuous linear functional. This fact can be used, for example, to obtain a Riesz Representation for a continuous price functional on a marketed subspace of an $L^q(P)$ space. Refer ahead to Exercise 9.5 for an application.

EXERCISE 7.12   A linear functional f on a subspace M of an ordered vector space L is *strictly positive* if $f(m) > 0$ for any non–zero $m \in M \bigcap L_+$. Show that any strictly positive linear functional f on a vector subspace M of a Euclidean space L has a strictly positive linear extension $F : L \to R$. *Hint:* Use Stiemke's Lemma.

EXERCISE 7.13   Let L and N be vector spaces, with N ordered. A function $\phi : L \to N$ is *sublinear* if $\phi(x + y) \leq \phi(x) + \phi(y)$ for all x and y in L, and if $\phi(\alpha x) = \alpha \phi(x)$ for all $\alpha \in (0, \infty)$ and $x \in L$.

(A)   Prove the following topology–free extension theorem.

HAHN–BANACH EXTENSION THEOREM. *Suppose L is a vector space, M is a linear subspace of L, $p : M \to R$ is linear, $\phi : L \to R$ is sublinear, and $p \cdot x \le \phi(x)$ for all $x \in M$. Then there is a linear functional $q : L \to R$ extending p with $q \cdot x \le \phi(x)$ for all x in L.*

Hint: Use the Separating Hyperplane Theorem (Proposition 3F).

(B)   Prove the following topological version.

COROLLARY. *Suppose, under the conditions of the theorem, that L is normed, ϕ is continuous, and p is continuous. Then the extension q can be chosen to be continuous with the stated properties.*

EXERCISE 7.14   Suppose M is a vector subspace of an ordered vector space L. Then the pair (M, L) is defined to have the *subspace positive intersection property* if, for each $x \in L$,

$$[\exists y \in M : x + y \ge 0] \iff [\exists z \in M : x + z \le 0].$$

(A)   Prove the following application of the Hahn–Banach Extension Theorem.

MONOTONE EXTENSION THEOREM. *Suppose M is a vector subspace of an ordered vector space L, and (M, L) has the subspace positive intersection property. If p is a positive linear functional on M, then p has a positive linear extension to L.*

(B)   Prove the following related result.

KREIN–RUTMAN THEOREM. *Suppose L is a normed ordered vector space and that M is a vector subspace of L such that $M \cap \operatorname{int}(L_+)$ is not empty. Then any positive continuous linear functional p on M has a positive continuous linear extension $q : L \to R$.*

EXERCISE 7.15   Let $(\Omega, \mathcal{F}, P)$ be a probability space, and treat $d = \{d_1, \ldots, d_N\} \subset L^\infty(P)$ as a set of securities, with $d_n(\omega)$ the dividend of the n–th security in state ω. Suppose further that one of the securities is riskless, meaning that $d_1(\omega) = 1$ for all $\omega \in \Omega$. Let $\pi \in R^N$ denote the market value of these securities, and assume that the pair (π, d) is *weakly arbitrage–free*, in the sense that there is no portfolio $\theta \in R^N$ with the properties $\pi^\top \theta < 0$ and $\sum_{n=1}^{N} \theta_n d_n \ge 0$. Let $r = 1/\pi_1 - 1$ denote the interest rate on the riskless security (assuming $\pi_1 \neq 0$). Assuming $r > -1$, demonstrate the existence of a probability measure Q on $(\Omega, \mathcal{F})$ such that

$$\pi_n = \frac{1}{1+r} E^Q(d_n)$$

for all n, where E^Q denotes expectation for the probability space $(\Omega, \mathcal{F}, Q)$. *Hint:* Use the Krein–Rutman Theorem and the definition of a probability measure. It may help to read Paragraph 9A in advance and to use the Riesz Representation Theorem, but that is not strictly necessary. This is a major focal point of finance theory that reappears in a dynamic setting in Section 17.

Notes

For a discussion of vector subspaces and Hamel bases, see Holmes (1975) and, for more details, the monographs by Raikov (1965) and Day (1973). Raikov proves that every vector space has a Hamel basis. The discussion in this section is mainly a simple manipulation of definitions. The fact that any linear functional on a vector subspace has an extension to the whole space is reported in Holmes (1975). Stiemke's Lemma is from Corollary 2, page 49, of David Gale (1960).

8. Optimization Principles

A few guiding principles of optimization apply in any vector choice space. For an unconstrained problem, a differentiable functional is maximized at a point only if none of its derivatives are strictly positive at the point. If the functional is also concave, this condition is both necessary and sufficient. Given a solution to a constrained problem, there exists a corresponding unconstrained problem with the same solution whose objective functional is the sum of the original functional and a "Lagrange multiple" of the constraint function. The Lagrange multiplier, a dual vector, communicates the "shadow price" of the constraint. Although these principles call for carefully formulated definitions and a few regularity conditions, the generality of their application shows the power of a simple geometric approach to optimization. As an application, the exercises present versions of the representative agent problem.

A.   Throughout this section we fix f to be a functional on a subset X of a vector space L. Our aim is to establish conditions under which x_0

maximizes f on X, meaning $x_0 \in X$ and $f(x_0) \geq f(x)$ for all x in X. This is occasionally denoted by

$$x_0 \in \arg \max_{x \in X} \ f(x).$$

The familiar *first order necessary conditions* for optimality are loosely stated as: If x_0 maximizes f on X, then the rate of improvement of f is negative along every feasible direction from x_0. The set of *feasible directions* at x_0 is the set

$$F(x_0, X) = \{h \in L : \exists \epsilon \in (0, 1) : x_0 + \alpha h \in X, \quad 0 \leq \alpha \leq \epsilon\}.$$

Of course $F(x, L) = L$ for all x in L. By definition, $x \in \mathrm{core}(X) \iff F(x, X) = L$.

A notion of the rate of improvement of f as x moves from x_0 along a feasible direction $h \subset L$ is given the following form. Suppose, for $x \in X$, that $h \in F(x, X)$, and that the limit

$$\lim_{\alpha \downarrow 0} \frac{f(x + \alpha h) - f(x)}{\alpha} \tag{1}$$

exists. Then the limit (1) is denoted $f'(x; h)$ and defines the *Gateaux (or directional) derivative of f at x in the direction of h*. The statement: "$f'(x; h)$ exists", for some $h \in L$, includes the assertion that $h \in F(x; X)$. This convention makes for simple wording but places an onus of care on the reader.

Here are the first order necessary conditions more carefully stated.

PROPOSITION. *Suppose x_0 maximizes f on X. Then $f'(x_0; h) \leq 0$ for any h in L such that $f'(x; h)$ exists.*

PROOF: For any $h \in F(x_0, X)$ and corresponding scalar $\delta > 0$ sufficiently small, we have $f(x_0 + \alpha h) \leq f(x_0)$, for all α in $[0, \delta]$. The result follows from the definition of $f'(x_0; h)$. ∎

Suppose, for some $x \in X$, that $f'(x; h)$ exists for all h in L. We then say f is *Gateaux differentiable* at x. In that case the functional $f'(x; \cdot) : L \to R$, if linear, is the *gradient of f* at x, denoted $\nabla f(x)$, an element of the dual space L'.

Example. Suppose $X = L = R^n$. If, for $x = (x_1, \ldots, x_n) \in R^n$, the row vector of partial derivatives

$$\frac{\partial f(x)}{\partial x} = \left[\frac{\partial f(x)}{\partial x_1}, \ldots, \frac{\partial f(x)}{\partial x_n} \right]$$

exists, then

$$f'(x; h) \equiv \nabla f(x) \cdot h = \frac{\partial f(x)}{\partial x} h \quad \left(\equiv \sum_{i=1}^{n} \frac{\partial f(x)}{\partial x_i} h_i \right), \quad \in R^n.$$

Thus, the functional $\nabla f(x)$ can be identified with the vector $\partial f(x)/\partial x$. In fact, it is typical to write "$\nabla f(x) = \partial f(x)/\partial x$". The vector $\partial f(x)/\partial x$ is the direction of "fastest improvement", or "steepest ascent" of f at x, meaning $\partial f(x)/\partial x$ maximizes $f'(x; z/ \parallel z \parallel)$ over all non–zero z in L. ♠

We say f is *stationary* at $x \in X$ if $\nabla f(x)$ exists and is the zero functional (or $\nabla f(x) \cdot h = 0$ for all h in L). In other words, f is stationary at x if the rate of improvement of f is zero in every direction from x. Exercise 8.4 asks the reader to prove the following classical statement of first order conditions.

COROLLARY. *Suppose x_0 maximizes f on X. If $\nabla f(x_0)$ exists, then f is stationary at x_0. Conversely, if f is concave and stationary at $x_0 \in X$, then x_0 maximizes f on X.*

B.   Now we add structure by posing an *optimization problem* (f, X, g, Y), usually expressed as: $\max_{x \in X} f(x)$ subject to $g(x) \leq 0$, where g maps X into an ordered vector space Y. We say x_0 *solves* (f, X, g, Y) if $x_0 \in X$, $g(x_0) \leq 0$, and $f(x_0) \geq f(x)$ for all x in X satisfying $g(x) \leq 0$. We call (f, X, g, Y) a *concave program* if f is a concave functional, X is a convex set, and g is convex from X into Y. An example of a concave program is a *linear program* (f, X, g, Y), for which $X = R^n, f : R^n \to R$ is linear, $Y = R^m$, and $g : R^n \to R^m$ is affine.

We recall that Y'_+ denotes the set of positive linear functionals on the vector space Y. The *Lagrangian* for an optimization problem (f, X, g, Y) is the functional $\mathcal{L}$ on $X \times Y'_+$ defined by

$$\mathcal{L}(x, \lambda) = f(x) - \lambda \cdot g(x), \quad x \in X, \lambda \in Y'_+.$$

The dual vector $\lambda \in Y'_+$ of the Lagrangian is sometimes termed a *Lagrange multiplier*. A point (x_0, λ_0) in $X \times Y'_+$ is a *saddle point* of $\mathcal{L}$ provided

$$\mathcal{L}(x, \lambda_0) \leq \mathcal{L}(x_0, \lambda_0) \leq \mathcal{L}(x_0, \lambda), \quad (x, \lambda) \in X \times Y'_+.$$

In other words, (x_0, λ_0) is a saddle point of $\mathcal{L}$ if x_0 maximizes $\mathcal{L}(\cdot, \lambda_0)$ on X and λ_0 minimizes $\mathcal{L}(x_0, \cdot)$ on Y'_+.

THEOREM (SADDLE POINT THEOREM). *Let (f, X, g, Y) be a concave program.*

I. *(Optimality Implies a Saddle Point and Complementary Slackness.) Suppose there exists $x_1 \in X$ such that $-g(x_1) \in \text{core}(Y_+)$. If $x_0 \in X$ solves the concave program then there exists $\lambda_0 \in Y'_+$ such that (x_0, λ_0) is a saddle point of $\mathcal{L}$, the Lagrangian for this program. Furthermore, we have complementary slackness: $\lambda_0 \cdot g(x_0) = 0$.*

II. *(A Saddle Point Implies Optimality.) Suppose $(x_0, \lambda_0) \in X \times Y'_+$ is a saddle point of the Lagrangian $\mathcal{L}$ for this program, Y is normed, λ_0 is continuous, and Y_+ is closed. Then x_0 solves the given program.*

PROOF: (Part I)   Construct:

$$A = \{(r, y) \in R \times Y \cdot \exists r \in X; r \le f(x), y \ge g(x)\}$$

$$B = \{(r, y) \in R \times Y : r \ge f(x_0), y \le 0\}.$$

By the definition of optimality, $\text{core}(B) \cap A = \emptyset$, and by assumption, $\text{core}(B) \ne \emptyset$. Both sets are convex by assumptions on f and g. By the Separating Hyperplane Theorem (Exercise 3.13), A and B can be separated by an element of $(R \times Y)' = R \times Y'$, say (ℓ, λ_0). (See Exercise 3.14.) It is easily verified that $\ell < 0$ and $\lambda_0 \ge 0$ from the hypothesized properties of x_1, so ℓ can be taken to be -1 without loss of generality. Since $(f(x_0), 0) \in A \cap B$, x_0 maximizes $\mathcal{L}(\cdot, \lambda_0)$ on X. Then, since $\lambda_0 \cdot g(x_0) \le 0$, we have

$$f(x_0) \ge f(x_0) - \lambda_0 \cdot g(x_0) \ge f(x_0),$$

implying $\lambda_0 \cdot g(x_0) = 0$. It follows that (x_0, λ_0) is a saddle point.

The proof of Part II is left as an exercise. ∎

Under the combined regularity conditions for Parts I and II of the Saddle Point Theorem, (x_0, λ_0) is a saddle point for the Lagrangian if and only if x_0 solves the optimization problem. It is frequently desirable in applying Part I of the Theorem to have the existence of a *continuous* Lagrange multiplier λ_0 on Y (where Y is, for example, a normed space). Appropriate strengthened hypotheses on Y_+ are given in Exercise 8.5. If Y is an L^q space, however, the continuity of any $\lambda \in Y'_+$ follows automatically by Proposition 6F. On the other hand, of the infinite–dimensional L^q spaces, only L^∞ spaces have a positive cone with a non–empty core or interior.

C.   In order to extend the first order necessary conditions stated in Proposition 8A to problems with constraints, we must first extend the definition of "gradient" to cover a function $g : X \rightarrow Y$, where Y is a normed space. Suppose, for some $x \in X$, that $F(x, X) = L$ and that the limit

$$\lim_{\alpha \to 0} \frac{g(x + \alpha h) - g(x)}{\alpha} \tag{2}$$

exists for all $h \in L$ and defines a function of h that is linear from L into Y. Then we denote the limit (2) by $\nabla g(x) \cdot h$, and call the linear mapping $\nabla g(x) : L \rightarrow Y$ that it defines the *gradient* of g at x. As before, the existence of $\nabla g(x)$ includes the assertion that $F(x, X) = L$.

Example.   Extending from Example A, suppose $X = L = R^n, Y = R^m$, and $g : R^n \rightarrow R^m$ is differentiable at $x \in R^n$. Then $\nabla g(x)$ exists, and

$$\nabla g(x) \cdot h = \frac{\partial g(x)}{\partial x} h, \qquad h \in R^n,$$

where $\partial g(x)/\partial x$ is the *Jacobian* of g at x, the m by n matrix whose (i, j)– element is $\partial g_i(x)/\partial x_j$. ♠

We now have a differential form of the Saddle Point Theorem.

THEOREM (KUHN–TUCKER). *Suppose x_0 solves an optimization problem (f, X, g, Y), where $\nabla f(x_0)$ and $\nabla g(x_0)$ exist, and there is some h in L such that $g(x_0) + \nabla g(x_0) \cdot h < 0$. Let $\mathcal{L}$ denote the Lagrangian for (f, X, g, Y). If $int\,(Y_+) \neq \emptyset$ then there exists $\lambda_0 \in Y_+^*$ such that*
(a) $\mathcal{L}(\cdot, \lambda_0)$ is stationary at x_0,
(b) $\mathcal{L}(x_0, \cdot)$ is stationary at λ_0, and
(c) $\lambda_0 \cdot g(x_0) = 0$.

Theorems 8B and 8C, whose proof is cited in the Notes, enable one to replace the original constrained optimization problem (f, X, g, Y) with the simpler unconstrained problem

$$\max_{x \in X}\quad f(x) + \lambda_0 \cdot g(x),$$

provided the correct Lagrange multiplier vector λ_0 can be found. In numerical approaches, one might begin with a trial value λ for λ_0 and adjust $x \in X$ and $\lambda \in Y'$ toward a saddle point. In some cases one can use the Kuhn–Tucker conditions to deduce a solution immediately.

D.   We turn to the role of superdifferentials in maximizing a concave functional f on a convex subset X of a vector space L. A dual vector $p \in L'$ is a *supergradient* of f at $x \in X$ provided $p \cdot (y - x) \geq f(y) - f(x)$

for all $y \in X$. The set of all supergradients of f at x is the *superdifferential* of f at x, denoted $\partial f(x)$. The functional f is *superdifferentiable* at x provided $\partial f(x)$ is not empty. In particular, if the gradient $\nabla f(x)$ exists, then $\nabla f(x) \in \partial f(x)$.

LEMMA. *If x is in the intrinsic core of X, then f is superdifferentiable at x.*

In particular, if $x \in \operatorname{core}(X)$, then $\partial f(x)$ is not empty.

PROPOSITION. *If x_0 maximizes a concave functional f on X and $p \in \partial f(x_0)$, then x_0 maximizes p on X.*

Exercise 8.7 calls for a proof of this simple proposition. The following converse result involves more detailed considerations; a proof is cited in the Notes.

THEOREM. *Suppose L is a normed space and f is concave and continuous at x_0. If x_0 maximizes some continuous $p \in \partial f(x_0)$ on X, then x_0 maximizes f on X.*

EXERCISES

EXERCISE 8.1 Show that, if X is a convex set, then $y - x \in F(x, X)$ for all x and y in X.

EXERCISE 8.2 Show that a convex functional on a convex set X is Gateaux differentiable at any point $x \in \operatorname{core}(X)$.

EXERCISE 8.3 Demonstrate a functional f that is Gateaux differentiable at a point x, but whose gradient does not exist at x.

EXERCISE 8.4 Prove Corollary 8A.

EXERCISE 8.5 Prove the following corollary to Part I of the Saddle Point Theorem. *Under the same conditions, if Y is a normed space and $\operatorname{int}(Y_+) \neq \emptyset$, then λ_0 is continuous.*

EXERCISE 8.6 Prove Part II of the Saddle Point Theorem 8B by showing that the conditions imply $g(x_0) \leq 0$, and then applying arguments used in the proof of Part I. *Hint:* Use Exercise 3.14.

EXERCISE 8.7 Prove Proposition 8D.

EXERCISE 8.8 Prove Lemma 8D.

EXERCISE 8.9   Prove the steepest ascent assertion of Example 8A.

EXERCISE 8.10   Show the detailed arguments for the following steps of the proof given for Part I of the Saddle Point Theorem:

    (a) $\text{core}(B) \cap A = \emptyset$,

    (b) $\text{core}(B) \neq \emptyset$,

    (c) A and B are convex,

    (d) $\ell < 0$ and $\lambda_0 \geq 0$,

    (e) $\ell = -1$ is without loss of generality,

    (f) x_0 maximizes $\mathcal{L}(\cdot, \lambda_0)$ on X,

    (g) $f(x_0) \geq f(x_0) - \lambda_0 \cdot g(x_0)$; $f(x_0) - \lambda_0 \cdot g(x_0) \geq f(x_0)$, and

    (h) λ_0 minimizes $\mathcal{L}(x_0, \cdot)$ on Y'_+.

EXERCISE 8.11   Let L be a vector space, X be a subset of L, and $\succeq$ be a preference relation on X defined by a functional $u : X \to R$. Suppose $x_0 \in X$ is an optimal choice given the endowment $\omega \in L$ and given the non–zero price vector $p \in L'$, meaning x_0 solves the problem

$$\max_{x \in X} \quad u(x) \quad \text{subject to} \quad p \cdot x \leq p \cdot \omega.$$

Assume that the gradient $\nabla u(x_0)$ exists and is non–zero, and show that $p = k \nabla u(x_0)$ for some strictly positive scalar k.

EXERCISE 8.12   Let L be a vector space, X be a convex subset of L, and $\succeq$ be a preference relation on X represented by a concave (utility) functional $u : X \to R$. Let $g : L \to R$ be convex, defining the production set $Y = \{x \in L : g(x) \leq 0\}$. Suppose $x_0 \in X$ solves the problem

$$\max_{x \in X} \quad u(\omega + x) \quad \text{subject to} \quad g(x) \leq 0,$$

where ω is an endowment in L. Assume that $\nabla u(\omega + x_0)$ and $\nabla g(x_0)$ exist, and are both non–zero. Prove that $(x_0 + \omega, x_0, \nabla g(x_0))$ is an equilibrium for the single–agent production–exchange economy $\mathcal{E} = ((X, \succeq); Y; \omega; 1)$ on the choice space L, as defined by relation (3.1). Show that the price vector $\nabla g(x_0)$ is a strictly positive scalar multiple of $\nabla u(x_0)$.

EXERCISE 8.13   Let L be an ordered vector space and, for each i in $\{1, \ldots, I\}$, let $\omega_i \in L$ be an endowment for agent i, X_i be a convex choice set for agent i, and $\succeq_i$ be a preference relation on X_i represented by a concave functional $u_i : X_i \to R$. Let Y be the set $\{z \in L : g(z) \leq 0\}$, where g is a convex functional. For an economy with agents $(X_i, \succeq_i, \omega_i)$, $i \in$

$\{1, \ldots, I\}$, and the single production set Y, suppose $(x_1, \ldots, x_I, y)$ is an efficient allocation. Suppose further that $\nabla u_1(x_1), \ldots, \nabla u_I(x_I)$ and $\nabla g(y)$ exist and are non–zero.

(A)   Show that the price vector $p = \nabla g(y)$ strictly supports the allocation $(x_1, \ldots, x_I, y)$, in the sense of (3.3)–(3.4). In particular, if $\theta_1, \ldots, \theta_I$ are the agents' firm shares and $(x_1, \ldots, x_I, y, p)$ is an equilibrium, show that $p = k \nabla g(y)$ for some scalar $k > 0$.

(B)   (Representative Agent)   Suppose $X_i = L$ for all i, and consider the functional $u_\alpha : L \rightarrow R$ defined for some given (utility weights) $\alpha = (\alpha_1, \ldots, \alpha_I) \in R^I$ according to

$$u_\alpha(x) = \max_{z_1, \ldots, z_I} \sum_{i=1}^{I} \alpha_i u_i(z_i), \quad \text{subject to} \quad z_1 + \cdots + z_I < x. \quad (3)$$

Let $p = \nabla g(y)$, and consider $\overline{\alpha} = (1/\lambda_1, \ldots, 1/\lambda_I)$, where (x_i, λ_i) is a saddle point for the problem

$$\max_z \quad u_i(z) \quad \text{subject to} \quad p \cdot z \leq p \cdot \omega_i. \quad (4)$$

Show that y solves the problem

$$\max_z \quad u_{\overline{\alpha}} \left(z + \Sigma_{i=1}^{I} \omega_i \right) \quad \text{subject to} \quad g(z) \leq 0, \quad (5)$$

as well as the problem

$$\max_z \quad u_{\overline{\alpha}} \left(z + \Sigma_{i=1}^{I} \omega_i \right) \quad \text{subject to} \quad p \cdot z \leq p \cdot \left(y + \Sigma_{i=1}^{I} \omega_i \right). \quad (6)$$

(C)   For both (5) and (6), show that the nested maximization problem given by the definition of $u_{\overline{\alpha}}$ is solved by $x_1, \ldots, x_I$.

Notes

A classic reference on optimization with a vector space approach is Luenberger (1969). Section 14 of Holmes (1975) is a quick abstract review of the principles. Clarke (1983) has shown how to relax many of the typical differentiability assumptions while maintaining much of the historic elegance of this theory. For finite–dimensional theory and algorithms, see Rockafellar (1970), Hestenes (1975), and Luenberger (1984). Part I of Theorem 8B is an algebraic form of the Hurwicz Saddle Point Theorem. The proof is a trivial extension of Luenberger's. Theorem 8C is also from Luenberger (1969). The results of Paragraph D are summarized from Holmes (1975), with Theorem 8D being a corollary to Pshenichnii's Theorem. Further results showing the relationship between a supporting price vector and the gradients of the utility and production functions at an efficient allocation are found in Mas–Colell (1986b).

9.   Second Probability Concepts

We will continue the outline of basic probability concepts begun in Section 4. We consider different probability measures on the same tribe of events, and different tribes of events on the same underlying event space. The concept of conditional expectation is formalized. This is of critical importance in a multi–period economic setting or under asymmetric information. A general form of the "conditional" Jensen's inequality is stated. Finally, probabilistic independence is introduced along with a version of the law of large numbers.

A.   When considering two different probability measures P and Q on a measurable space $(\Omega, \mathcal{F})$, we should make a distinction between expectation under P (say "E^P") and expectation under Q ("E^Q"), between "P–almost surely" and "Q–almost surely", and so on. If P and Q have the same negligible events, they are *equivalent probability measures*. One might think of two individuals differing in their subjective probability assessments but agreeing on which events have probability zero, and therefore on which are almost sure. If $P(B) = 0$ implies $Q(B) = 0$ for any B in $\mathcal{F}$, then Q is *absolutely continuous* with respect to P, denoted $Q \prec P$. That is, every P–negligible event is Q–negligible, but not necessarily the converse. If $Q \prec P$ there exists a real–valued random variable ξ with the property, for any Q–integrable random variable x,

$$E^Q(x) \equiv \int_\Omega x(\omega)\, dQ(\omega) = \int_\Omega x(\omega)\xi(\omega)\, dP(\omega) = E^P(x\xi). \qquad (1)$$

This function ξ, often denoted dQ/dP, is the *Radon–Nikodym derivative* of Q with respect to P. By considering $x = 1_\Omega$ in (1), we see that $E^P(\xi) = 1$. It is also readily seen that ξ is positive Q–almost surely. If P and Q are equivalent, the Radon–Nikodym derivative dQ/dP is in fact strictly positive almost surely, which the reader is asked to show as an exercise. Reversing directions, suppose ξ is a positive real–valued random variable on $(\Omega, \mathcal{F}, P)$ with $E^P(\xi) = 1$. Then ξ defines a new probability measure Q on $(\Omega, \mathcal{F})$ by: $Q(B) = E^P(1_B \xi)$ for all B in $\mathcal{F}$. The Radon–Nikodym derivative of Q with respect to P is then $dQ/dP = \xi$.

B. When considering two different tribes $\mathcal{F}$ and $\mathcal{G}$ on a set Ω, we distinguish between those events and functions measurable with respect to $\mathcal{F}$, or $\mathcal{F}$–measurable, and those that are $\mathcal{G}$–measurable. We say $\mathcal{G}$ is a *sub–tribe* of $\mathcal{F}$ if $\mathcal{G} \subseteq \mathcal{F}$, with the implication that every $\mathcal{G}$–measurable function is $\mathcal{F}$–measurable, but not necessarily the converse. We could then say that $\mathcal{F}$ represents "more information" than $\mathcal{G}$, or that knowing the truth or falsehood of every event in $\mathcal{F}$ conveys more precise knowledge of the "true state" of the world than does the corresponding information from $\mathcal{G}$.

Example: For illustration, let $\Omega = \{1, \ldots, 10\}$ and let $\mathcal{F}$ and $\mathcal{G}$ be the tribes on Ω generated by the following partitions of Ω, respectively:

$$\mathcal{A} = \big\{\{1,2\}, \{3\}, \{4,5,6\}, \{7,8,9,10\}\big\}$$
$$\mathcal{B} = \big\{\{1,2,3,4,5,6\}, \{7,8,9,10\}\big\}.$$

If the true state of the world is 8, the two individuals whose information corresponds to $\mathcal{F}$ and $\mathcal{G}$ respectively will both find out that the true state lies in $\{7,8,9,10\}$. If the true state is 2, the individual with partition $\mathcal{A}$ has more precise knowledge. When, as here, every element of partition $\mathcal{B}$ is the union of elements of partition $\mathcal{A}$, we say $\mathcal{A}$ is a *refinement* of $\mathcal{B}$, and that $\mathcal{B}$ is a *coarsening* of $\mathcal{A}$. Whenever a partition $\mathcal{A}$ is a refinement of $\mathcal{B}$, it follows that $\mathcal{G} = \sigma(\mathcal{B})$ is a sub–tribe of $\mathcal{F} = \sigma(\mathcal{A})$. ♠

C. To begin a discussion of conditional expectation, we start with the simple concept of conditional expectation "given that an event B has occurred". Let $(\Omega, \mathcal{F}, P)$ be a probability space, x an integrable random variable on this space, and $B \in \mathcal{F}$ with $P(B) > 0$. The usual conditioning rule and notation is:

$$E(x \mid B) = \frac{1}{P(B)} \int_B x(\omega)\, dP(\omega) = \frac{1}{P(B)} E(1_B x).$$

In particular, the conditional probability of event A given B is

$$P(A \mid B) \equiv E(1_A \mid B) = \frac{1}{P(B)} \int_B 1_A(\omega)\, dP(\omega)$$
$$= \frac{1}{P(B)} \int_{A \cap B} dP(\omega) = \frac{P(A \cap B)}{P(B)}.$$

We next consider conditioning on events whose outcomes are uncertain. For example, we could consider the events to be revealed by observing the outcome of some real–valued random variable y. We recall that y generates a tribe, $\sigma(y)$. In a certain sense $\sigma(y)$ includes precisely those events that the outcome of y will reveal to be true or false. Consider for example $A = \{\omega \in \Omega : y(\omega) \leq 0\} \in \sigma(y)$. We could think of "$P(A \mid y)$", or equivalently "$P(A \mid \sigma(y))$" as the random variable whose outcome is 1 if the outcome of y is negative, and 0 otherwise. Similarly, "$E(x \mid y)$" or "$E(x \mid \sigma(y))$" can sometimes be thought of as the random variable whose outcome is $E[x \mid y = y(\omega)]$ if state $\omega \in \Omega$ occurs. This way of thinking is not always consistent. For example, the event that y is equal to $y(\omega)$ may have zero probability. The notation suggests conditioning with respect to an arbitrary sub–tribe $\mathcal{G}$ of $\mathcal{F}$. Roughly speaking, "$E(x \mid \mathcal{G})$" is the random variable whose outcome is the expectation of x given all of the information to be revealed by $\mathcal{G}$. This is a good point to introduce the formal definition of conditional expectation.

Let $(\Omega, \mathcal{F}, P)$ be a probability space, $\mathcal{G}$ a sub–tribe of $\mathcal{F}$, and x a Z–valued integrable random variable for some measurable outcome space Z. A version of $E(x \mid \mathcal{G})$, the *conditional expectation* of x given $\mathcal{G}$, is any $\mathcal{G}$–measurable Z–valued integrable random variable y satisfying

$$\int_B x(\omega)\, dP(\omega) = \int_B y(\omega)\, dP(\omega) \text{ for all } B \in \mathcal{G}.$$

The term making this definition precise is "version". It is generally possible for there to exist different versions of $E(x \mid \mathcal{G})$. We often fix a particular version of $E(x \mid \mathcal{G})$ for consideration. Incidentally, the conditional expectation $E(x \mid \mathcal{G})$ exists whenever x is real–valued ($Z = R$), and much more generally. For any random variable y, $E(x \mid y)$ denotes $E(x \mid \sigma(y))$.

D.   We list a few important properties of conditional expectation on a probability space $(\Omega, \mathcal{F}, P)$ given sub–tribes $\mathcal{G}$ and $\mathcal{H}$ of $\mathcal{F}$.

(a) If x is an integrable $\mathcal{G}$–measurable random variable and $\mathcal{G} \subseteq \mathcal{F}$, then

$$E(x \mid \mathcal{G}) = x \qquad \text{a.s.} \tag{2}$$

(b) If $\mathcal{G} \subseteq \mathcal{H} \subseteq \mathcal{F}$ then, for any integrable random variable x,

$$E\big[E[x \mid \mathcal{H}] \mid \mathcal{G}\big] = E[x \mid \mathcal{G}] \qquad \text{a.s.} \tag{3}$$

Relation (3) is known as the *law of iterated conditional expectations*. In particular, taking the *trivial tribe* $\mathcal{G} = \{\emptyset, \Omega\}$ in relation (3),

$$E\big[E[x \mid \mathcal{H}]\big] = E[x]. \tag{4}$$

(c) If x is real–valued and integrable, y is real–valued and $\mathcal{G}$–measurable, and xy is integrable, then

$$E[xy \mid \mathcal{G}] = yE[x \mid \mathcal{G}] \qquad \text{a.s.} \tag{5}$$

E. We extend the definition of expectation (or equivalently, integration) to cover the case of a random variable x on a probability space $(\Omega, \mathcal{F}, P)$, taking values in a separable Banach space Z normed by $| \cdot |$. Although further extensions are possible, separable Banach spaces cover any application we will meet. Let $| x |$ denote the real–valued random variable defined by $| x | (\omega) = | x(\omega) |$. Then x is *integrable* by definition whenever $| x |$ is integrable, and the expectation (integral) of x is the unique element $E(x) \equiv \int_\Omega x \, dP$ of Z with the property: $p \cdot E(x) = E(p \cdot x)$ for any continuous linear functional p on Z. Here $p \cdot x$ denotes the real–valued random variable defined by $[p \cdot x](\omega) = p \cdot (x(\omega))$, $\omega \in \Omega$. As in Section 6, it is common to identify random variables that are equal almost surely. Let $L_Z^1(\Omega, \mathcal{F}, P)$ denote the vector space of equivalence classes of versions of Z–valued integrable random variables, with norm $\| \cdot \|_1$ defined by

$$\| x \|_1 = E(| x |), \qquad x \in L_Z^1(\Omega, \mathcal{F}, P).$$

Under this norm $L_Z^1(\Omega, \mathcal{F}, P)$ is itself a Banach space, a fact to be used in constructing conditional expectations (Exercise 9.3).

Example 1. Let x be an R^N–valued integrable random variable on a probability space $(\Omega, \mathcal{F}, P)$. Then $E(x) = [E(x_1), E(x_2), \ldots, E(x_N)] \in R^N$. ♠

Example 2. Let Z denote the vector space of real–valued integrable functions of the time interval $[0, 1]$, taking the usual (Lebesgue) integral $\int_0^1 f(t) \, dt$, and identifying functions equal almost everywhere on $[0, 1]$. Then Z is a separable Banach space under the norm $| f |_Z \equiv \int_0^1 | f(t) | \, dt$. Let $(\Omega, \mathcal{F}, P)$ be a probability space. Then $L_Z^1(\Omega, \mathcal{F}, P)$ is the space of $\mathcal{F}$–measurable "stochastic processes" x on $\Omega \times [0, 1]$, such that $x(\omega) \in Z$ for all $\omega \in \Omega$ and $\| x \|_1 = E(| x |_Z) = E(\int_0^1 | x(\cdot, t) | \, dt) < \infty$. The expectation $E(x)$ is a function of time $t \in [0, 1]$. A full definition of stochastic processes appears in Section 14. ♠

F. There are many applications in economics for Jensen's Inequality: a convex function of the expectation of a random variable is less than or equal to the expectation of the convex function of the random variable. Some regularity conditions are required when the random variable takes values in an infinite–dimensional space. A functional f on a subset X of a normed vector space is *lower semicontinuous* if $\{x \in X : f(x) \leq \alpha\}$ is closed for any scalar α. Of course a continuous functional on a closed set is lower semicontinuous.

THEOREM (JENSEN'S INEQUALITY). *Suppose* $(\Omega, \mathcal{F}, P)$ *is a probability space, C is a closed convex subset of a separable Banach space, f is a convex lower semicontinuous functional on C, and x is a C–valued integrable random variable such that $f(x) \equiv f \circ x$ is integrable. Let $\mathcal{G}$ be a sub–tribe of $\mathcal{F}$. Then*

$$f\left[E(x \mid \mathcal{G})\right] \leq E\left[f(x) \mid \mathcal{G}\right] \quad \text{a.s.} \tag{6}$$

If we take $\mathcal{G}$ to be the trivial sub–tribe $\{\Omega, \emptyset\}$ of $\mathcal{F}$, we recover the classical Jensen's Inequality: $f[E(x)] \leq E[f(x)]$. A proof of the above general version of Jensen's Inequality is cited in the Notes. We state a direct corollary.

COROLLARY. *Suppose x is an integrable real–valued random variable on a probability space $(\Omega, \mathcal{F}, P)$, f is a convex functional on R such that $f \circ x$ is integrable, and $\mathcal{G}$ is a sub–tribe of $\mathcal{F}$. Then relation (6) holds.*

G.   Given a probability space $(\Omega, \mathcal{F}, P)$, a family $\{A_\lambda : \lambda \in \Lambda\}$ of events is *independent* if, for any finite subset $\{A_{\lambda_1}, \ldots, A_{\lambda_N}\}$,

$$P\left(\bigcap_{n=1}^N A_{\lambda_n}\right) = \prod_{n=1}^N P(A_{\lambda_n}).$$

More generally, a family $\{x_\lambda : \lambda \in \Lambda\}$ of random variables on $(\Omega, \mathcal{F}, P)$ into measurable outcome spaces $\{Z_\lambda : \lambda \in \Lambda\}$ is independent if, for any finite subset $\{x_{\lambda_1}, \ldots, x_{\lambda_N}\}$ and any bounded measurable functions $f_n : Z_{\lambda_n} \to R$,

$$E\left[\Pi_{n=1}^N f_n(x_{\lambda_n})\right] = \prod_{n=1}^N E\left[f_n(x_{\lambda_n})\right].$$

Most generally, a family $\{\mathcal{G}_\lambda : \lambda \in \Lambda\}$ of sub–tribes of $\mathcal{F}$ is independent if any family of events of the form $\{A_\lambda \in \mathcal{G}_\lambda : \lambda \in \Lambda\}$ is independent.

The following version of the *law of large numbers*, whose proof is cited in the Notes, has extensions that relax the independence assumption as well as the uniform bound on variances. An exercise applies the law of large numbers to portfolio diversification.

THEOREM (LAW OF LARGE NUMBERS). *Let $\{x_n\}$ be a sequence of independent real–valued random variables on a probability space $(\Omega, \mathcal{F}, P)$. Suppose that $E(x_n) = 0$ for all n, and there is a constant k such that $\mathrm{var}(x_n) < k$ for all n. Then the limit in $L^2(P)$ of $\{N^{-1} \sum_{n=1}^{N} x_n\}$, as $N \to \infty$, exists and is zero almost surely.*

EXERCISES

EXERCISE 9.1   Suppose P and Q are equivalent probability measures on the same measurable space. Prove that dQ/dP and dP/dQ are strictly positive almost surely.

EXERCISE 9.2   Let $(\Omega, \mathcal{F}, P)$ be a probability space and x be a real–valued random variable on $(\Omega, \mathcal{F}, P)$ whose variance exists, that is, $x \in L^2(\Omega, \mathcal{F}, P)$. For any sub–tribe $\mathcal{G}$ of $\mathcal{F}$, demonstrate the existence of $E(x \mid \mathcal{G})$ by applying the Riesz Representation Theorem (Theorem 6E). *Hint:* Look for a particular element of $L^2(\Omega, \mathcal{G}, \widehat{P})$, where $\widehat{P}$ is the restriction of P to $\mathcal{G}$.

EXERCISE 9.3   Let Z be a separable Banach space, $(\Omega, \mathcal{F}, P)$ a probability space, and $\mathcal{G}$ a sub–tribe of $\mathcal{F}$. Let x be a simple Z–valued random variable, and construct $E(x \mid \mathcal{G})$. Now let $x \in L^1_Z(\Omega, \mathcal{F}, P)$. By the separability of Z, x is the $\| \cdot \|_1$– limit of a sequence $\{x_n\}$ of simple Z–valued random variables. Show that $\{E(x_n \mid \mathcal{G})\}$ converges in $\| \cdot \|_1$, and that the limit is equal to $E(x \mid \mathcal{G}) \in L^1_Z(\Omega, \mathcal{F}, P)$. *Hint:* Show that $E(\cdot \mid \mathcal{G})$ is a norm reducing linear operator on $L^1_Z(\Omega, \mathcal{F}, P)$, and use the definition of $\| \cdot \|_1$ as a Banach space norm. (A *linear operator* is merely a linear function on one vector space into another.)

EXERCISE 9.4   Let $(\Omega, \mathcal{F}, P)$ be a probability space and let L be the choice space $L^q(P)$, for some $q \in [1, \infty)$. Consider an exchange economy on this choice space with at least one agent having the choice set L_+, endowment $\widehat{x} \in L_+$, and a strictly monotonic preference relation $\succeq$ on L_+. Suppose p is an equilibrium price functional for this economy. Prove the following:

(A)   If $p \cdot \widehat{x} > 0$, then p is a *strictly positive continuous linear functional* on L, that is, $p \cdot x > 0$ for any non–zero $x \in L_+$.

(B)   If $\widehat{x}$ is strictly positive almost surely and p is a non–zero positive linear functional on L, then $p \cdot \widehat{x} > 0$, and the conclusion of part (A) applies.

(C)   If $p \cdot \widehat{x} > 0$ there exists a probability measure Q on $(\Omega, \mathcal{F})$ such that p has the representation:

$$p \cdot x = kE^Q(x), \quad x \in L,$$

where k is a strictly positive constant. Furthermore, P and Q are equivalent measures.

EXERCISE 9.5   Show that any convex functional on a Euclidean space is continuous. (One can actually show that such a functional is differentiable at every point except for points in a set of Lebesgue measure zero.)

EXERCISE 9.6   Let $(\Omega, \mathcal{F}, P)$ be a measure space. The *symmetric difference* of two subsets A and B of Ω is defined as $A \triangle B = \{(A \bigcup B) \backslash (A \bigcap B)\}$, that is, the set of elements of A or B that are not in both A and B. For any sub–tribe $\mathcal{G}$ of $\mathcal{F}$, show that

$$\widehat{\mathcal{G}} = \{A \triangle B : A \in \mathcal{G}, B \in \mathcal{F}, P(B) = 0\}$$

is a sub–tribe of $\mathcal{F}$. This tribe $\widehat{\mathcal{G}}$ is the *completion* of $\mathcal{G}$. The completion of $\mathcal{F}$ itself is defined differently as

$$\widehat{\mathcal{F}} = \{A \triangle B : A \in \mathcal{F}, B \subset C \in \mathcal{F}, P(C) = 0\}.$$

Define $\widehat{P} : \widehat{\mathcal{F}} \to [0,1]$ by $\widehat{P}(A \triangle B) = P(A)$ for any $A \in \mathcal{F}$ and $B \subset C \in \mathcal{F}$ with $P(C) = 0$. Show that the *completion of the measure space* $(\Omega, \mathcal{F}, P)$, defined to be $(\Omega, \widehat{\mathcal{F}}, \widehat{P})$, is also a measure space. A measure space is *complete* if it coincides with its completion.

EXERCISE 9.7   Prove the law of iterated conditional expectation, relation (9.3), in the case of a probability space $(\Omega, \mathcal{F}, P)$ for which Ω is a finite set.

EXERCISE 9.8   (Diversification)   Suppose $(\Omega, \mathcal{F})$ is a measurable space. A *charge* (also know as a *bounded additive set function* or a *finitely–additive measure*) is a function $\mu : \mathcal{F} \to [0, \infty)$ with the properties: $\mu(\emptyset) = 0$ and, for any finite sequence $\{B_1, B_2, \ldots, B_N\}$ of disjoint measurable sets, $\mu\left(\bigcup_{n=1}^{N} B_n\right) = \sum_{n=1}^{N} \mu(B_n)$. In other words, μ would be a measure if it maintained this additivity property for any infinite disjoint sequence $\{B_n\}$. As is well known, any positive continuous linear functional f on the vector space ℓ^∞ of bounded sequences (with the norm $\| x \| = \sup_n |x_n|$) can be represented by a unique charge μ_f on the measurable space of the positive integers $\{1, 2, \ldots\}$ (with the power set tribe), in the form $f \cdot x = \int x \, d\mu_f$

for all $x \in \ell^\infty$. (We do not define the integral here, although it is straight-forward to do so.)

(A)   Show that the function $f : \ell^\infty \to R$ defined by

$$f(x) = \lim_{N \to \infty} \frac{1}{N} \sum_{n=1}^{N} x_n$$

is positive, linear, and continuous. Thus, by the above, we may think of $f(x)$ as a weighted sum $\int x \, d\mu_f$ of the elements of a sequence x, where the weights are given by a charge μ_f.

(B)   Suppose, to extend the construction of portfolios given in Section 7 that $\mathcal{A}$ indexes a collection of securities, defined by a set $\{x_a : a \in \mathcal{A}\}$ of uniformly bounded real–valued random variables on some probability space $(\Omega, \mathcal{T}, P)$, where $\mathcal{A}$ is countable. The dividend paid by security a in state ω is $x_a(\omega)$. A *portfolio* is here defined to be a charge φ on $\mathcal{A}$ (with the tribe of all subsets of $\mathcal{A}$). If the prices of the securities are given by a bounded function $p : \mathcal{A} \to R$, then the market value of a portfolio φ can be defined as the integral $\int p(a) \, d\varphi(a)$. The total dividend accruing to a portfolio φ in a state $\omega \in \Omega$ is similarly defined by $\int x_a(\omega) \, d\varphi(a)$. If $\mathcal{A}$ contains an infinite subset of securities with independent dividends, show the existence of a portfolio φ whose payoff is a constant (almost surely). For any such portfolio φ, state the value of its (constant) dividend as an integral of the expectations of the securities' dividends with respect to φ.

EXERCISE 9.9   Prove the claim of Example 1 of Paragraph 9E.

Notes

The concepts presented here may be found in any advanced mathematical treatment of probability, such as the classic by Meyer (1966). Vector–valued integration is dealt with in Rudin (1973). The Radon–Nikodym derivative is dealt with in vast generality by Bourgin (1983), where one may find a definition of conditional expectation of Banach space–valued random variables. The form of Jensen's Inequality given here is a special case of Theorem 7 of Kozek and Suchanecki (1980). A simpler form is given by Ting and Yip (1975). For an unconditional form of Jensen's Inequality in otherwise great generality, see Perlman (1974).

For the law of large numbers, Feller (1968), Chapter X, is a standard source, where our version may be found. See Feller (1971) for somewhat stronger versions of the law of large numbers. The exercise applying the law of large numbers to portfolio diversification is from an idea used by

Ross (1976a) for arbitrage pricing. Our notion of diversification exploits the theory of charges, as suggested by Feldman and Gilles (1985). This is consistent with the diversification approach of Connor (1984). Hartigan (1983) reviews Bayes Theory, which is essentially the calculation of conditional probabilities, with some philosophical underpinnings.

10.   Risk Aversion

Although we have a vaguely common perception of "risk aversion", and could all easily confect examples, we might be hard pressed to agree on a satisfactory general definition. Since risk attitudes are so fundamental to economic behavior in markets, we present one formulation of the concept, and show its relationship with other candidate formulations.

A.   We fix a probability space $(\Omega, \mathcal{F}, P)$, a separable Banach space Z such as R^n, and the vector space Y of Z–valued random variables on $(\Omega, \mathcal{F}, P)$ that are integrable, that is, whose expectations exist. In the notation of Section 9, $Y = L^1_Z(\Omega, \mathcal{F}, P)$. A special case is $Y = L^1(P)$ (for $Z = R$). A preference relation $\succeq$ on a subset X of Y is *risk averse* if

$$x \succeq x + y \tag{1}$$

for any x in X and any non–zero y in Y satisfying $x + y \in X$ and $E\left[y \mid x\right] = 0$. Intuitively, an agent is risk averse if the addition of a prospect that has no incremental effect on expected value is undesirable. The preference relation $\succeq$ is *strictly risk averse* provided $x \succ x + y$ for any x and y with the properties in relation (1). Finally, if $x \sim x + y$ (indifference) for any x and y with these properties, then $\succeq$ is *risk neutral*.

B.   There is some connection between convexity of preferences, concavity of an expected utility representation of preferences, and risk aversion, but these are not equivalent properties. We will need the following technical lemma, to be proven as an exercise.

LEMMA. *Suppose $u : Z \to R$ satisfies, for some fixed scalar $\alpha \in (0, 1)$,*

$$u(\alpha a) + u\left[(1 - \alpha)b\right] \geq \alpha u(a) + (1 - \alpha)u(b)$$

for all a and b in Z. Then u is concave.

A probability space $(\Omega, \mathcal{F}, P)$ is *trivial* if there is no event B with $P(B) \in (0, 1)$.

THEOREM. *Suppose $(\Omega, \mathcal{F}, P)$ is not trivial, Z is a separable Banach space, and $\succeq$ is a preference relation on $Y = L_Z^1(\Omega, \mathcal{F}, P)$ with an expected utility representation given by a function $u : Z \to R$. Then A: (the risk aversion of $\succeq$) and B: (the concavity of u) are equivalent. Either A or B implies C: (the convexity of $\succeq$).*

PROOF: $A \Rightarrow B$: Choose $\alpha \in (0,1)$ such that there exists an event B with $P(B) = \alpha$, and any outcomes a and b in Z. Let $x = (\alpha a + (1-\alpha)b)1_\Omega$ and $y = a1_B + b1_{\Omega\setminus B} - x$. Since $E[y \mid x] = E[y]1_\Omega = 0$, risk aversion implies $x \succeq x + y$, or $\alpha u(a) + (1-\alpha)u(b) = E[u(x+y)] \leq E[u(x)] = u(\alpha a + (1-\alpha)b)$, implying concavity of u by the previous lemma, since a and b are arbitrary.

$B \Rightarrow A$: Suppose x and y in Y satisfy $E[y \mid x] = 0$. By Jensen's Inequality as stated by Theorem 9F, $E[u(x + y) \mid x] \leq u(E[x + y \mid x])$. However,

$$u(E[x + y \mid x]) = u(E[x \mid x] + E[y \mid x]) = u(E[x \mid x]) = u(x) \quad \text{a.s.}$$

Taking expectations again and using the law of iterated expectations (9.4),

$$E\big[E[u(x + y) \mid x]\big] = E[u(x + y)] \leq E[u(x)].$$

Thus $x \succeq x + y$, implying that $\succeq$ is risk averse.

$A \Rightarrow C$: Suppose $\alpha \in [0,1]$, u is concave, and x and y are elements of Y. Then

$$E[u(\alpha x + (1-\alpha)y)] \geq E[\alpha u(x) + (1-\alpha)u(y)] = \alpha E[u(x)] + (1-\alpha)E[u(y)],$$

implying quasi–concavity of the functional $E[u(\cdot)]$ representing $\succeq$, or equivalently the convexity of $\succeq$. ∎

Much of the above proof applies if the preference relation is defined merely over a convex subset of Y.

C. If the outcome space Z is the real line (or a real interval), there is a convenient relationship between risk aversion and *stochastic dominance*. Let x and y be real–valued random variables with cumulative distribution functions F and G, respectively. Then x has *second order stochastic dominance* over y, denoted $x \succeq_2 y$, if

$$\int_{-\infty}^T [G(t) - F(t)]\, dt \geq 0, \qquad T \in R.$$

PROPOSITION. *Suppose $\succeq$ is a state–independent preference relation on the set X of bounded real–valued random variables on a probability space. Then $\succeq$ is risk averse if and only if $x \succeq_2 y \Rightarrow x \succeq y$ for all x and y in X.*

PROOF: (if) For any $t \in R$, let $v_t : R \to R$ be defined by $v_t = -(t - x)^+$. Then v_t is concave. Choose any x and z in X satisfying $E(z \mid x) = 0$ a.s. By the theorem of Paragraph B,

$$E[v_t(x)] \geq E[v_t(x + z)], \quad t \in R. \tag{2}$$

Let F and G be the cumulative distribution functions of $x + z$ and x respectively, and define $H : R \to [0, 1]$ by $H(t) = G(t) - F(t)$, $t \in R$. By relation (2),

$$0 \leq \int_{-\infty}^{t} (t - s)\, dH(s) = tH(t) - \int_{-\infty}^{t} s\, dH(s), \quad t \in R. \tag{3}$$

Integrating by parts, and applying the bounds on x and z,

$$\int_{-\infty}^{t} H(s)\, ds = tH(t) - \int_{-\infty}^{t} s\, dH(s), \quad t \in R. \tag{4}$$

Combining relations (3) and (4), we have $\int_{-\infty}^{t}[G(s) - F(s)]\, ds \geq 0$ for all t in B, implying that $x \succeq_2 x + z$. Then, since $x \succeq_2 x + z \Longrightarrow x \succeq x + z$ by assumption, $\succeq$ is risk averse by definition.

The *only if* part of the proof is rather lengthy and delicate, and may be found in a source cited in the Notes. ∎

EXERCISES

EXERCISE 10.1   Prove Lemma 10B.

EXERCISE 10.2   Suppose $\succeq$ is a risk averse preference relation on a set x of integrable random variables on a probability space $(\Omega, \mathcal{F}, P)$. Suppose x and $E(x)1_\Omega$ are in X. Show that $E(x)1_\Omega \succeq x$.

Notes

The major impetus for this section is the paper by Rothschild and Stiglitz (1970, 1972). The central result, Theorem 10B, is not, however, directly comparable to the main result (Theorem 2) of Rothschild and Stiglitz, whose proof implies the *only if* part of Proposition 10C. Although there is a close connection, Rothschild and Stiglitz characterize an equivalence between partial orders on random variables, while here we characterize certain properties of preferences. Recent developments in the theory of stochastic dominance and risk aversion include the results of Jewitt (1987), Scarsini (1986), and Mulière and Scarsini (1987). For further results on risk aversion, see Arrow (1970), Huang and Litzenberger (1987), Machina (1982), as well as Rothschild and Stiglitz (1971), to list but a small sample of the literature.

11. Equilibrium in Static Markets Under Uncertainty

A classical finance model is built around the means and covariances of the payoffs of securities in a static market under uncertainty. Given an assumption of "variance aversion" on agents' preferences, this model is a rich source of intuition and the basis for many practical financial decisions. This section is a brief survey of the theory of market equilibrium in that setting. The principle results are necessary conditions for equilibrium pricing, in particular the Capital Asset Pricing Model, and sufficient conditions for the existence of an equilibrium.

A. Our basic primitive for uncertainty is a probability space $(\Omega, \mathcal{F}, P)$, with Ω to be thought of as the set of states of the world, upon which the payoffs of securities depend. Our choice space is $L = L^2(P)$, the vector space of real–valued random variables on $(\Omega, \mathcal{F}, P)$ whose variances exist, treating any random variables that are equal almost surely as the same vector. A more formal definition of $L^2(P)$ may be found in Section 6, along with several properties to be applied in this section. For concreteness, we may think of a vector x in L as a random variable whose payoff, $x(\omega)$ in state ω of Ω, is measured in "consumption". One commonly refers to a vector x in L as an *asset*. With reinterpretation, some results apply more generally, for instance in Section 16 to vectors that are stochastic processes. We might recall from Exercise 6.5 that the expectation of any x in L exists.

B. We begin in the general case of incomplete markets, taking $A \subset L$ as the subset of traded securities and $M = \text{span}(A)$ as the marketed space. As explained in Section 7, M is merely the subset of L that can be achieved by forming portfolios of traded securities. If M is finite–dimensional or if $M = L$ (complete markets), then M is trivially closed. A given non–zero linear functional p on M assigns market values to marketed assets. Of course if A is a finite set of securities, then M is finite–dimensional and p is continuous.

PROPOSITION. *Suppose the marketed space M is closed and a linear price functional p on M is continuous. Then there exists a unique asset π in M such that, for all x in M,*

$$p \cdot x = E(x\pi) = E(\pi)E(x) + \operatorname{cov}(x, \pi). \tag{1}$$

PROOF: We have noted in Section 6 that $L^2(P)$ is a Hilbert space under the inner product $(x, y) \mapsto E(xy)$, and that any closed vector subspace of a Hilbert space is a Hilbert space under the same inner product. Then, by the properties of a Hilbert space stated in Paragraph 6G, for any continuous linear functional p on M, there exists a unique π in M such that $p \cdot x = (\pi \mid x) = E(x\pi)$ for all x in M. This proves the first equality of relation (1); the second follows from the definition of covariance. ∎

The marketed asset π satisfying relation (1) is the *pricing asset*. For any asset x in M whose market value $p \cdot x$ is not zero, the *return* of x is the random variable

$$\mathcal{R}_x \equiv \frac{x}{p \cdot x}.$$

The *expected return* of any x in M with non–zero market value is $\mu_x \equiv E(\mathcal{R}_x)$. For any asset z in $L^2(P)$ whose variance and price are both non–zero, the *beta* of any asset x in $L^2(P)$ relative to z is $\operatorname{cov}(\mathcal{R}_x, \mathcal{R}_z)/\operatorname{var}(\mathcal{R}_z)$, denoted β_{xz}. The following corollary's proof is left as an exercise.

COROLLARY. *Under the assumptions of the proposition, suppose $E(\pi) \neq 0$ and $\operatorname{var}(\pi) \neq 0$, where π is the pricing asset of relation (1). Let $r = 1/E(\pi)$. Then any marketed asset x whose market value is not zero satisfies*

$$(\mu_x - r) = \beta_{x\pi}(\mu_\pi - r). \tag{2}$$

Relation (2) is known as a *beta model* of rates of return. The scalar r is merely the return on the riskless asset 1_Ω, if 1_Ω is actually marketed. Otherwise, an interpretation of r as a *zero–beta* return is given in an exercise.

C.   Two basic approaches to asset pricing in our current setting are widely used in practical applications: the *Capital Asset Pricing Model* or *CAPM*, and the *Arbitrage Pricing Theory*, or *APT*. It is difficult to favor one over the other as they are not directly comparable. The CAPM makes strong assumptions concerning the probability distributions of security pay-offs, or about agents' preference relations, or about both. As a result the pricing asset π of relations (1) and (2) is identified as a linear combination of the *market portfolio* (the total of all net trades) and the riskless asset as a necessary condition for market equilibrium. The APT makes strong assumptions concerning equilibrium rates of return of securities. As a result, the pricing portfolio π is identified as the sum of a number of "factors", random variables in $L^2(P)$ that affect securities' rates of return. Because the APT does not specifically identify these factors, one might think of the CAPM as a special single–factor example of the APT, at least in terms of conclusions. Neither of the two models' assumptions imply the other's assumptions. We will review the CAPM and refer readers to the Notes and exercises for the APT.

D. A preference relation $\succeq$ on a subset X of $L^2(P)$ is *variance–averse* if $x \succeq x + y$ whenever x and $x + y$ are in X and $E(y) = \text{cov}(x, y) = 0$. The definition states that an increase in variance is disliked if it does not affect expected value. One may wish to compare this condition with risk–aversion, defined in Paragraph 10A. The relation $\succeq$ is *strictly variance* averse if, under the same conditions on x and y, $y \neq 0$ implies $x \succ x + y$.

Example 1 (Expected Quadratic Utility)   Suppose the preference relation $\succeq$ on $X \subset L^2(P)$ is represented by the expected utility functional $E[u(\cdot)]$, where

$$u(\alpha) = A\alpha - B\alpha^2 + C, \quad \alpha \in R, \tag{3}$$

for some scalars A, B, and C. If $B \geq 0$ then $\succeq$ is variance–averse. ♠

Example 2 (Normally Distributed Payoffs)   Suppose the vector space M has a Hamel basis of jointly normal random variables. Then if $\succeq$ is a risk–averse preference relation on a subset X of M, it follows that $\succeq$ is variance–averse. The reader is asked to prove this, an easy exercise given the following property. ♠

FACT.   *Suppose x and y are jointly normally distributed random variables. Then $E(xy) = E(y) = 0$ implies $E(y \mid x) = 0$.*

In each of the examples above, variance–aversion applies because the agent's preferences are given directly in terms of the means and variances of an asset, and for a given mean, more variance is worse. Nothing in the definition of variance–aversion, however, requires that preferences depend only on mean and variance.

E. We next review the Capital Asset Pricing Model. For simplicity, we choose the setting of an exchange economy $\mathcal{E} = (X_i, \succeq_i, \omega_i) \, i \in \mathcal{I}$ for the choice space $L^2(P)$, as described in Paragraph 3A. Let $A \subset L^2(P)$ denote a security set for $\mathcal{E}$. One should recall from Paragraph 7D the definition of an equilibrium $(\phi_1, \ldots, \phi_I, p)$ for $(\mathcal{E}, A)$. The total endowment $m = \sum_{j=1}^{J} y_j$

is known as the *market portfolio*. We recall that the market subspace M is the span of A.

THEOREM (CAPITAL ASSET PRICING MODEL). *Given an equilibrium for the security market exchange economy* $(\mathcal{E}, A)$ *for the choice space* $L^2(P)$, *suppose:*

(a)   *the preference relation of each agent is strictly variance–averse,*

(b)   *the endowment* ω_i *of each agent* i *is in the marketed subspace* M,

(c)   *the marketed subspace* M *is finite–dimensional,*

(d)   *each agent's choice set is* $L^2(P)$,

(e)   *the riskless asset* 1_Ω *is marketed and has non–zero market value,*

(f)   *the market portfolio* m *has a non–zero variance.*

Then any asset x *in* M *with non–zero market value satisfies the Capital Asset Pricing Model:*

$$(\mu_x - r) = \beta_{xm}(\mu_m - r). \tag{4}$$

Furthermore, the same result applies if condition (c) *is weakened to:*

(c′) *the marketed subspace* M *is closed; the equilibrium price functional* p *is continuous.*

PROOF: Let $(\cdot \mid \cdot)$ denote the inner product on M defined by $(x \mid y) = E(xy)$. Under condition (c) or (c′), M is a Hilbert space under $(\cdot \mid \cdot)$. For any agent's equilibrium allocation $x \in M$, let $\hat{x}$ denote the orthogonal projection of x into $\text{span}(\{1_\Omega, \pi\})$, where $\pi \in M$ denotes the pricing asset of relation (2) for the equilibrium price functional p. Let $y = \hat{x} - x$. By the Hilbert Space Projection Theorem, $(y \mid \pi) = (y \mid 1_\Omega) = (y \mid \hat{x}) = 0$, implying that $p \cdot \hat{x} = p \cdot x$ and that $\hat{x}$ is strictly preferred to x unless $\hat{x} = x$. This implies that $x = \hat{x}$ and thus that the total net trade m is in $\text{span}(\{1_\Omega, \pi\})$. It follows that $m = A + B\pi$ a.s., for some scalars A and B. Then (4) follows provided $\text{var}(m) \neq 0$ by Corollary 11B. ∎

An alternative proof of the CAPM based on the representaitive agent construct is given in Exercise 25.14. framework.

F.   Having discussed necessary conditions for equilibrium pricing, we move on to sufficient conditions for the existence of an equilibrium. In the case of an exchange economy on $L^2(P)$, known conditions for the existence of an equilibrium are more stringent than the Debreu conditions of Paragraph 3G for a Euclidean choice space. A key additional condition is placed on preferences. Let Z denote any ordered vector space normed by $\| \cdot \|$. A preference relation $\succeq$ on a set containing the positive cone $Z_+ = \{x \in Z : x \geq 0\}$ of Z is *proper* at $x \in Z_+$, provided there exists a scalar $\epsilon > 0$ and a vector $v \in Z_+$ such that: $x - \alpha v + z \succeq x$ for some $z \in Z$ and $\alpha \in [0, \infty)$ implies that $\| z \| \geq \alpha \epsilon$. In a sense, this condition places bounds on the marginal rates of substitution between v and any other choice vector z in Z. The vector v is "so good" that the loss of αv is compensated for by the gain of z only if z is at least a certain size relative to αv, that is, $\| z \| \geq \alpha \epsilon$. Given a subset X of Z_+ and a pair $(v, \epsilon) \in Z_+ \times (0, \infty)$, if $\succeq$ is proper at all $x \in X$ with respect to (v, ϵ), we define $\succeq$ to be *v–proper* on X.

Example. Consider the choice space $L^2(P)$ of Paragraph A. Let u : $R_+ \to R$, a concave function, define a preference relation $\succeq$ on $L^2(P)_+$ by the "expected utility" functional $U(x) = E[u(x)], x \in L^2(P)_+$. By concavity, the right derivative of u at any $\alpha \in (0, \infty)$ exists and is defined by the scalar

$$D^+ u(\alpha) = \lim_{\beta \downarrow \alpha} \frac{1}{\beta - \alpha}[u(\beta) - u(\alpha)].$$

The right derivative of u at zero, however, may be $+\infty$ or finite. If $D^+ u(0)$ is finite, then $\succeq$ is 1_Ω–proper on any set of the form $[0, \bar{x}] \equiv \{x \in L^2(P)_+ : x \leq \bar{x}\}$, for a given $\bar{x} \in L^2(P)_+$. The reader is asked to verify this as an exercise. Of course, "expected utility" implies the independence axiom, a severe restriction not at all implicit in properness. ♠

A preference relation $\succeq$ on Z_+ is *uniformly proper* if there exists some $v \in Z_+$ such that $\succeq$ is v–proper on Z_+. The following results on proper preferences have extensions and proofs cited in the Notes.

PROPOSITION. *Suppose $Z = L^q(P)$ for some measure space $(\Omega, \mathcal{F}, P)$ and some $q \in [1, \infty]$. If $\succeq$ is a continuous and uniformly proper preference relation on Z_+, then $\succeq$ has a continuous utility representation $u : Z_+ \to R$.*

THEOREM. *Suppose $Z = L^q(P)$ for some measure space $(\Omega, \mathcal{F}, P)$ and some $q \in [0, \infty]$, and suppose that $Z_+ \subset D$ and $D \subset D + Z_+$ for some closed convex subset D with non–empty interior. Suppose $\succeq$ is a non–satiated monotone preference relation on D represented by a concave function $u :$ $D \to R$. Then, for any $\bar{x} \in Z_+$, there exists some $v \in Z_+$ such that $\succeq$ is v–proper on $[0, \bar{x}]$.*

The last result is a generalization of our example, since it applies to any preference relation on $L^q(P)_+$ represented by a function u that can be extended to a set D with the stated properties.

G.   Let $(\Omega, \mathcal{F}, P)$ be any measure space, say a probability space, and consider the choice space $L^2(P)$. The following theorem of existence of equilibria depends on proper preferences; there are counterexamples when the assumption is dropped.

THEOREM. *Let* $\mathcal{E} = (X_i, \succeq, \widehat{x}_i)$, $i \in \mathcal{I}$, *be an exchange economy for the choice space* $L^2(P)$. *Let* $\overline{x} = \sum_{i=1}^{I} \widehat{x}_i$. *Suppose, for each agent* $i \in \mathcal{I}$, *that the endowment* $\widehat{x}_i \in L^2(P)_+$ *is not zero, that* $X_i = L^2(P)_+$, *and that* $\succeq_i$ *is convex, continuous, locally non–satiated at any* $x \in [0, \overline{x}]$, *and* $\overline{x}$–*proper on* $[0, \overline{x}]$. *Then* $\mathcal{E}$ *has an equilibrium.*

The assumption of local non–satiation is implied by strict monotonicity. The proof, cited in the Notes, also applies to the following extension to the choice space H of R^M–valued measurable functions x on $(\Omega, \mathcal{F}, P)$ satisfying

$$\| x \| = \left(\int_{\Omega} x^{\top} x \, dP \right)^{1/2} < \infty.$$

(To be exact, the elements of H are equivalence classes of versions, as with $L^2(P)$, so that H is a Hilbert space under $\| \cdot \|$, an easy exercise.) We may think of H as the space of random claims to M different commodities, the payoff of each having finite variance. We take the product order on H, defining the positive cone $H_+ = \{ x \in H : x_1 \geq 0, x_2 \geq 0, \ldots, x_M \geq 0 \}$.

PROPOSITION. *Suppose* $\mathcal{E}$ *is an exchange economy on the choice space* H *satisfying the conditions of Theorem 11G, with* H *replacing* $L^2(P)$. *Then* $\mathcal{E}$ *has an equilibrium whose price functional* p *is represented by a unique element* $\pi = (\pi_1, \ldots, \pi_M)$ *of* H *as*

$$p \cdot x = \sum_{m=1}^{M} \int_{\Omega} \pi_m(\omega) x_m(\omega) \, dP(\omega), \quad x \in H. \tag{5}$$

If $(\Omega, \mathcal{F}, P)$ is a probability space, then relation (5) is equivalent to $p \cdot x = E(\sum_{m=1}^{M} \pi_m x_m)$ for each x in H. We note that the result is stated for any measure space $(\Omega, \mathcal{F}, P)$, not merely probability spaces. The result applies to far more general choice spaces and, under suitable conditions on production sets, with production.

For technical reasons, we will later need additional conditions ensuring that the representations $\pi_1, \ldots, \pi_M$ of the equilibrium price functional shown in (5) are essentially bounded. Since $L^{\infty}(P)$ is the topological dual of $L^1(P)$, we should not be overly surprised that the conditions of the following corollary are sufficient. A proof is cited in the Notes. The analogue to the $L^1(P)$–norm for H is the norm $\| \cdot \|_1$ on H defined by

$$\| \, x \, \|_1 = \int_\Omega \sum_{m=1}^{M} | \, x_m(\omega) \, | \; dP(\omega), \quad x \in H.$$

COROLLARY. *If, furthermore, $P(\Omega) < \infty$ and $\succeq_i$ satisfies the conditions of Theorem 11G with the $\| \cdot \|_1$–norm topology on H, then there exists an equilibrium whose price functional p is represented by (5) with $\pi_m \in L^\infty(P)$, $1 \le m \le M$.*

Neither the results of Paragraph G nor their extensions to production are sufficient conditions for the Capital Asset Pricing Model as stated in Theorem 11E. Sufficient conditions are cited in the Notes.

EXERCISES

EXERCISE 11.1   Suppose A is a finite subset of a normed space L and $M = \mathrm{span}(A)$. Prove that M is closed.

EXERCISE 11.2   Suppose A is a finite subset of a normed space L, that $M = \mathrm{span}(A)$, and that p is a linear functional on M. Show that p is continuous.

EXERCISE 11.3   Prove directly that if M is a closed vector subspace of $L^2(\Gamma)$, then M is a Hilbert space under the inner product $(x, y) \mapsto E(xy)$. Extend this result to the choice space H of Proposition 11G under a natural inner product.

EXERCISE 11.4   Suppose M is a closed vector subspace of $L^2(P)$ and 1_Ω is not in M. Let p be a non–zero continuous price functional on M with pricing asset $\pi \in M$ as in relation (1). Assume $E(\pi) \ne 0$ and show that $r = 1/E(\pi)$ is the unique expected return on any marketed asset z satisfying $\mathrm{cov}(\pi, z) = 0$, $p \cdot z \ne 0$, and $E(z) \ne 0$. This is known as the zero–beta return since $\beta_{z\pi}$ is zero for any such z.

EXERCISE 11.5   As remarked in this section, one of the main occupations of financial economists is the identification of the pricing asset π of relations (1) and (2). In this exercise we will identify π on the basis of the observed market values and covariance structure of securities. There is assumed to be a finite number of securities $x_1, \ldots, x_N$ available for trade, each of which is in $L^2(P)$. Let Σ denote the N by N matrix whose (i, j)–element is $\mathrm{cov}(x_i, x_j)$. Let $q \in R^N$ denote the vector whose n–th element is $E(x_n)$.

Assume that the matrix $Q = \Sigma + qq^{\top}$ is nonsingular. Let $v \in R^N$ denote the vector whose n–th element is the market value of x_n. Then show that relation (1) holds for $\pi = \sum_{n=1}^{N} \alpha_n x_n$, where $(\alpha_1, \ldots, \alpha_N) = \gamma Q^{-1} v$ for some scalar γ. Calculate γ.

EXERCISE 11.6   Suppose M is a closed vector subspace of $L^2(P)$ and 1_Ω, the *riskless security*, is not in M. If p is a continuous linear functional on M, show the existence of a unique π in M such that $p \cdot x = \mathrm{cov}(\pi, x)$ for all x in M.

EXERCISE 11.7   Let X be a subset of $L^2(P)$ and $\succeq$ be a preference relation on X. The preference relation $\succeq$ is *mean–variance* if $x \succeq z$ whenever $E(x) = E(z)$ and $\mathrm{var}(x) \leq \mathrm{var}(z)$, for any x and z in X. Show that a mean–variance risk averse preference relation is variance–averse. Is there a counterexample to the converse?

EXERCISE 11.8   Prove the conclusion of Example 2 of Paragraph D, which states roughly that risk aversion and normally distributed choices implies variance aversion. Does strict risk aversion imply strict variance aversion in this setting?

EXERCISE 11.9   Suppose M is a closed vector subspace of $L^2(P)$ with $1_\Omega \in M$, and p is a non–zero continuous linear price functional on M. By previous work there exists π in M such that $p \cdot x = E(\pi x)$ for all x in M. Assume $p \cdot 1_\Omega \neq 0$. Suppose w in M satisfies $w = \alpha + \gamma\pi$ for some scalars α and γ. Provided $\mathrm{var}(w) \neq 0$, show that, for any x in M with $p \cdot x \neq 0$,

$$\lambda_x = \beta_{xw}\lambda_w,$$

where, for any x in M, $\lambda_x = x/p \cdot x - 1/p \cdot 1_\Omega$. We may think of λ_x as the *excess expected return* of x; specifically $\lambda_x = \mu_x - r$.

EXERCISE 11.10   Prove the claims of Example 11F. That is, if $u : R_+ \to R$ is concave, then $D^+u(\alpha)$ exists and is finite for all $\alpha \in (0, \infty)$. If $D^+u(0)$ exists and is finite, then u has a bounded right derivative, and the preference $\succeq$ on $L^2(P)_+$ represented by the functional $U(x) = E[u(x)]$, $x \in L^2(P)_+$, is 1_Ω–proper on any set of the form $[0, \bar{x}]$ for $\bar{x} \in L^2(P)_+$.

EXERCISE 11.11   Suppose $\succeq$ is a monotonic preference relation on the positive cone of a normed ordered vector space L. Prove that $\succeq$ is v–proper on L_+ for any $v \in \mathrm{int}(L_+)$. (An example is $L = L^\infty(P)$.)

Notes

The Capital Asset Pricing Model is credited to both Sharpe (1964) and Lintner (1965). The proof used here is essentially that of Chamberlain (1985), who provides conditions for a generalization to dynamic markets. The Arbitrage Pricing Theory began with Ross (1976a); a complete proof is given by Huberman (1982). A connection between the APT and equilibrium theory is given by Connor (1984). Chamberlain and Rothschild (1983) and Chamberlain (1983b) have given additional characterization of the APT and an asymptotic approach to an "approximate factor structure". They have also adopted Hilbert space techniques to analyze linear pricing in L^2 markets; some of these techniques appear here. Chamberlain (1983a) gives a complete characterization of the class of random variables whose distributions are given in terms of mean and variance alone. Thus Example 2 of Paragraph 11D can be extended to this class.

A precursor to Theorem 11E and the concept of proper preferences are due to Mas-Colell (1986a) in a more general setting. Example 11F was privately related to the author by Chi-fu Huang and Scott Richard. As stated, Theorem 11G and Proposition 11G are special cases of a result due to Zame (1987). Other extensions are due to Yannelis and Zame (1986), Richard (1986), Zame (1987), Mas-Colell and Richard (1987), Araujo and Monteiro (1986), and Duffie and Zame (1987). Corollary 11G is proved in Duffie (1986a). Sufficient conditions for proper preferences are given by Richard (1985) as well as Richard and Zame (1985). In particular, Richard (1985) proves a generalization of Proposition 11F and Richard and Zame (1985) prove an extension of Theorem 11F. An extension of Mas-Colell's existence theorem for general (possibly incomplete and non-transitive) preferences may be found in Yannelis and Zame (1986).

Zame (1987), Mas-Colell (1986b), and Richard (1987) extend the existence of equilibrium using proper preferences to a production economy. For production equilibria in this setting, see also Aliprantis, Brown, and Burkinshaw (1987). These existence results apply, under some additional assumptions, to many other choice spaces.

The *Zero Beta Capital Asset Pricing Model* is due to Black (1972). Sufficient conditions for equilibrium with the Capital Asset Pricing Model, in the original and zero-beta versions, were only recently provided by Nielson (1985, 1987), extending the earlier work of Hart (1974) showing existence of equilibrium without lower bounds on choice sets. This lack of bounds is an important aspect of security markets, which generally allows negative holdings, or *short sales*. Hart's work is also extended with a different application by Werner (1985a).

Chapter II

STOCHASTIC ECONOMIES

This chapter applies the static theory developed in Chapter I to the study of stochastic economies. We begin in Section 12 with the simplest possible stochastic setting, a finite event tree. This serves to develop much of the intuition for later more general results. The single most important concept here is the spanning role of securities in a dynamic setting. If there are insufficient securities to provide the effect of complete markets, even with the opportunity for repeated trade of the same securities as information is resolved, equilibrium allocations are not generally Pareto efficient. Nevertheless, equilibria exist under weak conditions. Production is added in Section 13. There is still no satisfactory general paradigm for the financial and production decisions of the firm in incomplete markets. An introduction to stochastic processes is found in Section 14. The central primitive for information revelation is a *filtration*. An event tree has a corresponding filtration, as does a "state variable process", whether in a continuous or discrete time. In Section 15, we present the stochastic integral as a model for financial gains from trade. The latter part of Section 15 is advanced, but not necessary for an informal appreciation of the continuous–time results of the remaining sections. Section 16 addresses the dynamic spanning role of securities in a general continuous–time stochastic equilibrium. By using a special normalization of prices, the equilibrium shown has the following property: Any stochastic process describing cumulative financial gains from security trade is a martingale. Section 17 shows that this is not at all a surprise. Under regularity conditions, this will be the case in any economy lacking arbitrage opportunities, once two basic normalizations are allowed. The first transformation expresses market values with respect to a chosen numeraire security. The second transformation is an adjustment of probability assessments.

12.   Event Tree Economies

This section presents a stochastic model of security and spot market equilibrium in a simple finite–dimensional setting, with information modeled by an event tree. Most of the key issues can be transparently worked out in this framework. Several important effects, however, are better illustrated under the gradual transitions in probability assessments afforded by certain continuous–time information structures, in particular the models of Chapter IV based on uncertainty generated by Brownian Motion. A mathematical apparatus suited to the general case is assembled in later sections. In this section we deal exclusively with exchange; production is added in Section 13. The central theme is the dynamic spanning ability of security markets. By repeated trade, a small number of securities can permit a much higher dimensional marketed space of choices. Once this marketed space is fixed, the economy is essentially the same as the static incomplete markets model of Section 7.

A.   All agents in our economy are assumed to learn information according to an event tree, such as that depicted in Figure 12.1. A formal model of information structures, identifying event trees as special cases, will appear in Section 14. Formally speaking, an *event tree* is a pair $(\Xi, \mathcal{A})$ consisting of a set $\Xi = \{\xi^1, \ldots, \xi^{\overline{K}}\}$ of *vertices* , and a set $\mathcal{A} \subset \Xi \times \Xi$ of *arcs*. A vertex represents a particular time and state of the world. If (ξ, η) is an arc, we treat η as a state of the world and time that could immediately follow ξ, or η is an *immediate successor* of ξ. Similarly, if $(\xi, \eta) \in \mathcal{A}$, the vertex ξ is the *immediate predecessor* of η. A *walk* is a sequence $\{\eta_1, \ldots, \eta_K\} \subset \Xi$ such that $(\eta_i, \eta_{i+1}) \in \mathcal{A}$ for $1 \leq i \leq K - 1$. The following properties define $(\Xi, \mathcal{A})$ to be an event tree, a special type of directed graph:

(a) ξ^1 is the *root vertex*, the unique vertex with no immediate predecessor,

(b) any vertex ξ other than ξ^1 has a unique immediate predecessor denoted ξ_-, and

(c) there is no *cycle*, a walk $\{\eta_1, \ldots, \eta_K\} \subset \Xi$ with $\eta_K = \eta_1$, $K \neq 1$.

The number of immediate successor vertices of any ξ in Ξ is denoted $\#\xi$. A vertex $\xi \in \Xi$ is *terminal* if $\#\xi = 0$, and otherwise *non–terminal*. The immediate successor vertices of any non–terminal vertex $\xi \in \Xi$ are labeled $\xi_{+1}, \ldots, \xi_{+K}$, where $K = \#\xi$. The *sub–tree* with root $\xi \in \Xi$ is the subset $\Xi(\xi)$ of Ξ whose elements are in a walk with first element ξ. In particular, $\Xi = \Xi(\xi_0)$. This notation is illustrated in Figure 12.1.

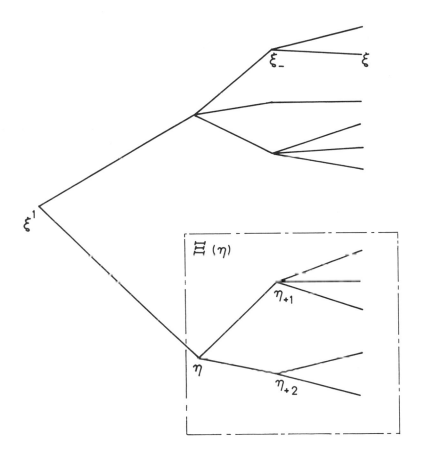

Figure 12.1   Event Tree Notation

At a particular vertex, the selection of an immediate successor vertex is treated as a random event, introducing risk. The likelihood of a given successor vertex is not modeled by explicitly introducing a probability space, although it could be, and will be in Section 14. Agents may have their own subjective probability assessments reflected in their preferences over consumption at each vertex. Although the number of vertices in Ξ is assumed to be finite, many results apply as well to infinite trees.

B.   At each vertex the agents of an economy are imagined to meet at spot commodity markets and security markets to conduct trade at given prices for that vertex. For any integer $n \geq 1$, let F_n denote the space of R^n-valued functions on Ξ. With ℓ commodities available for consumption at each vertex, the choice space for the economy is thus the vector space $L = F_\ell$. Since F_ℓ is finite–dimensional, we can give it the Euclidean norm. Any function on Ξ is referred to as a *process* throughout this section, portending the more general stochastic models of later sections. A *consumption process* $x \in L$ represents spot consumption $x(\xi) \in R^\ell$ at a typical vertex $\xi \in \Xi$. A *spot price process* is also a vector $\psi \in L$, with $\psi(\xi) \in R^\ell$ denoting the vector of unit commodity prices at a given vertex ξ. We assume spot markets are complete.

A *security* is a process $d \in F_1$ of spot market "dividends". We speak simply of "security d" rather than "the security claiming dividends defined by the process d". The holder of a unit of security d is entitled at vertex ξ to any spot market consumption bundle $z \in R^\ell$ of market value $\psi(\xi){\cdot}z = d(\xi)$. Other models treat a "security" as a claim to a consumption process $x \in L$. Under that convention, the holder at vertex ξ of a security claiming x is entitled to collect the consumption bundle $x(\xi) \in R^\ell$. With complete spot markets, this is equivalent to a claim to the dividend process $\psi \mathbin{\square} x \in F_1$ defined by

$$[\psi \mathbin{\square} x](\xi) = \psi(\xi) \cdot x(\xi). \tag{1}$$

The number of securities is some integer $N \geq 1$. The case $N = 0$ is ignored notationally, although the results to follow trivially carry over to this case. Each security d_n, for $1 \leq n \leq N$, is assigned a real–valued *price process* $S_n \in F_1$. In other words, $S_n(\xi)$ is the market value of d_n at vertex $\xi \in \Xi$. It will be convenient to treat $S_n(\xi)$ as the market value of d_n after the dividend $d_n(\xi)$ has been "declared", (that is, after vertex ξ occurs), but before the dividend has been paid. The vector $d = (d_1, \ldots, d_N) \in F_N$ of dividend processes is thus assigned a vector $S = (S_1, \ldots, S_N) \in F_N$ of price processes.

Commodity and security markets are commonly denominated, so a portfolio $\alpha \in R^N$ of securities can be sold at vertex ξ for any spot consumption vector of total market value $\alpha \cdot S(\xi)$. Then, barring arbitrage, it will be the case at any terminal vertex ξ in Ξ that $S(\xi) = d(\xi)$. To simplify the exposition, we adopt this *no terminal arbitrage* condition as a convention for all price processes.

A triple $(d, S, \psi) \in F_N \times F_N \times F_\ell$ is a complete characterization of trading opportunities, or a *market system*. There is an implicit assumption that all securities may be traded at all vertices, or that the securities are "long–lived". "Short–lived" securities, those traded only at a subset of vertices, can be dealt with by a natural extension treated in a source cited in the Notes.

C. Let ξ^0 denote a *pre–trade vertex*, let $\Xi' = \Xi \bigcup \{\xi^0\}$, and let $(\Xi', \mathcal{A}')$ denote the event tree formed by taking ξ^0 to be the root vertex and unique predecessor of ξ^1. A *trading strategy* is an element $\theta = (\theta_1, \ldots, \theta_N)$ of the space Θ of R^N–valued functions on Ξ'. The scalar $\theta_n(\xi)$ represents the number of units of security d_n held at vertex ξ when strategy θ is followed. We adopt the convention that $\theta(\xi)$ represents the portfolio held after trading at vertex ξ has occurred, but before dividends $d(\xi) \in R^N$ are paid. That is, a spot market value $\theta(\xi) \cdot d(\xi)$ accrues to strategy θ at vertex ξ. Because trades occur at the pre–dividend security values $S(\xi)$, our conventions are consistent. The portfolio of securities purchased by θ at any vertex $\xi \in \Xi$ is denoted $\Delta\theta(\xi) = \theta(\xi) - \theta(\xi_-)$. The market value of the portfolio of securities purchased at vertex ξ under strategy θ is then $\Delta\theta(\xi) \cdot S(\xi)$. The dividend process *generated* by a trading strategy θ is the process d^θ in F_1 defined by

$$d^\theta(\xi) = -\Delta\theta(\xi) \cdot S(\xi) + \theta(\xi) \cdot d(\xi). \tag{2}$$

A trading strategy θ *finances* a consumption process x if $d^\theta \geq \psi \,\square\, x$.

D. We are ready to formulate equilibrium in a simple setting. A *dynamic exchange economy* is a triple $(\mathcal{E}, (\Xi, \mathcal{A}), d)$ consisting of an event tree $(\Xi, \mathcal{A})$, a security vector $d \in F_N$, and an exchange economy

$$\mathcal{E} = (X_i, \succeq_i, \omega_i), \quad i \in \mathcal{I} = \{1, \ldots, I\}, \tag{3}$$

on the vector space $L = F_\ell$. That is, agent i has an endowment process $\omega_i \in L$ and a preference relation $\succeq_i$ on a choice subset $X_i \subset L$ of consumption processes.

Taking a market system (d, S, ψ) as given, a *budget feasible plan* for agent i is a pair $(\theta_i, x_i) \in \Theta \times F_\ell$ made up of a consumption process $x_i \in X_i$ and a trading strategy θ_i financing the net trade $x_i - \omega_i$, with $S(\xi^0) \cdot \theta_i(\xi^0) = 0$. A budget feasible plan (θ_i, x_i) is *optimal* if there is no other budget feasible plan (θ_i', x_i') for agent i such that $x_i' \succ_i x_i$. A collection $((S, \psi), (\theta_i, x_i))$, $i \in \mathcal{I}$, is an *equilibrium* for the economy $(\mathcal{E}, (\Xi, \mathcal{A}), d)$ provided (θ_i, x_i) is an optimal plan for each agent i given market system (d, S, ψ), and provided *markets clear:*

$$\sum_{i=1}^{I} x_i - \omega_i = 0$$

$$\sum_{i=1}^{I} \theta_i = 0. \tag{4}$$

E.   We next study the connection between static and dynamic market equilibria. For a given market system (d, S, ψ), let D denote the set of dividend processes generated by trading strategies, or $D = \{d^\theta : \theta \in \Theta\}$. Let M denote the set of consumption processes $x \in L$ such that $\psi \, \square \, x \in D$. That is, M is the *marketed subspace* of L, that set of consumption processes financed by some trading strategy without excess dividends. Contrary to the static incomplete markets model of Section 7, the marketed subspace depends endogenously on security and spot prices. An exercise shows D and M to be vector spaces.

We question the possibility of some dividend process being generated by two different trading strategies θ^A and θ^B such that

$$\beta = \theta^A(\xi^0) \cdot S(\xi^1) - \theta^B(\xi^0) \cdot S(\xi^1) \neq 0. \qquad (5)$$

This can indeed happen in equilibrium, although it would be pathological. If a security market system (d, S) permits such a pathology, it is termed *slack*, and otherwise *tight*. Suppose some agent i is *non–satiated* in M at the equilibrium allocation x_i, or more precisely, suppose there exists $x' \in X_i$ with $x' - \omega_i \in M$ such that $x' \succ_i x_i$. We claim that (d, S) is tight. For a proof by contradiction, suppose (d, S) is not tight. Let $\widehat{\theta}$ be any trading strategy financing x' and let $\alpha = \widehat{\theta}(\xi^0) \cdot S(\xi^1)$, the initial portfolio market value required. Now construct the trading strategy $\theta' = \widehat{\theta} - (\alpha/\beta)(\theta^A - \theta^B)$, where β, θ^A, and θ^B are as shown in relation (5). This trading strategy θ' also finances x' since $\theta^A - \theta^B$ finances the zero process, and $\theta'(\xi^0) \cdot S(\xi^1) = 0$ by construction. Thus (θ', x') is a budget feasible plan strictly preferred to (θ_i, x_i), a contradiction of the optimality of (θ_i, x_i). We have proven the following result.

PROPOSITION. *Suppose (d, S) is a security market system for $(\mathcal{E}, \Xi, d)$ at which, for some $i \in \mathcal{I}$, $\succeq_i$ is non–satiated in the marketed subspace M at an optimal plan. Then (d, S) is tight.*

Suppose (d, S) is tight. Let $\Pi : D \to R$ be defined by

$$\Pi(d^\theta) = \theta(\xi^0) \cdot S(\xi^1), \quad \theta \in \Theta.$$

That is, Π defines the unique initial portfolio market value required to generate a given dividend process that can be "reached" by some trading strategy. The reader can easily verify that Π is a linear functional. In fact, since the total number of vertices in Ξ is the integer $\overline{K}$, D is identified with a vector subspace of $R^{\overline{K}}$. Since Π can be linearly extended to $R^{\overline{K}}$, there exists some $q \in F_1$ such that

$$\Pi(d) = \sum_{\xi \in \Xi} q(\xi)d(\xi) \quad \text{for all } d \in D.$$

The scalar $q(\xi)$ may be thought of as "shadow price of wealth" at vertex ξ. If, for some vertex $\xi \in \Xi$, there exists a trading strategy θ such that $d^\theta(\xi) = 1$ and $d^\theta(\xi') = 0$ for $\xi' \neq \xi$, then $q(\xi)$ is actually the implied initial market value of a security paying one unit of spot market value at vertex ξ. Of course, each of the underlying dividend processes $d_1, \ldots, d_N$ is in D, so for any n, we know that $\Pi(d_n) = S_n(\xi^1)$.

F.   If (d, S) is tight, a linear functional p on the marketed space M is defined by

$$p \cdot x = \Pi(\psi \ \Box \ x), \quad x \in M.$$

As defined, p is the *implicit price functional*, specifying the market value of the initial portfolio required to finance any given marketed consumption process. As far as any agent is concerned, the marketed subspace M and implicit price functional $p \in M'$ is a complete characterization of the range of budget feasible consumption choices. Each agent i searches for an optimal net trade $x_i - \omega_i$ in M subject to $p \cdot (x_i - \omega_i) \leq 0$. Any such choice can be implemented in dynamic trade by choosing a trading strategy θ financing $x_i - \omega_i$. By the definition of p, the strategy θ satisfies the zero initial wealth restriction $\theta(\xi^0) \cdot S(\xi^1) \leq 0$.

The following connection between static and dynamic equilibria should already have occurred to any reader familiar with Section 7. The proof is left as an exercise. The net trade economy $\mathcal{E}^M$ induced by a vector subspace M is as defined by relation (7.2).

PROPOSITION. *Suppose* $((S, \psi), (x_i, \theta_i))$, $i \in \mathcal{I}$, *is an equilibrium for the dynamic exchange economy* $(\mathcal{E}, (\Xi, \mathcal{A}), d)$, *where* (d, S) *is a tight security market system, with marketed subspace* $M \subset L$ *and implicit price functional* $p \in M'$. *Then* $(\hat{x}_1, \ldots, \hat{x}_I, p)$ *is an equilibrium for the (static) economy* $\mathcal{E}^M$ *on the choice space* M, *where* $\hat{x}_i = x_i - \omega_i$, $i \in \mathcal{I}$.

G.   Under what conditions on the market system (d, S, ψ) is the marketed subspace M equal to the whole choice space L, or *complete financial markets*? This is basically a property of the security price process, $S = (S_1, \ldots, S_N)$, as we now demonstrate.

At any vertex $\xi \in \Xi$ with $K = \#\xi \geq 1$ successors, let

$$S(\xi_+) = \begin{pmatrix} S_1(\xi_{+1}) & S_1(\xi_{+2}) & \cdots & S_1(\xi_{+K}) \\ S_2(\xi_{+1}) & S_2(\xi_{+2}) & \cdots & S_2(\xi_{+K}) \\ \vdots & \vdots & \ddots & \vdots \\ S_N(\xi_{+1}) & S_N(\xi_{+2}) & \cdots & S_N(\xi_{+K}) \end{pmatrix}_{N \times K}$$

denote the matrix of security values at the $K = \#\xi$ immediate successor vertices of ξ. In choosing a portfolio $\theta(\xi)$ of securities at a vertex $\xi \in \Xi$ with K successor vertices, we will suppose that an agent has a specific target V_k for the pre–trade market value $\theta(\xi) \cdot S(\xi_{+k})$ of the security portfolio to be held at vertex ξ_{+k}. Given such a "wealth target" V_k for each of the K successor vertices, we desire a single solution $\theta(\xi) \in R^N$ to the system of linear equations

$$\theta(\xi) \cdot S(\xi_{+k}) = V_k, \quad 1 \le k \le K,$$

or more simply,

$$\theta(\xi)^\top S(\xi_+) = V \equiv (V_1, \dots, V_K). \tag{6}$$

If V is an arbitrary vector in R^K, the existence of a solution is purely a matter of the *column rank* of $S(\xi_+)$, the number of linearly independent column vectors of $S(\xi_+)$, which is denoted rank$[S(\xi_+)]$. The following is a standard result of linear algebra.

LEMMA. *There exists a solution $\theta(\xi) \in R^N$ to* (6) *for any $V \in R^K$ if and only if the column rank of $S(\xi_+)$ is K.*

Thus the presence of complete financial markets depends entirely on the rank of $S(\xi_+)$ at each vertex.

PROPOSITION. *A market system (d, S, ψ) has a complete marketed subspace $M = L$ if and only if*

$$\text{rank}[S(\xi_+)] = \#\xi \tag{7}$$

for all non–terminal vertices ξ in the underlying event tree Ξ.

Given the scenario proceeding the last lemma, this proposition is easily proved by backward induction. The vector security price process S is naturally defined to be *market completing* if condition (7) is met.

A dividend–price pair $(d, S) \in F_N \times F_N$ is *arbitrage–free* if, for any trading strategy θ generating a positive non–zero dividend process d^θ, the required investment $\theta(\xi^0) \cdot S(\xi^1)$ is strictly positive. This is a stronger condition than tightness. The following corollary, whose proof is assigned as an exercise, states that the number of securities required for a complete marketed subspace $(M = L)$ without arbitrage is the *spanning number* $N(\Xi, \mathcal{A}) \equiv \max\{\#\xi : \xi \in \Xi\}$, the greatest number of immediate successors of any vertex. A subset A of an open Euclidean set B is *generic* if the complement $B \setminus A$ is closed and has Lebesgue measure zero. The notion of a "generic result" is that it is unlikely to fail in general, since the complement of a generic subset is negligible for most purposes.

COROLLARY. *If the number of securities N is strictly less than $N(\Xi, \mathcal{A})$, then the marketed subspace M is not equal to L. Conversely, there is a generic subset $\mathcal{D}$ of $F_{N(\Xi, \mathcal{A})}$ such that, for all $d \in \mathcal{D}$, there is a market completing price process $S \in F_{N(\Xi, \mathcal{A})}$ such that (d, S) is arbitrage–free.*

We claim in this corollary that the spanning number, the maximum number of branches leaving any vertex in the event tree Ξ, is a necessary and sufficient number of securities for arbitrage–free complete financial markets. Along with the usual preference and endowment assumptions, this is also enough for the existence of efficient equilibrium allocations, as we shall soon see.

H. In this paragraph we study a simple and illustrative convention for pricing securities. Later we show that an equilibrium can be constructed satisfying this convention. Let $\Lambda : F_N \to F_N$ be the function assigning security prices to dividend processes according to $S = \Lambda(d)$, where

$$S(\xi) = \Lambda(d)_\xi \equiv \sum_{\eta \in \Xi(\xi)} d(\eta), \quad \xi \in \Xi. \tag{8}$$

The "current value" of a security at vertex ξ is "announced" under Λ to be the sum of its dividends in the entire sub-tree $\Xi(\xi)$. It is easily verified that for each vector price process S there is a unique vector dividend process d such that $\Lambda(d) = S$. In other words, Λ is invertible, and we may speak of the dividend process $\Lambda^{-1}(S)$ underlying a given vector price process S. The following lemma, also proved by a backward induction argument, will soon be of use.

LEMMA. *For any market system of the form $(d, \Lambda(d), \psi)$, if a consumption process x and trading strategy θ satisfy $d^\theta = \psi \square x$, then*

$$\theta(\xi_-) \cdot S(\xi) = \sum_{\eta \in \Xi(\xi)} \psi(\eta) \cdot x(\eta) \quad \text{for all } \xi \in \Xi.$$

In particular, $(d, \Lambda(d), \psi)$ is tight and the implicit price functional p on the marketed subspace M can be defined by

$$p \cdot x = \sum_{\xi \in \Xi} \psi(\xi) \cdot x(\xi), \quad x \in M. \tag{9}$$

I. Now our task is to complete the circle connecting static and dynamic equilibria begun with Proposition 12F. Let $(x_1, \ldots, x_I, p)$ be a (static) equilibrium for

$$\mathcal{E} = (X_i, \succeq_i, \omega_i), \quad i \in \mathcal{I} = \{1, \ldots, I\},$$

an exchange economy on the vector space $L = F_\ell$. Since F_ℓ is Euclidean, any linear functional on L, for instance the given equilibrium price functional p, can be represented by some spot price process ψ in the form

$$p \cdot x = \sum_{\xi \in \Xi} \psi(\xi) \cdot x(\xi), \qquad x \in L. \tag{10}$$

Combining the spot price process ψ given by (10) with any market completing security price process S, and taking the canonical underlying dividend process $d = \Lambda^{-1}(S)$, we have a candidate market system (d, S, ψ). The following result uses this market system to provide a dynamic equilibrium implementation of the given static equilibrium $(x_1, \ldots, x_I, p)$.

PROPOSITION. *There exists a trading strategy θ_i for each agent i such that there is an equilibrium for the economy $(\mathcal{E}, (\Xi, \mathcal{A}), d)$ of the form $((S, \psi), (\theta_i, x_i))$.*

PROOF: Step 1: Since S is market completing by construction, $M = L$. Thus, for any agent i there exists some trading strategy θ_i for agent i financing the net trade $x_i - \omega_i$. By Lemma 3B, $p \cdot (x_i - \omega_i) = 0$. Then (θ_i, x_i) is a budget feasible plan for agent i since, by Lemma 12H and relation (10),

$$\theta_i(\xi^0) \cdot S(\xi^1) = \sum_{\xi \in \Xi} \psi(\xi) \cdot [x_i(\xi) - \omega_i(\xi)] = p \cdot (x_i - \omega_i) = 0. \tag{11}$$

If there is only one agent, we move on to Step 2. Otherwise, we assign trading strategies (θ_i) with the above property for any $I - 1$ of the agents, say the first $I - 1$. Let $\theta_I = -\sum_{i=1}^{I-1} \theta_i$. The reader can verify that (θ_I, x_I) is a budget feasible plan for agent I as well.

Step 2: Markets clear obviously from Step 1. Suppose some agent, say i, has a strictly preferred budget feasible plan (θ', x'); that is, $x' \succ_i x_i$. Then, by definition of (static) equilibrium, $p \cdot x' > p \cdot x_i$, and

$$p \cdot (x' - \omega_i) > p \cdot (x_i - \omega_i) = 0,$$

contradicting the assumption that (θ', x') is actually a budget feasible plan for agent i, since any budget feasible plan must satisfy (11). Thus, each agent's plan (θ_i, x_i) is optimal. ∎

Given securities d such that $\Lambda(d)$ is market completing (and such securities exist since Λ is invertible), we have reduced the task of demonstrating an equilibrium for $(\mathcal{E}, (\Xi, \mathcal{A}), d)$ to the existence of a (static) equilibrium for $\mathcal{E}$. Sufficient conditions for this are well known. For example, we can apply the Debreu Conditions of Section 3.

THEOREM. *Suppose the securities d are such that $\Lambda(d)$ is market completing, and $\mathcal{E}$ satisfies the Debreu Conditions. Provided $\omega_i \in \text{int}(X_i)$ for each i in $\mathcal{I}$, the (static) economy $\mathcal{E}$ has a static equilibrium. The dynamic exchange economy $(\mathcal{E}, (\Xi, \mathcal{A}), d)$ then also has an equilibrium.*

PROOF: We can apply Proposition 3G and Theorem 3G for the existence of a static equilibrium, and then Proposition 12I. ∎

J. We also have sufficient conditions for the existence of dynamic exchange equilibria with the marketed subspace M a proper subspace of the choice space L, or *incomplete financial markets.*

THEOREM. *Suppose $(\mathcal{E}, (\Xi, \mathcal{A}), d)$ is a dynamic exchange economy with Euclidean spot consumption spaces. If $X_i = L_+$; $\succeq_i$ is continuous, convex, and strictly monotonic, and $\omega_i \in \text{int}(L_+)$ for all $i \in \mathcal{I}$, then a dynamic exchange equilibrium exists.*

The proof of this theorem, although longer than we have room for here, uses standard fixed point analysis. A theorem with significantly weaker endowment assumptions is cited in the Notes. Notably, there are no conditions on the securities d.

A *security market system* $(d, S) \in F_N \times F_N$ is *arbitrage–free* if

$$\{\theta \in \Theta : \theta(\xi^0) = 0,\ d^\theta \geq 0,\ d^\theta \neq 0\} = \emptyset,$$

that is, if it is impossible to generate positive non–zero dividends without any initial endowment of securities. The theorem above is proved by fixing any price process S for the available securities d such that the security market system (d, S) is arbitrage–free, and then adjusting the spot market price process ψ to an equilibrium. For example, we could fix $S = \Lambda(d)$. We can state this method of proof as a useful result in its own right.

PROPOSITION. *For an economy $(\mathcal{E}, (\Xi, \mathcal{A}), d)$ satisfying the assumptions of Theorem 12J, let $\widehat{S}$ be any security price process such that the security market system $(d, \widehat{S})$ is arbitrage–free; for example, let $\widehat{S} = \Lambda(d)$. Then there exists an equilibrium $\left((\widehat{S}, \psi), (x_i, \theta_i) \right)$.*

In simple terms, any arbitrage–free security price process can be embedded in an equilibrium. This means that the spot price process ψ can be adjusted to clear both spot and security markets.

K. It should be cautioned that the previous results concerning the existence of equilibria depend critically on the definition of a security as a claim to a stream of financial dividends, rather than a claim to a consumption process or a *real security*. With the latter convention, an adjustment of the spot price process from ψ to ψ' changes the financial nature of the security claiming a consumption process $x \in L$ from $\psi \,\square\, x$ to $\psi' \,\square\, x$. This can cause severe problems in demonstrating an equilibrium. The distinction between *purely financial securities* (our model above) and *real securities* is thus fundamental. Counterexamples to the existence of equilibria are cited in the Notes, and apply to economies satisfying stringent regularity conditions. We can, however, demonstrate the generic existence of equilibria with real securities, that is, equilibria for a generic set of economies. We let $L_{++} = \text{int}(L_+)$ and consider the following regularity conditions on a utility representation $u_i : L_{++} \to R$ for the preference relation $\succeq_i$ on L_{++}. For the following conditions, we can treat L as a Euclidean space.

(U.1) u_i has two continuous derivatives, denoted $\nabla u_i(x)$ and $\nabla^2 u_i(x)$ at a point $x \in L_{++}$,

(U.2) $\nabla u_i(x) \in L_{++}$ for all x in L_{++} (strict monotonicity),

(U.3) for all x in L_{++}, $h^{\top} \nabla^2 u_i(x) h < 0$ for all $h \neq 0$ with $\nabla u_i(x) \cdot h = 0$, and

(U.4) $\{x \in L_{++} : u_i(x) \geq u_i(\overline{x})\}$ is a closed subset of L for all $\overline{x}$ in L_{++}.

Condition (U.3) characterizes *differentiably strictly convex preferences*; (U.4) is a *preference boundary condition*. An example of a utility function satisfying these conditions is given in Paragraph 13B.

We change the definition of an economy only by replacing the purely financial dividend vector $d \in F_N$ with a real dividend vector $d \in L^N$. The only change in the definition of an equilibrium is the dividend process $d^{\theta} \in F_1$ generated by a trading strategy θ. We now obviously have

$$d^{\theta}(\xi) = -\Delta\theta(\xi) \cdot S(\xi) + \sum_{n=1}^{N} \theta_n(\xi)\psi(\xi) \cdot d_n(\xi), \quad \xi \in \Xi. \qquad (2')$$

THEOREM. *Suppose that each agent i has the consumption set $X_i = L_{++}$ and a preference relation $\succeq_i$ on L_{++} with a utility representation u_i satisfying conditions (U.1)–(U.4). Then, for any number $N \geq 0$ of real securities, there is a generic subset E of $L_{++}^I \times L^N$ with the property: for each $(\omega, d) \in E$ there exists an equilibrium for $((X_i, \succeq_i, \omega_i), (\Xi, \mathcal{A}), d)$.*

The result shows that the set of endowments and securities for which there is no equilibrium is "small" indeed. A proof, extending the result to include purely financial, real, and mixed securities, as well as linear restrictions on trading strategies, is cited in the Notes. Section 13 contains the extension to stock market economies.

L. A *state price process* is a process $q \in (F_1)_{++} \equiv \text{int}[(F_1)_+]$, that can be used to infer security prices in the following manner. First, for any state price process q, let $\Lambda_q : F_N \to F_N$ be defined by

$$[\Lambda_q(d)](\xi) = \frac{1}{q(\xi)} \sum_{\eta \in \Xi(\xi)} q(\eta)d(\eta), \quad \xi \in \Xi. \tag{12}$$

A special case is $q(\xi) = 1$ for all ξ, which gives the previously defined operator Λ.

PROPOSITION. *A security market system $(d, S) \in F_N \times F_N$ is arbitrage–free if and only if there exists a state price process $q \in (F_1)_{++}$ such that $S = \Lambda_q(d)$. Furthermore, there is a unique state price process with this property if and only if S is market completing.*

The proof is left as an exercise. It should be clear that there is a large margin for normalization of prices in a dynamic economy.

LEMMA. *Consider an economy $(\mathcal{E}, (\Xi, \mathcal{A}), d)$, where $d \in F_N$ is a purely financial vector dividend process. There is a generic subset Q of $(F_1)_{++}$ such that, for any state price process $q \in Q$, there exists an equilibrium of the form $((\Lambda_q(d), \psi'), (x_i, \theta_i'))$, where the consumption allocation (x_i) is invariant over Q.*

Again, proof is left as an exercise.

EXERCISES

EXERCISE 12.1 Show that the spaces $D = \{d^\theta : \theta \in \Theta\}$ and $M = \{x \in L : \psi \square x \in D\}$ are vector spaces, where ψ is a spot price process. The notation is as defined in this section.

EXERCISE 12.2 Show that the functionals Π on D and p on M, defined in Paragraphs E and F respectively, are linear.

EXERCISE 12.3 Prove Proposition 12F.

EXERCISE 12.4 Prove Proposition 12G.

EXERCISE 12.5 Prove Lemma 12H.

EXERCISE 12.6   Show, as claimed in the proof of Proposition 12I, that $(-\sum_{i=1}^{I-1} \theta_i, x_I)$ is indeed a budget feasible plan for agent I.

EXERCISE 12.7   For a given event tree $(\Xi, \mathcal{A})$ and tight security market system (d, S), suppose S is market completing. Let ψ denote a given spot price process and p the implicit price functional for the market system (d, S, ψ). Show the existence of a linear function Λ^* mapping any new dividend process δ to a security price process $S^* = \Lambda^*(\delta)$ such that the adjoined market system $((d_1, \ldots, d_N, \delta), (S_1, \ldots, S_N, S^*), \psi)$ has the same implicit price functional p.

EXERCISE 12.8   Show that arbitrage–free implies tight. Demonstrate a tight security market system that is not arbitrage–free.

EXERCISE 12.9   Prove Theorem 12J and Proposition 12J. Hint: Fix the security prices and proceed in the manner suggested in the discussion following the statement of the theorem, using the fixed point argument outlined in Exercise 3.18 as a basis for extension to incomplete markets.

EXERCISE 12.10   Prove Proposition 12L. Hint: Use Exercise 7.12.

EXERCISE 12.11   Prove Lemma 12L.

Notes

The seminal paper on the spanning role of securities with dynamic trading is Arrow (1953). General equilibrium in the event tree setting is found in Debreu (1953). Kreps (1982) originated the idea of Proposition 12G and its corollary. Friesen (1974) is an early related paper. For a formal definition of an event tree as a directed graph, see Avondo–Bodino (1962) for a simple source. Extensions of Proposition 12I may be found in Duffie and Huang (1985) and further literature cited in Section 16. Duffie (1987) proves Theorem 12J and its corollary under weaker endowment assumptions, and allowing "short–lived" securities, not traded at given vertices in the event tree. This would permit, for example, one period loan markets, or financial futures markets that open at fixed intervals before delivery. This work on incomplete financial markets follows on the seminal equilibrium existence proofs of Werner (1985b) and Cass (1984).

Radner (1972) demonstrates existence of exchange equilibria with real securities in the event tree setting, using a lower bound on trading strategies. Hart (1975) has given counterexamples to the existence of equilibrium for markets with real securities, pointing out that Radner's assumption of an a priori lower bound on security portfolios is critical to the existence and nature of the equilibrium. Radner (1967) is a precursor to much of this theory.

Generic existence in the case that the number of real securities is at least as large as the spanning number of the event tree is due to Repullo (1986), McManus (1984), and Magill and Shafer (1984, 1985). For related results, one may see Wiesmuth (1987), Shefrin (1981), Nermuth (1985, 1987), and Brown (1987). The general case, Theorem 12K and its extensions, is found in Duffie and Shafer (1985, 1986a, 1986b). Alternative proofs are given by Husseini, Lasry, and Magill (1986) as well as Geanakoplos and Shafer (1987). Geanakoplos and Polemarchakis (1986) have pointed out that securities paying real numeraire goods only do not cause problems for the existence of equilibria. Chae (1985) has a generalization of this result. All of these existence results are based on security dividends that are linear functions of spot prices. A typical nonlinear case is options, for which there is a robust example of non–existence of equilibrium due to Polemarchakis and Ku (1986). Krasa (1987), however, shows that the fraction of options economies without equilibria is small, with sufficient variation in the supply of commodities across states, in a precise sense.

Geanakoplos and Polemarcharkis (1986) have results on the generic lack of constrained optimality of equilibrium allocations with incomplete markets, provided the set of agents is sufficiently small. They use a stronger criterion for constrained optimality than that used here. Mas–Colell (1987) showed that constrained efficiency, in the sense of Geanakoplos and Polemarchakis, applies to equilibrium allocations of economies with a sufficiently diverse set of preferences. Hart (1975) also shows that the addition of new security markets may result in a movement from one equilibrium allocation to another that dominates it. Debreu (1953) has an early proof of existence of complete markets dynamic equilibria with event tree uncertainty.

For studies of the indeterminacy in the equilibrium allocation with incomplete financial markets, see Geanakoplos and Mas Colell (1985), Cass (1985), Balasko and Cass (1986), and Werner (1986, 1987). Following Debreu (1970), who studied the case of complete markets, Duffie and Shafer (1986b) show finiteness of the set of equilibrium allocations (or "determinacy") in the pure exchange case with only real securities, and indeterminacy with production. Balasko and Cass (1985, 1986) examine related issues. The *smooth preference* assumptions (U.1)–(U.4) of Paragraph 12K are due to Debreu (1970, 1972, 1976). For the general theory of economies with smooth preferences, one may consult the monographs of Mas–Colell (1985) or Balasko (1986).

13. A Dynamic Theory of the Firm

This section continues in the event tree framework of the last, adding firms.
In a setting of dynamically complete markets, the theory has settled into
a fairly clear framework. We will look over the formulation of equilibrium,
the financial decisions of the firm and the Modigliani–Miller irrelevance
principle, and finally the production decisions of the firm. In the absence
of a sound theoretical model without dynamically complete markets, the
concluding paragraphs are loosely argued.

A.   Continuing with the setup of Section 12, let $(\Xi, \mathcal{A})$ denote a given
finite event tree and F_n denote the vector space of R^n–valued processes
on $(\Xi, \mathcal{A})$. The consumption space is $L = F_\ell$, where ℓ is the number of
spot commodities. For a simple exposition, we leave out securities in zero
net supply. The general case is covered in a paper cited in the Notes.
A *stochastic production economy* is then a pair $(\mathcal{E}, (\Xi, \mathcal{A}))$, where $\mathcal{E}$ is a
production–exchange economy

$$((X_i, \succeq_i \omega_i); (Y_j); (\alpha_{ij})), \quad i \in \mathcal{I} \equiv \{1, \ldots, I\}, \quad j \in \mathcal{J} \equiv \{1, \ldots, J\},$$

on L. In particular, $Y_j \subset L$ is the *production set* of firm j and $\alpha_{ij} \geq 0$ is
the pre–trade share of the initial market value of firm j held by agent i.
We take the common normalization $\sum_{i=1}^{I} \alpha_{ij} = 1$ for each of the J firms.

Suppose firm j chooses a production process $y_j \in Y_j$ and that a spot
price process ψ is given. We recall that $\psi(\xi) \cdot z$ is the market value at
vertex ξ of the spot consumption vector $z \in R^\ell$. Firm j thus issues the
common share security $d_j = \psi \square y_j$, as defined in Section 12. This means
that the firm's share pays at a given vertex ξ in the event tree the spot
market value $d_j(\xi) = \psi(\xi) \cdot y_j(\xi)$ of its production at that vertex. Later we
introduce financial policies for the firm, allowing it to adjust the definition
of its common share.

We treat firms as though they maximize the market value of their
common shares. In order for firms to evaluate the effect of production
decisions on share value, we assume they take as given a state price process
$q \in (F_1)_{++} \equiv \text{int}[(F_1)_+]$, which is used to price all securities according
to the function $\Lambda_q : F_1 \to F_1$ defined in Paragraph 12L. As shown there,
security price processes are arbitrage–free if and only if they are determined
by a state price process in this manner. (In general, however, the state price
process is not uniquely determined merely by the absence of arbitrage.)
Given a spot price process $\psi \in L$, the initial share value of a production
choice $y_j \in Y_j$ is $v_{q,\psi}(y_j)$, where $v_{q,\psi} : L \to R$ is the linear functional

defined by $v_{q,\psi}(y) = [\Lambda_q(\psi \,\square\, y)](\xi^1)$. Firm j thus faces the problem

$$\max_{y \in Y_j} \; v_{q,\psi}(y). \tag{1}$$

A production choice $y_j \in Y_j$ is *value–maximizing* for firm j if y_j solves this optimization problem. As shown in an exercise, this problem is equivalent to the problem of maximizing current market value at all vertices, taking past production decisions as given.

Taking a spot price ψ and a state price process q as given, each agent evaluates the price process $S_j = \Lambda_q(d_j) \in F_1$ for each security d_j. As with the exchange economy of Section 12, a budget feasible plan for agent i, given $(q, \psi, d) \in (F_1)_{++} \times L \times F_J$, is a pair (θ_i, x_i) consisting of a consumption process $x_i \in X_i$ and a trading strategy $\theta_i \in \Theta$ financing the net trade $x_i - \omega_i$, with pre–trade portfolio $\theta_i(\xi^0)_j = \alpha_{ij}$. Such a plan (θ_i, x_i) is *optimal* for agent i, we recall, if there is no other budget feasible plan (θ', x') for agent i such that $x' \succ_i x_i$. A *stock market equilibrium* for $(\mathcal{E}, (\Xi, \mathcal{A}))$ is a collection

$$((\psi, q); (\theta_i, x_i), (y_j)), \qquad i \in \mathcal{I}, \; j \in \mathcal{J},$$

where ψ is a spot price process and q is a state price process, such that: for each firm j, the production choice y_j is value–maximizing; for each agent i, the plan (θ_i, x_i) is optimal; and markets clear:

$$\sum_{i=1}^{I} x_i - \omega_i = \sum_{j=1}^{J} y_j$$

$$\sum_{i=1}^{I} \theta_{ij}(\xi) \equiv 1, \quad j \in \mathcal{J}, \; \xi \in \Xi.$$

This formulation is extended in later paragraphs in order to study the effect of financial policies for the firm.

B. Sufficient conditions for the existence of a stock market equilibrium, in a generic sense, are given in a paper cited in the Notes. We illustrate our model with a simple example having an infinite set of equilibrium allocations.

Example. We consider an example with $I = 2$ agents, $J = 1$ firm, $\ell = 1$ commodity, and an event tree $(\Xi, \mathcal{A})$ of the form $\Xi = \{\xi^1, \xi^2, \xi^3\}$ with $\xi^2_- = \xi^3_- = \xi^1$. That is, we have two periods and $S = 2$ states in the second period. For any consumption process $x \in L$, we write $x_0 = x(\xi^1)$, $x_1(1) = x(\xi^2)$, $x_1(2) = x(\xi^3)$, and $x_1 = \big(x_1(1), x_1(2)\big) \in R^2$. Each agent's choice set is $X_i = L_{++} = \mathrm{int}(L_+)$. The agents' preferences are represented by the utility functions $u_i : L_{++} \to R$ defined by

$$u_i(x) = \log(x_0) + \beta_1^i \log\big(x_1(1)\big) + \beta_2^i \log\big(x_1(2)\big), \quad x \in L_{++},$$

for some $\beta^i \in R_{++}^2$, $i \in \{1, 2\}$. We note that u_i satisfies conditions (U.1)–(U.4) of Paragraph 12K. The firm's production set is

$$Y_1 = \Big\{ y \in L : y_0 \le 0,\ y_1 \ge 0,\ \|y_1\| \le \sqrt{(-y_0)} \Big\} - L_+.$$

That is, a feasible output of the firm in period 2 is any (positive) vector whose norm is less than the square root of the input in period 1, with the added possibility of free disposal shown by subtraction of the positive cone L_+. Taking the state price vector $\bar{q} = (1, 1)$ and normalizing the spot price vector $\psi \in L_{++}$ by choosing $\psi_0 = 1$, the market value maximizing production choices are:

$$y_0 = \frac{-\psi_1 \cdot \psi_1}{4}$$

$$y_1(s) = \frac{\psi_1(s)}{2}, \quad s \in \{1, 2\}. \tag{2}$$

The initial market value of the firm, denoted $p \cdot y$, is thus $(\psi_1 \cdot \psi_1)/4$.

The problem of agent i is reduced to choosing the fraction $\gamma^i \equiv \theta_i(\xi^1)$ of the firm to hold. The first order condition for optimal γ^i is

$$\frac{-p \cdot y - y_0}{w_0^i} + \gamma^i(y_0 - p \cdot y) + \alpha_i p \cdot y + \sum_s \frac{\beta_s^i y_1(s)}{w_1^1(s) + y_1(s)\gamma^i} = 0. \tag{3}$$

Substituting the market value maximizing y yields

$$\frac{-\psi_1 \cdot \psi_1}{w_0^i + \left(\frac{\alpha_i}{4} - \frac{\gamma^i}{2}\right)\psi_1 \cdot \psi_1} + \sum_s \frac{\beta_s^i \psi_1(s)}{w_1^i(s)} + \frac{\psi_1(s)\gamma^i}{2} = 0, \quad i \in \{1, 2\}. \tag{4}$$

We note that $\gamma^1 + \gamma^2 = 1$ implies spot market clearing, and that the set of equilibria is therefore equivalent to the set of $(\psi_1, \gamma^1, \gamma^2)$ solving the two equations given by the market clearing equation $\gamma^2 = 1 - \gamma^1$ and relation (4). The set of equilibria turns out to be infinite for a generic subset of endowments $(\omega^1, \omega^2) \in L_+^2$.

Distinct $(\psi_1, \gamma^1, \gamma^2)$ and $(\bar{\psi}_1, \bar{\gamma}^1, \bar{\gamma}^2)$ solving both (4) and $\gamma^1 + \gamma^2 = \bar{\gamma}^1 + \bar{\gamma}^2 = 1$ correspond to distinct allocations for the agents. To see this, suppose not. Then $\psi_1 = \bar{\psi}_1$, for otherwise the corresponding production

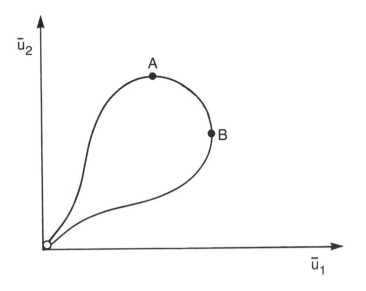

Figure 13.1   Equilibrium Utilities in Incomplete Markets

choices y and $\bar{y}$ differ. Furthermore $\psi_1 \gamma^1 = \overline{\psi}_1 \overline{\gamma}^1$, for otherwise the corresponding consumption choices x_1 and $\overline{x}_1$ differ. Thus $\gamma^1 = \overline{\gamma}^1$.

Special Case: Let $\omega^i = (1,0,0)$, $\beta_1^i + \beta_2^i = 1$, and $\alpha_i = 1/2$ for $i \in \{1,2\}$. Then (4) reduces to

$$\frac{\psi_1 \cdot \psi_1}{2 + \left(\frac{1}{4} - \gamma^i\right)\psi_1 \cdot \psi_1} - \frac{\beta_1^i + \beta_2^i}{\gamma^i} = 0, \quad i \in \{1,2\}.$$

Taking $\gamma^2 = 1 - \gamma^1$ and solving for $\psi_1 \cdot \psi_1$ and γ^1, we have $\gamma^1 = 1/2$ and $\psi_1 \cdot \psi_1 = 8/3$. Thus the set of spot price vectors $\psi_1 \gg 0$ on the circle of radius $\sqrt{8/3}$ is in one-to-one correspondence with the set of equilibrium consumption allocations.

We graph the equilibria in terms of the monotonic transformation of utility

$$\overline{u}_i(x) = e^{2u_i(x)}, \quad i \in \{1,2\}.$$

The graph of equilibrium utilities for $\beta^1 = \left(\frac{1}{3}, \frac{2}{3}\right)$ and $\beta^2 = \left(\frac{2}{3}, \frac{1}{3}\right)$ is shown in Figure 13.1 as the set of non–zero solutions to the cubic equation $\overline{u}_1^3 + \overline{u}_2^3 = k\overline{u}_1\overline{u}_2$ for some scalar k. ♠

C.   We introduce security trading by a firm. Taken liberally, this is what a firm's financial policy amounts to. For example, a firm can sell bonds, commonly termed "debt financing", deal in futures contracts, buy and sell competitors' shares, issue its own securities, and so on. We begin by allowing firm j to adopt any trading strategy $\gamma_j \in \Theta$ subject to the initial endowment restriction: $\gamma_j(\xi^0) = 0$. A *plan* for firm j is then a pair (γ, y) consisting of a trading strategy γ and a production plan $y \in Y_j$. Given a spot price process ψ and a state price process q, plans (γ_j, y_j), $j \in \mathcal{J}$, for the firms determine, under a mild regularity condition to be explored shortly, a dividend process d_j and security price process S_j. The careful reader will notice a simultaneity issue here: the dividend of firm j depends on the prices of all securities, which in turn depend on the dividends of all securities. This is resolved by the following result, whose proof is left as an exercise. Given a trading strategy γ_j for each firm j, for any vertex $\xi \in \Xi$, let $\gamma(\xi)$ denote the $J \times J$ matrix whose (j, k)–element is $\gamma_j(\xi)_k$, the number of shares of firm k held by firm j. The trading strategies $(\gamma_1, \dots, \gamma_J)$ of the J firms are defined to be *regular* if $[I - \gamma(\xi)]$ is non–singular for all non–terminal vertices in $(\Xi, \mathcal{A})$.

LEMMA. *Let ψ be a spot price process, q be a state price process, and $((\gamma_1, y_1), \dots, (\gamma_J, y_J))$ be a collection of firms' plans. Then the securities' dividend processes (d_j) and price processes (S_j) are uniquely determined by $S_j = \Lambda_q(d_j)$ and $d_j = d^{\gamma_j} + \psi \square y_j$ if and only if $(\gamma_1, \dots, \gamma_J)$ is regular.*

We see that firms are in a rather special position vis-à-vis individual agents, who do not issue their own common share securities. As far as budgetary restrictions are concerned, a firm can theoretically choose its trades on financial markets and its production plans at will. The resulting dividend stream "picks up the remaining cash flow." One often assumes, however, that a firm has *limited liability*: (γ_j, y_j) must be chosen such that the dividend process d_j is positive. The existence of a limited liability plan obviously depends on the spot price process ψ, but follows trivially if $0 \in Y_j$.

Now it is an easy matter to give an extended definition of a *stock market equilibrium* for the stochastic production economy $(\mathcal{E}, (\Xi, \mathcal{A}))$, as a collection

$$((q, \psi), (\theta_i, x_i), (\gamma_j, y_j)), \quad i \in \mathcal{I}, \; j \in \mathcal{J},$$

such that

(a) $(\gamma_1, \dots, \gamma_J)$ is regular,

(b) for each agent $i \in \mathcal{I}$, (θ_i, x_i) is an optimal plan given $((q, \psi), (\gamma_j, y_j))$,

(c) for each firm $j \in \mathcal{J}$, there is no plan (γ', y'), such that the collection $(\gamma_1, \dots, \gamma_{j-1}, \gamma', \dots, \gamma_J)$ of strategies is regular, with larger market value $[\Lambda_q(\psi \square y' + d^{\gamma'})](\xi^1) > [\Lambda_q(\psi \square y_j + d^{\gamma_j})](\xi^1)$, and

(d) markets clear: $\sum_i x_i - \omega_i = \sum_j y_j$ and

$$\sum_i \theta_i(\xi)_k + \sum_j \gamma_j(\xi)_k = 1, \quad k \in \mathcal{J}, \xi \in \Xi.$$

D. Can a firm increase its share value by changing its financial policy? Taking a state price process q and a spot price process ψ as given, the answer is "No," as stated by the following proposition, whose proof is left as an exercise.

MODIGLIANI–MILLER THEOREM (PART I). *Suppose a state price process q, a spot price process ψ, and a collection of firms' plans $((\gamma_j, y_j))$, $j \in \mathcal{J}$, are given. If $\gamma = (\gamma_1, \ldots, \gamma_J)$ is regular then, for any firm j,*

$$[\Lambda_q(\psi \square y_j + d^{\gamma_j})](\xi^1) = [\Lambda_q(\psi \square y_j)](\xi^1).$$

The result shows that the initial price of the common stock of a firm is independent of its security trading strategy, under the competitive price–taking assumption. The following paragraph shows that price–taking is at least consistent with changes in financial policy.

E. The market value S_j of the security claiming the dividend process d_j of firm j is also termed the *equity*, or *shareholder value* of firm j. Since the dividend process d_j adjusts in response to the firm's policy γ_j for trading securities, it is conceivable that the financial policy of the firm might have repercussions throughout the economy. Another firm $k \in \mathcal{J}$, for example, could hold shares of d_j in its portfolio at certain vertices. A change in γ_j changes d_j, shifting S_j, and thereby potentially moving the marketed subspace $M \subset L$ of consumption processes reachable by some trading strategy. If M shifts, the forces of supply and demand meet on new terrain; spot prices will react, and agents could be affected in "real" allocational terms. As it turns out, provided one completely accounts for the effect of all firms trading strategies simultaneously on the dividends and share prices of all firms, the marketed subspace is not actually affected by shifts in the financial policy of firms. For any change in a firm's financial policy in equilibrium, there is indeed a new equilibrium with the same allocations and valuation of securities. We state this extension of the *Modigliani–Miller Theorem* more carefully.

MODIGLIANI–MILLER THEOREM (PART II). *Let $((q, \psi), (\theta_i, x_i), (\gamma_j, y_j))$ be an equilibrium for the economy $(\mathcal{E}, (\Xi, \mathcal{A}))$. Let $(\widehat{\gamma}_1, \ldots, \widehat{\gamma}_J)$ be any regular set of trading strategies for the firms. Then there exist trading* *strategies* $(\widehat{\theta}_1, \ldots, \widehat{\theta}_I)$ *for agents such that* $(q, \psi, (\widehat{\theta}_i, x_i), (y_j, \widehat{\gamma}_j))$ *is also an equilibrium.*

The proof, left as an exercise, can easily be extended in a number of directions, for example, the inclusion of additional zero–net–supply securities such as bonds and forward contracts. To repeat, a new financial trading strategy for any firm (or alternatively, a new dividend strategy) can be embedded in a new equilibrium without changes in consumption allocations. Agents can counteract potentially adverse budget effects of a firm's financial policy changes by making compensating changes in their own portfolio strategies, without real effects. Furthermore, it is optimal for agents to do so.

F.   The *market value process*

$$V_j = \{V_j(\xi) = S_j(\xi) - \gamma_j(\xi_-) \cdot S(\xi) : \ \xi \in \Xi\}$$

of firm j is the sum of its equity value and total debt. Under the assumptions of Theorem 13D the market value process of a firm does not depend on its financial policy given a production plan y_j. This could be stated as a corollary to both Theorem 13D and Theorem 13E, but we choose the latter for simplicity. Proof is again left as an exercise.

COROLLARY. *Further to the statement of Theorem 13E, the market value process of any firm* j *for the original equilibrium* $((q, \psi), (\theta_i, x_i), (\gamma_j, y_j))$ *is identical to the market value process of firm* j *in the new equilibrium* $((q, \psi), (\widehat{\theta}_i, x_i), (\widehat{\gamma}_j, y_j))$.

G.   We could easily extend our model to include more than a single security issued by any given firm. Many firms introduce, in addition to an equity or common share security, their own corporate bonds, preferred shares of various classes, convertible bonds, and so on. Usually the dividend processes for these corporate securities are defined jointly in some precedence relation, with the common shares claiming the residual value. With care in modeling their joint definition, one can avoid complications when bankruptcy is considered. (This idea is picked up in Paragraph H.)

The decision to issue (or retire) securities, as distinct from their sale or purchase, is itself an important financial decision. By augmenting (or deleting from) the set of securities, a firm can change the marketed subspace M of "reachable" consumption processes. This can have wide–ranging consequences. Whether such a change will help or hurt particular shareholders in the movement to a new equilibrium is a complex issue, beyond the domain of our current analytical ability. With a complete marketed subspace

$M = L$, issuing new securities has no real effects. Provided the marketed subspace cannot be made incomplete by retiring a security, this action is also free of real effects. By "no real effects", we mean there exists a new equilibrium embedding the financial alterations with the original equilibrium allocation.

In any case, taking the spot price process ψ and the state price process q as given, issuing securities has no effect on the initial share price of the firm. To see this, we merely note that the functional $[\Lambda_q(\cdot)](\xi^1)$ assigning an initial market value to dividend processes is linear. By issuing a financial security $\delta \in F_1$, any firm j with a plan (γ_j, y_j) has the new initial share value

$$[\Lambda_q(\psi \,\square\, d^{\gamma_j} - \delta)](\xi^1) + [\Lambda_q(\delta)](\xi^1) = [\Lambda_q(\psi \,\square\, y_j)](\xi^1), \tag{5}$$

where the left hand side is the initial market value of the dividend stream generated by the plan (γ_j, y_j) after paying out δ, plus the initial value received for the sale of δ. Equality with the right hand side follows from linearity of Λ_q and by Theorem 13D. Thus financial policy is completely irrelevant for share value, taking prices as given.

As long as short selling is permitted, any adjustment in the production plan of a firm can have a major effect on an economy regardless of the number and size of firms and agents (not taking prices as given). With a short sales restriction, however, one may expect that a change in a firm's plan would have a relatively small effect on the overall economy if the firm itself is small.

It has been implicit in the analysis that firms and individuals have common access to security markets. In reality, bilateral contracts such as individualized loans are popular. We have spoken of firms (but not individual agents) introducing new securities. How the structure of security markets is determined has been left out of the story. Presumably entrepreneurs balance the costs of setting up and maintaining a market, enforcing security contracts, and executing trades, against the profits to be made by selling transactions services to potential traders who may benefit from the addition of securities. A simple example is cited in the Notes.

The results of Section 7 on efficiency with incomplete markets are easily extended to this stochastic setting via the connection between static and stochastic equilibria established in Section 12. A stochastic equilibrium given firms' plans is M–constrained efficient, where M is the marketed subspace, under mild conditions. The Notes, however, cite work indicating generic failure of a stronger sense of constrained efficiency in a production equilibrium.

H.   At this point some comments on the tyranny of complete and symmetric models of contingencies seem called for. A naïve but reasonable question about this whole exercise might be: "How should agent i be expected to know in advance precisely the endowment $\omega_i(\xi)$, the dividend vector $d(\xi)$, the spot price vector $\psi(\xi)$, and the security price vector $S(\xi)$, for each vertex ξ in the event tree?" It is with little choice but probably some embarrassment that the modeler should respond, "If, for example, the dividend $d(\xi)$ at vertex ξ is not known in advance by all agents, then we're simply barking up the wrong event tree. If $d(\xi)$ is a random variable with, say, fifty possible outcomes then we must replace this event tree $(\Xi, \mathcal{A})$ with one having fifty different vertices in place of ξ. If at some point the dividend paid by a security is a random variable with an uncountable set of potential outcomes, then we must scrap the notion of using an event tree model of contingencies, and move on to more general models." This glib response seems unsatisfactory. None of us have a complete description of how the state of the world evolves, event tree or otherwise, in which every relevant piece of information for our choice problem is catalogued contingency by contingency, date by date. Even if we did, our models would not likely be the same. This lack of a perfect model for information and inattention to computational limitations and costs is not a special feature of stochastic market theory; it pervades most of economic theory. Readers must deal with this on their own terms.

Just as it is difficult to imagine how individual agents make the same spot price conjectures without the aid of a Walrasian auctioneer, so is it difficult to accept a model of market valuation by firms in which all firms choose the same state–price vector without coordination.

The fact that $(\Xi, \mathcal{A})$ is assumed to be an exhaustive model of contingencies also explains why bankruptcy does not interfere with our analysis. No firm, for example, could default on payments due a bondholder. If some firm has sold a security ("bond") promising to pay a dividend of, say, $d(\xi) = 1$ at vertex ξ, and the holder of this security is at risk because the firm may not be able to make that payment, then something is wrong with the definition of $d(\xi)$ or ξ. Vertex ξ signals a complete description of the financial position of the firm in question at that vertex. Either the firm is able to pay a unit dividend to each such bondholder at ξ (and every agent knows this), or it cannot, and every agent knows that this bond actually pays some specific dividend less than unity at vertex ξ. Every security is treated by agents as a claim to "actual" rather than "advertised" dividends. It may be embarrassing to rely on this tautology so conveniently, but one has no other choice in a model presumed to include all relevant contingencies.

I. The objectives of a firm are difficult to characterize in incomplete markets. An easy justification for the criterion of market value maximization can be given only when the firm cannot change the subspace of the choice space spanned by trade. In that case, every positive shareholder supports market value maximization as the firm's objective, since the firm affects shareholders only insofar as their initial budgets. A larger budget implies a larger set of budget feasible choices, and therefore a superior consumption choice. That is, if regardless of the actions of firm j the marketed subspace M is the entire choice space L, then a production process y_j maximizing the total initial value of firm j is optimal for every initial shareholder. By maintaining the same production plan y_j, firm j also maximizes its total market value $V_j(\xi)$ at each vertex $\xi \in \Xi$. Total value, however, is not equity value. Under the conditions of Proposition 12F, at each vertex ξ, positive equity shareholders nevertheless agree on the same value maximizing production plan at ξ. In short, in a stochastically complete markets equilibrium, at each vertex every positive shareholder of a firm supports market value maximization. Suppose, on the other hand, that by adjusting its production plan, a firm can shift the marketed subspace M. If shareholders do not take account of this possibility, and instead take the marketed subspace M as given, then once again shareholders unanimously support market value maximizing production choices by firms. If shareholders do not take M as given, however, they generally disagree with market value maximization (as indicated in a paper cited in the Notes), and indeed disagree with one another. As we have already pointed out, even if one accepts the goal of market value maximization by firms, the goal is difficult to implement without a model determining state prices, and there is currently no indication of how to pick a particular state–price vector in the absence of complete markets.

In general, let us suppose that initial shareholders acting by some unspecified group decision mechanism have directed firm j to adopt a particular production–financial plan. Shareholders at a subsequent vertex, of course, have the ability to revise this plan to suit their own interests. Future shareholders will not, however, revise the plan to the detriment of original shareholders. Original shareholders have chosen from the set of plans supported by subsequent shareholders. This is an incentive compatibility constraint. More precisely, original shareholders choose from those plans that, if overturned, are not revised to the detriment of original shareholders. It would be irrational folly, for example, for today's shareholders to map out a plan for the firm meeting their best interests in each future contingency, but failing to be supported in some contingencies by tomorrow's shareholders. The reasoning, at a crude level, is as follows. Suppose there is a single firm and security markets consist entirely of that firm's common share. The firm's only current decision is therefore current production. We suppose that, for any given distribution of shareholders of the firm at a given terminal vertex and any previous history of the economy, there is a unique outcome of the terminal shareholders' final period production decision. At each penultimate vertex, and each possible history of the economy up to that vertex, a given action by current shareholders thus induces a corresponding action by terminal shareholders at each terminal vertex, as stated in the previous sentence. The penultimate shareholders will then formulate a two period production plan that can be continued by terminal shareholders as a one period plan. The analysis continues by backward induction to the root vertex, and original shareholders choose from the set of "sequentially incentive compatible" production plans. Of course uniqueness of choice presents a problem. If shareholders at a future vertex are indifferent between two production choices, but original shareholders are not indifferent, the event tree must be enlarged to account for this endogenous piece of uncertainty. Similarly, if agents' trading strategies are not uniquely determined, uncertainty governing the distribution of shares at a given vertex may also force enlargement of the tree. If carried out formally, the analysis might be intractable. The principle remains, however, that a production plan chosen rationally by initial shareholders should not theoretically be revised to their strict disadvantage.

EXERCISES

EXERCISE 13.1 Suppose y^j solves the initial market value maximization problem (1) of firm j. Let $\xi \in \Xi$ be arbitrary, and let $Y_j(\xi) = \{y \in Y_j : \forall \eta \notin \Xi(\xi), \quad y(\eta) = y_j(\eta)\}$. Thus $Y_j(\xi)$ is the set of feasible production processes that are consistent with y_j up until vertex ξ. Show that y_j also solves the *current market value maximization* problem:

$$\max_{y \in Y_j(\xi)} \quad [\Lambda_1(\psi \square y)](\xi).$$

Thus maximizing initial market value is identical with maximizing current market value at all times and in all states of the world.

EXERCISE 13.2 Verify the solution (2) to the market value maximizing production choices for the example of Paragraph B.

EXERCISE 13.3 Verify the first order conditions (3) to the problem of agent i in the example of Paragraph B.

EXERCISE 13.4   Prove Lemma 13C. *Hint:* Calculate the dividends and share prices of the firms vertex by vertex recursively from terminal vertices.

EXERCISE 13.5   Prove Theorem 13D, Part I of the Modigliani–Miller Theorem. *Hint:* Show as a preliminary lemma that if S is the security price process for $\gamma = 0$ and S' is the security price process for some regular trading strategies $\gamma = (\gamma_1, \ldots, \gamma_J)$, then $S'(\xi) = [I - \gamma(\xi_-)]^{-1} S(\xi)$ for any vertex $\xi \in \Xi$.

EXERCISE 13.6   Prove Theorem 13E, Part II of the Modigliani–Miller Theorem. *Hint:* Use the lemma suggested in the previous exercise to construct the agents' "new" trading strategies.

EXERCISE 13.7   Prove Lemma 13F.

Notes

The surveys of Kreps (1979) and Hart (1987), and Marimon (1987) may be consulted for some of the literature on material going beyond that surveyed in this section. The theory has not settled into a satisfactory whole by any means. Early notable papers are those by Diamond (1967), Drèze (1974), and Ekern and Wilson (1974). The second generation of literature, not taking the marketed space as fixed, is represented by Grossman and Stiglitz (1976), Grossman and Hart (1979), and other papers by these economists. A third generation, deriving "competitive" assumptions under which the goal of the firm is value maximization, includes for example Hart (1979a, 1979b), Makowski (1983), and Haller (1984). A general model of the decisions of the firm in incomplete markets remains to be settled. Another unresolved issue is the effect of the limited liability restriction, largely ignored here, which leads to a theory in which the financial policy of the firm is important in supporting production choices that must otherwise involve negative dividends. Conditions for generic existence of stock market equilibria for the model given in Paragraph A are found in Duffie and Shafer (1986b), as is the example of Paragraph B. Existence conditions in Radner's setting are given by Burke (1986). The infinite multiplicity of allocations in this example is a generic property of the general model of Duffie and Shafer (1986b) under incomplete markets. Lemma 13C is from Duffie and Shafer (1986b), as is Theorem 13D. The (better) proof of Theorem 13D suggested in Exercise 13.5 is due to DeMarzo (1986), as is Theorem 13E. The original versions of these results are due to Modigliani and Miller (1958). For other versions, see Stiglitz (1972, 1974), Fama (1978), and Hellwig (1981). Lemma 13F is an obvious extension of a result in Modigliani and Miller (1958). The endogenous market structure example mentioned in Paragraph 13G is in Duffie and Jackson (1986b). A recent addition to this literature is due to Allen and Gale (1987).

The firms' objective, in the existence results of Drèze (1974) and Grossman and Hart (1979), are of the form: maximize a "pseudo–value" given by taking prices to be the sum of shareholders' "marginal rates of substitution" for future consumption, weighted by shareholdings. The pseudo–prices will thus differ according to the firm under consideration. This style of objective leads to difficulties in the multi–period setting, as indicated in Paragraph I. The "state–price" formulation used in Paragraph A can be traced back to the revision of Arrow (1953) published in Arrow (197), and suffers from the lack of a model for the determination of state prices. Here, state prices are effectively "announced by an auctioneer" in the Walrasian tradition. The set of state prices consistent with arbitrage–free pricing and equilibrium with incomplete markets is multi–dimensional. Breeden and Litzenberger (1978) have shown a method of calculating consistent state prices from the values of options, but this implicitly assumes complete markets. Since different firms can compute different consistent state prices in incomplete markets, the problem of state price determination calls for further investigation.

The result of competitive disagreement of shareholders with market value maximization referred to in Paragraph I is from Duffie and Shafer (1986b). The inefficiency of production allocations in incomplete markets is well known. Drèze (1976) is an excellent introduction. Stiglitz (1982) is a typical inefficiency result. Geanakoplos, Magill, Quinzii, and Drèze (1987) show the failure of constrained efficiency in a sense extended from Geanakoplos and Polemarchakis (1986).

Recently, more attention has been focused on the capital structure of the firm, for example by Aghion and Bolton (1986), Grossman and Hart (1987), Harris and Raviv (1987), Hart (1987), and Shah and Thakor (1987).

14. Stochastic Processes

This section expands our ability to model dynamics under uncertainty, or "stochastics", beyond the event tree paradigm of Sections 12 and 13. The central concept here is the *filtration*, an abstract model of the revelation of information through time.

A.   Let T denote an ordered set of positive real numbers; T is the *time set*. In *continuous–time*, we might have $T = [0, \infty)$; for *discrete–time*, $T = \{0, 1, 2, \ldots\}$; variations are common. We take the first element of T

to be 0. Let Ω denote the relevant set of "states of the world." A *filtration* (for Ω and T) is a family $F = \{\mathcal{F}_t : t \in T\}$ of tribes on Ω. A filtration is a complete specification of the revelation of information through time. For example, if some subset A of Ω is an element of the tribe $\mathcal{F}_t$, then at time t, intuitively speaking, one "knows" whether the "correct" state of the world is an element of A, that is, whether A is "true" or "false". To formalize the notion that such a fact is never forgotten, we always assume that a filtration F is *increasing* or $\mathcal{F}_t \subset \mathcal{F}_s$ whenever $s \geq t$.

B.   Let Z denote a measurable outcome space. Typically $Z = R^d$ for some integer dimension d. A Z–valued *stochastic process* is merely a function, say X, mapping $\Omega \times T$ into Z. One speaks of $X(\omega, t) \in Z$ as the outcome of X in state $\omega \in \Omega$ at time $t \in T$, and $X(\cdot, t) : \Omega \to Z$ (also denoted "$X(t)$" or "X_t") as the (random) value of X at time t. This definition of a stochastic process is rather barren, making no connection between the value of a process at a particular time and how uncertainty about that value is resolved. This connection is made by defining the process X to be *adapted* to the filtration $F = \{\mathcal{F}_t : t \in T\}$ provided X_t is measurable with respect to $\mathcal{F}_t$ for all t in T. In other terms, X is adapted if, for any time t, X_t is a random variable on $(\Omega, \mathcal{F}_t)$. The economic significance of adaptedness is crucial. First, this is an informational restriction on actions by agents. A filtration F is the general model of how information is revealed to agents through time. Any action the agent takes can only depend on the available information. The phrase: "action X_t depends only on information available at time t" is merely an informal way of stating that the function X_t on Ω is measurable with respect to $\mathcal{F}_t$. If $X = \{X_t : t \in T\}$ is a stochastic process describing actions taken through time, a minimum informational restriction is therefore that X must be F–adapted. Adaptedness is similarly a criterion for determining whether a given stochastic process is "observed" by a given agent. If the agent's information filtration is F and a given stochastic process X is F adapted, then the outcome of X_t may be treated as information known by this agent at a given time t.

Example.   (Two Coin Tosses in Sequence). Let $\Omega = \{HH, HT, TH, TT\}$, where HT is mnemonic for "Heads followed by Tails", and so on. We take the time set $T = \{0, 1, 2\}$ and construct the filtration corresponding to the information received by observing the first coin toss at time 1 and the second at time 2. The associated event tree is illustrated in Figure 14.1. At time 0, "nothing" is known, so $\mathcal{F}_0 = \{\Omega, \emptyset\}$. Initially, that is, there are no events other than Ω and the null set that an observer of the coin tosses can claim to know as being true or false. Suppose that the first toss (at time 1) is revealed to be heads. Then an observer knows that the event $\{HH, HT\}$

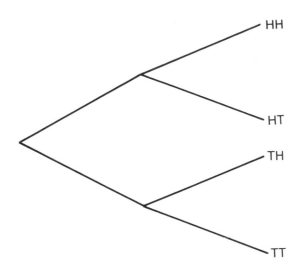

Figure 14.1   The Two–Coin–Toss Event Tree

is true and that the event $\{TH, TT\}$ is false. Similarly, if the outcome of
the first toss is tails, these same two events have known outcomes. An
observer could not say at this stage whether the event $\{HH\}$, for example,
is true or false; that remains to be observed at time 2. At time 1, then, the
relevant tribe of events is $\mathcal{F}_1 = \{\Omega, \emptyset, \{HH, HT\}, \{TH, TT\}\}$. At time 2,
every possible event is known, and $\mathcal{F}_2 = 2^\Omega$, the set of all subsets of Ω.

Suppose X is a stochastic process describing, say, a time stream of
"payoffs" depending on the coin tosses. At each time t in $\mathcal{T}$ there are
two possible payoffs, zero and one, so we let the outcome space Z be
$\{0, 1\}$, with measurable subsets $Z, \emptyset$, (the empty set) $\{0\}$, and $\{1\}$. The
relevant payoff at time 1 is the random variable X_1, and the outcome
of X_1 can only depend on information known at that time: whether the
first toss is heads or tails. In other words, X_1 must be measurable with
respect to $\mathcal{F}_1$. It would be wrongheaded, for instance, to assign payoffs
$X(HH, 1) = 1$ and $X(HT, 1) = 0$, for how could X_1 depend non–trivially
on information revealed by the coin toss only at time 2? Indeed, it is
easily checked that this X_1 is not measurable with respect to $\mathcal{F}_1$ and that
the corresponding stochastic process X of payoffs is therefore not adapted
to $F = \{\mathcal{F}_0, \mathcal{F}_1, \mathcal{F}_2\}$. Of course, if the filtration $G = \{\mathcal{G}_0, \mathcal{G}_1, \mathcal{G}_2\}$ is constructed by setting $\mathcal{G}_0 = \mathcal{G}_1 = \mathcal{G}_2 = \mathcal{F}_2$, then any Z–valued stochastic process is G–adapted. With information revealed by G, however, one knows
the outcome of both coin tosses at time 0, which is not our intention. ♠

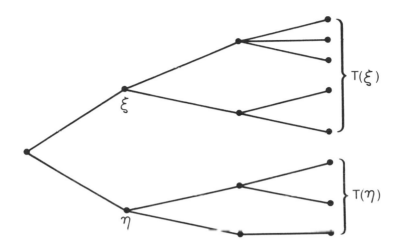

Figure 14.2   An Event Tree

C.   Without other guidance about the filtration under consideration, a stochastic process X is usually discussed in the context of the filtration it generates: $F^X = \{\mathcal{F}_t^X : t \in T\}$, where $\mathcal{F}_t^X = \sigma(\{X_s : 0 \leq s \leq t\})$ for all t in T. We recall from Section 4 that $\sigma(\{X_s : 0 \leq s \leq t\})$ denotes the tribe on Ω generated by the family of functions $\{X_s : 0 < s < t\}$ on Ω. As a crude illustration, if the event A is in $\mathcal{F}_t^X$ then one will know at time t whether or not A is "true" by observing the past behavior of the process X. The filtration generated by a given stochastic process may be treated as a model of the information received through time by observing that process. By definition, a stochastic process is adapted to the filtration it generates.

We turn to the filtration generated by an event tree, taking a discrete–time set $T = \{0, 1, \ldots\}$ for simplicity. This merely formalizes the previous example. We take an event tree $(\Xi, \mathcal{A})$ and the terminology surrounding it devised in Section 12. For any vertex ξ in Ξ, let $T(\xi)$ denote the set of terminal vertices in the sub–tree $\Xi(\xi)$, as illustrated in Figure 14.2. The set of all terminal vertices in Ξ is then $\Omega \equiv T(\xi^1)$, where ξ^1 is the root vertex of Ξ. We associate time $0 \in T$ with the root vertex ξ^1, time 1 with each successor vertex of ξ^1, time 2 with each immediate successor of any of the successor vertices of ξ^1, and so on. Let ξ^t denote the subset of vertices associated with time $t \in T$, and let Λ_t denote the partition $\{T(\xi) : \xi \in \xi^t\}$ of Ω, recalling the definition of a partition from Section 4. (We can always extend the tree without changing its informational content so that every

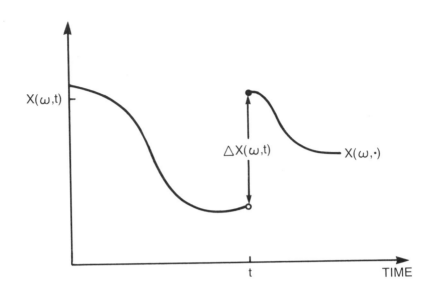

Figure 14.3   A Right–Continuous Left–Limits Sample Path

path from the root vertex to a terminal vertex includes the same number of vertices.) The filtration generated by Ξ is then $F = \{\mathcal{F}_t = \sigma(\Lambda_t) : t \in T\}$, remembering that $\sigma(\Lambda_t)$ is the tribe on Ω generated by the partition Λ_t. In Example 14B, for instance, $\Lambda_1 = \{\{HH, HT\}, \{TH, TT\}\}$, and $\mathcal{F}_1 = \sigma(\Lambda_1)$.

Any specific filtration we will discuss is generated either by a stochastic process or by an event tree.

D.   If f is a real–valued function of a real interval, the notation $\lim_{s\downarrow t} f(s)$ means the limit, when it exists, of any sequence $\{f(s_n)\}$, where $\{s_n\}$ is a sequence of scalars strictly larger than t converging to t. In continuous–time, a real–valued stochastic process X is *right–continuous* provided, for each state ω in Ω, the "ω–sample path" function $X(\omega, \cdot) : T \to R$, is right–continuous, meaning that for any time t, $\lim_{s\downarrow t} X(\omega, s) = X(\omega, t)$. A sample path of a right–continuous process is illustrated in Figure 14.3. Similarly, X is a *left–limits* process provided, for each ω in Ω, the sample path $X(\omega, \cdot)$ is a left–limits function on T, meaning that $\lim_{s\uparrow t} X(\omega, s)$ exists for all t in T, ignoring $t = 0$. The sample path depicted in Figure 14.3 is also a left–limits function. The definitions of *left–continuous* and *right–limits* are then the obvious analogues.

A stochastic process that is both right–continuous and left–limits is labeled *RCLL*. One commonly hears the term càdlàg (for "*continué à droite, limité à gauche"*) in place of RCLL, and occasionally the term *Skorohod* (for an associated mathematician). If X is an RCLL process, X_{t-} denotes the left limit of X at time t (sample path by sample path), and $\Delta X_t \equiv X_t - X_{t-}$ denotes the "jump" of X at time t, again illustrated in Figure 14.3. By convention, $X_{0-} \equiv X_0$. A *continuous* process is a stochastic process all of whose sample paths are continuous functions of time. An *increasing* process is a stochastic process all of whose sample paths are increasing functions of time. We are implicitly speaking of real–valued processes here; the extensions of the definitions to Euclidean–valued processes are the obvious ones.

A filtration $F = \{\mathcal{F}_t : t \in T\}$ is *right–continuous* provided $\mathcal{F}_t = \bigcap_{s>t} \mathcal{F}_s$ for all t in T. Continuing to provide loosely worded interpretations: One receives information from a right–continuous filtration provided, for any time t, any information known at all times after t is also known at time t. This definition is interesting only in continuous–time settings.

E. Now we add probability to the story. Let $(\Omega, \mathcal{F}, P)$ be a probability space and, for some time set T, let $F = \{\mathcal{F}_t : t \in T\}$ denote a filtration of sub–tribes of $\mathcal{F}$. The quadruple $(\Omega, \mathcal{F}, F, P)$ is a *filtered probability space*, a highly compact notation for a completely abstract model of multiperiod uncertainty. Once given a particular filtered probability space, we relax the definitions of right–continuous, left–continuous, continuous, and increasing processes to include those adapted processes having the respective properties almost surely.

For technical reasons, we sometimes replace the filtration $F = \{\mathcal{F}_t : t \in T\}$ with the *augmented* filtration $F^\sim = \{\mathcal{F}_t^\sim : t \in T\}$, where $\mathcal{F}_t^\sim$ denotes the tribe generated by the union of $\mathcal{F}_t$ and all subsets of zero probability elements of $\mathcal{F}$. This is analogous to the completion of a tribe. Since the continuous–time assumptions that a filtration is increasing, right–continuous, and augmented are so common, they have an official name: *the usual conditions*.

An *integrable process* is an adapted real–valued process X such that $E(|X_t|)$ is finite for all $t \in T$. A *martingale* (with respect to $(\Omega, \mathcal{F}, F, P)$) is an integrable process X with the property: $E(X_t \mid \mathcal{F}_s) = X_s$ a.s. whenever $t > s$. The essence of a martingale is that its conditional expected future value is its current value, for any future and current times.

F. We now review two basic classes of stochastic processes: *Brownian Motion* and *Poisson* processes. We fix a probability space $(\Omega, \mathcal{F}, P)$ and the continuous–time set $T = [0, \infty)$. A real–valued stochastic process B is a *Standard Brownian Motion* on $(\Omega, \mathcal{F}, P)$ provided:

(a) for any $0 \le s < t < \infty$, $B_t - B_s$ is a normally distributed random variable with expected value equal to zero and variance equal to $t - s$,

(b) for any $0 \le t_0 < t_1 < \cdots < t_l < \infty$, the random variables $B(t_0)$ and $B(t_k) - B(t_{k-1})$, $1 \le k \le l$, are independent, and

(c) $P(\{B_0 = 0\}) = 1$.

No filtration has been mentioned! Without guidance on this point one usually discusses a Brownian Motion B on the filtration $F = \{\mathcal{F}_t : t \in [0, \infty)\}$ where $\mathcal{F}_t = \sigma(\{B_s : 0 \le s \le t\})^\sim$, the augmented filtration generated by B, which is sometimes called the *standard* or *natural* filtration of B. In this setting of course, B is a martingale and a continuous process. A *Standard Brownian Motion in R^d*, for some integer dimension d, is an R^d–valued stochastic process $B = (B^1, \ldots, B^d)$, where B^i is a Standard Brownian Motion for each $i \in \{1, \ldots, d\}$, and where the processes $B^1, \ldots, B^d$ are independent.

A real–valued stochastic process N is a *Poisson process* on $(\Omega, \mathcal{F}, P)$ with parameter $\lambda > 0$ provided:

(a) for any $0 \le s < t < \infty$, $N_t - N_s$ is a random variable with Poisson distribution having expected value $\lambda(t - s)$,

(b) for any $0 \le t_0 < t_1 < \cdots < t_l < \infty$, the random variables $N(t_0)$ and $N(t_k) - N(t_{k-1})$, $1 \le k \le l$, are independent, and

(c) $P\{N_0 = 0\} = 1$.

Again, without other guidance, a Poisson process is usually discussed with respect to its standard filtration. In that case, the process $\{N_t - \lambda t : t \ge 0\}$ is a martingale.

G.   For a given filtered probability space $(\Omega, \mathcal{F}, F, P)$ on a time set $\mathcal{T}$, a positive real–valued random variable τ is a *stopping time* provided the event $\{\omega \in \Omega : \tau(\omega) \le t\}$ is in $\mathcal{F}_t$ for all t in $\mathcal{T}$. If X is an F–adapted process and τ is a stopping time, then X^τ denotes the process X "stopped" at time τ. That is, $X^\tau(t) = X(t)$ for all $t \le \tau$ and $X^\tau(t) = X(\tau)$ for all $t > \tau$. Another common notation for $X^\tau(t)$ is $X_{\tau \wedge t}$, since $Y \wedge Z$ denotes the random variable $\min\{Y, Z\}$ for any two real–valued random variables Y and Z.

We can characterize processes that are "locally" in a particular class using the stopping concept. For example, an adapted process X is a *local martingale* if there exists a sequence $\{\tau_1, \tau_2, \ldots\}$ of stopping times such that $\tau_n \le \tau_{n+1}$ almost surely for all n with $\lim_{n \to \infty} \tau_n = \infty$ almost surely, and for which X^{τ_n} is a martingale for each n. In particular, a martingale is a local martingale.

We next define semimartingales, perhaps the most general type of stochastic security price process for which one can define gains from trading securities. First, Y is a *finite variation process* if $Y = A - B$, where A and B are increasing adapted processes. A *semimartingale* is a stochastic process X of the form $X = M + Y$ where M is a local martingale and Y is a finite variation process. In discrete–time, every adapted process is a semimartingale.

EXERCISES

EXERCISE 14.1 Prove that the "wrongheaded payoff" process X of Example 14B is not adapted to the filtration F constructed there, where we recall that $X(HH, 1) = 1$ and $X(HT, 1) = 0$.

EXERCISE 14.2 Construct the filtration $F = \{\mathcal{F}_t : t \in \mathcal{T}\}$ generated by the coin toss information of Example 14B for the continuum time set $\mathcal{T} = [0, 2.5]$, ensuring that the filtration is right–continuous. That is, state the elements of $\mathcal{F}_t$ for each $t \in [0, 2.5]$.

EXERCISE 14.3 Suppose $N = \{N_t : t \geq 0\}$ is a Poisson process on some probability space with parameter $\lambda = 1$. Verify that $\{N_t - t : t > 0\}$ is a martingale with respect to the filtration generated by N.

EXERCISE 14.4 Consider the following description. "An economy can be in any of three mutually exclusive states in any period. There is an initial period and two subsequent periods. Label the states 1 for good, 2 for average, and 3 for bad. An agent learns information by observing the state of the economy in each period, starting at the initial period in an average state. The transitions between states are independent events with probabilities given by the following transition matrix:

$$\pi = \begin{pmatrix} 0.3 & 0.3 & 0.4 \\ 0.4 & 0.2 & 0.4 \\ 0.3 & 0.3 & 0.4 \end{pmatrix},$$

where π_{ij} denotes the probability of the economy changing from state i to state j in one period. Let a security have a dividend process d that pays two units of dividends whenever the economy is in a good state, one unit in an average state, and nothing in a bad state."

The above scenario has a reasonably clear economic interpretation. Formalize this scenario by constructing a filtered probability space and time set $\mathcal{T}$ consistent with the above description. (There are actually two obvious ways to do this; either is acceptable.) Completely specify the stochastic process describing the dividend process d, as well as the stochastic process G describing at each period the current conditional expected value of the total of all past, current, and future dividends. Prove that G is a martingale.

EXERCISE 14.5 Let Ω be a finite set and $F = \{\mathcal{F}_0, \mathcal{F}_1, \ldots, \mathcal{F}_T\}$ be a filtration of tribes on Ω with $\mathcal{F}_0 = \{\Omega, \emptyset\}$. Construct the event tree determined by F in the obvious way.

EXERCISE 14.6 Show that a martingale is a local martingale. This is intended to be easy.

Notes

This section is mainly interpretive. The definitions, and many implications ignored here, can be found in any mathematical treatment of stochastic processes, for example Chung and Williams (1983) or Durrett (1984). The definition of the filtration generated by an event tree is certainly not the most reasonable one if each vertex in the tree is already primitively associated with an element of a given time set. In that case, the construction of a filtration is also a simple exercise. Advanced abstract sources on stochastic processes include Dellacherie and Meyer (1978, 1982) and Jacod (1979).

15. Stochastic Integrals and Gains From Security Trade

Economists have used many models for the stochastic process describing cumulative financial gains from security trade, taking as data the stochastic processes defining the market values and dividends of the securities themselves, as well as the processes describing the number of units of each security held at each time. All of these models are equivalent to stochastic integration. The stochastic integral will be motivated here at a basic level. Subsequent sections will add properties and generalizations. In particular, Section 21 outlines the Ito calculus, the theory of integration with respect to Brownian Motion.

A.   First we take the easiest case, discrete–time. A probability space $(\Omega, \mathcal{F}, P)$, the time set $\mathcal{T} = \{0, 1, 2, \ldots\}$, and a filtration $F = \{\mathcal{F}_t : t \in \mathcal{T}\}$ of sub–tribes of $\mathcal{F}$ are fixed for this paragraph. For simplicity alone, we assume that $\mathcal{F}_0$ is *trivial*, that is, $\mathcal{F}_0 = \{\Omega, \emptyset\}$. Let S be a real–valued F–adapted stochastic process. For readers tracking the parallel stories of gain from trade and stochastic integration, the random variable S_t may be thought of as the market value of a given security at time t. For a simple story, we assume the security pays no dividends. The equilibrium model of Section 16 incorporates dividends.

A stochastic process is *predictable*, in this discrete–time setting, if adapted to the filtration $G = \{\mathcal{G}_t : t \in \mathcal{T}\}$, where $\mathcal{G}_t = \mathcal{F}_{t-1}$ for $t \geq 1$, and $\mathcal{G}_0$ is trivial. A process θ is predictable, in interpretation, if θ_t can be chosen on the basis of information available at time $t - 1$. For convenience, whenever we say "predictable" in this section we also mean real–valued. In the security trading story, a predictable process θ might describe the number of units of the security held, θ_t units at time t. The gain in value realized from time $t - 1$ to time t is $\theta_t(S_t - S_{t-1})$, the amount held multiplied by the change in the market value of the security. If one is not limited to predictable trading strategies, and could choose an arbitrary F–adapted "trading strategy" process θ, one could select θ_t on the basis of all information available at time t, including $S_t - S_{t-1}$. If $S_t - S_{t-1} \neq 0$, the gain $\theta_t(S_t - S_{t-1})$ could then be made arbitrarily large. It is essentially for this reason that the predictable class of processes is appropriate for trading strategies.

For any $T \in \mathcal{T}$ let

$$\left(\int \theta \, dS \right)_T \equiv \int_0^T \theta \, dS \equiv \sum_{t=1}^T \theta_t(S_t - S_{t-1}). \tag{1}$$

The process $\int \theta \, dS$ defined by (1) for $T = 1, 2, \ldots$, is the *stochastic integral* of θ with respect to S, taking $(\int \theta \, dS)_0 = 0$ as a convention. The notation should be suggestive: "$\int$" is for "sum" (or "$\sum$"); and "dS" is for "difference" (or "$S_t - S_{t-1}$"). We will write $\int \theta_t \, dS_t$ interchangeably with $\int \theta \, dS$.

Major parts of the theories of stochastic integration and financial gains from trade revolve around the case of a martingale integrator S. If the price process S is a martingale, we want a theory in which $\int \theta \, dS$ is also a martingale under appropriate regularity conditions. It must be viewed as a pathology to trade a security that never has expected changes in value using a trading strategy yielding non–zero expected gains from trade. A process θ is *bounded* if there is a scalar K such that $| \theta(\omega, t) | \leq K$ for all (ω, t) in $\Omega \times \mathcal{T}$. The reader is asked to prove the following result as an exercise.

PROPOSITION. *Suppose S is a martingale and θ is a bounded predictable process. Then $\int \theta \, dS$ is a martingale.*

Boundedness is a regularity condition that can be relaxed; it provides inte-grability. Predictability is an informational restriction of particular interest to economists. All of this is obvious in discrete–time, but it pays to limber up one's intuition for the following extension to continuous–time.

B.   We fix the time set T as either a real interval $[0, T]$ or $[0, \infty)$, mak-ing a specific choice whenever convenient. Let $(\Omega, \mathcal{F}, P)$ be a complete probability space and $F = \{\mathcal{F}_t : t \in T\}$ be a filtration of sub–tribes of $\mathcal{F}$ satisfying *usual conditions*, as defined in Paragraph 14E. The filtered probability space $(\Omega, \mathcal{F}, F, P)$ is the ambient frame of reference for the re-mainder of this section.

Two adapted processes X and Y are *versions* of one another if $X_t = Y_t$ almost surely for each t in T. It saves a lot of ink and costs little in understanding to identify martingales with a common version as the same process. That is, if X and Y are martingales and $P(\{X_t = Y_t\}) = 1$ for all t in T, then X and Y are treated as the same process; we write "$X = Y$". It turns out that every martingale has an RCLL version. It is convenient, whenever the need to deal with sample paths arises, to work with a fixed RCLL version of each martingale. The reader will not be reminded that this is now our practice.

A martingale S is *square–integrable* if S_t^2 is an integrable random variable for all t in T. This integrability condition, that the variance of S_t is finite for all t, is a technical expedient. Given a square–integrable martingale S, our goal is to specify a class of processes such that, for any θ in this class, there is a construction $\int \theta \, dS$ making reasonable sense as a stochastic integral. We also want the continuous–time analogue to Proposition 15A: the process $\int \theta \, dS$ should be a martingale under regularity conditions. To this end, we add a couple of definitions to our arsenal. First comes an appropriate definition of "predictable" for continuous–time. Let $\mathcal{P}$ denote the tribe on $\Omega \times T$ generated by the set of left–continuous adapted processes. A stochastic process (which, after all, is no more than a function on $\Omega \times T$) is *predictable* if $\mathcal{P}$–measurable. The left–continuity condition is the analogue to our discrete–time definition of predictable. One can "predict" the value of a left–continuous process in the sense that, given the sample path of the process up to but not including any time t, the value of the process at time t is known to be the left–limit of the sample path at t. We note, however, that a predictable process need not itself be left–continuous, but rather must depend on the information generated by left–continuous processes, or more precisely, be $\mathcal{P}$–measurable. By definition, any adapted left–continuous process, in particular any adapted continuous process, is predictable.

Let $\mathcal{M}^2$ denote the space of square–integrable martingales whose value at time zero is zero. (An example is Standard Brownian Motion with respect to its standard filtration.) The *quadratic variation* of a martingale $S \in \mathcal{M}^2$ is the unique increasing process denoted $[S]$ such that, for each time t,

$$[S]_t = \lim_{n \to \infty} \sum_{i=0}^{2^n - 1} \left[S(t_{i+1}^n) - S(t_i^n) \right]^2, \tag{2}$$

where $t_i^n = i 2^{-n} t$ for $0 \le i \le 2^n$. (The limit is in the $L^1(P)$ norm sense; its existence is beyond our scope here.) Thus the quadratic variation $[S]_t$ is roughly the limit of sums of squared movements of the process during $[0, t]$, taking the limit as the size of the time intervals over which the movements are measured converges to zero. For a Standard Brownian Motion B, one can deduce that $[B]_t = t$ for all $t \ge 0$. In fact, this can be taken as the defining property of Brownian Motion.

PROPOSITION. *Suppose $S \in \mathcal{M}^2$ is continuous. Then S is a Standard Brownian Motion if and only if $[S]_t = t$ for all $t \ge 0$.*

C. Now we begin to construct the stochastic integral in continuous time. First we recall the definition of deterministic integration. Suppose $F : [0, \infty) \to R$ is a (deterministic) right–continuous function of time of finite variation. (By *finite variation*, we mean only that F is of the form $G - H$, where G and H are increasing functions of time.) Further, suppose $g : [0, \infty) \to R$ is continuous. We then have the definition: for any time $t \in [0, \infty)$,

$$\int_0^t g(s) \, dF(s) = \lim_{n \to \infty} \sum_{i=0}^n g(t_{i+1}^n)[F(t_{i+1}^n) - F(t_i^n)] \tag{3}$$

is the *Stieltjes integral* of g with respect to F, where t_i^n is defined as for relation (2). If S is a right–continuous stochastic process of finite variation and θ is a continuous process, we can therefore define the stochastic integral $\int \theta \, dS$, separately for each fixed time t and each fixed state of the world ω, as the Stieltjes integral $\int_0^t \theta(\omega, s) \, dS(\omega, s)$. This *random Stieltjes integral* is merely the limit of the discrete–time integral given by (1) as the intervals of time converge to zero in size. A random Stieltjes integral can be defined "ω by ω" in this manner under weaker restrictions on θ and S. References to the theory are cited in the Notes. The ultimate class of "Stieltjes integrable" pairs (θ, S), however, is not large enough to illustrate several valuable economic principles. For these applications, we must sacrifice an "ω by ω" definition of $\int \theta \, dS$ and settle for a stochastic integral, a probabilistic specification of $\int \theta \, dS$ as a stochastic process with integral–like behavior. The reader is assured, however, that the stochastic and random Stieltjes integrals coincide when the latter is well–defined.

D. Let $S \in \mathcal{M}^2$ and let $L^2[S]$ denote the set of predictable processes θ such that the random Stieltjes integral $\int_0^t \theta_\tau^2 \, d[S]_\tau$ has finite expectation for each t in $\mathcal{T}$. As $[S]$ is increasing and θ^2 is positive, these Stieltjes integrals do indeed exist, and can be shown to be random variables (measurable). In the case of Brownian Motion, since $[B]_t = t$, we know that $L^2[B]$ is the set of predictable θ such that $E[\int_0^t \theta_s^2 \, ds] < \infty$ for all t. A proof of the lemma below is omitted.

LEMMA. *For any square–integrable martingale S, $L^2[S]$ is a vector space.*

In order to define stochastic integration, we first restrict ourselves to a time interval $\mathcal{T} = [0, T]$ of finite length. Later we extend the definition to the inifinite horizon case. A stochastic process θ is *elementary* provided there is a partition of $\mathcal{T}$ of the form $\{(0, t_1], (t_1, t_2], \ldots, (t_k, T]\}$ such that θ_t is a constant over each set in the partition. In words, an elementary process is piecewise constant and left–continuous. Figure 15.1 illustrates a typical sample path of an elementary process.

The set of elementary processes in $L^2[S]$ is denoted $L^2[S]_{\mathcal{E}}$. For any θ in $L^2[S]_{\mathcal{E}}$, the stochastic integral $\int \theta \, dS$ is defined as the random Stieltjes integral $\int \theta \, dS$. This Stieltjes integral is obviously well defined since, for any (ω, t) in $\Omega \times \mathcal{T}$, $[\int \theta \, dS](\omega, t)$ is a sum of the form (1); no limits are involved. The following lemma, offered without proof, is of the nature of Proposition 15A.

LEMMA. *If $S \in \mathcal{M}^2$ and $\theta \in L^2[S]_{\mathcal{E}}$, then $\int \theta \, dS \in \mathcal{M}^2$.*

A positive functional $\| \cdot \|_S$ is defined on $L^2[S]$ by

$$\| \theta \|_S = \left(E \left[\int_0^T \theta_t^2 \, d[S]_t \right] \right)^{1/2}, \qquad \theta \in L^2[S].$$

A Hilbert space norm $\| \cdot \|_{\mathcal{M}^2}$ is defined on $\mathcal{M}^2$ by

$$\| S \|_{\mathcal{M}^2} = \sqrt{\operatorname{var}(S_T)}, \qquad S \in \mathcal{M}^2.$$

Interested readers may refer to the Notes for a proof of the following result defining stochastic integration.

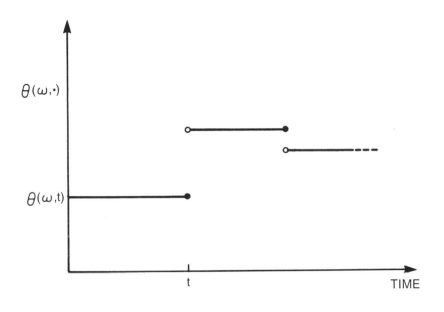

Figure 15.1   A Sample Path of an Elementary Process

THEOREM (DEFINITION OF STOCHASTIC INTEGRATION). *For any martingale* $S \in \mathcal{M}^2$ *and any* θ *in* $L^2[S]$, *there exists a sequence* $\{\theta_n\}$ *in* $L^2[S]_{\mathcal{E}}$ *such that* $\| \theta_n - \theta \|_S \to 0$. *There is a unique martingale denoted* $\int \theta \, dS \in \mathcal{M}^2$ *such that, for any such sequence* $\{\theta_n\}$, *the sequence of martingales* $\{\int \theta_n \, dS\}$ *converges in* $\| \cdot \|_{\mathcal{M}^2}$ *to* $\int \theta \, dS$.

The martingale $\int \theta \, dS$ given by this theorem is the *stochastic integral* of θ with respect to S. The proof of this theorem is based on showing that $\| \theta \|_S = \| \int \theta \, dS \|_{\mathcal{M}^2}$, a useful fact for other purposes.

Extending the definition of the stochastic integral from $\mathcal{T} = [0, T]$ to $\mathcal{T} = [0, \infty)$ is a trivial matter. For any martingale $S \in \mathcal{M}^2$ and any θ in $L^2[S]$, we define $\int \theta \, dS$ up to any time $T > 0$ as the martingale defined by the above Theorem, restricting θ and S to $\Omega \times [0, T]$. Since this applies for all $T > 0$, we have thereby defined $\int \theta \, dS$ on all of $\Omega \times [0, \infty)$.

There are fancier and quicker ways to define the stochastic integral, but this one yields some idea of its meaning. For any ϕ in $L^2[S]$ one can get arbitrarily close in norm to $\int \phi \, dS$ with some $\int \theta \, dS$, where θ is elementary.

Of course, if θ is elementary, then $\int \theta \, dS$ has a clear economic meaning as a finite sum of the form (1). We also note the extension of Proposition 15A included in the above definition of $\int \theta \, dS$. If θ is in $L^2[S]$ then $\int \theta \, dS$ is a martingale, implying no expected financial gains from trade in the application to security trading.

E.   Having defined stochastic integration with respect to martingales in $\mathcal{M}^2$, we will at least allude to generalizations. The first extension is integration with respect to a general local martingale M. The definition of $\int \theta \, dM$ is analogous to the case $M \in \mathcal{M}^2$, and we refer readers to the Notes for sources with details. The next extension is integration with respect to semimartingales. As with martingales, we identify a semimartingale with one of its RCLL versions. If S is a semimartingale and θ is a predictable process satisfying regularity conditions, we can define the stochastic integral $\int \theta \, dS$ if there exists a decomposition of S as the sum $M + A$ of a local martingale M and a finite variation adapted process A, such that $\int \theta \, dM$ is well defined as a stochastic integral and $\int \theta \, dA$ is well defined as a random Stieltjes integral. In this case, $\int \theta \, dS$ is defined as $\int \theta \, dM + \int \theta \, dA$, which is also a semimartingale. The class of predictable processes integrable in the stochastic sense with respect to a given semimartingale S is denoted $L[S]$. We let $L^1[S]$ denote the set of predictable processes θ in $L[S]$ such that $E[(\int_0^t \theta^2 \, d[S])^{1/2}] < \infty$ for all t in $\mathcal{T}$, where $[S]$ is the (here undefined) quadratic variation of S. If S is itself a local martingale and θ is in $L^1[S]$, then $\int \theta \, dS$ is a martingale.

The last extension is to the case of integration with respect to $S = (S^1, \ldots, S^N)$, an R^N-valued semimartingale (that is, the components of S are semimartingales). The vector space of R^N-valued predictable processes $\theta = (\theta^1, \ldots, \theta^N)$ such that $\int \theta \, dS$ exists is denoted $L[S]$. Again, we do not define this extension, deferring to sources cited in the Notes. The integral $\int \theta \, dS$ is safely interpreted as $\sum_{n=1}^N \int \theta^n \, dS^n$, but is not always defined precisely as such. Of course, if $\theta^1 \in L[S^1]$ and $\theta^2 \in L[S^2]$, then $\theta = (\theta^1, \theta^2) \in L[S]$, where $S = (S^1, S^2)$, and $\int \theta \, dS = \int \theta^1 \, dS^1 + \int \theta^2 \, dS^2$. If S is an R^N-valued local martingale, then $L^1[S]$ again denotes the set of θ in $L[S]$ such that $\int \theta \, dS$ is a martingale. The following properties of stochastic integration are carryovers from Stieltjes integration.

(a) Suppose S is an R^N-valued semimartingale. For any scalars α and β and any θ and ϕ in $L[S]$,

$$\alpha \int \theta \, dS + \beta \int \phi \, dS = \int \alpha \theta \, dS + \int \beta \phi \, dS = \int (\alpha \theta + \beta \phi) \, dS. \quad (4)$$

(b) For any t in $\mathcal{T}$, and any θ in $L[S]$,

$$\Delta\left(\int \theta\, dS\right)_t = \theta_t \cdot \Delta S_t. \tag{5}$$

(c) For any R^N-valued semimartingales S and X with sum $Y = S + X$, if $\theta \in L[S] \cap L[X]$, then $\theta \in L[Y]$ and

$$\int \theta\, dY = \int \theta\, dS + \int \theta\, dX. \tag{6}$$

Properties (4) and (6) are the *linearity of stochastic integration.* Property (5) states that the jump of a stochastic integral process is the value of the integrand multiplied by the jump of the integrator (or their inner product in the multidimensional case).

Example. (Integration with Respect to Ito Processes) Suppose $B = (B^1, \ldots, B^N)$ is a Standard Brownian Motion in R^N with respect to the filtered probability space $(\Omega, \mathcal{F}, F, P)$. Let a be a real–valued predictable process and $b = (b^1, \ldots, b^N)$ be an R^N-valued predictable processes such that the Lebesgue integrals $\int_0^t |a_s|\, ds$ and $\int_0^t b_s \cdot b_s\, ds$ are finite almost surely for all t. Then, for any scalar starting point S_0, a semimartingale S is well defined by

$$S_t = S_0 + \int_0^t a_s\, ds + \sum_{n=1}^N \int_0^t b_s^n\, dB_s^n.$$

In this case, we call S an Ito process. If $\theta \in L[S]$, then the process Y defined by $Y_T = \int_0^t \theta_t\, dS_t$ is also an (Ito) semimartingale, with

$$Y_T = \int_0^T \theta_t a_t\, dt + \sum_{n=1}^N \int_0^T \theta_t b_t^n\, dB_t^n,$$

which is more commonly written in the *stochastic differential form*

$$dY_t = \theta_t\, dS_t = \theta_t a_t\, dt + \theta_t b_t\, dB_t. \tag{7}$$

We note that $Y_0 = 0$. Following the notation of (7), if $dS_t = a_t\, dt + b_t\, dB_t$ and likewise X is an Ito process defined by $dX_t = \widehat{a}\, dt + \widehat{b}_t\, dB_t$, then the process Z defined by $Z_t = S_t + X_t$ is an Ito process with the stochastic differential representation

$$dZ_t = (a_t + \widehat{a}_t)\, dt + (b_t + \widehat{b}_t)\, dB_t, \tag{8}$$

and so on, following the rules given by relations (4) and (6). Of course, an Ito process such as S has no jumps; that is, $\Delta S_t = 0$ almost surely for all t. Some basics of the theory of Ito processes are outlined in Section 21. ♠

F.   For a given filtered probability space $(\Omega, \mathcal{F}, F, P)$, suppose there exists an R^N–valued martingale $S = (S^1, \ldots, S^N)$ such that any square–integrable martingale X can be written as $X = X_0 + \int \theta \, dS$ for some θ in $L[S]$. Then we say S is a *martingale generator*. If N is the smallest number of martingales forming a martingale generator, then S is a *martingale basis* and N is the *martingale multiplicity* of $(\Omega, \mathcal{F}, F, P)$. These definitions generalize, as indicated in the Notes.

Example.   Suppose $(\Omega, \mathcal{F}, F, P)$ is a filtered probability space for the time set $[0, \infty)$ on which is defined a Standard Brownian Motion B in R^N. If F is the standard filtration of B, then B is itself a martingale basis. Specifically, for any square–integrable martingale X on $(\Omega, \mathcal{F}, F, P)$ there exists a predictable R^N–valued process θ such that, for any time $t \geq 0$, $E([\int_0^t \theta_\tau \cdot \theta_\tau \, d\tau]) < \infty$ and $X_t = X_0 + \int_0^t \theta \, dB$. In this case, $\int \theta_\tau \, dB_\tau = \sum_{n=1}^N \int \theta_\tau^n \, dB_\tau^n$. ♠

Other examples are cited in the Notes.

G.   Since the definition of a stochastic integral is in part a property of the probability measure of the underlying filtered probability space, not to mention the filtration, it is worthwhile recording the following invariance properties for changes of probability measure. Let S be an R^n–valued semimartingale on the filtered probability space $(\Omega, \mathcal{F}, F, P)$ for a time set $\mathcal{T} = [0, \infty)$ or $\mathcal{T} = [0, T]$, where $F = \{\mathcal{F}_t : t \in \mathcal{T}\}$ is a filtration of sub–tribes of $\mathcal{F}$ satisfying the usual conditions. We take a new probability measure Q on $(\Omega, \mathcal{F})$ equivalent to P. The following results have slightly more complicated versions when Q is merely absolutely continuous with respect to P. We note that F also satisfies the usual conditions under Q and emphasize our convention of identifying a semimartingale with one of its RCLL versions. Let $L_P[S]$ denote the space of predictable R^n–valued processes such that $\int \theta \, dS$ is a well defined stochastic integral on $(\Omega, \mathcal{F}, F, P)$. This is the space $L[S]$ alluded to, but not precisely defined, in Paragraph E. We have merely made the dependence on the probability measure P explicit in our notation. We also show this dependence by writing $_P\!\int \theta \, dS$ for the stochastic integral under P. We use the notation $L_Q[S]$ and $_Q\!\int \theta \, dS$ likewise.

PROPOSITION.   *If S is an R^n–valued semimartingale for $(\Omega, \mathcal{F}, F, P)$ and Q is equivalent to P, then S is also an R^n–valued semimartingale for*

$(\Omega, \mathcal{F}, F, Q)$. *The spaces $L_P[S]$ and $L_Q[S]$ coincide, and for any θ in $L_P[S]$, the two stochastic integrals $_P\int \theta \, dS$ and $_Q\int \theta \, dS$ have a common version. If S is a real–valued semimartingale under P, then its quadratic variation process $[S]$ under P is a version of its quadratic variation process under Q.*

EXERCISES

EXERCISE 15.1 Prove Proposition 15A.

EXERCISE 15.2 Suppose B is a Standard Brownian Motion. Show that $[B]_t = t$ for all $t \geq 0$.

EXERCISE 15.3 Suppose $(\Xi, \mathcal{A})$ is a finite event tree. Take the filtration of tribes F generated by $(\Xi, \mathcal{A})$, as constructed in Section 14, for the measurable space $(\Omega, \mathcal{F})$, where Ω is the set of terminal nodes of $(\Xi, \mathcal{A})$ and $\mathcal{F}$ is the set of all subsets of Ω. Take any probability measure P on $(\Omega, \mathcal{F})$ such that $P(B) > 0$ for any non–empty B in $\mathcal{F}$. That is, the probability of "reaching" any terminal node under P is strictly positive. Show that the martingale multiplicity of the resulting filtered probability space is one less than the maximum number of immediate successors of any node in the tree, or $N(\Xi, \mathcal{A}) - 1$ in the notation of Section 12.

Notes

The presentation here is designed for economists, drawing on the now standard theory of stochastic integrals, as exposed for example in Chung and Williams (1983). Durrett (1984) and Kopp (1984) also address this topic. Comprehensive sources are Jacod (1979) and Dellacherie and Meyer (1982). The theory of Stieltjes integration is presented in Bartle (1976) (for the Riemann–Stieltjes integral), and Royden (1968) (for the Lebesgue–Stieltjes integral). For readers familiar with the theory, our definition of stochastic integration avoids the use of the *predictable compensator* $\langle S, S \rangle$ of a square integrable martingale S, sometimes called the *sharp brackets process* for S, substituting instead the simpler quadratic variation process $[S]$. Theorem 15D is then a consequence of Dellacherie and Meyer (1982) VIII-5 and the fact that $\langle S, S \rangle$ is the dual predictable projection of $[S]$. See Dellacherie and Meyer (1982) VIII-30. (This substitution wouldn't save any effort if we actually had to prove the theorem!)

For an abstract summary of integration with respect to R^n–valued semimartingales and of martingale multiplicity theory, see Duffie (1985a). For a set of examples of martingale multiplicity, see Jacod (1977). Harrison and Kreps (1979), Harrison and Pliska (1981, 1983), Pliska (1982), and Stricker (1984) are responsible for extending the "diffusion" models of financial gains from trade to general stochastic integrals. Lemma 15D is a corollary to the Kunita–Watanabe Inequality, which may be found in Jacod (1979). For comparison with the Stratonovich definition of the integral in finance application, see Lehoczky and Sethi (1981).

16.   Stochastic Equilibria

We now study stochastic exchange equilibria in continuous–time, the setting for Chapter IV. Our model is a direct extension of the event–tree economy of Section 12, where the concept of probability is not needed thanks to finite–dimensionality. Our attention is directed mainly at the formulation and existence of equilibria. We will also see the extension of the spanning number concept of Section 12 to continuous–time. Indeed, we use spanning in order to demonstrate the existence of equilibria.

A.   As usual, we fix our basic primitives: the time set $T = [0, T]$ for some positive time horizon T, and a filtered probability space $(\Omega, \mathcal{F}, F, P)$ for this time set, where the information filtration F satisfies the *usual conditions*, as previously defined. For an integer number $\ell \geq 1$ of commodities, let L denote the vector space of R^ℓ–valued predictable processes $c = (c^1, \dots, c^\ell)$ satisfying $E(\int_0^T c_t \cdot c_t \, dt) < \infty$. An element c of L is a *consumption rate* process. Here, $c^k(\omega, t)$ is the prescribed rate of consumption of the k–th commodity in state $\omega \in \Omega$ at time $t \in T$. The predictability of c implies that c_t can only be chosen on the basis of information available up to time t. It is left as an exercise to show that this choice space L is a Hilbert space under the inner product

$$(c, \psi) \mapsto E \left(\int_0^T \psi_t \cdot c_t \, dt \right).$$

An element ψ of L can also be treated as a *spot price process*, $\psi^k(\omega, t)$ being the unit price of the k–th good in state ω at time t.

Let $\mathcal{E} = (X_i, \succeq_i, e^i)$, $i \in \mathcal{I} \equiv \{1, \dots, I\}$, be an exchange economy on L. We recall that for each agent i, $X_i \subset L$ is a choice set of consumption processes, $\succeq_i$ is a preference relation on X_i, and $e^i \in L$ is an endowment. Let $\mathcal{D}$ denote the space of integrable RCLL processes. A *security* is identified with a *dividend process* $D \in \mathcal{D}$, where D_t is the cumulative dividends paid by the security up to and including time t. We associate with each security D an adapted real–valued *price process* S, where S_t denotes the random market value for security D at time t. We treat S_t by convention as the post–dividend market value of the security at time t. In other words, if the dividend process jumps at time t, the market value S_t reflects the jump as already having been paid out, or S_t is *ex dividend*. As an illustration, an agent buying one unit of security D at time t and selling it at a later time s receives a total amount of dividends $D_s - D_t$ in the interim, and realizes a further net "capital" gain (or loss) from the two transactions of $S_s - S_t$. If the dividend process jumps at time s, then $\Delta D_s = D_s - D_{s-}$ is paid as a lump sum dividend to each shareholder at time s. The total gain from trade is $G_s - G_t$, where $G \equiv S + D$ is the *gain process*. Letting $\mathcal{G}$ denote the space of semimartingales, we assume that agents take as given a *gain operator*, a linear function $\Pi : \mathcal{D} \to \mathcal{G}$ with the property that security D has the gain process $\Pi(D)$. The *price process* for D is then $S = \Pi(D) - D$. This is the most general model allowing us to define gains from trade as a stochastic integral $\int \theta \, dG$, where θ is the corresponding trading process, θ_t denoting the number of units of the security held at time t. The intention, of course, is that $\int \theta \, dG = $ "$\int \theta \, dS + \int \theta \, dD$", but the right hand side, the sum of capital gain and dividend gain, need not be well–defined unless both stochastic integrals are. The *cum dividend* market value of θ_t units of security D at time t is $\theta_t (S_t + \Delta D_t)$.

To be precise about trading strategies, let $D = (D^0, D^1, \ldots, D^N) \in \mathcal{D}^{N+1}$ be the vector of $N + 1$ securities available for trade, and $S = (S^0, S^1, \ldots, S^N)$ be a vector of price processes for D. For simplicity we distinguish the security paying D^0 as a riskless bond; that is, we assume that $D^0(t) = 0, 0 \le t < T$, and that $D^0(T) \equiv 1$. Also for simplicity, we assume that the "risky securities" are continuous. For example, a security paying dividends at the rate δ, for some adapted process δ, defines a continuous cumulative dividend process $D_t = \int_0^t \delta(s) \, ds$ (provided D is integrable). The general case is cited in the Notes. An R^{N+1}–valued process $\theta = (\theta^0, \theta^1, \ldots, \theta^N)$ is a *trading strategy* if $\theta \in L^1[G]$. Referring to Section 15, this implies first that the stochastic integral $\int \theta \, dG$, interpreted as $\sum_{n=0}^N \int \theta^n \, dG^n$, is well defined, and second: that if the components of G are martingales, then $\int \theta \, dG$ is also a martingale.

A *stochastic economy* is a triple $(D, \mathcal{E}, F)$ where D is a vector of securities, $\mathcal{E}$ is an exchange economy on L, and F denotes the information filtration available to all agents. Given a spot price process ψ and a gain operator Π, let $S^n = \Pi(D^n) - D^n$ for $0 \le n \le N$. A consumption process c and trading strategy θ form a *budget feasible plan* (c, θ) for agent i if c is in X_i,

$$\theta_t \cdot (S_t + \Delta D_t) = \int_0^t \psi_\tau \cdot (e_\tau^i - c_\tau) \, d\tau + \int_0^t \theta_\tau \, dG_\tau \quad \text{a.s., } t \in [0, T], \quad (1)$$

and

$$\theta_T \cdot (S_T + \Delta D_T) \geq 0 \qquad \text{a.s.} \tag{2}$$

Implicit in relation (1) is the requirement that the initial market value $\theta_0 \cdot S_0$ of the trading strategy θ is zero; there are no initial endowments of securities. Interpreting, relation (1) is merely an accounting identity stating that the current market value of the portfolio of securities held (cum dividend) is the initial value plus the accumulated sale value of spot market consumption endowments net of purchases, plus accumulated financial gains from security trading. Relation (2) precludes terminal debt. A pair (c, θ) is an *optimal plan* for agent i given (ψ, Π) provided (c, θ) is a budget feasible plan and $c \succeq_i b$ for any other budget feasible plan (b, φ). A collection $(\psi, \Pi, (c^i, \theta^i)), i \in \mathcal{I}$, is an *equilibrium* for $(D, \mathcal{E}, F)$ if, for each agent i, (c^i, θ^i) is an optimal plan given the spot price process ψ and gain operator Π, and if markets clear: $\sum_{i=1}^{I} c^i - e^i = 0$ and $\sum_{i=1}^{I} \theta^i = 0$.

B.   To demonstrate an equilibrium for a stochastic economy, we will set up security markets in which any given consumption process can be financed at a fixed initial investment cost by some trading strategy. The vector dividend process D is *spanning* given a gain operator Π provided, for any spot price process $\psi \in L$ and any consumption process $c \in L$, there exists a trading strategy θ such that:

$$\theta_t \cdot (S_t + \Delta D_t) = \theta_0 \cdot S_0 - \int_0^t \psi_\tau \cdot c_\tau \, d\tau + \int_0^t \theta_\tau \, dG_\tau \quad \text{a.s.}, \ t \in [0, T], \ (1')$$

and such that

$$\theta_T \cdot (S_T + \Delta D_T) = 0 \qquad \text{a.s.} \tag{2'}$$

That is, for any consumption process c, there exists a trading strategy θ requiring an initial investment of $\theta_0 \cdot S_0$ that finances the spot market payments required over time to purchase the consumption plan c, leaving no terminal financial obligation or surplus. In this case, we say θ *finances* c *with initial investment* $\theta_0 \cdot S_0$.

We will consider the gain operator $\overline{\Pi}$ defined by

$$\overline{\Pi}(D)_t = E(D_T \mid \mathcal{F}_t), \quad t \in [0, T]. \tag{3}$$

The price process for a security, under the gain operator $\overline{\Pi}$, is merely the conditional expected total future dividends of the security. The resulting gain process $G = \overline{\Pi}(D)$ is a martingale.

We recall from Section 15 that an R^N–valued martingale m is a *martingale generator* if any square–integrable martingale X can be written in the form $X_t = X_0 + \int_0^t \theta_s \, dm_s$, where $\theta = (\theta^1, \ldots, \theta^N)$ is in the space $L^1[m]$ of predictable processes integrable with respect to m. In a sense, m dynamically "spans" the space of all martingales. A vector $D = (D^0, D^1, \ldots, D^N)$ of securities is *fundamental* if D^0 is a riskless bond (as previously defined) and if there is a martingale generator $m = (m^1, \ldots, m^N)$ such that:

$$D_T^n = m_T^n, \qquad 1 \le n \le N.$$

Under the gain operator $\overline{\Pi}$, the gain process for a fundamental vector of securities D is $G = \overline{\Pi}(D) = (\mathbf{1}, m^1, \ldots, m^N)$, where $\mathbf{1}$ denotes the identically 1 martingale, and m is a martingale generator.

PROPOSITION. *A fundamental vector D of securities is spanning given the gain operator $\overline{\Pi}$.*

PROOF: Let ψ and c in L be arbitrary, and let $m = (m^1, \ldots, m^N)$ be the martingale generator underlying D. Then $G = D + S = (\mathbf{1}, m^1, \ldots, m^N)$, where $S = \overline{\Pi}(D) - D$. Let X be the martingale defined by:

$$X_t = E\left(\int_0^T \psi_s \cdot c_s \, ds \,\middle|\, \mathcal{F}_t \right), \qquad t \in [0, T]. \tag{4}$$

Since m is a martingale generator, by definition there exists φ in $L^1[m]$ such that $X - X_0 = \int \varphi \, dm$. Define the process θ^0 by

$$\theta_t^0 = X_t - \int_0^t \psi_\tau \cdot c_\tau \, d\tau - \sum_{n=1}^N \varphi_t^n (S_t^n + \Delta D_t^n), \qquad t \in [0, T]. \tag{5}$$

Let $\theta = (\theta^0, \varphi^1, \ldots, \varphi^N)$. Since $G^0 \equiv 1$ and θ^0 is predictable (an exercise), we know $\theta^0 \in L^1[G^0]$ and $\int \theta^0 \, dG^0 \equiv 0$. Thus $\theta \in L^1[G]$ is a well defined trading strategy. Then $\int \theta \, dG = \int \theta^0 \, dG^0 + \int \varphi \, dm = \int \varphi \, dm$. From (4), (5), and arithmetic, relations (1') and (2') are satisfied. ∎

COROLLARY.   *Under the same assumptions, for a given spot price process ψ and consumption process c, any trading strategy θ in $L^1[\overline{\Pi}(D)]$ financing c has the unique initial investment $\theta_0 \cdot S_0 = E[\int_0^T \psi_t \cdot c_t \, dt]$.*

A proof of this corollary is merely a matter of the definitions of X and θ^0 given in the proof of the proposition.

C.   Suppose D is a fundamental vector of securities. One basic route to the existence of equilibria for the stochastic economy $(D, \mathcal{E}, F)$ is: (i) demonstrate an equilibrium $((c^i), p)$, $i \in \mathcal{I}$, for the static economy $\mathcal{E}$ on

L; (ii) let the spot price process ψ be chosen to be the Hilbert space dual representation of p; and (iii) apply the dynamic spanning property of a fundamental vector of securities under the conditional expectation gain operator $\overline{\overline{\Pi}}$ in order to demonstrate trading strategies (θ^i) financing $(c^i - e^i)$ at zero initial investments. The remaining properties of an equilibrium then fall easily into place. The following result applies conditions for the existence of a static equilibrium presented in Section 11. Our choice space L fits into that setting since L is equivalent to the space of R^ℓ-valued functions on the finite measure space $(\Omega \times [0, T], \mathcal{P}, \mu)$, with $\mathcal{P}$ as usual denoting the predictable tribe, and where the measure μ on $\mathcal{P}$ is given by $\mu(A) = E[\int_0^T 1_A(\omega, t) \, dt]$ for any measurable set A.

THEOREM. *Suppose D is a fundamental vector of securities for $(\Omega, \mathcal{F}, F, P)$ and the static economy $\mathcal{E}$ satisfies the conditions of Corollary 11G. Then the stochastic economy $(D, \mathcal{E}, F)$ has an equilibrium.*

PROOF: By Proposition 11G, $\mathcal{E}$ has a static equilibrium $((c^i), p)$, $i \in \mathcal{I}$, where p is continuous on L. Since L is a Hilbert space under the stated inner product, there is a unique spot price process ψ in L such that

$$p \cdot c = E \left(\int_0^T \psi_t \cdot c_t \, dt \right), \quad c \in L.$$

By the stronger continuity assumption of Corollary 11G, ψ is essentially bounded. We take the conditional expectation gain operator $\overline{\overline{\Pi}}$. Since D is fundamental, D is spanning given $\overline{\overline{\Pi}}$ by Proposition 16B. Then for each $i \in \{1, \ldots, I-1\}$ there exists a trading strategy θ^i satisfying $(1')$ and $(2')$ for $c = c^i - e^i$. Let $\theta^I = -\sum_{i=1}^{I-1} \theta^i$. By the linearity of stochastic integration [relation (15.4)] and the fact that market clearing in the static equilibrium implies $c^I - e^I = -\sum_{i=1}^{I-1}(c^i - e^i)$, we deduce that θ^I also satisfies $(1')$ and $(2')$ for $c = c^I - e^I$. Furthermore, by Corollary 16B, we have

$$p \cdot (c^i - e^i) = E \left(\int_0^T \psi_t \cdot (c_t^i - e_t^i) \, dt \right) = \theta_0^i \cdot S_0, \quad \forall i \in \mathcal{I}.$$

Since $((c^i), p)$ is an equilibrium for $\mathcal{E}$, we know $p \cdot (c^i - e^i) = 0$ by Lemma 3B, so $\theta_0^i \cdot S_0 = 0$ for all i. Thus (c^i, θ^i) satisfies (1) and (2), and is therefore a budget feasible plan for each agent $i \in \mathcal{I}$ given $(\psi, \overline{\overline{\Pi}})$. By construction, markets clear: $\sum_{i=1}^I (c^i - e^i) = 0$ and $\sum_{i=1}^I \theta^i = 0$.

We have verified all properties of equilibrium for $(\psi, \overline{\overline{\Pi}}, (c^i, \theta^i))$, $i \in \mathcal{I}$, with the possible exception of optimality. Suppose, with the goal of a contradiction, that there exists for some agent i a budget feasible plan

(b, φ) with $b \succ_i c^i$. By the definition of an equilibrium for $\mathcal{E}$, this implies that $p \cdot b > p \cdot c^i = 0$. Since (b, φ) is budget feasible, $\varphi_0 \cdot S_0 = 0$, and (1)–(2) imply that $\varphi_T \cdot (S_T + \Delta D_T) = \int_0^T \varphi \, dG - \int_0^T \psi_t \cdot (b_t - e_t^i) \, dt \geq 0$. Taking expectations we have

$$E \left(\int_0^T \varphi \, dG \right) - E \left[\int_0^T \psi_t \cdot (b_t - e_t^i) \, dt \right] \geq 0.$$

Since $p \cdot (b - e^i) = E(\int_0^T \psi_t \cdot (b_t - e_t^i) \, dt) > 0$, we have $E(\int_0^T \varphi \, dG) > 0$, which contradicts the fact that $Y = \int \varphi \, dG$ is a martingale with initial value $Y_0 = 0$. ∎

The equilibrium just shown has several important properties:

(a) since $\int \theta \, dG$ is a martingale for any trading strategy θ, there are no expected financial gains from trade,

(b) markets are *dynamically complete*. any consumption process can be financed at a given initial investment,

(c) the (stochastic) equilibrium allocation (c^i) is Pareto optimal since it is given by a Pareto optimal static equilibrium allocation, and

(d) the number of securities is no less than the martingale multiplicity of $(\Omega, \mathcal{F}, F, P)$ plus one, and is equal to that number when the martingale generator underlying the fundamental securities is a martingale basis.

Actually, there are regularity conditions cited in the Notes under which the minimum number of securities supporting dynamically complete markets is the same number: one plus the martingale multiplicity. This will therefore be called the *spanning number*. Making a connection with the event tree setting of Section 12, we can identify the spanning number when the filtration is generated by an event tree as the maximum number of branches leaving any node in the tree. See Exercise 15.3 and Corollary 12G.

Example. (Brownian Information) Suppose that F is the standard filtration of a Standard Brownian Motion $B = (B^1, \ldots, B^N)$ in R^N, for some $N \geq 1$. Then B is itself is a martingale generator; indeed B is a martingale basis as claimed in Example 15F. Let D^0 be a riskless bond and let $D^n = B^n$, $1 \leq n \leq N$. Then $D = (D^0, \ldots, D^N)$ is fundamental, and there exists an equilibrium with price process $S = (1, 0, 0, \ldots, 0)$ under the assumptions of Corollary 11G on preferences and endowments. For a more general setting, let $X = (X^1, \ldots, X^N)$ be any R^N-valued semimartingale of the form:

$$X_t = X_0 + \int V_t \, dB_t, \qquad 0 \leq t \leq T, \quad X_0 \in R^N, \tag{6}$$

where V is a bounded predictable $N \times N$ matrix valued process with a bounded inverse. The conditions on V can be greatly relaxed. Then a vector of securities $D \in \mathcal{D}^{N+1}$ is fundamental if D^0 is a riskless bond and $D^n(T) = X^n(T)$. We return to this example in Section 25 in order to obtain restrictions on equilibrium rates of returns. ♠

EXERCISES

EXERCISE 16.1 Prove that the vector space L of consumption processes defined in Paragraph A is a Hilbert space under the stated inner product.

EXERCISE 16.2 Let $(\Omega, \mathcal{F}, F, P)$ be any filtered probability space for any time set $\mathcal{T}$, and D be any dividend process. Prove that $\overline{\Pi}(D)$ is a martingale, where $\overline{\Pi}$ is as defined in relation (3).

EXERCISE 16.3 Show that the trading strategy θ^0 defined in the proof of Proposition 16B is in fact predictable.

EXERCISE 16.4 Perform the "arithmetic" referred to in the last sentence of the proof of Proposition 16B, and verify Corollary 16B.

EXERCISE 16.5 Perform the detailed calculations verifying the claim in the proof of Theorem 16C that θ^I satisfies relations (1') and (2') for $c = c^I - e^I$.

Notes

The seminal formulation of stochastic equilibria is due to Radner (1972), albeit in a somewhat different setting. The approach taken here to demonstrate stochastic equilibria began with Kreps (1982), following a line of work dating to Black and Scholes (1973). Kreps' work was extended to continuous–time in Duffie and Huang (1985) by making use of the concept of martingale multiplicity and relying on the work of Harrison and Kreps (1979) and Harrison and Pliska (1981). Theorem 16C is generalized in Duffie (1986c). For a production–exchange setting, see Duffie and Huang (1986b). The allocational role of financial securities applied here dates all the way back to Arrow (1953). See Huang (1987) and Duffie and Zame (1987) (which is summarized in Section 25) for an application of Example 16C to the demonstration of equilibrium with diffusion price processes. For a specific closed form solution to the case given in Example 16C, see Lehoczky and Shreve (1986). The generality of preferences allowed in this section is illusory. Our definition of optimality implicitly assumes that a plan is optimally not revised as time passes and information is obtained. This implicit assumption on preferences can be formalized as a rather strong consistency condition, and has been in other settings by Epstein and Zin (1987).

17. Transformations to Martingale Gains from Trade

In Section 16 we demonstrated equilibria with no expected financial gains from trade. This was done by assigning a security paying cumulative dividends $D = \{D_t : t \geq 0\}$ a price process $S = \{S_t : t \geq 0\}$ such that the total gain from trade process $G = D + S$ is a martingale. In this section our goal is to show that martingale gains from security trade is a necessary condition for stochastic equilibria, at least after two transformations. The first transformation re–expresses market values relative to the value of a given security, which is then a numeraire. The second transformation adjusts probability assessments, roughly along the lines of assigning the probability of an event A to be the initial investment required for a trading strategy with no intermediate dividends or investment, and with terminal market value 1_A (1 if A occurs, 0 otherwise). An extension of this idea applies in incomplete markets. Under these two transformations the necessity of martingale gains from trade in equilibrium is almost trivial, and in fact follows under much weaker assumptions than the presence of an equilibrium. The connection between martingales and stochastic equilibria is thus fundamentally general and important, for it brings the full power of martingale theory and stochastic integration to bear on the problem of security pricing and equilibrium without restrictive preference or distributional assumptions. Aside from Paragraph A, this section is advanced, and should be avoided on a first reading. Section 22 is a simpler and more concrete introduction to this theory.

A. Most of this section is motivated by the following simple observation. Let $\Omega = \{1, \ldots, m\}$ be a finite set of states, and let $d_1, \ldots, d_n$ be vectors in R^m representing the dividends paid in the m states by each of n securities. Let $S \in R^n$ denote the vector of market values of these securities before the true state is revealed. The securities are *arbitrage–free* if there is no portfolio $\theta \in R^n$ with the properties: $\sum_{j=1}^{n} \theta_j d_j \geq 0$ (positive payoffs in every state) and $S^{\top}\theta < 0$ (strictly negative market value). The securities are arbitrage–free, as we learned in Exercise 7.8, if and only if there is a positive *state–price vector* $\lambda \in R^m_+$, a vector of "shadow prices" for dividends in the various states with the property: $S_j = \lambda^{\top} d_j$ for each j. Assuming $S \neq 0$, it follows that $\lambda \neq 0$. With arbitrage–free securities, we can then construct a probability measure Q on the tribe $\mathcal{F} = 2^{\Omega}$ of all subsets of Ω by:

$$Q(\{i\}) = \frac{\lambda_i}{k}, \qquad 1 \le i \le m,$$

where $k = \sum_{i=1}^{m} \lambda_i$. Treating d_j as a random variable on $(\Omega, \mathcal{F}, P)$ in the obvious way, it follows that

$$S_j = kE(d_j), \qquad 1 \le j \le n.$$

We take $M = \mathrm{span}(d_1, \ldots, d_n)$ and $p : M \to R$ as the linear functional defined by:

$$p \cdot x = kE(x), \qquad x \in M.$$

It follows that $p \cdot x$ is the market value of a portfolio of securities that pays the random dividend x.

Suppose one of the securities, say the first, is a *numeraire*, meaning that $d_1 = (1, \ldots, 1) \in R^m$ and that $S_1 = 1$. It follows that $k = 1$. Then the market value of any portfolio is merely the expected value of its random dividend, using the constructed probability measure Q. If none of the securities are numeraires, but one of them, say the first, has strictly positive dividends in each state, then we can re–express values relative to security number one as: $\widehat{S} = S/S_1$ and

$$\widehat{d}_j = \left(\frac{d_{j1}}{d_{11}}, \ldots, \frac{d_{jm}}{d_{1m}} \right), \qquad 1 \le j \le n.$$

Let $\widehat{M} = \mathrm{span}(\widehat{d}_1, \ldots, \widehat{d}_n)$ and let $\widehat{p} : \widehat{M} \to R$ be represented by $\widehat{S}$ in the same manner that p was represented by S. We then have

$$\widehat{p} \cdot \widehat{x} = \widehat{E}(\widehat{x}), \qquad \widehat{x} \in \widehat{M}, \qquad\qquad (*)$$

where $\widehat{E}$ denotes expectation with respect to the probability measure $\widehat{Q}$ constructed from a state–price vector $\widehat{\lambda}$ for $(\widehat{S}, \widehat{d})$. Other exercises in Section 7 make for easy extensions of this result to infinite–dimensional spaces. Most of this section is concerned with a general stochastic analogue for the representation of security market values given by $(*)$. After normalization to a numeraire and a change of probability measure, the current market value of any attainable payoff is the current conditional expectation of the payoff.

B.   Henceforth the central primitive is a complete probability space $(\Omega, \mathcal{F}, P)$ and a filtration $F = \{\mathcal{F}_t : t \in [0, T]\}$ of sub–tribes of $\mathcal{F}$ satisfying the usual conditions. The initial tribe $\mathcal{F}_0$ is almost trivial, meaning that no information is available at time 0. Also given is a vector

$D = (D^0, D^1, \ldots, D^N)$ of securities (integrable RCLL cumulative dividend processes) and corresponding price processes $S = (S^0, S^1, \ldots, S^N)$. The sum $D + S \equiv G \equiv (G^0, G^1, \ldots, G^N)$ is assumed to be a vector semimartingale, the most general known class of stochastic processes defining gains from trade. By convention, S is ex dividend and $S_T = 0$. As usual, we work with RCLL versions of semimartingales for simplicity. Let $L^1(P)$ denote the vector space of integrable real–valued random variables. This is treated as the space of random wealth at time T. We suppose that a particular agent has a preference relation $\succeq$ on $L^1(P)$. As the saying goes, "you can't eat money," and several scenarios are later explored for the derivation of such a preference relation. The reader may temporarily imagine, for example, that goods are consumed only at time T and measured in units of wealth.

C. A trading strategy, as we saw in Section 16, is an R^{N+1}-valued predictable process $\theta = (\theta^0, \theta^1, \ldots, \theta^N)$ in $L^1[G]$. If the components of G are martingales, we know that $\int \theta \, dG$ is also a martingale. A trading strategy θ is *self–financing* provided

$$\theta_t \cdot (S_t + \Delta D_t) = \theta_0 \cdot S_0 + \int_0^t \theta \, dG, \quad t \in (0, T]. \tag{1}$$

Self–financing, in other words, means that $\theta_t \cdot (S_t + \Delta D_t)$, the cum dividend market value of the portfolio held at any time t, is the initial portfolio value $\theta_0 \cdot S_0$ plus the intermediate gains from trade $\int_0^t \theta \, dG$. There are no net intermediate dividends from a self–financing strategy, nor are additional investments required.

D. Let Θ denote the space of self–financing trading strategies, a vector space by the linearity of stochastic integration, relation (15.4). Let $W(\theta)$ denote the terminal wealth generated by a given strategy θ in Θ, or $W(\theta) = \theta_T \cdot \Delta D_T$. The *marketed subspace* of $L^1(P)$ is the set of terminal wealth choices that can be achieved by self–financing trading strategies, or $M = \{W(\theta) : \theta \in \Theta\}$. Because Θ is a vector subspace of the space $L^1[G]$ of all trading strategies and again because of the linearity of stochastic integration, it follows that the marketed subspace M is a vector subspace of $L^1(P)$. The initial investment corresponding to a trading strategy θ is the scalar $\theta_0 \cdot S_0$. It may happen, even in equilibrium, that there exist θ and γ in Θ such that $W(\theta) = W(\gamma)$, but that $\theta_0 \cdot S_0 \neq \gamma_0 \cdot S_0$, meaning that a given terminal wealth can be achieved at two different initial investments. If this possibility exists, we say that (D, S) is *slack*, and otherwise that (D, S) is *tight* (following the terminology of Section 12). We suppose that the agent in question has some initial scalar wealth w. Then a self–financing trading

strategy θ is *budget–feasible* provided $\theta_0 \cdot S_0 \leq w$. A budget feasible strategy θ is *optimal* if there does not exist a budget–feasible strategy $\gamma \in \Theta$
such that $W(\gamma) \succ W(\theta)$. The agent is *non–satiated* in M at $x \in M$ if there
exists $y \in M$ such that $y \succ x$. The following result is proved in exact
parallel with Proposition 12E.

PROPOSITION. *Suppose an agent with preference relation $\succeq$ on $L^1(P)$ is
non–satiated in the marketed subspace M at the terminal wealth $W(\theta)$ of
an optimal trading strategy θ. Then (D, S) is tight, and there exists a
linear functional π on M giving the unique initial investment $\pi \cdot x$ required
for any marketed terminal wealth choice x, or*

$$\pi \cdot W(\theta) = \theta_0 \cdot S_0, \quad \theta \in \Theta.$$

As in Section 12, we call π the *implicit price functional*.

THEOREM. *Suppose that $M \cap L^1(P)_+ \neq \{0\}$ and that $\succeq$ is algebraically
continuous, convex, and strictly monotonic. If an optimal trading strategy
exists, then (D, S) is tight and the corresponding implict price functional
π on M is represented by a probability measure Q on $(\Omega, \mathcal{F})$ via*

$$\pi \cdot x = kE^Q(x), \quad x \in M, \tag{2}$$

*where k is a strictly positive scalar and E^Q denotes expectation under Q.
Furthermore, P and Q are equivalent and the Radon–Nikodym derivative
$\frac{dQ}{dP}$ is essentially bounded.*

Before proving the theorem, we note that continuity of $\succeq$ is a sufficient
condition for its algebraic continuity.

PROOF: By the strict monotonicity assumption on $\succeq$ and the fact that
$M \cap L^1(P)_+ \neq \{0\}$, we know that $\succeq$ is non–satiated at the choice $W(\theta)$
corresponding to an optimal trading strategy θ. Let M^w denote the set of
budget feasible choices, or $M^w = \{x \in M : \pi \cdot x \leq w\}$, where w denotes
initial scalar wealth. Let $Y = \{x \in L^1(P) : x \succ W(\theta)\}$. Then M^w
and Y are disjoint convex sets, the latter having non–empty core by the
algebraic continuity of $\succeq$. The Separating Hyperplane Theorem in the form
of Exercise 3.13 thus implies the existence of a non–zero linear functional
p on $L^1(P)$ such that $p \cdot x \geq p \cdot x'$ for any x in Y and x' in M^w. Suppose y
is a non–zero element of $L^1(P)_+$. Then $W(\theta) + y \in \text{core}(Y)$ by the strict
monotonicity and algebraic continuity of $\succeq$, implying $p \cdot (W(\theta) + y) >
p \cdot W(\theta)$, or $p \cdot y > 0$. Thus p is a strictly positive linear functional on
$L^1(P)$. By assumption, there exists a non–zero $\widehat{y} \in M \cap L^1(P)_+$, and as
above, $\beta \equiv p \cdot \widehat{y} > 0$. Since $\succeq$ is strictly monotonic, $\alpha \equiv \pi \cdot \widehat{y} > 0$. Let

ψ denote the linear functional $(\alpha/\beta)p$. Then $\psi \cdot \widehat{y} = (\alpha/\beta)p \cdot \widehat{y} = \pi \cdot \widehat{y}$. We claim ψ is an extension of π to $L^1(P)$, for suppose not. Then there exists $m \in M$ such that $\psi \cdot m - \pi \cdot m > 0$. Let c be a scalar such that $\pi \cdot m = \pi \cdot (c\,\widehat{y})$ and let $\widehat{x} = W(\theta) + m - c\,\widehat{y}$. Then $\pi \cdot \widehat{x} = \pi \cdot W(\theta)$, so $\widehat{x}$ is in M^w, a budget feasible choice. Thus $\psi \cdot \widehat{x} \leq \psi \cdot W(\theta)$ by the separation property that ψ inherits from p. However,

$$\psi \cdot \widehat{x} = \psi \cdot (W(\theta) + m - c\,\widehat{y})$$

$$= \psi \cdot W(\theta) + \psi \cdot m - c\psi \cdot \widehat{y}$$

$$> \psi \cdot W(\theta) + \pi \cdot m - c\pi \cdot \widehat{y} = \psi \cdot W(\theta),$$

a contradiction. Thus ψ is indeed an extension of π.

Because ψ is a positive linear functional on $L^1(P)$, ψ is continuous by Proposition 0F. By the Riesz Representation Theorem 6G, there exists a unique $v \in L^\infty(P)$ such that

$$\psi \cdot x = E(vx), \quad x \in L^1(P).$$

Let k denote the scalar $E(v)$. Then v/k is the Radon–Nikodym derivative dQ/dP for a probability measure Q on $(\Omega, \mathcal{F})$ and $\psi \cdot x = E(vx) = E[k(dQ/dP)x] = kE^Q(x)$ for all x in $L^1(P)$. Since ψ is an extension of π, relation (2) follows. Suppose $B \in \mathcal{F}$ with $P(B) > 0$. Since ψ is strictly positive, $E^Q(1_B) > 0$, or $Q(B) > 0$, implying P and Q are equivalent. Because $v \in L^\infty(P)$, the Radon–Nikodym derivative dQ/dP is also in $L^\infty(P)$. ∎

E. A probability measure Q on $(\Omega, \mathcal{F})$ is an *equivalent uniform martingale measure* for (D, S) provided Q and P are equivalent, dQ/dP is bounded, and $\int \theta \, dG$ is a martingale on $(\Omega, \mathcal{F}, F, Q)$ for any trading strategy θ. This would imply zero expected financial gains from trade under Q, and of course that the gain processes $G^0, G^1, \ldots, G^N$ are themselves Q–martingales. In particular, we would have $S_t = E^Q[D_T - D_t \mid \mathcal{F}_t]$ for any time t, meaning the current price is the conditional expectation (under Q) of the remaining dividends. We recall that the set of trading strategies $L^1[G]$ is defined with the use of the probability measure P. For example, if G is real–valued, then θ is in $L^1[G]$ provided (i) θ is predictable and (ii) the expectation under P of $v(\theta) \equiv \left(\int_0^T \theta_t^2 \, d[G]_t \right)^{1/2}$ is finite. If dQ/dP is essentially bounded, say by the scalar k, then

$$E^Q[v(\theta)] = E^P\left(\frac{dQ}{dP} v(\theta) \right) \leq E^P[kv(\theta)] = kE^P[v(\theta)] < \infty.$$

Thus, if $\theta \in L^1[G]$ under P, then θ satisfies the identical restriction under an equivalent uniform martingale measure Q. The same conclusion is drawn when G is multidimensional. Thus we have the following technical result.

LEMMA. *Suppose Q and P are equivalent measures and dQ/dP is essentially bounded. If $G = D + S$ is a vector martingale on $(\Omega, \mathcal{F}, F, Q)$, then Q is an equivalent uniform martingale measure for (D, S).*

We are implicitly using the fact here that $\int \theta \, dG$ defines the same semimartingale on $(\Omega, \mathcal{F}, F, P)$ that it does on $(\Omega, \mathcal{F}, F, Q)$. This is indeed the case when Q and P are equivalent, as stated more carefully in Paragraph 15G.

We are left with the following main result of the section. For simplicity, we make use of the following technical assumptions, which are relaxed in a paper cited in the Notes. We first record an assumption that the security numbered zero pays no intermediate dividends and acts as a numeraire, or

Assumption A:
$$D_t^0 \equiv S_t^0 - 1 \equiv 0, \quad t \in [0, T)$$
$$D_T^0 \equiv 1.$$

Security zero is then effectively a nominally riskless bond with zero interest rate. Later we carry out a transformation yielding the effect of this assumption under general conditions. As a technical integrability condition, we also state

Assumption B:
$$E\left([G^n]_T^{1/2} \right) < \infty, \quad n \in \{0, 1, \ldots, N\},$$

where, as usual, $[G^n]$ denotes the quadratic variation process for G^n.

Assumption C: *The risky dividend processes $D^1, \ldots, D^N$ are continuous.* Paragraph G discusses an extension of the following result for the case of discontinuous dividend processes.

THEOREM. *Suppose $\succeq$ is continuous, convex, and strictly monotonic. Under Assumptions A, B, and C, suppose an optimal trading strategy exists. Then there exists an equivalent uniform martingale measure for (D, S).*

PROOF: By Assumption A, $1_\Omega \in M$, so all of the conditions of Theorem 17D are satisfied. There exists therefore a probability measure Q on $(\Omega, \mathcal{F})$

equivalent to P such that dQ/dP is essentially bounded and such that the initial investment functional π has the representation $\pi \cdot x = kE^Q(x)$, $x \in M$, where k is a strictly positive scalar. By the existence of a riskless numeraire (Assumption A), we have $k = 1$.

Of course $G^0 \equiv 1$ is a martingale under any probability measure. For $n \neq 0$, pick any two times s and t in $[0, T]$ with $s > t$, and any event B in $\mathcal{F}_t$. Let $\theta = (\theta^0, \theta^1, \ldots, \theta^N)$ denote the self–financing trading strategy constructed as follows. For $m \neq 0$ or $m \neq n$, let $\theta^m \equiv 0$. Let $\theta^n = 1_A$, where A is the set $B \times (t, s] \subset \Omega \times [0, T]$. (That is, θ^n "buys" one unit of security n at time t provided event B is true, and sells this security at time s.) Define the numeraire trading strategy θ^0 by:

$$\theta_\tau^0 = \int_0^T \theta^n \, dG^n - \theta_\tau^n (S_\tau^n + \Delta D_\tau^n), \quad \tau \in [0, T]. \tag{3}$$

This defines a predictable numeraire trading strategy θ^n. We have

$$\theta_\tau^0 (S_\tau^0 + \Delta D_\tau^0) + \theta_\tau^n (S_\tau^n + \Delta D_\tau^n) = \int_0^T \theta^n \, dG^n, \quad \tau \in [0, T].$$

Because $\int \theta^0 \, dG^0 \equiv 0$, the resulting strategy θ is self-financing. The total gain from trade is $\int_0^T \theta^n \, dG^n = (G_s^n - G_t^n)1_B$. Since the initial investment required is zero,

$$\pi \cdot \left[(G_s^n - G_t^n) 1_B \right] = E^Q \left[(G_s^n \quad G_t^n) 1_B \right] - 0,$$

leaving, since B is arbitrary,

$$E^Q \left[(G_s^n - G_t^n) 1_B \right] = 0, \quad \forall B \in \mathcal{F}_t.$$

By the definition of conditional expectation, $E^Q(G_s^n - G_t^n \mid \mathcal{F}_t) = 0$ almost surely. Since s and t are arbitrary, G^n is by definition a martingale for $(\Omega, \mathcal{F}, F, Q)$. Since n is arbitrary, the result follows by the previous technical lemma. ∎

This theorem represents the initial investment required to reach a given random terminal wealth as the expected value of that wealth under a probability measure Q with the following special property. The process defined by adding the market value of a security to the cumulative dividends of the security is a martingale under Q. In particular, if a security has no intermediate dividends, its price process is a Q–martingale.

F.   Assumption A, the existence of a "riskless" security, is restrictive. We have the freedom of choosing any numeraire, of course. One of the securities, again that numbered zero for convenience, may satisfy the following weakening of Assumption A.

Assumption D: The price process S_0 is predictable, $D_t^0 \equiv 0$, $t \in [0,T)$, and there exist scalars $\overline{K}$ and $\underline{K}$ such that $\overline{K} \geq S_t^0 + \Delta D_t^0 \geq \underline{K} > 0$ for all $t \in [0,T]$.

A simple example is riskless bond with price process $S_t^0 = e^{-(T-t)r}$ for some deterministic interest rate r. Under Assumption D we can treat security number zero as a numeraire and re–express all security market values and dividends relative to the current cum–dividend value of this numeraire security, defining $(\widehat{D}, \widehat{S})$ by,

$$\widehat{S}_t^n = \frac{S_t^n}{S_t^0 + \Delta D_t^0}, \quad t \in [0,T],$$

$$\widehat{D}_t^n = \int_0^t \frac{1}{S_\tau^0 + \Delta D_\tau^0} \, dD_\tau^n, \quad t \in [0,T].$$

The resulting set of gain processes $\widehat{G}^n = \widehat{S}^n + \widehat{D}^n$, $n = 0,1,2,\ldots N$, satisfies the original Assumption A. If Assumption B holds for (D,S), then it also holds for $(\widehat{D}, \widehat{S})$ given the bounds $\overline{K}$ and $\underline{K}$. Of course Assumption C also carries over with this normalization. One can further weaken Assumption A, as indicated in the Notes.

We should verify the obvious intuition that a change of numeraire has no effect on budget feasible choices. Let $\widehat{\Theta}$ denote the space of self–financing trading strategies corresponding to $(\widehat{D}, \widehat{S})$. If $(\widehat{D}, \widehat{S})$ is tight, let $\widehat{\pi}$ denote the corresponding initial investment functional on the marketed space $\widehat{M}$ for $(\widehat{D}, \widehat{S})$. The notation Θ, D, S, π, and M refers to the original "pre–normalization" security market system.

PROPOSITION. *Suppose Assumption D holds. Then*

(a) $\widehat{\Theta} = \Theta$,

(b) $m \in M \Longleftrightarrow m/(S_T^0 + \Delta D_T^0) \in \widehat{M}$, and

(c) $(\widehat{D}, \widehat{S})$ *is tight if and only if* (D,S) *is tight, and in that case,*

$$\widehat{\pi}\left(\frac{m}{S_T^0 + \Delta D_T^0}\right) = \frac{1}{S_0^0}\pi(m), \quad m \in M. \tag{4}$$

Relation (4) gives the following story for the invariance of choice of numeraire. Suppose m is the random terminal wealth generated by a chosen trading strategy θ for the "original" security market system (D, S). Then m can be obtained at an initial investment of $\pi(m) = \theta_0 \cdot S_0$. Taking the security numbered zero as a numeraire, the terminal value of m is $\widehat{m} = m/(S_T^0 + \Delta D_T^0)$. Part (b) of the proposition states that $\widehat{m}$ can be obtained by trade with respect to the normalized security market system $(\widehat{D}, \widehat{S})$. Part (c) states that the required initial investment is $(1/S_0^0)\pi(m)$, but in terms of the original security prices, this is precisely the original cost $\pi(m)$. Thus the normalization has no effect.

The proof of part (a) is rather technical, and cited in the Notes. In discrete time, of course, this is trivial. For part (b), suppose $m \in M$. Then $m = \theta_T \cdot (S_T + \Delta D_T)$ for some $\theta \in \Theta$, implying by part (a) that

$$\theta_T \cdot (\widehat{S}_T + \Delta \widehat{D}_T) = \frac{\theta_T \cdot (S_T + \Delta D_T)}{S_T^0 + \Delta D_T^0} = \frac{m}{S_T^0 + \Delta D_T^0} \in \widehat{M},$$

which yields part (b) once the same argument is repeated in reverse. Part (c) is left as a simple exercise.

One can now merely repeat Theorem 17E in a more general framework.

THEOREM. *Suppose $\succeq$ is continuous, convex, and strictly monotonic. Under Assumptions B, C, and D, suppose an optimal trading strategy exists. Then there exists an equivalent uniform martingale measure for $(\widehat{D}, \widehat{S})$, the normalized security market system.*

G. The careful reader will note a slight technical problem when the risky securities' dividends have discontinuous sample paths. In that case, we have not shown that the numeraire trading strategy defined by (3) is predictable. Under Assumption A, we can easily relax to an adapted numeraire trading strategy. This is innocuous since $G^0 \equiv 1$ under Assumption A implies that $\int \theta^0 \, dG^0 \equiv 0$ is the only possible definition of the financial gains from trading the numeraire. Furthermore, this is quite natural, corresponding to automatic deposit or withdrawal from a checking account of any excess or insufficient cash flow. Since the riskless bond is a numeraire, there is no speculative motive for its trade. In general, adaptedness is too weak a measurability restriction to preclude arbitrage opportunities; here it is strong enough. For Theorem 17F, however, the original numeraire gain process G^0 is not necessarily constant under Assumption D. Thus, the adaptedness measurability restriction for a numeraire trading strategy may be too weak with normalization. We have therefore restricted ourselves here to continuous risky dividend processes, since the numeraire trading strategy is predictable in this case. Thus, for example, if dividends are paid at "rates" one need not relax the predictability restriction on a numeraire trading strategy. The technical issue of whether an adapted numeraire strategy should be permitted after normalization from (D, S) to $(\widehat{D}, \widehat{S})$ is then avoided.

H.   We have been working with a preference relation $\succeq$ over the space $L^1(P)$ of random variables representing terminal wealth for an economy with time set $[0, T]$. Suppose, more generally, that there is an integer number ℓ of consumption goods available at time T. We take the product choice space $L = \prod_{k=1}^{\ell} L^2(P)$ of R^{ℓ}–valued random variables on $(\Omega, \mathcal{F}, P)$, normed by $x \mapsto \left[E(x^{\top}x)\right]^{1/2}$ for any $x = (x_1, \ldots, x_{\ell})$ in L. We also represent random spot prices for goods at time T as a vector $\psi = (\psi_1, \ldots, \psi_{\ell})$ in L, where $\psi_k(\omega)$ represents the spot price of the k–th good in state $\omega \in \Omega$. The total (random) market value for a choice x in L with spot prices $\psi \in L$ is $\psi^{\top}x = \sum_{k=1}^{\ell} \psi_k x_k$. By the Cauchy–Schwarz inequality, $\psi_k x_k \in L^1(P)$ for each k, so $\psi^{\top}x \in L^1(P)$. Having done this spadework, suppose the agent has a preference relation $\succeq_L$ over choices in L. This induces a preference relation $\succeq$ on the space $L^1(P)$ of terminal wealth by the definition

$$W_1 \succeq W_2 \quad \Longleftrightarrow \quad \left[\psi^{\top}x_2 \leq W_2 \Rightarrow \exists x_1 \in L : x_1 \succeq_L x_2, \psi^{\top}x_1 \leq W_1\right] \quad (5)$$

for any W_1 and W_2 in $L^1(P)$ and x_2 in L. This equivalence means merely that random wealth W_1 is preferred to random wealth W_2 whenever any consumption choice x_2 that can be obtained for less than W_2 is bettered by some choice x_1 costing less than W_1. In even less precise terms, $W_1 \succeq W_2$ means that the agent prefers the random spot market budget W_1 to W_2.

PROPOSITION. *Suppose the primitive preference relation $\succeq_L$ on the consumption choice space L is strictly monotonic. Then the preference relation $\succeq$ induced by (5) on the random terminal wealth space $L^1(P)$ is strictly monotonic.*

PROOF: Suppose $W_1 \geq W_2$ and $W_1 \neq W_2$ for any W_1 and W_2 in $L^1(P)$. Suppose $x_2 \in L$ satisfies $\psi^{\top}x_2 \leq W_2$, and let y be any non–zero element of L_+ such that $\psi^{\top}y \leq W_1 - W_2$. The existence of such a y is simple to show (Exercise 17.6). Then $x_2 + y \succ_L x_2$, so $W_1 \succ W_2$. ∎

LEMMA. *Suppose the preference relation $\succeq_L$ on L is convex. Then the preference relation $\succeq$ induced on the terminal wealth space $L^1(P)$ by relation (5) is also convex.*

PROOF: Suppose $v \succeq_L x$ and $z \succeq_L x$ for some $x, v,$ and z in L. Then, for any $\alpha \in [0, 1], W_{\alpha} = \alpha\psi^{\top}v + (1 - \alpha)\psi^{\top}z \in L^1(P)$ is sufficient wealth for $\alpha v + (1 - \alpha)z$. Thus, $\succeq$ is convex on $L^1(P)$ whenever $\succeq_L$ is convex on L. ∎

The representation (2) of the required investment for a given marketed choice extends to this setting. To see this, let $M_L = \{x \in L : \psi^\top x \in M\}$, where $M \subset L^1(P)$ is the marketed subspace of random terminal wealth. Provided (D, S) is tight, we can let π_L denote the linear functional on M_L defining the required initial cost of a marketed consumption choice, or $\pi_L \cdot x = \theta_0 \cdot S_0$, where $W(\theta) = \psi^\top x$. Then we have the representation, under the conditions of Theorem 17C,

$$\pi_L \cdot x = kE^Q \left(\psi^\top x \right), \quad x \in M_L,$$

for a strictly positive scalar k and a probability measure Q equivalent to P with dQ/dP essentially bounded. Under the conditions of Theorem 17E, Q is an equivalent martingale measure.

I. We turn to the choice space C of R^ℓ–valued predictable consumption processes on $\Omega \times [0, T]$ that was identified in Paragraph 16A. We recall that $c = (c^1, \ldots, c^\ell)$ is in C if $E \left(\int_0^T c_t \cdot c_t \, dt \right) < \infty$. The scalar $c^k(\omega, t)$ represents the amount of good k consumed in state $\omega \in \Omega$ at time $t \in [0, T]$. We relax the budget constraint (16.2) for a budget feasible plan (c, θ) for consumption $c \in C$ and trading strategy $\theta \in L^1[G]$ to allow for terminal wealth endowments. This is merely a device for inducing a preference relation on the space of random terminal wealth. For some terminal wealth W in $L^1(P)$, the terminal budget constraint (16.2) is modified to

$$\theta_T \cdot S_T + W \geq 0 \quad \text{a.s.} \tag{6}$$

We then say (c, θ) is W–*budget feasible* if budget feasible in the sense defined in Paragraph 16A, replacing (16.2) however with relation (6) above. If $W_1 \geq W_2 \in L^1(P)$, an agent will quite generally prefer to have terminal wealth endowment W_1. A preference relation $\succeq_C$ on C induces a preference relation $\succeq$ on $L^1(P)$ as follows. We write $W \succeq W'$, for W and W' in $L^1(P)$, provided, for any W'–budget feasible plan (c', θ') there exists a W–budget feasible plan (c, θ) such that $c \succeq_C c'$. One can immediately record results analogous to those of the last paragraph. For example, under an equivalent martingale measure Q the required initial investment for a consumption process $c \in C$ is $E^Q(\int_0^T \psi_t \cdot c_t \, dt)$, where ψ is the spot price process of the economy. Of course, one need not actually include terminal wealth endowments in the economy. Even if wealth endowments are zero the preference relation induced on $L^1(P)$ is well defined.

The induced preference relations of the preceding paragraphs depend on the regime of security and spot prices in place. That is consistent with the intentions of this section: to characterize the given price system for an economy.

EXERCISES

EXERCISE 17.1   (Planetary Finance)

(A)   On the planet Valdar, a stock appreciates in market value by 25 percent in a "good year" and by -5 percent in a "bad" year. (There are only two kinds of years on Valdar.) The Valdarian bond appreciates by 10 percent per year, regardless. The unit of currency on Valdar is the valdar. State the exact current arbitrage–free value, in valdars, of a Valdarian security that pays 100 valdars after two good years, 100 valdars after a good year followed by a bad year, 160 valdars after a bad year followed by a good year, and 50 valdars after two bad years. Is there an example of a valdarian security that does not have a unique arbitrage–free price ? If so, provide such an example. If not, briefly prove so. Assume Valdar has perfect capital markets (no taxes, transactions costs, short sales restrictions, and so on).

(B)   On the sister planet Dalvar, there are three kinds of years: "good," "so–so," and "rotten." Dalvarians have access to Valdarian security markets, and can spend valdars along with their own currency (dalvars, of course). The exchange rate fluctuates randomly, and is always non–zero. Good years occur on Dalvar precisely when they occur on Valdar. (That means that a bad year on Valdar could be either so–so or rotten on Dalvar.) Based on stated assumptions concerning exchange rates, state a contingent claim to dalvars one year from now that does not have a unique arbitrage– free price today. Based on your assumption about exchange rates, what is the minimum number of securities that the Dalvarian Securities Commission could approve in order to guarantee Dalvarian traders effectively complete markets for contingent claims to dalvars one year from now? Does the answer depend on exchange rates? Why or why not? State such a sufficient set of additional securities, and prove that this set is satisfactory. (Dalvarians also have perfect capital markets.)

EXERCISE 17.2   Suppose $(\pi, (d_1, \ldots, d_n))$ is a collection of security prices $S \in R^n$ and dividends $d_j \in R^m$, as in the framework of Paragraph A, that is *strictly arbitrage–free*, meaning that the securities are arbitrage– free and that any portfolio $\theta \in R^n$ with positive non–zero payoff vector $\sum_{j=1}^n \theta_j d_j \in R^m$ has strictly positive market value $S^\top \theta$. Show that the probability measure Q constructed in Paragraph A to represent portfolio market values can be taken to have the property $P(A) > 0$ whenever A is a non–empty event. *Hint:* Use Stiemke's Lemma of Section 7.

EXERCISE 17.3   (Bond Forward Arbitrage)   Recall that a *forward contract* at time t for delivery of an asset at a later time T at the forward price

F_t is an agreement between two parties, buyer and seller, made at time t, for the buyer to give F_t units of account (say dollars) to the seller at time T and for the seller to give one unit of the asset to the buyer at time T. At time t, suppose markets for the following instruments are currently open:

(a) A forward contract, delivering at the end of 1987, for one year Treasury Bills. The current forward price is g_t; the contract delivers a U.S. Treasury Bill paying 10,000 dollars to the bearer at the end of 1988.

(b) A forward contract, delivering at the end of 1988, for U.S. Treasury Bonds. The current forward price is G_t; the contract delivers a U.S. Treasury Bond paying the face value of 100,000 dollars to the bearer at the end of year 2009. This bond, issued in 1979, pays annual coupons of 11.75 percent of face value, paid at the end of each year. Assume that the coupon for 1988 is paid just milliseconds before the forward contract delivery time. That is, the forward contract delivers the bond with the coupon for 1988 already clipped.

(c) The 11.75 percent U.S. Treasury Bond of 2009 described under (b) is currently available for sale at the price s_t.

(d) The two year U.S. Treasury Note maturing at the end of 1988 is currently selling for p_t. This note pays the face value of 100,000 dollars to the bearer at the end of 1988. Assume it pays no coupons. (This is not realistic.)

(A)   Assuming no transactions costs, write a formula for the unique bond forward price G_t that precludes arbitrage, based only on the variables s_t, g_t, and p_t.

(B)   Assume the following bid and ask prices in these markets. The December 1988 T–Note price p_t, bid: 89.00 percent of face value, ask: 89.04 percent of face value. The $11\frac{3}{4}$ bond of 2009, s_t, bid: 123.16 percent of face value, ask: 123.20 percent of face value. Assume all other transactions are costless, with the forward price for December 87 delivery of one year T–Bills, g_t currently at 91.22 percent of face value. Give the highest value of G_t that precludes arbitrage and the lowest value of G_t that precludes arbitrage.

(C)   Suppose the two year Treasury Note of December 1988 pays a coupon of 7 percent of face value at the end of 1987. Under the conditions of Part (A), is there still a unique arbitrage–free bond forward price G_t? If so, state the formula for G_t in terms of the other available data. If not, why not?

EXERCISE 17.4   Suppose the marketed subspace M is dense, meaning that the closure of M is $L^1(P)$. Show that the probability measure Q representing π via relation (2) is unique.

EXERCISE 17.5   Show that the numeraire trading strategy θ^0 defined by relation (3) is predictable under Assumption C.

EXERCISE 17.6   Prove Part (c) of Proposition 17F.

EXERCISE 17.7   With regard to the proof of Proposition 17H, suppose $W_1 - W_2 \in L^1(P)_+ \setminus \{0\}$ and $\psi \in L = \prod_{k=1}^{\ell} L^2(P)$. Prove the existence of $y \in L_+ \setminus \{0\}$ such that $\psi^\top y \le W_1 - W_2$.

Notes

Most of the results of this section originate with Harrison and Kreps (1979). Extensions in Paragraphs B through F are mainly of a technical nature, and have been worked out here and in a series of papers with others goals: Harrison and Pliska (1981), Huang (1985a), Duffie and Huang (1986a), Huang (1985b), Harrison and Pliska (1983), Müller (1983, 1984, 1985), Föllmer and Sondermann (1986), and Duffie (1986c). Proposition 17G is equivalent to results in Huang (1985b), although in a different setting. Huang (1985b) also further weakens Assumptions A and C. The results of Paragraphs G through I are original, and remain to be worked out in fuller detail. For an alternative no–free–lunch version of Thereom 17E, see Duffie and Huang (1986a). For other extensions, see Sun (1986). Ohashi (1987) has pointed out that, with continuous–trading, Proposition 5.1 of Duffie and Huang (1986a) (stated without proof) is incorrect. That is, it is not the case that the absence of arbitrage implies that the terminal cum dividend price of a security is equal to the terminal dividend payoff.

Arrow, in a revision of his 1953 paper on the role of securities published in Arrow (1970), gave an early demonstration that the price of a security could be treated as its expected payoff under a change of probability assessments. The basic idea of representing arbitrage–free security prices by a positive linear extension of the pricing functional from the marketed subspace is due to Ross (1978), a precursor to the dynamic model of Harrison and Kreps (1979). Prisman (1985) and Ross (1987) extend some of the results of this section to markets with taxes or transactions costs.

Chapter III
DISCRETE–TIME ASSET PRICING

Chapters III and IV outline asset pricing theory in discrete and continuous time stochastic market models. The unifying principle of equilibrium asset pricing theory is that the market value of any asset is obtained by discounting the dividend it pays in each date and state, then adding up; the discount factor applied to a given date and state is the marginal utility for aggregate consumption (in that date and state) of a "representative agent". This applies essentially whenever equilibrium allocations are efficient. In the discrete–time models of Section 20, equilibria are automatically efficient since there is but a single agent in the economy. In Section 25, efficiency follows instead from the effect of complete markets, achieved by the ability to continually trade a "dynamically spanning" set of securities.

In these two chapters we often specialize the models of Chapter II to uncertainty generated by an underlying *Markov state–variable process*. This allows for simple representations of market values as well as agents' optimal consumption and portfolio plans. As stated mathematically in Section 18, the expectation of any function of future values of a Markov process depends only on the current value of the Markov process, the defining property of *Markov*. Section 18 is devoted mainly to the mathematical background for discrete–time Markov processes valued in a Borel state space. Section 18 also characterizes the arbitrage–free valuation of securities in a Markov setting. The *principle of dynamic programming* states that the current value of a dynamic program is the supremum, over the set of possible current actions, of the current reward plus the expected value of the dynamic program at the next period. This principle is laid out more carefully in Section 19, where it is allied with the concept of a Markov state process in order to derive the famous *Bellman Equation* for optimal stochastic control. As an illustration, we work out simple closed–form solutions to infinite–horizon investment problems. In Section 20 the Bellman Equation yields a simple Markov equilibrium asset pricing model for a discrete–time stochastic economy. This setting for equilibrium illustrates the main economic principles at work in a stochastic economy.

18.   Markov Processes and Markov Asset Valuation

The essential defining property of a Markov process is that the conditional distribution of its future values given all current information is the same as the conditional distribution of its future values given only its current value. In this section we give a precise meaning to this property in several settings, mainly in discrete–time. A natural and general setting calls for developing the definition of a Borel space. As an application, we show how the martingale security pricing model of Section 17 specializes to a Markov setting.

A.   We begin simply in the finite–state discrete–time setting of a Markov chain. A (possibly finite) sequence $X = (X_1, X_2, \ldots)$ of random variables on a given probability space $(\Omega, \mathcal{F}, P)$, valued in $Z = \{1, 2, \ldots, n\}$, is an n–state *Markov chain* provided, for any time t and state i in Z,

$$P(X_{t+1} = i \mid X_1, \ldots, X_t) = P(X_{t+1} = i \mid X_t). \tag{1}$$

(As usual, we write "$X_{t+1} = i$" as informal notation for the event $\{\omega \in \Omega : X_{t+1}(\omega) = i\}$.) Loosely speaking, old history is irrelevant given the current location of the chain. We must always make a clear distinction between a state $i \in Z$ of the chain X and a state of the world $\omega \in \Omega$. It is often convenient to take Ω to be the *sample path space* $Z \times Z \times Z \times \cdots$ of all possible sample paths of a process valued in Z, to denote a particular state of the world $\omega \in \Omega$ as $(\omega_1, \omega_2, \ldots)$, and to let $\mathcal{F}$ denote the set of all subsets of Ω. The *canonical state process* is then defined as the sequence of random variables $Y = (Y_1, Y_2, \ldots)$ given by $Y_t(\omega) = \omega_t$. If the canonical state process is a Markov chain, we say that P has the *Markov chain property*. In particular, when we are only interested in properties of the distribution of a process, we work directly with a measure P on $(\Omega, \mathcal{F})$, and the reader is to understand that we have the canonical process in mind.

B.   An n–state *transition matrix* is an $n \times n$ positive matrix whose rows each sum to one. We have the following characterization of a Markov chain in terms of its transition matrices.

PROPOSITION. *A sequence $X = (X_1, X_2, \ldots)$ of random variables on a given probability space with values in the state space $Z = \{1, 2, \ldots, n\}$*

is an n–state Markov chain if and only if there exist n–state transition matrices $Q_1, Q_2, \ldots$ with the property: for any time t and any state j,

$$P(X_{t+1} = j \mid X_0, \ldots, X_t) = (Q_t)_{X(t)j}. \tag{2}$$

Moreover, for any initial state i and any n–state transition matrices Q_1, Q_2, ..., there is a unique probability measure P with the Markov chain property on the sample path space $Z \times Z \times \cdots$ satisfying both (2) and $P(X_1 = i) = 1$, where X denotes the canonical state process.

Proof is left as an exercise. In order to extend the idea behind relation (2) to a suitably general state space, certain technical concepts are introduced in the following paragraphs.

C. For a given set A, a positive real valued function d on $A \times A$ is a *metric* on A provided, for any a, b, and c in A,

(a) $d(a, b) = 0 \iff a = b$,

(b) $d(a, b) = d(b, a)$, and

(c) $d(a, c) \le d(a, b) + d(b, c)$.

We may think of $d(a, b)$ as the distance between a and b. A pair (A, d), where d is a metric on the set A, is a *metric space*. If (A, d) is a metric space, a subset B of A is *open* if, for any $b \in B$, there exists $\epsilon \in (0, \infty)$ such that $\{a \in A : d(a, b) \le \epsilon\} \subset B$. This defines the *metric topology*.

Example 1. Suppose A is a subset of a vector space L normed by $\| \cdot \|$. Then the metric d on A defined by $d(x, y) = \|x - y\|$ has the same topology as the norm topology. ♠

Example 2. If A is a finite set, the *discrete metric* d is defined by $d(a, b) = 1$ if $a \ne b$ and $d(a, a) = 0$, and induces the *discrete topology*. ♠

A sequence $\{x_n\}$ in a metric space (A, d) is *Cauchy* provided, for any $\epsilon \in (0, \infty)$, there exists an integer N so large that $d(x_n, x_m) \le \epsilon$ for all n and m larger than N. A sequence $\{x_n\}$ in (A, d) *converges* if there exists $x \in A$ such that $d(x_n, x) \to 0$. A metric space is *complete* if any Cauchy sequence converges. These are natural extensions of the corresponding definitions for a normed space. A *Polish space* is a complete separable metric space. For example, any closed subset of a Euclidean space is a Polish space when given the metric of the Euclidean norm. A *Borel space* is a Borel measurable subset of a Polish space. Any closed or open subset of a Euclidean space is thus a Borel space. A Borel space, unless otherwise

specified, is given the metric of the underlying Polish space, as well as the
Borel tribe of measurable subsets.

Example 3. For any Borel space B, let $C(B)$ denote the space of bounded
continuous real–valued functions on B. Then $C(B)$ is a complete metric
space under the *uniform metric d* defined by $d(f,g) = \sup_{x \in B} | f(x) -
g(x) |$. If B is compact, for example if $B = [0,1]$, then $C(B)$ is separable
and therefore a Polish space as well as a Borel space. These facts are proven
in a source cited in the Notes. ♠

Example 4. For any Borel space B, with Borel tribe $\mathcal{B}$, let $\mathcal{P}(B)$ denote
the space of probability measures on $(B,\mathcal{B})$. Then, under a metric cited
in the Notes, $\mathcal{P}(B)$ is itself a Borel space. Furthermore, a sequence $\{P_n\}$
converges in $\mathcal{P}(B)$ to P if and only if, for any $f \in C(B)$,

$$\int_B f(x)\,dP_n(x) \rightarrow \int_B f(x)\,dP(x),$$

that is, $E^{P_n}(f) \rightarrow E^P(f)$. The topology on $\mathcal{P}(B)$ is known variously as
the *vague topology*, the *weak topology*, or more formally, the *topology of
weak convergence relative to $C(B)$*. ♠

If (A_1,d_1) and (A_2,d_2) are metric spaces, a function $F : A_1 \rightarrow A_2$ is
continuous provided $\{F(x_n)\}$ converges in (A_2,d_2) to $F(x)$ whenever $\{x_n\}$
is a sequence in A_1 converging to x. For example, if A and B are Borel
spaces, then a function $F : A \rightarrow \mathcal{P}(B)$ is continuous if and only if, for any
sequence $\{a_n\}$ in A converging to a and any $f \in C(B)$, $E^{a_n}(f) \rightarrow E^a(f)$,
where E^a denotes expectation under the measure $F(a)$. Equivalently, F is
continuous if and only if the function $g : A \rightarrow R$ defined by $g(a) = E^a(f)$
is continuous for any $f \in C(B)$.

If (A_1,d_1) and (A_2,d_2) are metric spaces, then the product space $A_1 \times
A_2$ is given the *product metric d* defined by

$$d[(a_1,a_2),(b_1,b_2)] = d_1(a_1,b_1) + d_2(a_2,b_2),$$

for any (a_1,a_2) and (b_1,b_2) in $A_1 \times A_2$. If A_1 and A_2 are Borel spaces, so
is the product space $A_1 \times A_2$. Similarly, any finite product $A_1 \times \cdots \times A_N$
of Borel spaces $A_1,\ldots,A_N$ is a Borel space under the (obviously defined)
product metric. Any countable product $\prod_{n=1}^\infty A_n$ of Borel spaces $A_1, A_2, \ldots$
is also a Borel space; the details are cited in the Notes.

D. Given Borel spaces X and Y and a measure $P \in \mathcal{P}(X \times Y)$, the *marginal* of P on X is the measure $P_X \in \mathcal{P}(X)$ defined by $P_X(A) = P(A \times Y)$ for any event A in X. For illustration, suppose that W is an X-valued random variable and V is a Y-valued random variable, and that (W, V) has *joint distribution* P. Then P_X is the distribution of W. A *version of the conditional* of P on Y is any measurable function $Q : X \to \mathcal{P}(Y)$ with the property: for any measurable subsets A of X and B of Y,

$$P(A \times B) = \int_A [Q(x)](B) \, dP_X(x),$$

meaning that $Q(x)$ can be treated as the conditional distribution of V given an observed outcome x of W. The existence of a version of the conditional is non-trivial, and is cited in the Notes. A conditional is unique in the sense that, for any two versions Q and Q' of the conditional of P on Y, we have $Q(x) = Q'(x)$ almost surely with respect to the marginal P_X. For this reason, we typically refer to any version of the conditional as *the conditional*.

Given any measure $Q_1 \in \mathcal{P}(X)$ and any measurable function $Q_2 : X \to \mathcal{P}(Y)$, we can also construct a unique measure $P \in \mathcal{P}(X \times Y)$ such that Q_1 is the marginal P_X and Q_2 is the conditional of P on Y. To see this, for any $B \in X \times Y$, let $B_x = \{y \in Y : (x, y) \in B\}$. Then the measure P defined by

$$P(B) = \int_X [Q_2(x)](B_x) \, dQ_1(x) \tag{3}$$

indeed has the marginal $P_X = Q_1$ on X and a conditional Q_2 on Y. Proof is assigned as an exercise. Furthermore, P is unique in this regard, but we refer to the Notes for a proof of uniqueness.

E. For most of our purposes, a *state space* is any Borel space Z. For a finite time set $\{1, \ldots, T\}$, we let Z^T denote the T-fold product $\prod_{t=1}^{T} Z$, the *sample path space*. For each time $t \in \{1, \ldots, T-1\}$, suppose we are given a measurable function $Q^t : Z^t \to \mathcal{P}(Z)$, to be thought of as governing the transition of some underlying Z-valued stochastic process X. That is, given a *sample path history* at time t of $z^t = (z_1, \ldots, z_t) \in Z^t$, one is to think of $Q^t(z^t)$ as the conditional distribution of X_{t+1} given that $(X_1, \ldots, X_t) = z^t$. We are also given an *initial distribution* $P^1 \in \mathcal{P}(Z)$, treated as the distribution of X_1. Based on the construction in Paragraph D, we have a measure $P^2 \in \mathcal{P}(Z^2)$ whose marginal is P^1 and whose conditional is Q^1. In other words, P^2 may be thought of as the joint distribution of (X_1, X_2). By induction, for any t, we have a measure $P^t \in \mathcal{P}(Z^t)$ whose marginal on Z^{t-1} is P^{t-1} and whose conditional is Q^{t-1}. We can extend this to the infinite horizon case as follows.

THEOREM. Let $Z_1, Z_2, \ldots$ be a (possibly finite) sequence of Borel spaces. Let $P^1 \in \mathcal{P}(Z_1)$. For any $t \geq 1$, let $Z^t = Z_1 \times \cdots \times Z_t$ and let $Q^t : Z^t \to \mathcal{P}(Z_{t+1})$ be measurable. There exist unique $P^1 \in \mathcal{P}(Z^1)$, $P^2 \in \mathcal{P}(Z^2), \ldots,$ and $P \in \mathcal{P}(Z_1 \times Z_2 \times \cdots)$ such that, for any non–terminal time $t \geq 1$, P^t is the marginal of P on Z^t and Q^t is a version of the conditional of P^{t+1} on Z_{t+1}.

As an application, we can take $Z_t = Z$ for all t in a finite time set $\mathcal{T} = \{1, 2, \ldots, T\}$ or in the infinite time set $\mathcal{T} = \{1, 2, \ldots\}$, and let $\Omega = \prod_{t \in \mathcal{T}} Z$. The canonical process $X : \Omega \times \mathcal{T} \to Z$ is defined by $X\big((z_1, z_2, \ldots), t\big) = z_t$. If $P^1 \in \mathcal{P}(Z)$ is taken as an initial distribution and $Q^t : Z^t \to \mathcal{P}(Z)$ is the measurable transition function at time t, we may apply the previous theorem to obtain a distribution $P \in \mathcal{P}(\Omega)$ on the sample paths of the canonical process X such that the distribution under P of X_1 is P^1, and such that (almost surely) the conditional distribution of X_{t+1} given $(X_1, \ldots, X_t)$ is $Q^t(X_1, \ldots, X_t)$. Let $B(Z)$ denote the space of bounded measurable real–valued functions on Z. For any $f \in B(Z)$, the conditional expectation under P of $f(X_{t+1})$ given $X_1, \ldots, X_t$ is

$$E[f(X_{t+1}) \mid X_1, \ldots, X_t] = \int_Z f(z) \, d[Q^t(X_1, \ldots, X_t)](z) \quad \text{a.s.} \quad (4)$$

If the transition functions $\{Q^t\}$ are of the form $Q^t(z_1, \ldots, z_t) = Q_t(z_t)$ for some $Q_t : Z \to \mathcal{P}(Z)$, $t \geq 1$, we see that X has the Markov property: the conditional distribution of X_{t+1} given $X_1, \ldots, X_t$ depends only on X_t. More formally, we define a stochastic process X on some probability space with sample paths in Ω to be Markov if, for any $f \in B(Z)$ and any times t and $s \geq t$,

$$E[f(X_s) \mid X_1, \ldots, X_t] = E[f(X_s) \mid X_t] \quad \text{a.s.} \quad (5)$$

PROPOSITION. A stochastic process X on some probability space with sample paths in Ω is Markov if and only if, for any time t, there exists a measurable function $Q_t : Z \to \mathcal{P}(Z)$, such that for any $f \in B(Z)$,

$$E[f(X_{t+1}) \mid X_1, \ldots, X_t] = \int_Z f(z) \, d[Q_t(X_t)](z) \quad \text{a.s.} \quad (6)$$

Moreover, given any $P^1 \in \mathcal{P}(Z)$ and any such $Q_t : Z \to \mathcal{P}(Z)$, $t \geq 1$, there is a unique measure $P \in \mathcal{P}(\Omega)$ such that the canonical process X satisfies (6) and such that X_1 has distribution P^1.

A Markov process X with transition functions $Q_1, Q_2, \ldots$ characterized by this proposition is time–homogeneous provided there is a transition function $Q : Z \to \mathcal{P}(Z)$ such that $Q_t = Q$ for any (non–terminal) time t.

F. A *transition operator* on $B(Z)$, where Z is a Borel space, is a linear function $V : B(Z) \to B(Z)$ with the properties:

(a) $Vf \geq 0$ for any $f \geq 0$, and

(b) $V1_Z = 1_Z$.

(Note the shorthand convention "Vf" for the evaluation $V(f)$ of any $f \in B(Z)$.) The spaces of transition operators and transition functions are in one–to–one correspondence by associating $Q : Z \to \mathcal{P}(Z)$ with $V_Q : B(Z) \to B(Z)$ via $[V_Q f](z) = \int_Z f(z') \, d[Q(z)](z')$ for any $f \in B(Z)$, and via $[Q(z)](A) = [V_Q 1_A](z)$, for any measurable subset A of Z. We often work directly with the operator V_Q rather than Q because of the convenient property:

$$E[f(X_{t+1}) \mid X_t] = [V_Q f](X_t) \quad \text{a.s.} \tag{7}$$

for any $f \in B(Z)$, where X is any time–homogeneous Markov process with sample paths in Z and transition function Q, as given by Proposition 18E. (Property (7) is proven by a standard argument cited in the Notes.)

G. Let Z be a Borel space and T be a finite time set $\{1, \ldots, T\}$ or the infinite time set $\{1, 2, \ldots\}$. Repeating an earlier given definition, the sample path space $\Omega = \prod_{t \in T} Z$ determines the *canonical process* $X : \Omega \times T \to Z$ by $X((z_1, z_2, \ldots), t) = z_t$. Given a family $\{V_t : t \in T\}$ of transition operators on $B(Z)$, any initial distribution $P^1 \in \mathcal{P}(Z)$ gives us a unique measure $P \in \mathcal{P}(\Omega)$ under which X_1 has distribution P^1 and

$$E[f(X_{t+1}) \mid X_t] = [V_t f](X_t) \quad \text{a.s.}, \quad t \in T, \ f \in B(Z).$$

For any functions $U : B(Z) \to B(Z)$ and $W : B(Z) \to B(Z)$, we use the notation UW for the composition $U \circ W$; that is $[UW]f = U[Wf]$ for any $f \in B(Z)$. If, for any t, we define the transition operator $_tV_{t+2}$ on $B(Z)$ by $_tV_{t+2} = V_t V_{t+1}$, the law of iterated conditional expectation generates the expression, for any $f \in B(Z)$,

$$
\begin{aligned}
E[f(X_{t+2}) \mid X_t] &= E\big[E[f(X_{t+2}) \mid X_{t+1}] \mid X_t\big] \\
&= E\big[[V_{t+1}f](X_{t+1}) \mid X_t\big] = [V_t(V_{t+1}f)](X_t) \\
&= [_tV_{t+2}f](X_{t+1}) \quad \text{a.s.}
\end{aligned}
$$

In general, we define $_tV_s$ for any times t and $s \geq t$ by the composition

$$_tV_s = V_t \circ V_{t+1} \circ \cdots \circ V_{s-1},$$

with the convention: $_tV_t = I$, where I is the *identity operator* ($If = f$). Repeated application of the law of iterated conditional expectation then yields the convenient relation

$$E[f(X_s) \mid X_t] = [_tV_s f](X_t) \quad \text{a.s.} \tag{8}$$

By the same token, we have the *Chapman–Kolmogorov Equation*:

$$_tV_s = {}_tV_\tau \; {}_\tau V_s, \tag{9}$$

whenever $t \leq \tau \leq s$. For any $V : B(Z) \to B(Z)$ we define $V^0 = I$ and $V^t = V \circ V^{t-1}$ for $t \geq 1$. If X is a time–homogeneous Markov process with transition operator V, we have

$$E[f(X_s) \mid X_t] = [V^{s-t}f](X_t) \quad \text{a.s.} \tag{10}$$

for any $f \in B(Z)$, whenever $s \geq t$.

H. Given a Borel state space Z, a *sub–Markov transition operator* is a linear function $V : B(Z) \to B(Z)$ with the properties:

(a) $Vf \geq 0$ for any $f \geq 0$, and

(b) $V1_Z \leq 1_Z$.

We are to imagine that $1 - [V1_Z](z)$ is the probability of "no transition", or "death", in state z. In order to make a formal connection with probability theory, however, we must deal with the gap in the total probability of transition by augmenting a state † typically called the *cemetery*. We have the *augmented state space* $Z^\dagger = Z \cup \{\dagger\}$, which is a Borel space when the underlying metric d is extended to the metric $d^\dagger$ on $Z^\dagger$, defined for any a and b in Z by:

(a) $d^\dagger(a, b) = d(a, b)$, and

(b) $d^\dagger(a, \dagger) = d^\dagger(\dagger, a) = 1$.

Any $f \in B(Z)$ is extended to $f^\dagger \in B(Z^\dagger)$ by $f^\dagger(\dagger) = 0$. Then V can be uniquely extended to a transition operator $V^\dagger : B(Z^\dagger) \to B(Z^\dagger)$ with the properties:

(a) $[V^\dagger g](\dagger) = 0$ for any $g \in B(Z^\dagger)$, and

(b) $V^\dagger f^\dagger = Vf$ for any $f \in B(Z)$.

Given a finite time set $\mathcal{T} = \{1, \ldots, T\}$ or the infinite time set $\mathcal{T} = \{1, 2, \ldots\}$, Proposition 18E and the comments of the previous paragraph give us a time–homogeneous Markov process $X^\dagger$ with sample paths in $\Omega^\dagger = \prod_{t \in \mathcal{T}} Z^\dagger$, and with the transition property

$$E[g(X_{t+1}^\dagger) \mid X_t^\dagger] = [V^\dagger g](X_t^\dagger) \quad \text{a.s., } g \in B(Z^\dagger). \tag{11}$$

The †–augmented notation is cumbersome however, so we generally work with the sample path space $\Omega = \prod_{t \in T} Z$ and a *time–homogeneous sub–Markov process* X with sample paths in Ω and sub–Markov transition operator V. The relationship

$$E[f(X_{t+1}) \mid X_t] = [Vf](X_t), \quad f \in B(Z), \tag{12}$$

is entirely clear, but has formal meaning only via the definition of $X^\dagger$. More generally, given a family $\{V_t : t \in T\}$ of sub–Markov transition operators, we have a corresponding *sub–Markov process* X defined in the obvious way. The additional property $V_t 1_Z = 1_Z$ for all t gives rise to the terminology *proper Markov*, meaning Markov in the usual sense.

I. We next examine the arbitrage–valuation of securities in a Markov setting. Let Z be a Borel state space and let $Q^* \subset \mathcal{P}(Z)$ be given as a *reference measure*. In this paragraph, all equalities of the form "$f - g$," for f and g in $B(Z)$, are to be taken in the sense "$f = g$ Q^*–almost surely", a technical limitation. We consider a security market as follows. Let $\mathcal{T}$ be a finite time set $\{1, \dots, T\}$ or the infinite time set $\{1, 2, \dots\}$. For each non–terminal time t, let $\pi_t \in B(Z)$ denote the *discount rate* on short term riskless borrowing at time t. That is, $\pi_t(z)$ is the market value in state z of a claim to one unit of account in any state $z' \in Z$ at time $t+1$. There are N securities of the form

$$(d, p) = \{(d_{nt}, p_{nt}) \in B(Z) \times B(Z) : n \in \{1, \dots, N\}, \ t \in \mathcal{T}\},$$

where, at any time t and state $z \in Z$, $d_{nt}(z)$ is the current dividend of security n in units of account and $p_{nt}(z)$ is the current *ex dividend* market value of a claim to all future dividends of security n. The set of total payoffs in units of account at time $t+1$ that can be formed by short term borrowing and purchases of security portfolios in the *marketed subspace*

$$M_t = \mathrm{span}\big(\{1_Z, p_{1,t+1} + d_{1,t+1}, \dots, p_{N,t+1} + d_{N,t+1}\}\big) \subset B(Z). \tag{13}$$

A payoff $m \in M_t$ can be achieved as some combination of α_0 units of riskless borrowing, α_1 units of security one, α_2 units of security two, and so on, for the total payoff function

$$m = \alpha_0 1_Z + \alpha_1(d_{1,t+1} + p_{1,t+1}) + \cdots + \alpha_N(d_{N,t+1} + p_{N,t+1}),$$

at an investment cost at time t of

$$V_t(m) \equiv \alpha_0 \pi_t + \alpha_1 p_{1,t} + \cdots + \alpha_N p_{N,t}. \tag{14}$$

Of course $V_t(m)$ is a state–dependent function; the particular cost in state $z \in Z$ is $[V_t(m)](z)$ units of account. The function $V_t : M_t \rightarrow B(Z)$ defined by (14) is clearly linear. Furthermore, V_t is *positive*, by definition, if $V_t m$ is a positive function for any positive function m in M_t. But this is our notion of *no–arbitrage*: a positive payoff m can be achieved only at a positive investment $[V_t(m)](z) \geq 0$, regardless of the current state z. Defining the marketed subspaces $\{M_t : t \in \mathcal{T}\}$ and corresponding *valuation functions* $V_t : M_t \rightarrow B(Z)$, $t \geq 1$, we thus characterize (p, d, π) as *arbitrage–free* if V_t is positive for all (non–terminal) t. In this setting, we will say that interest rates are positive if $\pi_t \leq 1_Z$ for all (non–terminal) t. (The interest rate r in state z is defined by $(1 + r)\pi_t(z) = 1$ if $\pi_t(z) > 0$.) Although we defer to the Notes for a proof of the following extension result, the case of a finite state space is examined in an exercise.

PROPOSITION. *Suppose M is a linear subspace of $B(Z)$, $1_Z \in M$, and $V : M \rightarrow B(Z)$ is linear, positive, and satisfies $V(1_Z) \leq 1_Z$. Then V has an extension $\overline{V} : B(Z) \rightarrow B(Z)$ with the same properties. That is, $\overline{V}(m) = V(m)$ for all m in M, $\overline{V}(f) \geq 0$ for all $f \geq 0$, and $\overline{V}(1_Z) \leq 1_Z$.*

This proposition immediately gives us *Markov valuation of securities* in this setting.

THEOREM. *Suppose (p, d, π) is arbitrage–free and $\pi_t \leq 1_Z$ for all t (positive interest rates). Then there exists a sub–Markov process X with sample paths in $\Omega = \prod_{t \in \mathcal{T}} Z$ such that, for any times t and $s > t$, and any security n,*

$$p_{nt}(X_t) = E\left[p_{ns}(X_s) + \sum_{\tau=t+1}^{s} d_{n\tau}(X_\tau) \,\middle|\, X_t \right] \quad \text{a.s.} \quad (15)$$

PROOF: By the previous proposition, the valuation functions $\{V_t : M_t \rightarrow B(Z)\}$ have extensions $\overline{V}_t : B(Z) \rightarrow B(Z)$ with the properties of sub–Markov transition operators. The discussion in Paragraphs E through H gives the construction of a sub–Markov process X with the transition operator $\overline{V}_t$ for time t. Relation (15) then follows from (14) for $\alpha_n = 1$, $\alpha_k = 0$, $k \neq n$, and from induction in time. ∎

We remark on the similarity with the martingale valuation model of Section 17. Here, however, normalization to a numeraire security is unnecessary given the sub–Markov property. The normalization is implicit in the "death probability" of X. Indeed, the survival probability $E[1_Z(X_s) \mid X_t]$ from time t to time s is precisely the discount rate on riskless borrowing between times t and s (should such borrowing be possible). Further characterization is given in the exercises and cited in the Notes.

J. For general reference, we provide an abstract definition of Markov processes in discrete or continuous time settings. Let $(\Omega, \mathcal{F}, F, P)$ be a filtered probability space for a time set T, where $F = \{\mathcal{F}_t : t \in T\}$ is an information filtration. An F–adapted stochastic process X is *Markov* with respect to $(\Omega, \mathcal{F}, F, P)$ if, for any time $t \in T$ and any bounded real-valued random variable Y measurable with respect to the tribe $\sigma(\{X_s : s \geq t\})$ generated by future values of X,

$$E[Y \mid \mathcal{F}_t] = E[Y \mid X_t] \quad \text{a.s.} \tag{16}$$

In imprecise terms, X is a Markov process if at any time t the conditional distribution of X_s for any $s \geq t$ depends only on X_t. Given the current value X_t, in other words, all other known events provide no additional information on the future behavior of X. This definition places no restrictions on the outcome space for the process in question; X can take values in any measurable space $(Z, \mathcal{Z})$. When no filtration is stated, the filtration generated by X is assumed to be the ambient information structure. That is, a stochastic process X whose values $\{X_t : t \in T\}$ are random variables on a probability space $(\Omega, \mathcal{F}, P)$ is *Markov* if Markov with respect to the filtration generated by X.

EXERCISES

EXERCISE 18.1 Show that any finite set with the discrete metric forms a Polish space as well as a Borel space.

EXERCISE 18.2 Prove Proposition 18B.

EXERCISE 18.3 Let $B = [0, 1]$ be given the usual metric $d(x, y) = \mid x - y \mid$. Show that B is a Polish space. Show that $C(B)$, under the uniform metric, is a Polish space. *Hint:* Show that the simple functions of the form $f(x) = \sum_{n=1}^{N} 1_{[a_n, b_n]}(x) c_n$, where a_n, b_n, and c_n are rational numbers, form a countable set that is *dense*, that is, whose closure is $C(B)$.

EXERCISE 18.4 Let Z be a Borel space and $V_Q : B(Z) \to B(Z)$ denote the transition operator corresponding to a transition function $Q : Z \to \mathcal{P}(Z)$. Show that Q is continuous if and only if $V_Q f \in C(Z)$ for all $f \in C(Z)$.

EXERCISE 18.5 Show that any compact metric space is a Polish space.

EXERCISE 18.6 Let X and Y be Borel spaces, let $Q_1 \in \mathcal{P}(X)$, and let $Q_2 : X \to \mathcal{P}(Y)$ be measurable. Show that relation (3) defines a measure $P \in \mathcal{P}(X \times Y)$, that P has marginal $P_X = Q_1$ on X, and that P has Q_2 as a version of its conditional on Y.

EXERCISE 18.7   Suppose that U and W are transition operators on $B(Z)$ for some Borel space Z. Show that UW is a transition operator on $B(Z)$.

EXERCISE 18.8   Show that the function $V_t : M_t \to B(Z)$ defined by relation (14) is linear.

EXERCISE 18.9   Prove Proposition 18I in the case of a finite state space Z.

EXERCISE 18.10   Provide the details of the induction argument in the proof of Theorem 18I.

EXERCISE 18.11   For the state space $Z = \{1, \ldots, m\}$, and time set $\mathcal{T} = \{1, 2, \ldots\}$, let p and d be $m \times n$ matrices whose columns are the time–independent and state–dependent prices and dividends, respectively, of n securities. Assume there exists a portfolio $\bar{\theta} \in R^n$ with strictly positive total payoff in each state $[(p+d)\bar{\theta} \gg 0]$. Also assume that (p, d) is (strictly) arbitrage–free, in the sense that $(p + d)\theta > 0$ implies that $p\theta \gg 0$ for any portfolio $\theta \in R^n$. Finally, assume the growth condition

$$\max_k | \, p_{kj} \, | < \max_k | \, p_{kj} + d_{kj} \, |, \quad j \in \{1, \ldots, n\}, \tag{17}$$

indicating that the required investment in any security is less than its maximum payoff in the following period.

(A)   Demonstrate the existence of an m–state sub–Markov transition matrix Q, all of whose elements are strictly positive, with the property $p = Q(p + d)$. *Hint:* Use Stiemke's Lemma.

(B)   Interpret (A) by demonstrating the existence of a time–homogeneous sub–Markov process X with state space $\{1, \ldots, m\}$ and the property:

$$p_k = E[p_{X(t+1)} + d_{X(t+1)} \mid X(t) = k]$$

for any state k and time t. (Here, p_k denotes the k–th row of p, and d_k denotes the k–th row of d.)

(C)   From part (A), show that $(I - Q)$ is non–singular and that $p = [(I - Q)^{-1} + I]d$. Interpret this in terms of the Markov process X by showing that

$$p_k = E\left[\sum_{s=t+1}^{\infty} d_{X(s)} \,\middle|\, X(t) = k \right]$$

for any state k and time t. Demonstrate, in particular, that the expectation indeed exists.

(D)   Find a sufficient condition for (17) in terms of interest rates when riskless short–term borrowing is possible.

EXERCISE 18.12 An *eigenvalue* $\lambda \in R$ and corresponding *eigenvector* $q \in R^m$ of an $m \times m$ matrix Q are defined by the property: $Qq = \lambda q$. (We ignore complex eigenvalues, as they are not required here.) The *spectral radius* of Q, denoted $r(Q)$, is the maximum absolute value of any eigenvalue. The *Frobenius–Perron Theorem* states that if Q is positive, then $r(Q)$ is an eigenvalue of Q with a positive eigenvector.

(A) Given a Borel space Z and a (measurable) transition function $f : Z \to \mathcal{P}(Z)$, we define $\widehat{f} : \mathcal{P}(Z) \to \mathcal{P}(Z)$, denoting $\widehat{f}(\mu)$ as $\widehat{f}\mu$, by:

$$[\widehat{f}\mu](A) = \int_Z [f(z)](A)\, d\mu(z), \quad z \in Z,$$

for any event A of Z. In other words, if X is a Z–valued time–homogeneous Markov process with transition function f and initial distribution μ for X_1, then $\widehat{f}\mu$ is the distribution of X_2. Similarly, define $\widehat{f}^t : \mathcal{P}(Z) \to \mathcal{P}(Z)$ for $t \in \{0, 1, 2, \ldots\}$ inductively by $\widehat{f}^0\mu = \mu$ and $\widehat{f}^t\mu = \widehat{f}(\widehat{f}^{t-1}\mu)$, $t \geq 1$. A measure $\mu \in \mathcal{P}(Z)$ is a *steady–state distribution* for f (that is, for any time–homogeneous Markov process with transition function f) if $\widehat{f}\mu = \mu$, that is, if μ is a fixed point of $\widehat{f}$. (A steady–state distribution is also known as an *invariant measure*.) Equivalently, μ is a steady–state distribution of an underlying process X with transition function f if, once given an initial distribution μ for X_1, X_t has distribution $\widehat{f}^t\mu = \mu$ for all t. Show that if Z is finite, then any transition function $f : Z \to \mathcal{P}(Z)$ has a steady–state distribution. *Hint:* Show that the spectral radius of a transition matrix is unity, and use the Frobenius–Perron Theorem.

Remark: If $\widehat{f}$ is continuous and Z is a compact metric space, the *Schauder Fixed Point Theorem* implies the existence of a steady–state distribution. We do not provide the details of this fixed point theorem or its application here.

(B) A measure $\mu \in \mathcal{P}(Z)$ is *ergodic* for a measurable transition function $f : Z \to \mathcal{P}(Z)$ on a Borel space Z if, for any $\mu^0 \in \mathcal{P}(Z)$, $\lim_{t \to \infty} \widehat{f}^t\mu^0(A) = \mu(A)$ for any event A of Z. Suppose that Z is finite and that f corresponds to a strictly positive transition matrix Q. Show that f has a (unique) ergodic measure μ.

EXERCISE 18.13 In the context of Exercise 18.11, show that any such strictly positive sub–Markov transition matrix Q has a spectral radius $\lambda \in (0, 1)$ and a corresponding strictly positive eigenvector q whose elements sum to one. Show that

$$q^\top p = \frac{1}{1-\lambda} q^\top d. \tag{18}$$

Interpret probabilistically in terms of a "sub–steady–state" distribution for the sub–Markov process demonstrated in Exercise 18.11. Also interpret λ as a "steady–state" discount factor. If Q is a proper Markov transition matrix, show that q corresponds to its ergodic measure.

Notes

The material in Paragraphs A through H is completely standard. An excellent introductory treatment is Freedman (1983b). For Example 3 of Paragraph C, see Bertsekas and Shreve (1978). For Example 4 of Paragraph C, see Billingsley (1968). The metric on $\mathcal{P}(B)$ referred to in this example is the *Prohorov metric*. The fact that a countable product of Borel spaces is a Borel space can be found, for example, in Bertsekas and Shreve (1978). The existence of a version of the conditional on Y of any probability measure on the product $X \times Y$ of Borel spaces is recorded, among other places, in Chapter 7 of Bertsekas and Shreve (1978). This source can also be cited for the uniqueness of a measure on $X \times Y$ with a given marginal on X and a conditional on Y. Theorem 18E is also found in the same source. Proposition 18E can be deduced from Meyer (1967). Paragraph I is from Duffie and Garman (1985) and Duffie (1985b), and is extended there. Exercises 11 and 12 are special cases of some of these extensions for a finite state space. Parthasarathy (1967) is a standard treatment of probability measures on Borel spaces. General treatments of discrete–time Markov processes are given by Hunt (1966), Meyer (1967), and Revuz (1975).

19.   Discrete–Time Markov Control

In multi–period optimization models, the problem of selecting actions for all periods can be decomposed into a family of single–period problems. In each period, one merely chooses an action maximizing the sum of the reward for that period and the value of beginning the problem again in the following period. In a stationary infinite–horizon setting, where the efforts of this chapter are concentrated, this turns out to be a particularly simple decomposition, for the value of beginning in any period is the same. We will motivate the dynamic programming concept with a simple deterministic example and then turn to a Markovian setting for uncertainty. A discrete–time Markov process taking values in a Borel state space is then chosen as the framework for the general results of this section. As an example, we work out an application to optimal investment under stochastic returns as a prelude to the equilibrium asset pricing model of Section 20.

A. We start with a simple deterministic control example. Given an understanding of this informal example, not a great deal of additional intuition is required for more general stochastic control problems, although there are admittedly quite a few additional technical details.

Robinson Crusoe has been left with x bushels of corn, some of which may be planted and the remaining portion eaten immediately. Both portions must be positive of course. Each bushel planted yields γ bushels at the beginning of the following year, when Robinson will be faced with the same decision, and so on forever. Here γ is a strictly positive scalar; there is no uncertainty. Robinson evaluates a time sequence $c = \{c_1, c_2, c_3, \ldots\}$ of corn consumption with the utility functional $U(c) = \sum_{t=1}^{\infty} \rho^t u(c_t)$, where $\rho \in (0, 1)$ is a discount factor and u is a real–valued function on $[0, \infty)$. Suppose, for each initial stock x of corn, there exists an optimal consumption sequence $c^* = \{c_1^*, c_2^*, \ldots\}$, and let $V(x) = U(c^*)$. We call V the *value function* for the control problem; $V(x)$ is the indirect utility for any initial stock $x \geq 0$. Let $\hat{c}$ denote the consumption sequence $\{\hat{c}_1 = c_2^*, \hat{c}_2 = c_3^*, \ldots\}$. In other words, $\hat{c}$ is the consumption sequence starting one period later with the new stock of corn $\hat{x} = (x - c_1^*)\gamma$ resulting from the initial consumption choice c_1^*. We note that

$$U(c^*) = \rho u(c_1^*) + \rho \sum_{t=1}^{\infty} \rho^t u(c_{t+1}^*) = \rho u(c_1^*) + \rho U(\hat{c}).$$

We claim that $U(\hat{c}) = V(\hat{x})$, for otherwise there is an optimal consumption sequence b for initial stock $\hat{x}$ such that $U(b) > U(\hat{c})$. But then the sequence $\tilde{c} = \{c_1^*, b_1, b_2, \ldots\}$ would be strictly preferred to c^* since $U(\tilde{c}) = \rho u(c_1^*) + \rho U(b) > \rho u(c_1^*) + \rho U(\hat{c}) = U(c^*)$, contradicting the optimality of c^*. Thus, indeed, $U(\hat{c}) = V(\hat{x})$. Combining $V(x) = \rho u(c_1^*) + \rho U(\hat{c})$ with $U(\hat{c}) = V(\hat{x}) = V[(x - c_1^*)\gamma]$, we have the optimality relation

$$V(x) = \rho u(c_1^*) + \rho V[(x - c_1^*)\gamma].$$

We also claim that, for any other initial consumption choice c_1,

$$V(x) \geq \rho u(c_1) + \rho V[(x - c_1)\gamma].$$

Indeed, if $c_1 \in [0, x]$ is such that $V(x) < \rho u(c_1) + \rho V[(x - c_1)\gamma]$ and $b = \{b_1, b_2, \ldots\}$ is optimal for initial stock $(x - c_1)\gamma$, then $d = \{c_1, b_1, b_2, \ldots\}$ has the value

$$\rho u(c_1) + \rho U(b) = \rho u(c_1) + \rho V[(x - c_1)\gamma] > V(x),$$

again contradicting the optimality of c^*. Combining what we have learned,

$$V(x) = \max_{c_1 \in [0,x]} \quad \rho u(c_1) + \rho V[(x - c_1)\gamma], \qquad x \geq 0,$$

which is known as the *Bellman Equation* for this problem. We have reduced the infinite–horizon control problem to a family of single period problems. At each period the optimal consumption choice c_1^* given the current stock of corn x is given by maximizing over current consumption choices $c_1 \in [0, x]$ the current reward $u(c_1)$ plus the value $V[(x - c_1)\gamma]$ of the problem starting in the following period with the new stock $(x - c_1)\gamma$. It remains to deduce a solution V to the Bellman Equation. With $u(a) = \sqrt{a}$, for example, and provided $\rho\sqrt{\gamma} < 1$, the function $V(x) = \rho\sqrt{x/(1 - \rho^2\gamma)}$ solves the Bellman equation. The optimal initial consumption choice is then $c_1^* = (1 - \rho^2\gamma)x$. These solutions are easily verified, and a method of deducing them is sketched out in Paragraph J. Significantly, the current consumption choice c_t in any period t is always the same function $(1-\rho^2\gamma)x_t$ of the current stock of corn, x_t in period t. We will now turn to a stochastic model for control with the same basic feature: the current optimal action c_t is a fixed function of the current state of the problem X_t. In future examples, however, the state variable X_t is random.

B.   For an easy introduction to discrete–time control under uncertainty, we will begin at an informal level, and take a finite *state space* $Z = \{1, \ldots, n\}$ and a finite *action space* $A = \{1, \ldots, m\}$. Let Δ denote the *simplex* $\{p \in R_+^n : p_1 + \cdots + p_n = 1\}$, to be thought of as the set of possible probability assessments over the n states. Without yet delving into measure–theoretic formalities, a state process $X = \{X_1, X_2, \ldots\}$ moves according to a transition function $Q : Z \times A \to \Delta$. For any time $t \geq 0$, we treat $Q(i, k)_j$ as the conditional probability that $X_{t+1} = j$ given that $X_t = i$ and that action k is taken at time t.

Also given as primitives are a *reward function* $r : Z \times A \to R$, a *discount factor* $\rho \in (0, 1)$, and an *admissible action correspondence* $\Gamma : Z \to 2^A$, with $\Gamma(i) \subset A$ denoting the non–empty subset of admissible actions in state i.

At each time t, an agent chooses an action in A that may depend on the current and past observations of the process X. That is, the action at time t is given by some function $c_t : Z^t \to A$, where Z^t denotes the t–fold product of Z, yielding the action $c_t(X_1, \ldots, X_t) \in A$. Of course the outcomes of $X_1, \ldots, X_t$ are random, depending in part on the previous control functions $c_1, \ldots, c_{t-1}$. A sequence $c = \{c_1, c_2, \ldots\}$ of such functions is a *control policy*, and is *admissible* if $c_t(X_1, \ldots, X_t) \in \Gamma(X_t)$ for all t. Let

$\mathcal{C}$ denote the space of admissible control policies. For any c in $\mathcal{C}$, let $X^{c,i}$ denote the state process that is defined by a particular control policy c and a particular starting point i in Z. The *value* of an admissible control policy c is the function V^c on Z defined by

$$V^c(i) = E\left[\sum_{t=1}^{\infty} \rho^t\, r\left(X_t^{c,i}, c_t\left(X_1^{c,i}, \dots, X_t^{c,i}\right)\right)\right],$$

where E denotes an expectation that must be treated informally for the present, despite the obvious intent. Although there will be some abuse of notation, we usually suppress the superscripts on X and the arguments of c_t. For example, we may instead write

$$V^c(i) - E\left[\sum_{t=1}^{\infty} \rho^t r(X_t, c_t) \,\middle|\, X_1 = i\right].$$

The *value of the control problem* $(Z, A, Q, \Gamma, r, \rho)$ is the function $V : Z \to R$ defined by $V(i) = \sup_{c \in \mathcal{C}} V^c(i)$. If c is an admissible control policy with $V^c = V$, then c is an *optimal control*.

For any given function $W : Z \to R$, let $\mathcal{U}W$ denote the function on Z defined by

$$[\mathcal{U}W](i) = \max_{a \in \Gamma(i)} \left[\rho r(i, a) + \rho \sum_{j=1}^{n} Q(i, a)_j W(j)\right].$$

The interpretation is clear: $[\mathcal{U}W](X_t)/\rho$ is the maximum possible sum of the current reward $r(X_t, a)$ and the expected value of $W(X_{t+1})$ given X_t, with the maximum taken over all admissible actions at time t.

LEMMA. *There is a unique* $W^* : Z \to R$ *satisfying the Bellman Equation* $\mathcal{U}W^* = W^*$.

PROOF: Consider the function $F : R^n \to R^n$ defined by

$$F(x)_i = \max_{a \in \Gamma(i)} \rho\left[r(i, a) + Q(i, a) \cdot x\right].$$

For given x and y in R^n, let $|x| = \max_i |x_i|$, and let $\alpha = |x - y|$. For $\mathbf{1} = (1, 1, \dots, 1) \in R^n$, we have $F(y + \alpha\mathbf{1}) = F(y) + \alpha\rho\mathbf{1}$. Since $y + \alpha\mathbf{1} \geq x$, we also have $F(y + \alpha\mathbf{1}) \geq F(x)$, implying that $F(x) - F(y) \leq \alpha\rho\mathbf{1}$. By symmetry, $F(y) - F(x) \leq \alpha\rho\mathbf{1}$. Thus $|F(x) - F(y)| \leq \alpha\rho = \rho\,|x - y|$. Define a sequence $\{x_k\}$ in R^n inductively by choosing x_1 arbitrarily and by letting $x_k = F(x_{k-1})$ for $k \geq 2$. We have shown that $\mid F(x_k) - F(x_{k-1}) \mid$ $\leq \rho \mid x_k - x_{k-1} \mid$, implying that

$$\mid x_{k+1} - x_k \mid \leq \rho \mid x_k - x_{k-1} \mid .$$

Since $\mid x_{k+1} - x_k \mid \leq \rho^k \mid x_1 - x_0 \mid$ and $\rho \in (0, 1)$, we know $\{x_k\}$ is a Cauchy sequence, and therefore has a limit point $x^* \in R^n$. It follows that $\mid F(x^*) - x^* \mid = 0$, or $F(x^*) = x^*$. There is no other point $y^* \in R^n$ with $F(y^*) = y^*$, for if so,

$$\mid x^* - y^* \mid = \mid F(x^*) - F(y^*) \mid \leq \rho \mid x^* - y^* \mid < \mid x^* - y^* \mid,$$

which is absurd. Let $W^* : Z \to R$ be defined by $W^*(i) = x_i^*$. Then $\mathcal{U}W^* = W^*$ is equivalent to $F(x^*) = x^*$. Moreover, W^* is unique in this regard. ∎

Notably, the proof includes an algorithm for determining the unique fixed point W^* of $\mathcal{U}$.

Let $f : Z \to A$ be defined by

$$f(i) \in \arg \max_{a \in \Gamma(i)} \left[r(i, a) + \sum_{j=1}^{n} Q(i, a)_j W^*(j) \right].$$

That is, $f(i)$ is an admissible action that attains the stated maximum. We will show that the *stationary Markov policy* $f^\infty \in \mathcal{C}$, defined by $f_t^\infty(X_1, \ldots, X_t) = f(X_t)$, is an optimal policy.

PROPOSITION. $W^* \geq V$.

PROOF: (Our proof is informal, since we use probability theory without a probability space!) Let $c \in \mathcal{C}$ be an arbitrary control. Since $\mathcal{U}W^* = W^*$, we have, for all t,

$$W^*(X_t) \geq \rho r(X_t, c_t) + \rho E_t[W^*(X_{t+1})],$$

where E_t means expectation conditional on X_t and c_t. Multiplying by ρ^{t-1} and rearranging,

$$\rho^{t-1} W^*(X_t) - \rho^t E_t[W^*(X_{t+1})] \geq \rho^t r(X_t, c_t).$$

Taking expectations again with respect to the initial data X_1, and using the law of iterated conditional expectation $\left[\text{or } "E_1\left[E_t(\cdot) \right] = E_1(\cdot)" \right]$, we have, for all t,

$$E_1[\rho^{t-1} W^*(X_t)] - E_1[\rho^t W^*(X_{t+1})] \geq E_1[\rho^t r(X_t, c_t)].$$

Summing this expression over t, from $t = 1$ to any time T, and using the successive canceling of terms on the left hand side, we have

$$E_1[W^*(X_1)] - E_1[\rho^T W^*(X_{T+1})] \geq E_1\left[\sum_{t=1}^{T} \rho^t r(X_t, c_t)\right].$$

Of course $E_1[W^*(X_1)] = W^*(X_1)$. Taking limits as $T \longrightarrow \infty$, since W^* is bounded, $\rho^T E[W^*(X_{T+1})] \to 0$, and we are left with

$$W^*(X_1) \geq E_1\left[\sum_{t=1}^{\infty} \rho^t r(X_t, c_t)\right] = V^c(X_1).$$

Since c is arbitrary, $W^*(X_1) \geq V(X_1)$. Since this is true for any outcome of X_1 in Z, the claim follows. ∎

THEOREM. *The value function V is the unique solution W^* to the Bellman Equation, or $\mathcal{U}V = V$. The given stationary feedback policy f^∞ is optimal.*

PROOF: It suffices to show that $W^* = V^{f^\infty}$, for then $W^* \leq V$ by the definition of V, and the previous proposition yields $V^{f^\infty} = W^* = V$. Because f was chosen with the property:

$$W^*(X_t) = \rho r(X_t, f(X_t)) + \rho F_t[W^*(X_{t+1})]$$

for all t, all of the inequalities stated in the proof of the previous proposition may be replaced with equalities if we take the control policy $c = f^\infty$. Thus

$$W^*(X_1) = E_1\left[\sum_{t=1}^{\infty} \rho^t r(X_t, f(X_t))\right] = V^{f^\infty}(X_1).$$

We have $W^* = V^{f^\infty}$. ∎

After discussing a more abstract control setting, we will return to state conditions yielding this same theorem for a general Borel state space Z.

C.   Most of our applications call for an infinite state space. This is the case, for instance, even in the deterministic investment problem of Paragraph A, which has the state space $[0, \infty)$ for current corn stocks. We now extend the finite state results of Paragraph B to a general Borel state space Z. We limit ourselves to the case of actions in a measurable subset A of some Euclidean space. (The theory extends with mild regularity conditions to a general Borel action space.) As in Section 18, let $B(Z)$

denote the space of bounded measurable real–valued functions on Z, and
let $C(Z)$ denote the subset of $B(Z)$ whose elements are continuous. Let
$\Omega = Z \times Z \times \cdots$ denote the *sample path space* of (infinite time horizon)
sample paths in Z. For the time set $\mathcal{T} = \{1, 2, \ldots\}$, let $X : \Omega \times \mathcal{T} \to Z$ be
the *canonical state process*, defined by $X[(z_1, z_2, \ldots), t] = z_t$. One must be
careful to distinguish between what we sometimes call a "state of world",
which is in this case a possible sample path $(z_1, z_2, \ldots) \in \Omega$, and a "state of
X at time t", say $z_t \in Z$. A *controlled expectation function* is a mapping
of the form $\mathcal{E} : A \times Z \times B(Z) \to R$. At any $f \in B(Z)$, any action $a \in A$,
and any given state $z \in Z$, the value of $\mathcal{E}$, denoted $\mathcal{E}_{az}(f)$ for convenience,
may be safely thought of as the conditional expectation of $f(X_{t+1})$ given
at time t the action a and the state $X_t = z$. We require as part of the
definition, of course, that $\mathcal{E}_{az}$ represents expectation with respect to some
probability measure on Z. We assume that $\mathcal{E}$ is *weakly continuous*, in the
sense that any $W \in B(Z)$ defines a measurable function $F : A \times Z \to R$
by $F(a, z) = \mathcal{E}_{az}(W)$, and that F is continuous provided W is continuous.

Example. Let the state space Z be a Euclidean space and let $g : Z \times A \times Z \to$
R be a continuous function. Let $\mathcal{E}^g : A \times Z \times B(Z) \to R$ be defined by

$$\mathcal{E}^g_{az}(W) = \int_Z W(x) g(z, a, x) \, dx. \tag{1}$$

It is known, and assigned as an exercise to prove, that $\mathcal{E}^g$ is then weakly
continuous. ♠

The *admissible action correspondence* is given by some function Γ on
Z into the space of non–empty compact subsets of A. We treat $\Gamma(z)$ as the
subset of actions admissible in state z. We assume that Γ is *upper semicontinuous*, meaning $\{z \in Z : \Gamma(z) \subset G\}$ is an open subset of Z whenever
G is an open subset of A. Equivalent definitions of upper semicontinuity
are explored in an exercise. A real–valued function W on a Borel space B
is *upper semicontinuous* if $\{b \in B : W(b) \geq x\}$ is closed for each $x \in R$.
The specifications of a *control problem* $(Z, A, \mathcal{E}, \Gamma, r, \rho)$ are completed by
a bounded upper semicontinuous *reward function* $r : Z \times A \to R$ and a
discount factor $\rho \in (0, 1)$. As a reminder of our other maintained assumptions: Z is a Borel state space; the action space A is a measurable subset
of a Euclidean space; the admissible action correspondence $\Gamma : Z \to 2^A$ is
non–empty–compact–valued and upper semicontinuous; and the controlled
expectation function $\mathcal{E} : A \times Z \times B(Z) \to R$ is weakly continuous, in the defined sense. The theory of stochastic control allows much weaker regularity
conditions; sources are cited in the Notes.

D. Given a control problem $(Z, A, \mathcal{E}, \Gamma, r, \rho)$, we first define, and then prove the existence of, a solution. At any time t, one has some observation $z^t = (z_1, \ldots, z_t)$ for $(X_1, \ldots, X_t)$ from the t–*sample path space* $Z^t = \prod_{s=1}^{t} Z$. Based on this observation, one takes an action $a \in A$. Formally, a *control policy* is a sequence $c = \{c_1, c_2, \ldots\}$, where $c_t : Z^t \to A$ is a measurable function for any time t. Under policy c, the action chosen at time t based on the observation $z^t \in Z^t$ is $c_t(z^t)$. A control policy c is *admissible* if, for any time t, $c_t(z^t) \in \Gamma(z_t)$ for all $z^t = (z_1, \ldots, z_t) \in Z^t$. Let $\mathcal{C}$ denote the space of *admissible control policies*. For any control policy c and time t, one has a measurable transition function $Q_c^t : Z^t \to \mathcal{P}(Z)$, where $\mathcal{P}(Z)$ denotes the space of probability measures on Z, defined by

$$[Q_c^t(z^t)](B) = \mathcal{E}_{c_t(z^t)z_t}(1_B),$$

for any measurable subset B of Z. That is, $[Q_c^t(z^t)](B)$ is taken as the conditional probability that $X_{t+1} \in B$ given the history $(X_1, \ldots, X_t) = z^t = (z_1, \ldots, z_t)$ and given that action $c_t(X_1, \ldots, X_t)$ is taken at time t. From our discussion in Paragraph 18E, for any control policy c and any starting point $z \in Z$ for the state process X, there is a unique probability measure denoted P_{cz} on the sample path space Ω under which the state process has transition functions $Q_c^1, Q_c^2, \ldots$, and such that $P_{cz}(X_1 = z) = 1$. Given an arbitrary control policy c, the state process X need not be a Markov process under P_{cz}. A control policy c is defined to be *Markov* provided there is a sequence $\{f_1, f_2, \ldots\}$ of measurable functions on Z into A such that, for any time t and any history $z^t = (z_1, \ldots, z_t) \subset Z^t$, we have $c_t(z^t) = f_t(z_t)$. In other words, c is Markov if the action taken at any time t depends only on the current state X_t, and not otherwise on the previous history $X_1, \ldots, X_{t-1}$. This does not, of course, mean that the process $\{f_1(X_1), f_2(X_2), \ldots\}$ is itself Markov. We have, instead, the following simple lemma, whose proof is left as an exercise.

LEMMA. *For any $z \in Z$ and any Markov control policy c, the state process X is Markov under the corresponding distribution P_{cz} on its sample paths.*

The reward function r is measurable since it is upper semicontinuous (which is also left as an exercise to prove). Since r is also bounded, any control policy c and starting point $z \in Z$ leaves an unambiguous value for the expectation

$$V^c(z) = E_{cz}\left[\sum_{t=1}^{\infty} \rho^t r\left(X_t, c_t(X_1, \ldots, X_t)\right) \right], \tag{2}$$

where E_{cz} denotes expectation under the probability measure P_{cz}. The value $V \in B(Z)$ of the control problem $(Z, A, \mathcal{E}, \Gamma, r, \rho)$ is defined by

$$V(z) = \sup_{c \in C} \quad V^c(z), \quad z \in Z.$$

That is, $V(z)$ is the least upper bound on the total expected discounted reward that can be achieved by any admissible control policy. An admissible control policy c is *optimal* for $(Z, A, \mathcal{E}, \Gamma, r, \rho)$ if $V(z) = V^c(z)$ for all $z \in Z$. A control policy c is *stationary Markov* if there exists a measurable function $f : Z \to A$ such that, for any time t and $z^t = (z_1, \dots, z_t) \in Z^t$, we have $c_t(z^t) = f(z_t)$. In this case, we denote c by f^∞. A stationary Markov policy is not only independent of old history given the current state X_t, it is also independent of time. Given a stationary Markov policy $c = f^\infty$ and any starting point $z \in Z$, the state process X is Markov and time–homogeneous under the induced distribution P_{cz}.

THEOREM. *There exists a stationary Markov control policy that is an optimal policy for the problem* $(Z, A, \mathcal{E}, \Gamma, r, \rho)$.

E. Having stated the main theorem of this section, we will provide a proof based on methods of independent interest. First we quote a combination of results on the existence of a measurable function that selects an optimal action in each state, in an abstract problem setting.

THEOREM (MEASURABLE SELECTION OF MAXIMUM). *Suppose Z is a Borel space; A is a Borel measurable subset of a Euclidean space; $\Gamma : Z \to 2^A$ is upper semicontinuous, non–empty valued, and compact–valued; and $w : Z \times A \to R$ is bounded above and upper semicontinuous. Then there exists a measurable function $f : Z \to A$ such that the function $v : Z \to R$ defined by $v(z) = w(z, f(z))$ is upper semicontinuous, bounded above, and such that, for any z in Z,*

$$f(z) \in \arg \max_{a \in \Gamma(z)} \quad w(z, a). \tag{3}$$

This widely applied result has many extensions and improvements, some of which are cited in the Notes.

F. An *operator* $T : B(Z) \to B(Z)$ is merely a function whose value at a function $v \in B(Z)$ is a function typically denoted Tv in $B(Z)$. We define $\mathcal{L}_a : B(Z) \to B(Z)$, $\mathcal{L}_f : B(Z) \to B(Z)$, and $\mathcal{U} : B(Z) \to B(Z)$ as follows, for arbitrary action $a \in A$, and measurable $f : Z \to A$. For any $v \in B(Z)$ and $z \in Z$, let

$$[\mathcal{L}_a v](z) = \rho \left[r(z, a) + \mathcal{E}_{az}(v) \right],$$
$$[\mathcal{L}_f v](z) = [\mathcal{L}_{f(z)} v](z), \text{ and}$$
$$[\mathcal{U}v](z) = \sup_{a \in \Gamma(z)} [\mathcal{L}_a v](z).$$

Interpreting, $[\mathcal{L}_a v](z)$ is the expected discounted value of $v(X_{t+1})$ in the next period plus the current reward $r(z, a)$, given the current action a and current state $X_t = z$. Then $[\mathcal{L}_f v](z)$ is the same quantity when the current action a is chosen by the function f in state z to be $f(z)$. Finally, $[\mathcal{U}v](z)$ is the supremum of this same quantity over all possible actions. This defines the *Bellman Operator* $\mathcal{U}$. Proofs of the following two results are left as exercises.

LEMMA. *If $W \in B(Z)$ is upper semicontinuous, then the function $w . Z \times A \to R$, defined by $w(z, a) = \rho[r(z, a) + \mathcal{E}_{za}(W)]$, is upper semicontinuous.*

PROPOSITION. *If $W \in B(Z)$ is upper semicontinuous, then $\mathcal{U}W$ is upper semicontinuous, and there exist measurable $f : Z \to A$ such that $\mathcal{U}W = \mathcal{L}_f W$.*

G. The following fixed point results will shortly be put to use in our control problem. Suppose (L, d) is a metric space. Then $T : L \to L$ is a *strict contraction* if there exists a scalar $\beta \in (0, 1)$ such that $d\left(T(x), T(y)\right) \le \beta d(x, y)$ for any x and y in L. A point $x \in L$ is a *fixed point* of T if $T(x) = x$.

PROPOSITION (CONTRACTION MAPPING PRINCIPLE). *If (L, d) is a complete metric space and $T : L \to L$ is a strict contraction, then T has a unique fixed point.*

Proof is left as an easy exercise. If L is an ordered vector space (or subset thereof) and T maps L into L, we typically use the notation "Tx" for $T(x)$. In this case, T is *monotonic* if $Tx \ge Ty$ whenever $x \ge y$. The ordered vector spaces $B(Z)$ and $C(Z)$ are complete metric spaces under the metric d defined by $d(f, g) = \sup_{z \in Z} | f(z) - g(z) |$.

BLACKWELL'S FIXED POINT THEOREM. *Suppose Z is a Borel space and $T : L \to L$ is monotonic, where $L = B(Z)$ or $L = C(Z)$. Suppose there exists $\beta \in (0, 1)$ such that, for any $\alpha \in [0, \infty)$ and any $f \in L$,*

$$T(f + \alpha 1_Z) \le Tf + \alpha \beta 1_Z. \tag{4}$$

Then T is a strict contraction and has a unique fixed point.

PROOF: Since L is complete, and by the Contraction Mapping Principle, we need only show that T is a strict contraction. Since, for any x and y in L, $x \leq y + d(x,y)1_Z$, we have $Tx \leq Ty + \beta d(x,y)1_Z$. By symmetry, $Ty \leq Tx + \beta d(y,x)1_Z$. Thus $d(Tx,Ty) \leq \beta d(x,y)$. ∎

H.   We can now prove the existence of stationary Markov optimal policies.

LEMMA. *The Bellman Operator $\mathcal{U}$ has a unique fixed point.*

PROOF: It is easy to verify that $\mathcal{U}$ satisfies that hypotheses of Blackwell's Fixed Point Theorem. ∎

PROPOSITION. *The unique fixed point W^* of $\mathcal{U}$ is upper semicontinuous, and there exists a measurable function $f : Z \rightarrow A$ such that $W^* = \mathcal{L}_f W^* = \mathcal{U}W^*$.*

PROOF: Let $W^0 \in B(Z)$ be given by $W^0(z) = 0$ for all z in Z. For any integer $t \geq 1$, let W^t be defined by $W^t = \mathcal{U}W^{t-1}$. The functions $\{W^t\}$ are upper semicontinuous by Lemma 19F. Since $\mathcal{U}$ is a strict contraction, $W^t \rightarrow W^*$, a fact also shown in an exercise. In order to show that W^* is upper semicontinuous, let b denote a bound on $\{|\,r(z,a)\,|: z \in Z, a \in A\}$. For each time t, let $J^t \in B(Z)$ be defined by

$$J^t(z) = W^t(z) + b \sum_{s=t+1}^{\infty} \rho^s. \tag{5}$$

We note that $J^t \downarrow W^*$. That is, for each z in Z, $\{J^1(z), J^2(z),\ldots\}$ is a decreasing sequence converging to $W^*(z)$. For any $\alpha \in R$, it follows that

$$\{z \in Z : W^*(z) \geq \alpha\} = \bigcap_{t=1}^{\infty}\{z \in Z : J^t(z) \geq \alpha\}.$$

Since J^t is upper semicontinuous and the intersection of closed sets is closed, we have shown that W^* is upper semicontinuous. Thus, by Proposition 19F, there exists a measurable function $f : Z \rightarrow A$ such that $\mathcal{L}_f W^* = \mathcal{U}W^* = W^*$. ∎

Theorem 19D follows from the next result.

THEOREM. *The unique fixed point of $\mathcal{U}$ is the value of $(Z, A, \mathcal{E}, \Gamma, r, \rho)$. There exists an optimal policy for this problem that is Markov and stationary.*

PROOF: For the unique fixed point W^* of $\mathcal{U}$, let $f : Z \to A$ be a measurable function satisfying $\mathcal{L}_f W^* = \mathcal{U} W^* = W^*$. (Such a function exists by the previous proposition.) Let f^∞ denote the corresponding (admissible) stationary Markov policy. Let c be any admissible policy, $z \in Z$ be any starting point, and $P_{cz} \in \mathcal{P}(\Omega)$ be the corresponding distribution of the canonical state process $X = \{X_1, X_2, \ldots\}$. Since $\mathcal{U} W^* = W^*$, the following inequality holds P_{cz}–almost surely for any time t:

$$W^*(X_t) \geq \rho r\big(X_t, c_t(X_1, \ldots, X_t)\big) + \rho \mathcal{E}_{c_t(X_1, \ldots, X_t)X_t}(W^*)$$
$$= \rho r(X_t, c_t(X_1, \ldots, X_t)) + \rho E_{cz}[W^*(X_{t+1}) \mid X_1, \ldots, X_t], \quad (6)$$

where E_{cz} denotes expectation under P_{cz}. Multiplying (6) through by ρ^{t-1} and rearranging, P_{cz}–almost surely:

$$\rho^{t-1} W^*(X_t) - \rho^t E_{cz}[W^*(X_{t+1}) \mid X_1, \ldots, X_t] \geq \rho^t r(X_t, c_t(X_1, \ldots, X_t)). \tag{7}$$

Taking expectations on both sides of (7) and using the law of iterated conditional expectation, for any time t:

$$E_{cz} \left[\rho^{t-1} W^*(X_t) - \rho^t W^*(X_{t+1}) \right] \geq E_{cz} \left[\rho^t r \left(X_t, c_t(X_1, \ldots, X_t) \right) \right]. \tag{8}$$

If we sum both sides of (8) for $t = 1$ to any time $T \geq 2$, the intermediate terms on the left hand side cancel telescopically, leaving

$$E_{cz} \left[W^*(X_1) - \rho^T W^*(X_{T+1}) \right] \geq E_{cz} \left[\sum_{t=1}^{T} \rho^t r[X_t, c_t(X_1, \ldots, X_t)] \right]. \tag{9}$$

Since $P_{cz}(X_1 = z) = 1$, and since W^* is a bounded function and $\rho^T \to 0$ as $T \to \infty$, we have the conclusion

$$W^*(z) \geq E_{cz} \left[\sum_{t=1}^{\infty} \rho^t r [X_t, c_t(X_1, \ldots, X_t)] \right] = V^c(z). \tag{10}$$

Since z is arbitrary and c is an arbitrary admissible policy, $W^* \geq V$. If we take, in particular, the policy $c = f^\infty$, each of relations (6), (7), (8), (9), and (10) hold with equality, and we conclude that $W^* = V^{f^\infty}$. This implies that $V^{f^\infty} \geq V$, but by the definition of V, we know that $V^{f^\infty} \leq V$. Thus $V^{f^\infty} = V = W^*$ and f^∞ is an optimal policy. ∎

COROLLARY (BELLMAN'S EQUATION). *The value V of $(Z, A, \mathcal{E}, \Gamma, r, \rho)$ is the unique function in $B(Z)$ satisfying Bellman's Equation $\mathcal{U}V = V$.*

We may write Bellman's Equation $\mathcal{U}V = V$ more elaborately as:

$$V(z) = \sup_{a \in \Gamma(z)} \rho\left[r(z, a) + \mathcal{E}_{az}(V)\right], \tag{11}$$

for all $z \in Z$. The Corollary states that any solution V is the value of the control problem.

I.   It is instructive to connect the values of the finite horizon problems for $(Z, A, \mathcal{E}, \Gamma, r, \rho)$ with the value V of the infinite horizon problem. For any time T, the T–horizon value $V_T \in B(Z)$ for $(Z, A, \mathcal{E}, \Gamma, r, \rho)$ is defined by

$$V_T(z) = \sup_{c \in C} \ E_{cz}\left[\sum_{t=1}^{T} \rho^t r\left[X_t, c_t(X_1, \ldots, X_t)\right]\right], \quad z \in Z.$$

An admissible policy $c \in C$ is T–horizon optimal for $(Z, A, \mathcal{E}, \Gamma, r, \rho)$ if

$$V_T(z) = E_{cz}\left[\sum_{t=1}^{T} \rho^t r\left[X_t, c_t(X_1, \ldots, X_t)\right]\right], \quad z \in Z.$$

(Of course $c_{T+1}, c_{T+2}, \ldots$ are irrelevant, but there is no need to define new classes of admissible controls for the finite horizon problems.) Let $V_0 \in B(Z)$ be the zero function; that is, $V_0(z) = 0$ for all z in Z.

THEOREM (PRINCIPLE OF OPTIMALITY). *For any time horizon T, $V_T = \mathcal{U}V_{T-1}$, V_T is upper semicontinuous, and there exists an optimal T–horizon policy that is Markov.*

PROOF: The case $T = 1$ follows from the definition of V_1, $\mathcal{U}$, and V_0, and by Proposition 19F. We prove the result by induction. Suppose, for some $T > 1$, that $V_{T-1} = \mathcal{U}V_{T-2}$ and that V_{T-1} is upper semicontinuous. Let c^{T-1} be an optimal $(T - 1)$–horizon policy that is Markov, and let $f :$ $Z \to A$ be a measurable function given by Proposition 19F with the property: $\mathcal{L}_f V_{T-1} = \mathcal{U}V_{T-1}$. Since c^{T-1} is Markov, for each t there exists measurable $g_t : Z \to A$ such that $c_t^{T-1}(z_1, \ldots, z_t) = g_t(z_t)$ for all $(z_1, \ldots, z_t) \in Z^t$. Let c^T be the policy defined by $c_1^T = f$ and $c_t^T(z_1, \ldots, z_t) = g_{t-1}(z_t)$ for all $(z_1, \ldots, z_t) \in Z^t$, for all $t > 1$. Since c^{T-1} is admissible and $f(z) \in \Gamma(z)$ for all $z \in Z$, the policy c^T is admissible. By definition, c^T is Markov. We claim that c^T is optimal. To prove this, let $\hat{c}$ be any admissible policy.

Let $z_0 \in Z$ be fixed, and let b be the policy defined by $b_t(z_1, \ldots, z_t) = \widehat{c}_{t+1}(z_0, z_1, \ldots, z_t)$. By definition of V_{T-1}, we have

$$V_{T-1}(z) \geq \widehat{V}_{T-1}(z) \equiv E_{bz} \left[\sum_{t=1}^{T-1} \rho^t r[X_t, b_t(X_1, \ldots, X_t)] \right]$$

for all $z \in Z$. By the definitions of $\mathcal{U}$ and f, and the law of iterated conditional expectation,

$$\rho r[z_0, f(z_0)] + \rho \mathcal{E}_{f(z_0)z_0}(V_{T-1}) \geq \rho r[z_0, \widehat{c}_1(z_0)] + \rho \mathcal{E}_{\widehat{c}_1(z_0)z_0}(V_{T-1})$$

$$\geq \rho r[z_0, \widehat{c}_1(z_0)] + \rho \mathcal{E}_{\widehat{c}_1(z_0)z_0}(\widehat{V}_{T-1})$$

$$= E_{\widehat{c}z_0} \left[\sum_{t=1}^{T} \rho^t r[X_t, \widehat{c}_t(X_1, \ldots, X_t)] \right].$$

By construction of c^T, we also have

$$E_{c^T z_0} \left[\sum_{t=1}^{T} \rho^t r[X_t, c_t^T(X_1, \ldots, X_t)] \right] = \rho r[z_0, f(z_0)] + \rho \mathcal{E}_{f(z_0)z_0}(V_{T-1}),$$

again using the law of iterated conditional expectation. This proves that $V_T = \mathcal{U} V_{T-1}$ and that c^T is a stationary Markov policy that is T–horizon optimal. In addition, V_T is upper semicontinuous by Lemma 19F. ∎

COROLLARY. *The T–horizon value V_T of $(Z, A, \mathcal{E}, \Gamma, r, \rho)$ converges to the (infinite horizon) value V as $T \to \infty$.*

PROOF: Since $V_T = \mathcal{U} V_{T-1}$, $T \geq 1$, the sequence $\{V_T\}$ converges in $B(Z)$ to the unique fixed point of $\mathcal{U}$ because $\mathcal{U}$ is a strict contraction, as shown in an exercise. The result follows from Corollary 19H. ∎

Although it is not necessarily a practical consideration, one can generate the value V of $(Z, A, \mathcal{E}, \Gamma, r, \rho)$ by taking an arbitrary upper semicontinuous initial guess $W^0 \in B(Z)$ for V and applying the Bellman Operator $\mathcal{U}$ repeatedly, generating $\{W^1, W^2, \ldots\}$. This "algorithm" converges since $\mathcal{U}$ is a strict contraction. Indeed, we used this fact in the proof of Proposition 19H, and the sequence $\{W^t\}$ generated there is in fact the sequence $\{V_t\}$ of t–horizon values.

J. We now study the investment problem of Paragraph A with the additional realism of uncertain returns. The existence of a stationary Markov optimal policy follows by the style of arguments used in the general model just presented. For a closed–form solution, however, we adopt a tractable class of reward functions that are unbounded, thus calling for additional arguments. Let $\{\gamma_n\}$ be a sequence of positive, independent, and identically distributed real–valued random variables on a given probability space, with γ_t to be treated as the random value at time t of one unit of wealth invested at time $t - 1$. We may think of an economy with a single commodity, say "wealth". We could also think of an economy with a single commodity in which the random return γ_t on investment in a given security at time t is determined endogenously as specified.

The state space $Z = R_+$ represents current wealth; the action space $A = R_+$ represents current consumption. The reward $r : Z \times A \to R$ is defined by $r(z, a) = u(a)$, where for the present $u : R_+ \to R$ is assumed to have a continuous strictly positive derivative u'. The admissible action correspondence Γ is defined by $\Gamma(z) = \{a \in A : a \leq z\}$, meaning that wealth is not permitted to be negative, a natural budget constraint. A discount factor $\rho \in (0, 1)$ is also given. An admissible control policy is defined, as usual, as a sequence $\{c_1, c_2, \ldots\}$, where $c_t : Z^t \to A$ is measurable and assigns the (consumption) action $c_t(z_1, \ldots, z_t) \in \Gamma(z_t)$ at time t on the basis of a given (wealth) state history $(z_1, \ldots, z_t) \in Z^t$. Rather than completing a formal definition of the control problem at this point, we first derive an equation related to the Bellman Equation. We then formally define the problem and confirm a conjectured solution.

If the value $V : Z \to R$ for a natural version of this problem is well defined, the Bellman Equation must be of the form: for each z in Z,

$$V(z) = \sup_{a \in [0,z]} \rho u(a) + \rho E\big[V[(z - a)\gamma_1]\big]. \tag{12}$$

The reasoning, just as in Paragraph A, is that an optimal consumption level is one that maximizes the reward $u(a)$ for current consumption plus the expected value of beginning in the next period with wealth $(z - a)\gamma_1$. Of course, it makes no difference whether we use γ_1 or any γ_t in this expression; they are equivalent in distribution. We suppose that V is continuously differentiable with derivative V'. Under technical regularity conditions that we ignore for the present, one calculates the derivative

$$\frac{d}{da} E\big[V[(z - a)\gamma_1]\big] = E\left[\frac{d}{da} V[(z - a)\gamma_1]\right] = E\big[-\gamma_1 V'[(z - a)\gamma_1]\big]. \tag{13}$$

The first order necessary condition for an interior solution $a^* \in (0, z)$ to (12) is thus

$$u'(a^*) = E\big[\gamma_1 V'[(z - a^*)\gamma_1]\big]. \tag{14}$$

Presuming a unique solution a^* to (14) for each initial wealth $z > 0$, we are given a real–valued function $f : Z \to A$ specifying an optimal (consumption) action $f(z)$ for each (wealth) state z. Presuming that f is differentiable and that interchange of differentiation and expectation is again justified, we may differentiate (12) with respect to z after replacing a^* with $f(z)$, to obtain

$$V'(z) = \rho u'[f(z)]f'(z) + \rho[1 - f'(z)]E\big(\gamma_1 V'\left[(z - f(z))\gamma_1\right]\big). \qquad (15)$$

Substituting (14) into (15) leaves $V'(z) = \rho u'[f(z)]$, and thus the so–called *Stochastic Euler Equation:*

$$u'[f(z)] = \rho E\left(\gamma_1 u'\big[f\left([z - f(z)]\gamma_1\right)\big]\right), \quad z \in (0, \infty), \qquad (16)$$

an equation involving a single unknown, the function f. In order to deduce a closed–form expression for f, we make the specific assumption $u(a) = a^\alpha$ for some $\alpha \in (0, 1)$. (The problem is solved for other reward functions in exercises.) Since we then have $u'(a) = \alpha a^{\alpha-1}$, relation (16) reduces to

$$f(z)^{\alpha-1} = \rho E\left[\gamma_1 \big[f\left([z - f(z)]\gamma_1\right)\big]^{\alpha-1}\right], \quad z \in (0, \infty), \qquad (17)$$

which has the solution $f(z) = \lambda z$ for some scalar λ satisfying $(1 - \lambda)^{1-\alpha} = \rho E[\gamma_1^\alpha]$. This suggests consuming a fixed fraction λ of current wealth, regardless of current wealth. If $\rho E[\gamma_1^\alpha] < 1$, the fraction λ is indeed in $(0, 1)$, and we will verify that this stationary policy is indeed optimal. First, for any admissible policy c, let

$$V^c(z) = E_{cz}\left[\sum_{t=1}^{\infty} \rho^t u[c_t(X_1, \ldots, X_t)]\right],$$

where E_{cz} denotes expectations for the state process X defined inductively by $X_1 = z$ and $X_t = [X_{t-1} - c_{t-1}(X_1, \ldots, X_{t-1})]\gamma_t$, $t > 1$. Since u is positive–valued, the expectation is well–defined. The value $V : Z \to [0, \infty]$ is defined by

$$V(z) = \sup_{c \in C} V^c(z), \quad z \in Z.$$

An admissible policy c is optimal, as usual, if $V(z) = V^c(z)$ for all $z \in Z$. The stationary Markov policy just discussed is denoted c^λ and formally defined by $c_t^\lambda(z_1, \ldots, z_t) = \lambda z_t$ for all $(z_1, \ldots, z_t) \in Z^t$ and any time t.

PROPOSITION. For $\alpha \in (0,1)$, let $u(a) = a^\alpha$, $a \in [0,\infty)$, and let $\beta = \rho E[\gamma_1^\alpha]$. Let $\lambda = 1 - \beta^{1/(1-\alpha)}$. If $\beta \in (0,1)$, then the stationary Markov policy c^λ, consume the fixed fraction λ of current wealth, is optimal. The value of wealth z is $V(z) = \rho\lambda^{\alpha-1}z^\alpha$.

PROOF: Let $0 \in C$ denote the admissible consumption policy defined by $0_t(z_1,\ldots,z_t) = 0$, and let $W : Z \to R$ be defined by $W(z) = \rho\lambda^{\alpha-1}z^\alpha$. Since $\{\gamma_1,\gamma_2,\ldots\}$ is an independent and identically distributed sequence, any admissible consumption policy $c \in C$ satisfies

$$
\begin{aligned}
E_{cz}[\rho^{t-1}W(X_t)] &= E_{cz}[\rho^t\lambda^{\alpha-1}X_t^\alpha] \\
&\leq E_{0z}[\rho^t\lambda^{\alpha-1}X_t^\alpha] \\
&= \rho^t\lambda^{\alpha-1}z^\alpha E\left[\Pi_{s=2}^t\gamma_s^\alpha\right] \\
&= \rho\lambda^{\alpha-1}z^\alpha\Pi_{s=2}^t\rho E[\gamma_1^\alpha] \\
&= \rho\lambda^{\alpha-1}z^\alpha\beta^{t-1}.
\end{aligned}
$$

Since $\beta \in (0,1)$, we deduce that $\lim_{t\to\infty} E_{cz}[\rho^{t-1}W(X_t)] = 0$. One easily shows that, for any $z \in Z$ and any $a \in [0,z]$,

$$
W(z) \geq \rho u(a) + \rho E\left[W\left((z-a)\gamma_1\right)\right].
$$

As shown in the proof of Theorem 19H, this implies that, for any time T,

$$
W(z) \geq E_{cz}\left[\sum_{t=1}^T \rho^t u[c_t(X_1,\ldots,X_t)]\right] + E_{cz}[\rho^T W(X_{T+1})]. \tag{18}
$$

Letting $T \to \infty$, we have $W(z) \geq V^c(z)$ for any admissible control c and any initial state z. Thus $W \geq V$. Repeating the calculations for the policy $c = c^\lambda$ shows that (18) holds with equality, or $W = V^{c^\lambda}$. Thus $V = V^{c^\lambda}$ and c^λ is an optimal policy. ∎

The only regularity assumption in the control problem $(Z, A, \mathcal{E}, \Gamma, u, \rho)$ of Theorem 19H that does not apply here is the boundedness of the reward function. Here, since u is unbounded, we substitute the condition $\beta < 1$ limiting the expected rate of growth of wealth relative to the discount rate ρ. This has sometimes been loosely referred to as a *transversality condition*.

EXERCISES

EXERCISE 19.1 (The Hotelling Problem).

(A)   Verify that $V(x) = \rho\sqrt{x/(1 - \rho^2\gamma)}$ is the value function for Robinson Crusoe's corn consumption problem of Paragraph 19A in the case: $u(a) = \sqrt{a}$ and $\rho\sqrt{\gamma} < 1$. *Remark:* It must be shown that a solution to the Bellman Equation is in fact the value function; there are pathological examples in which this is not the case.

(B)   Solve the same problem for the case $u(a) = a^\alpha$ for $\alpha \in (0,1)$, making an analogous regularity assumption on the parameters.

(C)   Solve the same problem for the case $u(a) = \log(a)$, stating appropriate regularity conditions. *Hint:* In this case, it is somewhat more difficult to show that a solution to the Bellman Equation is the value function. Why?

(D)   Solve the same problem for the case $u(a) = (a + k)^\alpha$, where k and α are constants, stating appropriate regularity conditions on ρ, α, γ, and k.

(E)   Solve the same problem for the case $u(a) = \log(a + k)$, where k is a constant, stating appropriate regularity conditions.

EXERCISE 19.2   Let X and Y be metric spaces. A *correspondence* Γ from X into Y, we recall, assigns a non–empty subset $\Gamma(x)$ of Y to each point $x \in X$, and is upper semicontinuous by definition if $\{x \in X : \Gamma(x) \subset G\}$ is open for each open $G \subset Y$.

(A)   Show that Γ is upper semicontinuous if and only if $\{x \in X : \Gamma(x) \cap F \neq \emptyset\}$ is closed for all closed $F \subset Y$.

(B)   The *graph* of Γ is the set $Gr(\Gamma) = \{(x,y) \in X \times Y : y \in \Gamma(x)\}$. Show that, if Y is compact and Γ is closed–valued, then Γ is upper semicontinuous if and only if $Gr(\Gamma)$ is closed.

(C)   Suppose X and Y are Polish spaces and that $\Gamma(x)$ is compact for all $x \in X$. Prove that $Gr(\Gamma)$ is closed if Γ is upper semicontinuous.

(D)   Suppose X and Y are Polish spaces. Prove that a compact–valued correspondence Γ from X into Y is upper semicontinuous if and only if it has the property: If $\{x_n\}$ converges in X to x, then any sequence $\{y_n\}$ with $y_n \in \Gamma(x_n)$ for all n has a subsequence converging in Y to a point $y \in \Gamma(x)$.

EXERCISE 19.3 Suppose X is a metric space and $f : X \to R$ is a function. Show that the correspondence Γ defined by $\Gamma(x) = \{y \in R : y \leq f(x)\}$ is upper semicontinuous if and only if f is upper semicontinuous.

EXERCISE 19.4 Prove Lemma 19D.

EXERCISE 19.5 Suppose B is a Borel space and $f : B \to R$ is upper semicontinuous. Show that f is measurable.

EXERCISE 19.6 Prove the Contraction Mapping Principle, Proposition 19G.

EXERCISE 19.7 Prove that the metric spaces $B(Z)$ and $C(Z)$ are complete if Z is a Borel space.

EXERCISE 19.8 Suppose T is a strict contraction on a complete metric space L. Let $x_0 \in L$ be chosen arbitrarily, and let $x_n = T(x_{n-1})$, $n \geq 1$. Show that the sequence $\{x_n\}$ converges to the unique fixed point of T.

EXERCISE 19.9 Show, as claimed in the proof of Proposition 19H, that $J^T \downarrow W^*$. *Remark:* See the previous exercise.

EXERCISE 19.10 Show that the Bellman Operator $\mathcal{U}$ indeed satisfies the conditions of Blackwell's Fixed Point Theorem.

EXERCISE 19.11 Prove that the controlled expectation function $\mathcal{E}^g$ defined by (1) is weakly continuous. *Hint:* This is intended for readers of some familiarity with the Lebesgue Dominated Convergence Theorem, which we have not provided.

EXERCISE 19.12 Prove Lemma 19F.

EXERCISE 19.13 For a Borel space Z, show that $W \in B(Z)$ is upper semicontinuous if and only if there exists a sequence $\{U_n\} \subset C(Z)$ such that $U_n \downarrow W$. That is, for each $z \in Z$, $\{U_n(z)\}$ is a decreasing sequence converging to $W(z)$.

EXERCISE 19.14 Verify, as claimed in the proof of Proposition 19J, that $V^{c^\lambda}(z) = \rho\lambda^{\alpha-1}z^\alpha$.

EXERCISE 19.15 Solve the problem presented in Paragraph 19J in closed form for the following reward functions:

(A) $u(a) = \log(a)$,

(B) $\quad u(a) = -e^{-\alpha a}, \quad \alpha \in (0, \infty)$,

(C) $\quad u(a) = a^{\alpha}/\alpha, \; \alpha < 1, \; \alpha \neq 0$.

Make assumptions analogous to $\rho E[\gamma_1^{\alpha}] < 1$ as necessary.

Notes

The theory of correspondences may be found in Hildenbrand (1974), Berge (1966), or Klein and Thompson (1984). A simple exposé of discrete–time Markov control may be found in the texts by Bertsekas (1976) and S.M. Ross (1983). Dynkin and Yushkevich (1979) as well as Bertsekas and Shreve (1978) are more advanced texts. The former includes a broad historical discussion of the literature. Wald (1950) is generally credited with the concept of Markov control, but the power of the theory lies with Bellman's (1957) principle of dynamic programming, and Howard's (1960) demonstration of its practicality. Blackwell (1965) originated the general approach taken here. Schäl (1975) as well as Himmelberg, Parthasarathy, and Van Vleck (1976) have more sophisticated control results than presented here. For an alternative general framework, see Shreve and Bertsekas (1979). For a pathological example of a Markov control problem with an optimal control but no optimal control that is stationary and Markov, see Dynkin and Yushkevich (1979).

The Measurable Selection of Maximum Theorem is actually a combination of results. The existence of a measurable selector is indicated by Schäl (1975). The upper semicontinuity of the maximum is due to Berge (1966), Chapter VI. A different measurable selection theorem is given by Himmelberg, Parthasarathy, and Van Vleck (1976). Shreve and Bertsekas (1979) quote a more advanced *Exact Selection Theorem*. For a general discussion of measurable selection and further results, see Part I.D of Hildenbrand (1974).

Hotelling (1931) formulated and solved an investment problem similar to that of Paragraph A. For the case of uncertainty, presented in Paragraph J, early results are due to Phelps (1962). Levhari and Srinivasan (1969) have solutions to the investment problem of Paragraph J. Multiple risky assets were introduced by Samuelson (1969). Hakansson (1970) extends the investment model of Paragraph J in several directions. One may also refer to Blume, Easley, and O'Hara (1982). Tong–sheng Sun has (as yet unpublished) results for other parametric investment examples. One may see the Notes to Section 24 for further references. Lang (1969), page 375, provides conditions under which one differentiate an integral by differentiating the integrand, as in relation (13).

20. Discrete–Time Equilibrium Pricing

This section characterizes security prices in a time–homogeneous Markov setting with a single agent. The central idea is apparent in a pure exchange economy. Exogenous uncertainty is given in the form of a time–homogeneous Markov process $X = \{X_1, X_2, \ldots\}$. Securities are given as a function d mapping the current state X_t to the current dividend vector $d(X_t)$. The single agent has utility of the form $E\left[\sum_{t=1}^{\infty} \rho^t u(c_t)\right]$ for a consumption process $c = \{c_1, c_2, \ldots\}$. An equilibrium is a function S mapping the current state X_t to the vector $S(X_t)$ of security prices such that, given the obviously defined control problem of maximizing utility subject to budget feasibility, the agent optimally chooses to hold precisely the total supply of each security and to consume precisely the total dividends paid by all securities. Production is added to the model as a function G mapping the current investment level I_t and the succeeding state X_{t+1} to the total capital stock K_{t+1} available in the following period. The uninvested capital stock $d_t = K_t - I_t$ is paid by the firm as a dividend. The firm chooses an investment policy maximizing the current market value of its common share, using Markov control. The state of the economy is captured by the augmented state process (X_t, K_t). An equilibrium is a value maximizing investment policy $\{I_t\}$ by the firm, at which the function S mapping the current market state (X_t, K_t) to the current value $S(X_t, K_t)$ of the firm's share is an equilibrium in the exchange sense for the endogenously defined dividend process $\{d_t = K_t - I_t\}$. The demonstration of an equilibrium may be thought of as a method of decentralizing a planned economy with the use of stock markets.

Advantages of the time–homogeneous Markov setting include its natural support of our intuition and the potential for statistical estimation and hypothesis testing. For Markov pricing with production, the state process $\{X_t\}$ must be augmented by an endogenously determined capital stock process $\{K_t\}$. Similarly, with the extension to heterogeneous agents, and without effectively complete markets, one must add additional state variables in order to preserve time–homogeneous Markov security pricing. For example, one must know at least the vector of wealth processes of the various agents, since the total current demand for securities at given prices depends on whose preferences correspond to which budget. The multi-agent case, however, is beyond our goals in this section; a relevant source is cited in the Notes.

A. The source of exogenous uncertainty for this entire section is a time–homogeneous Markov process $X = \{X_1, X_2, \ldots\}$ valued in a Borel space Z. The transition function of X, as discussed in Section 18, is a continuous function $Q : Z \to \mathcal{P}(Z)$, where $\mathcal{P}(Z)$ denotes the set of probability measures on Z. The value of Q at a state $z \in Z$, denoted Q_z, is safely thought of as the conditional distribution of X_{t+1} given that $X_t = z$, independent of the current time t. Preferences for current consumption of a single commodity are defined by a bounded continuous function $u : R_+ \to R$. A bounded continuous function $d : Z \to R_+^N$ defines the consumption dividends paid by N securities, the dividend vector $d(z)$ in state z. A discount rate $\rho \in (0,1)$ completes the specification of a *Markov exchange economy* (Z,Q,d,u,ρ).

B. Although one could envision an extremely large class of candidate security price processes, we limit ourselves to those given by a bounded continuous function $\mathcal{S} : Z \to \mathrm{int}(R_+^N)$. If the current state X_t is $z \in Z$, the vector of current security prices is $\mathcal{S}(z)$. We fix such a function $\mathcal{S}$ for all of Paragraphs B and C. In Paragraph D, under additional conditions, we demonstrate such a function $\mathcal{S}$ with an equilibrium property to be defined.

A *current action* is a point (a, α) in the *action space* $A = R^N \times R_+$, with a representing a portfolio of securities to be purchased, and α a possible consumption level. The *augmented state space* is $H = Z \times R_+$, with a typical element $h = (z, w)$ standing for current exogenous state z and current wealth w. The ∞–horizon sample path space is $H^\infty = H \times H \times \cdots$ with a typical element $h^\infty = [(z_1, w_1), (z_2, w_2), \ldots]$. Only the portion $h^t = [(z_1, w_1), \ldots, (z_t, w_t)] \in H^t$ of h^∞ is observed at time t. A *policy* is thus a sequence $(\theta, c) = \{(\theta_1, c_1), (\theta_2, c_2), \ldots\}$ of measurable functions of the form $\theta_t : H^t \to R^N$ and $c_t : H^t \to R_+$, that selects at time t the action $(\theta_t(h^t), c_t(h^t)) \in A$ on the basis of the observed portion $h^t \in H^t$ of the sample path of states and wealths. The *wealth process* $W^{\theta,w}$ generated by an initial wealth $w \in R_+$ and a policy (θ, c) is the real–valued process defined by $W_1^{\theta,w} = w$ and

$$W_t^{\theta,w} = \theta_{t-1}\left[(X_1, W_1^{\theta,w}), \ldots, (X_{t-1}, W_{t-1}^{\theta,w})\right] \cdot [\mathcal{S}(X_t) + d(X_t)], \quad t > 1.$$

A policy (θ, c) is *budget feasible* provided $c_t(h^t) + \theta_t(h^t) \cdot \mathcal{S}(z_t) \leq w_t$ for any history $h^t = [(z_1, w_1), \ldots, (z_t, w_t)] \in H^t$ and any time $t \in \{1, 2, \ldots\}$. Let F denote the space of budget feasible policies, and let

$$F_0 = \{(\theta, c) \in F : \theta_t(h^t) \geq 0, \quad \forall h^t \in H^t, \forall t\} \tag{1}$$

denote the subset of budget feasible policies precluding short sales. We recall from Section 18 that, given any initial state $z \in Z$, there is a unique distribution $P_z \in \mathcal{P}(Z \times Z \times \cdots)$ on the sample paths of X that is consistent with the given transition function Q and with $P_z(X_1 = z) = 1$. We also recall that $B(H)$ denotes the space of bounded measurable real–valued functions on H. Let $U : F \rightarrow B(H)$ be defined at the policy $(\theta, c) \in F$ as the function $U_{\theta,c} \in B(H)$ given by

$$U_{\theta,c}(z, w) = E_z \left[\sum_{t=1}^{\infty} \rho^t u \left(c_t[(X_1, W_1^{\theta,w}), \ldots, (X_t, W_t^{\theta,w})] \right) \right], \quad (z, w) \in H,$$

where E_z denotes expectation under the probability measure P_z. A policy $(\theta, c) \in F_0$ is *optimal* for the *agent problem* $(Z, Q, d, u, \rho, \mathcal{S})$ if, given any policy $(\theta', c') \in F_0$, we have $U_{\theta,c} \geq U_{\theta',c'}$. We later examine optimality relative to policies without short sales constraints.

We recall from Section 19 that a policy (θ, c) is *stationary Markov* if there exist measurable functions $f : H \rightarrow R^N$ and $g : H \rightarrow R_+$ such that $[\theta_t(h^t), c_t(h^t)] = [f(z_t, w_t), g(z_t, w_t)]$ for any $h^t = [(z_1, w_1), \ldots, (z_t, w_t)] \in H^t$ and any time t. Such a policy is denoted (f^∞, g^∞). In Paragraph C we prove the following Proposition by converting to the Markov control formulation of Section 19.

PROPOSITION. *There exists a stationary Markov optimal policy for the agent's consumption and portfolio control problem* $(Z, Q, d, u, \rho, \mathcal{S})$.

C.   We convert the problem of optimal portfolio and consumption policies in a time–homogeneous Markov setting to a standard Markov control formulation. Any current wealth $w \in R_+$ and state $z \in Z$ define the budget feasible set

$$\Gamma^{\mathcal{S}}(z, w) = \{(a, \alpha) \in A : \alpha + a^\top \mathcal{S}(z) \leq w, \quad a \geq 0\}$$

of actions. Thus $\Gamma^{\mathcal{S}}$ may be treated as an admissible action correspondence on the augmented state space $H = Z \times R_+$ into the subsets of $A = R^N \times R_+$. An exercise calls for proof of the following properties.

LEMMA. $\Gamma^{\mathcal{S}}$ *has non–empty, compact, and convex values, and is upper semicontinuous.*

For any random variable Y, it is convenient to let $\sim Y$ denote the distribution of Y. The controlled expectation function $\mathcal{E}^{\mathcal{S}} : A \times H \times B(H) \rightarrow R$ is specified by defining and denoting its value at a point $\big((a, \alpha), (z, w), U\big) \in A \times H \times B(H)$ as

$$\mathcal{E}_{az}^{\mathcal{S}}(U) = E\big[U\left(X', a^\top [\mathcal{S}(X') + d(X')]\right)\big], \quad \sim X' = Q_z.$$

We may think of U as a candidate function giving the indirect utility $U(z, w)$ of beginning in state z with wealth w, and treat $\mathcal{E}_{az}^{\mathcal{S}}(U)$ as the conditional expectation of $U(X_{t+1}, W_{t+1})$ given that $X_t = z$ and given the action (a, α) at time t. Of course, as indicated by our notation, this expectation does not depend on the current wealth w nor on current consumption α, but $\mathcal{E}^{\mathcal{S}}$ is formally defined on $A \times H \times B(H)$ in order to apply the results of Section 19, which call for a controlled expectation function of this general form. Recalling that "weak continuity" of $\mathcal{E}^{\mathcal{S}}$ merely means continuity of the map $(a, z) \mapsto \mathcal{E}^{\mathcal{S}}_{az}(U)$ for any continuous U in $B(H)$, we leave a proof of the following as an exercise.

PROPOSITION. *$\mathcal{E}^{\mathcal{S}}$ is weakly continuous.*

The reward function $r : H \times A \to R$ is defined in the obvious way by $r[h, (a, \alpha)] = u(\alpha)$.

THEOREM. *The Markov control problem $(H, A, \mathcal{E}^{\mathcal{S}}, \Gamma^{\mathcal{S}}, r, \rho)$ has a stationary Markov optimal policy.*

PROOF: In order to apply Theorem 19D, given the previous lemma and proposition, we need only to check that r is bounded and upper semicontinuous, an easy exercise. ∎

This is also a proof of Proposition 20B, since the values and constraints of policies in the problems defined by Proposition 20B and Theorem 20C are clearly identical.

D. A security price function $\mathcal{S}$ is an *equilibrium* for a given Markov exchange economy (Z, Q, d, u, ρ) if there exists a stationary Markov optimal policy (f^{∞}, g^{∞}) for the agent problem $(Z, Q, d, u, \rho, \mathcal{S})$ such that, for any state $z \in Z$, we have market clearing:

$$\left[f\left(z, \mathbf{1}^{\top}[\mathcal{S}(z) + d(z)] \right), g\left(z, \mathbf{1}^{\top}[\mathcal{S}(z) + d(z)] \right) \right] = [\mathbf{1}, e(z)], \qquad (2)$$

where $\mathbf{1} = (1, 1, \ldots, 1) \in R^N$ is the total supply of securities and $e : Z \to R_+$ is the aggregate consumption function defined by $e(z) = \mathbf{1}^{\top} d(z)$. We assume the following additional regularity condition for the remainder of Paragraph D.

CONDITION A. *The reward function u is strictly concave and monotonic, and has a derivative u' on $(0, \infty)$. Furthermore,*
(a) *$d(z)_n > 0$ for all $z \in Z$ and $n \in \{1, \ldots, N\}$, and $u'(0) \equiv \lim_{\alpha \downarrow 0} u'(\alpha)$ is finite, or*
(b) *there exists $\underline{d} \in \text{int}(R_+^N)$ such that $d(z) \geq \underline{d}$ for all $z \in Z$.*

Part (b) of Condition A is implied by compactness of Z if $d(z) \in \text{int}(R_+^N)$ for all $z \in Z$.

THEOREM. *The economy* (Z, Q, d, u, ρ) *has a unique equilibrium security price function* S *defined by*

$$S(z) = \frac{1}{\rho u'[e(z)]} \; E_z \left[\sum_{t=2}^{\infty} \rho^t u'[e(X_t)] d(X_t) \right], \quad z \in Z. \quad (3)$$

This theorem, the main result of Section 20, will be demonstrated in stages by applying properties of the value function $V \in B(H)$ of the Markov control problem $(H, A, \mathcal{E}^S, \Gamma^S, r, \rho)$. First, however, we claim (with proof left as an exercise) that the function S defined by (3) is in fact a valid security pricing function.

FACT 1. *As defined by* (3), S *is continuous and bounded on* Z *into* $\text{int}(R_+^N)$.

The proof of Fact 1 exploits the following useful fact. Again, proof is left as an exercise.

FACT 2. *There exists a constant* $K \in R_+$ *such that* $u'(\alpha)\alpha \le K$ *for all* $\alpha \in [0, \infty)$.

As shown in Section 19, the value V is upper semicontinuous and uniquely satisfies the Bellman Equation $V = \mathcal{U}V$, which may be written in the form: for all $(z, w) \in H$,

$$V(z, w) = \sup_{(a, \alpha) \in R_+^N \times R_+} \left[\rho u(\alpha) + \rho E \left[V \left(X', a^{\top} [S(X') + d(X')] \right) \right] \right], \quad (4)$$

where $\sim X' = Q_z$, subject to

$$\alpha + a^{\top} S(z) \le w. \quad (5)$$

We also leave the following as an exercise.

FACT 3. *For each* $z \in Z$, *the function* $V(z, \cdot) : R_+ \to R$ *is monotonic and strictly concave.*

The following result is slightly more delicate. We let (f^{∞}, g^{∞}) denote a stationary Markov optimal policy for $(H, A, \mathcal{E}^S, \Gamma^S, r, \rho)$.

FACT 4. *For given* $(z, \widehat{w}) \in Z \times R_+$ *with* $g(z, \widehat{w}) > 0$, *the function* $V(z, \cdot) : R_+ \to R$ *has a continuous derivative at* $\widehat{w}$, *denoted* $V_w(z, \widehat{w})$ *and equal to* $\rho u'[g(z, \widehat{w})]$.

PROOF: Since $g(z, \widehat{w}) > 0$, there is an interval $(\underline{w}, \overline{w}) \subset R_+$ containing $\widehat{w}$ such that a function $v : (\underline{w}, \overline{w}) \to R$ is well–defined by

$$v(w) = \rho u[g(z, \widehat{w}) + w - \widehat{w}] + \rho \mathcal{E}_{f(z, \widehat{w})z}(V).$$

Since V satisfies the Bellman Equation, we have $v(\widehat{w}) = V(z, \widehat{w})$ and $v(w) \leq V(z, w)$ for all $w \in (\underline{w}, \overline{w})$. Since $V(z, \cdot)$ is strictly concave at $\widehat{w}$ by the Fact 3, there is some $\beta \in R$ satisfying the inequality:

$$\beta(w - \widehat{w}) \geq V(z, w) - V(z, \widehat{w}) \geq v(w) - v(\widehat{w}), \tag{6}$$

for all $w \in (\underline{w}, \overline{w})$. We know that v is differentiable; indeed,

$$v'(w) = \rho u'[g(z, \widehat{w}) + w - \widehat{w}].$$

Dividing (6) through by $w - \widehat{w}$ for $w \neq \widehat{w}$ and letting $w \to \widehat{w}$ yields the existence of the required derivative $V_w(z, \widehat{w}) = v'(\widehat{w})$. The derivative of a strictly concave function is continuous. ∎

PROPOSITION. *If S is an equilibrium for (Z, Q, d, u, ρ), then S satisfies the equation: for all z in Z,*

$$S(z) = \frac{\rho}{u'[e(z)]} E\big[u'[e(X')][S(X') + d(X')]\big], \quad \sim X' = Q_z. \tag{7}$$

Before proving this key result, we leave it as an exercise that relations (3) and (7) are equivalent, thus yielding the uniqueness part of Theorem 20D. Relation (7), the so–called *Stochastic Euler Equation*, is often written in the conditional form: for any time t and any starting point $z \in Z$,

$$S(X_t) = \frac{\rho}{u'[e(X_t)]} E_t\big[u'[e(X_{t+1})][S(X_{t+1}) + d(X_{t+1})] \mid X_t\big] \quad \Gamma_z\text{–a.s.} \tag{8}$$

PROOF: We can re–write the Bellman equation (4), using strict concavity of u to replace α with $w - a^\top S(z)$, as: for all $(z, w) \in Z \times R_+$,

$$V(z, w) = \sup_{a \in R_+^N} \Big[\rho u\big[w - a^\top S(z)\big] + \rho E\big[V\big(X', a^\top[S(X') + d(X')]\big)\big]\Big], \tag{9}$$

where $\sim X' = Q_z$. If S is an equilibrium, then, at $(z, w) = (z, \mathbf{1}^\top[S(z) + d(z)])$, this supremum is attained at the interior point $a = \mathbf{1}$, where the first order necessary condition is

$$-u'[e(z)]S(z) + E\big[V_w\big(X', \mathbf{1}^\top[S(X') + d(X')]\big)[S(X') + d(X')]\big] = 0, \tag{10}$$

where $\sim X' = Q_z$. (The differentiation is justified by Condition A and Facts 3 and 4.) Since S is an equilibrium, we can use Fact 4 to substitute $\rho u'[e(X')]$ for $V_w\big(X', \mathbf{1}^\top[S(X') + d(X')]\big)$, yielding (7). ∎

PROOF: (Completion of the proof of Theorem 20D). To complete the proof of Theorem 20D, we can use the fact that (10) is not only necessary, but is also sufficient for optimality of $a = 1$ by the strict concavity of $V(z, \cdot)$ (Fact 3). Thus, if we specify $\mathcal{S}$ by (3), implying (7), we deduce that a stationary Markov optimal policy (f^∞, g^∞) can be chosen to satisfy $f\big(z, \mathbf{1}^\top[\mathcal{S}(z) + d(z)]\big) = 1$. This implies by budget feasibility that $g(z, \mathbf{1}^\top[\mathcal{S}(z) + d(z)]) = e(z)$, for all $z \in Z$. We therefore have market clearing (2), completing the proof, except for the following technicality.

Actually, although we shown that $a = 1$ is optimal for (9) by concavity and the first order conditions for optimality, the potential for linear dependence among the random variables

$$[\mathcal{S}_1(X') + d_1(X')], [\mathcal{S}_2(X') + d_2(X')], \ldots, [\mathcal{S}_N(X') + d_N(X')]$$

leaves open the possibility of other optimal portfolios. Thus, for a complete proof, we replace any stationary optimal policy (f^∞, g^∞) with a new policy $(\widehat{f}^\infty, \widehat{g}^\infty)$ defined by $\widehat{g} = g$ and by

$$\widehat{f}(z, w) = 1, \quad \text{if} \quad w = \mathbf{1}^\top[\mathcal{S}(z) + d(z)],$$

$$= f(z, w), \quad \text{otherwise.}$$

It is left as an exercise to show that this new policy is also optimal (in particular, that $\widehat{f}$ is measurable). ∎

In completing the proof of Theorem 20D, we have seen that Proposition 20D is indeed central in both the existence as well as the uniqueness arguments. The equivalent forms (3) and (7) of the equilibrium security price function can both be seen as natural multi–period extensions of the finite–dimensional equilibrium representative agent pricing condition deduced as relation (35) of Paragraph L of the Introduction. In the latter setting, however, the completeness of markets implies Pareto optimality, and therefore the existence of a representative satisfying the appropriate analogue to (7). In the present setting of incomplete markets, however, only the assumption of a single agent permits (7) to apply. With heterogeneous agents and incomplete markets, equilibria are not generally Pareto optimal, and there will not generally exist a representative agent. The existence of a stationary Markov equilibrium with heterogeneous agents nevertheless can be shown, as indicated in the Notes.

E. Our demonstration of stationary Markov equilibria in Markov exchange economies, Theorem 19D, suffers somewhat from the unnatural imposition of a *no–short–sales* constraint. We can relax this restriction if the state space Z is a finite set, as follows. For any vector $b \leq 0$ in R^N, let

$$F_b = \{(\theta, c) \in F : \theta_t(h^t) \geq b, \quad \forall h^t \in H^t \; \forall t\}$$

denote the subset of budget feasible policies with portfolios bounded below by b. Further, let $F_\infty = \bigcup_{b \leq 0} F_b$, the set of policies bounded below by some amount, but an amount not fixed in advance. We momentarily fix some bound $b \leq 0$. For a given security price function $\mathcal{S}$, and any $(z, w) \in Z \times R_+$, we let

$$\Gamma_b^{\mathcal{S}}(z, w) = \{(a, \alpha) \in A : \alpha + a^\top \mathcal{S}(z) \leq w, \; a \geq b, \; a^\top [\mathcal{S}(X') + d(X')] \geq 0\},$$

where X' has distribution Q_z. This defines an admissible action correspondence $\Gamma_b^{\mathcal{S}}$.

LEMMA. *$\Gamma_b^{\mathcal{S}}$ has non empty, compact, and convex values, and is upper semicontinuous.*

Proof is left as an exercise. A security price function $\mathcal{S}$ is an *equilibrium without restricted short sales* for the economy (z, Q, d, u, ρ) if there exists a stationary Markov policy $(\theta, c) = (f^\infty, g^\infty) \in F_\infty$ satisfying (2) (market clearing), and such that, for any policy $(\theta', c') \subset F_\infty$ and any state $z \subset Z$,

$$U_{\theta,c}\left(z, \mathbf{1}^\top [\mathcal{S}(z) + d(z)]\right) \geq U_{\theta',c'}\left(z, \mathbf{1}^\top [\mathcal{S}(z) + d(z)]\right). \tag{11}$$

PROPOSITION. *Suppose Condition A applies. Then the unique equilibrium $\mathcal{S}$ with unrestricted short sales is well–defined by relation (3).*

PROOF: Let $b = -1$ and let $(\theta, c) = (f^\infty, g^\infty)$ be a stationary Markov policy that is optimal for the control problem $(H, A, \mathcal{E}^{\mathcal{S}}, \Gamma_b^{\mathcal{S}}, r, \rho)$, where $\mathcal{S}$ is defined by (3). (This policy exists by the previous lemma.) By the proof of Theorem 19D, we can take it that (f, g) satisfies market clearing (2). Let $(\theta', c') \in F_\infty$ be arbitrarily chosen. Then (θ', c') and (θ, c) are in $F_{\hat{b}}$ for some $\hat{b} \leq 0$ in R^N by the definition of F_∞. Let $(\hat{\theta}, \hat{c}) = (\hat{f}^\infty, \hat{g}^\infty)$ be a stationary Markov optimal policy for $(H, A, \mathcal{E}^{\mathcal{S}}, \Gamma_{\hat{b}}^{\mathcal{S}}, r, \rho)$. Then $U_{\hat{\theta},\hat{c}} \geq U_{\theta',c'}$. In particular,

$$U_{\hat{\theta},\hat{c}}\left(z, \mathbf{1}^\top [\mathcal{S}(z) + d(z)]\right) \geq U_{c',\theta'}\left(z, \mathbf{1}^\top [\mathcal{S}(z) + d(z)]\right), \quad z \in Z. \tag{12}$$

Again, we can assume without loss of generality that $(\hat{f}, \hat{g})$ satisfies market clearing (2). This implies that

$$U_{\hat{\theta},\hat{c}}\left(z, \mathbf{1}^\top [\mathcal{S}(z) + d(z)]\right) = U_{\theta,c}\left(z, \mathbf{1}^\top [\mathcal{S}(z) + d(z)]\right), \quad z \in Z. \tag{13}$$

Together, (12) and (13) imply (11). ∎

The meaning of this result is as follows. Given the initial wealth endowment of all securities at their equilibrium prices (3), one can do no better than to continue holding all of the securities, always consuming their dividends, even without an exogenously set lower bound on portfolio holdings. (Of course, a lower bound b on portfolios may be binding at other levels of initial wealth.)

F.   We now make a modest extension of our model to allow for production. We limit ourselves to a single firm, a single technology, a single security (the firm's common share), and a single commodity, "consumption". Generalizations of each of these dimensional restrictions are conceptually straightforward. Heterogeneous agents present a greater challenge, but one that can undoubtedly be overcome. A *Markov production economy* is a collection (Z, Q, G, u, ρ), where the Borel state space Z, continuous transition function $Q : Z \to \mathcal{P}(Z)$, bounded continuous utility function $u : R_+ \to R$, and discount factor $\rho \in (0, 1)$ represent the same concepts presented in the exchange model of Paragraph A, and where $G : Z \times R_+ \to R_+$ is a bounded continuous *state–dependent growth function*. A given investment $y \in [0, \infty)$ of the consumption commodity generates a new stock $G(z, y)$ of the consumption commodity in the following period if the exogenous state in the following period is z. This new stock $\kappa' = G(z, y)$ is then partially allocated to investment y' in the following period, with any remainder $\alpha' = \kappa' - y'$ made available for consumption. We first describe a central planner's stochastic growth problem of determining a utility maximizing production plan. We follow this with a decentralization of the central planner's solution via a stock market for the shares of a firm controlling the production process as well as a spot market for consumption.

G.   The *central planner's problem* for a Markov production economy (Z, Q, G, u, ρ) is set up as follows. A consumption policy is defined, just as in the exchange case, as a sequence $c = \{c_1, c_2, \ldots\}$ of measurable functions of the form $c_t : H^t \to R_+$, where $H = Z \times R_+$ is the state space. In this (non–market) production problem, however, a typical element (z, κ) of H represents an exogenous state z and a current stock κ of the consumption commodity. A consumption policy c is *feasible* if $c_t(h^t) \le \kappa_t$ for any $h^t = [(z_1, \kappa_1), \ldots, (z_t, \kappa_t)]$ in H^t and for any time t. Taking the set $\Omega = Z \times Z \times \cdots$ of sample paths of the exogenous state process as the set of all possible states of the world, we recall that any initial state $z \in Z$ induces a unique measure $P_z \in \mathcal{P}(\Omega)$ corresponding to the distribution of the exogenous canonical state process $\{X_1, X_2, \ldots\}$ under the given transition function Q, with $P_z(X_1 = z) = 1$. For any feasible consumption policy c and any initial state $(z, \kappa) \in H$, let $K^{z, \kappa, c}$ denote the capital stock process defined inductively by $K_1^{z,\kappa,c} = \kappa$ and by

$$K_t^{z,\kappa,c} = G\left(X_t, K_{t-1}^{z,\kappa,c} - c_{t-1}\left[(X_1, K_1^{z,\kappa,c}), \ldots, (X_{t-1}, K_{t-1}^{z,\kappa,c})\right]\right), \quad t > 1.$$

For any feasible consumption policy c, let $U_c \in B(H)$ be defined at $(z, \kappa) \in H$ by

$$U_c(z, \kappa) = E_z\left[\sum_{t=1}^{\infty} \rho^t u\left(c_t\left[(X_1, K_1^{z,\kappa,c}), \ldots, (X_t, K_t^{z,\kappa,c})\right]\right)\right],$$

where E_z denotes expectation with respect to P_z. A feasible consumption policy c is *optimal* for (Z, Q, G, u, ρ) if $U_c \geq U_{c'}$ for any feasible consumption policy c'.

PROPOSITION. *There exists a stationary Markov optimal consumption policy for the central planner's problem defined by (Z, Q, G, u, ρ).*

PROOF: Let $(H, [0, \infty), \mathcal{E}, \Gamma, r, \rho)$ be the Markov control problem defined by

(a) $r[(z, \kappa), \alpha] = u(\alpha)$ for any $[(z, \kappa), \alpha] \in H \times [0, \infty)$,
(b) $\Gamma(z, \kappa) = [0, \kappa]$ for any $(z, \kappa) \in H$, and
(c) For any $[(z, \kappa), \alpha] \in H \times [0, \infty)$ and any $W \in B(H)$,

$$\mathcal{E}_{(z,\kappa)\alpha}(W) = E\left[W[X', G(X', \kappa - \alpha)]\right], \quad \sim X' = Q_z.$$

This is indeed a Markov control problem (satisfying the hypotheses of Theorem 19D), proving the result by the obvious equivalence with the stochastic growth problem (Z, Q, G, u, ρ). ∎

H. We decentralize the central planner's problem with markets and prices, as a production problem of maximizing the market value of the firm and a consumer's problem of optimal choice of consumption and investment in the firm's common stock, subject to the same budget constraint faced in a Markov exchange economy.

The firm takes as given some time–homogeneous Markov process $Y = \{Y_1, Y_2, \ldots\}$ with state space $H = Z \times R_+$. Let $J = H \times R_+$ define the firm's state space, with typical element $j = (h, \kappa)$ representing a given state h of H and stock κ of commodity on hand. A *dividend policy* is a sequence $D = \{D_1, D_2, \ldots\}$ of measurable functions of the form $D_t : J^t \to [0, \infty)$, mapping a history $j^t \in J^t$ to the consumption dividend $D_t(j^t)$ at time t. A dividend policy D is *feasible* if $D_t(j^t) \leq \kappa_t$ for any

$j^t = [(h_1, \kappa_1), \dots, (h_t, \kappa_t)] \in J^t$ and any time t. The firm assumes there is some function $\delta \in C(H)$ such that $\delta(z, \kappa) \leq \kappa$, and such that $Y_t = (X_t, \overline{K}_t)$, where $\overline{K}_1$ is given and

$$\overline{K}_t = G\left[X_t, \overline{K}_{t-1} - \delta(X_{t-1}, \overline{K}_{t-1})\right], \quad t > 1.$$

In other words, one part of the state Y_t is the exogenous state X_t; the other is a capital stock $\overline{K}_t$ that cannot be affected by the firm. This induces the transition function $Q^\delta : H \to \mathcal{P}(H)$ for Y defined by letting $Q^\delta_{(z,\kappa)}$ be the distribution of $(X', G[X', \kappa - \delta(z, \kappa)])$, where X' has distribution Q_z. A feasible dividend policy D and initial state $j = (h, \kappa) \in J$ of the firm determine the firm's stock process $K^{j,D}$ by $K_1^{j,D} = \kappa$ and

$$K_{t+1}^{j,D} = G\left(X_{t+1}, K_t^{j,D} - D_t\right), \quad t > 1,$$

dropping the arguments of D_t for notational simplicity. We emphasize the distinction between the capital stock $\overline{K}_t$ and the capital stock $K_t^{j,D}$ induced by the firm. It will turn out that these must be the same in a naturally defined equilibrium. Nevertheless, the firm must take $\overline{K}$ as fixed and $K^{j,D}$ as controllable.

Let $\pi \in C(H)$ denote a *state price function*, strictly positive valued, with $\pi(Y_t)$ to be thought of as the discount applied to dividends in a future period t in determining the contribution of those dividends to the current market value of the firm. We thus define the firm's current (*cum* dividend) market value in state $j = (h, \kappa) \in J$, given dividend policy D, as

$$F_D^{\pi\delta}(h, \kappa) = \frac{1}{\rho\pi(h)} \, E_h\left[\sum_{t=1}^{\infty} \rho^t \pi(Y_t) D_t\right], \tag{14}$$

where E_h denotes expectation over the space of sample paths of Y according to the distribution P_h given by the starting point h and the transition function Q^δ. A feasible dividend policy D is *value–maximizing* given (π, δ) provided $F_D^{\pi\delta}(j) \geq F_{D'}^{\pi\delta}(j)$ for any feasible dividend policy D', for any state $j \in J$. A *stationary Markov equilibrium* for (Z, Q, G, u, ρ) is a collection $(\delta, \mathcal{S}, \pi, d)$ satisfying the properties:

(a) $\mathcal{S}$ is an equilibrium for the Markov exchange economy $(H, Q^\delta, \delta, u, \rho)$,

(b) $D = d^\infty$ is a stationary Markov value–maximizing dividend policy given (π, δ),

(c) given any state $j = [(z, \overline{\kappa}), \kappa] \in J$ with $\overline{\kappa} = \kappa$, we have $d(j) = \delta(z, \kappa)$, and

(d) $\mathcal{S}(z, \kappa) = F_D^{\pi\delta}[(z, \kappa), \kappa] - \delta(z, \kappa)$ for any $(z, \kappa) \in H$.

Interpreting, (a) defines equilibrium in the markets for current consumption and the common share of the firm, (b) and (c) state that the firm's dividend policy is value–maximizing and consistent with the dividends assumed by the agent, and (d) states that the security price function taken by the agent is consistent with that determined by the firm's dividend policy and the valuation model assumed by the firm.

I. In order to show the existence of stationary Markov equilibria for (Z, Q, G, u, ρ), we adopt and maintain the following additional regularity conditions:

(a) u is monotonic, strictly concave, and differentiable on $(0, \infty)$, with $u'(0)$ finite when defined as $\lim_{\alpha \downarrow 0} u'(\alpha)$, and

(b) for all z in Z, the function $G(z, \cdot) : R_+ \to R_+$ is monotonic, strictly concave, and differentiable on $(0, \infty)$, with $G(z, 0) = 0$ and

$$\lim_{\kappa \downarrow 0} \frac{\partial G(z, \kappa)}{\partial \kappa} < 1/\rho.$$

We leave proof of the following improvement of Proposition 20G as an exercise.

LEMMA. *The central planner's problem for* (Z, Q, G, u, ρ) *has a unique stationary Markov optimal policy* δ^∞. *Furthermore,* δ *is bounded and continuous, and* $\delta(z, \kappa) \in (0, \kappa]$ *for any* $(z, \kappa) \in Z \times (0, \infty)$.

Fixing the dividend policy δ^∞ given by this lemma, consider the state price function $\pi \in C(H)$ defined by $\pi(z, \overline{\kappa}) = u'[\delta(z, \overline{\kappa})]$ and the security price function $S : H \to R_+$ defined by

$$S(h) = \frac{1}{\rho \pi(h)} E_h \left[\sum_{t=2}^{\infty} \rho^t \pi(Y_t) \delta(Y_t) \right]. \tag{15}$$

It can be seen as an easy exercise that S is well defined and in $C(H)$, and that condition (d) of an equilibrium is implied by equilibrium condition (c). A minor extension of the arguments given in the exchange case, accounting for the fact that δ may take the value 0, shows that S is an equilibrium for the exchange economy $(Z, Q^\delta, \delta, u, \rho)$.

One can formulate the firm's value maximization problem, given π and δ, as a Markov control problem, with reward $\pi(h)\alpha$ for dividend α in state (h, κ). Again as an exercise, we leave it to be shown that a value–maximizing stationary Markov dividend policy d^∞ exists. A proof of the following result uses an argument, like that of the proof of Fact 4 of Paragraph D, showing differentiability of the firm's value function with respect to the firm's capital stock, at interior dividend choices. This will imply that the first order conditions for the firm are implied by those of the central planner.

PROPOSITION. *For any state $j = [(z, \overline{\kappa}), \kappa] \in J$ for the firm with $\overline{\kappa} = \kappa$, the firm's value–maximizing dividend choice $d(j)$ is equal to the central planner's optimal consumption choice $\delta(z, \kappa)$.*

We have shown that equilibrium condition (c) applies to $(\delta, \pi, \mathcal{S}, d)$, proving the following claim.

THEOREM. *Under our maintained assumptions, there exists a unique stationary Markov equilibrium $(\delta, \pi, \mathcal{S}, d)$ for the Markov production economy (Z, Q, G, u, ρ), with the property that δ^∞ solves the central planner's problem defined by (Z, Q, G, u, ρ).*

EXERCISES

EXERCISE 20.1   Prove Lemma 20C.

EXERCISE 20.2   Prove Proposition 20C. *Hint:* The following facts are useful. Suppose X and Y are Borel spaces. The function $x \mapsto \delta_x$ is continuous from X into $\mathcal{P}(X)$, where $\delta_x \in \mathcal{P}(X)$ denotes the measure with $\delta_x(\{x\}) = 1$. The function $(\sim A, \sim B) \mapsto \sim(A, B)$ is also continuous from $\mathcal{P}(X) \times \mathcal{P}(Y)$ into $\mathcal{P}(X \times Y)$, where $\sim A$ denotes the distribution of a random variable A.

EXERCISE 20.3   Show that the reward function r defined in Paragraph C is upper semicontinuous.

EXERCISE 20.4   Prove Fact 1 of Paragraph D. *Hint:* The metric space $C(Z)$ is complete.

EXERCISE 20.5   Prove the existence of a solution $\mathcal{S}$ to relation (7) using Blackwell's Fixed Point Theorem.

EXERCISE 20.6   Prove Fact 2 of Paragraph D.

EXERCISE 20.7   In the proof of Fact 4 of Paragraph D, show that there indeed exists a scalar β satisfying relation (6). *Hint:* Review the definition of a superdifferential from Section 8.

EXERCISE 20.8 Prove Fact 3 of Paragraph D.

EXERCISE 20.9 Show that relations (3) and (7) are equivalent.

EXERCISE 20.10 Prove Lemma 20E.

EXERCISE 20.11 Suppose, in the framework of Paragraph 20B, that u is twice continuously differentiable, that the state process X is an i.i.d. strictly positive real–valued process, and that the economy includes a single security with dividends given by the function $d(z) = z$, $z \in R_+$. Show that the equilibrium security price function S demonstrated in Theorem 20C is differentiable and satisfies

$$\frac{zS'(z)}{S(z)} = -z\frac{u''(z)}{u'(z)}, \quad z \in R_+.$$

In neo–classical terms, this expression equates the elasticity of price with respect to income to the *Arrow Pratt measure of relative risk aversion*: $r(y) = -yu''(y)/u'(y), \quad y \ge 0$.

EXERCISE 20.12 (A General Markov Exchange Economy) Consider an extension of the notion of a Markov exchange economy defined by (Z, Q, d, b, u, ρ), where Z is a Borel space, $Q : Z \to \mathcal{P}(Z)$ is a continuous transition function, $d : Z \to \text{int}(R_+^{N\ell})$ is bounded and continuous, $b : Z \to R_+^{\ell}$ is bounded and continuous with some $\underline{b} \in \text{int}(R_+^{\ell})$ such that $b(z) \ge \underline{b}$ for all $z \in Z$, $u : Z \times R_+^{\ell} \to R$ is bounded and continuous, and $\rho : Z \to (0, \overline{\rho})$ is continuous for some $\overline{\rho} \in (0, 1)$. There are ℓ commodities; $d(z)$ is the $N \times \ell$ matrix whose (n, k)–element is the amount of commodity k paid by security n in state $z \in Z$; $b(z)$ is the commodity vector directly endowed to the agent in state z; $u(z, \alpha)$ is the reward (utility) of the agent in state z with total consumption $\alpha \in R_+^{\ell}$ of commodities; and $\rho(z)$ is the discount factor in state z. The total expected discounted utility for aggregate consumption, for example, is thus

$$E\left[\sum_{t=1}^{\infty} \rho(X_1)\rho(X_2)\cdots\rho(X_t)u[X_t, b(X_t) + \mathbf{1}^{\top}d(X_t)] \,\middle|\, X_1 = z\right],$$

for initial state $z \in Z$, where $X_1, X_2, \ldots$ is a time–homogeneous Z–valued Markov process with transition function Q. An *equilibrium* is a security price function $S : Z \to R_+^N$ and a commodity price function $p : Z \to R_+^{\ell}$ such that there exists an optimal stationary Markov portfolio and consumption strategy (f^{∞}, g^{∞}), with $f : Z \times R_+ \to R^N$ and $g : Z \times R_+ \to R_+^{\ell}$ satisfying $f(z, w) = \mathbf{1} \in R^N$ and $g(z, w) = b(z) + \mathbf{1}^{\top}d(z)$ whenever

$w = \mathbf{1}^{\top}[\mathcal{S}(z) + d(z)p(z)] + p(z)^{\top}b(z)$. (We have not, of course, given a definition of an optimal stationary Markov policy; that definition is part of this problem.)

(A)   Based on the understanding of this model, state the exact definition of an optimal stationary Markov policy, and guess the necessary form of an equilibrium $(\mathcal{S}, p)$ under appropriate assumptions such as differentiability of $u(z, \cdot)$ for all $z \in Z$. *Hint:* Choose a numeraire, for example: commodity number one.

(B)   Making minimal regularity assumptions, prove the existence of an equilibrium. If unsure about how to proceed at certain stages, sketch out the arguments for a proof of that point. This problem extends our original setting by allowing: (a) state–dependent discounting, (b) multiple commodities, (c) private endowments, and (d) state–dependent utility. If unable to deal with one of these, revert to the original simple formulation on that point.

(C)   Based on the chosen numeraire, give the term structure of interest rates in this model. That is, solve for the price $\phi_k(z)$ of a bond in zero net supply paying one unit of account k periods in the future, given current state $z \in Z$. *Hint:* See Exercise 20.14.

EXERCISE 20.13   In the context of the Markov equilibrium of Paragraph B, suppose the single agent has a utility function $u : R_+ \rightarrow R$ for current consumption such that

$$u(\alpha) = a + b\alpha - c\alpha^2, \qquad \alpha \in [0, \bar{e}],$$

for strictly positive scalars a, b, and c, where $\bar{e}$ is an upper bound for e, the aggregate endowment function. Assume that $b - 2c\bar{e} \geq 0$. The *expected rate of return* on security n is the function $\mu_n : Z \rightarrow R$ defined by

$$\mu_n(z) = \frac{1}{\mathcal{S}^n(z)} E[\mathcal{S}^n(X') + d^n(X')], \qquad \sim X' = Q_z.$$

The *expected rate of growth of aggregate consumption* is similarly defined as the function $\mu_C : Z \rightarrow R$ given by

$$\mu_C(z) = \frac{1}{e(z)} E_z[e(X')], \qquad \sim X' = Q_z.$$

The *beta* between security n and aggregate consumption is defined as the function β_n given by

$$\beta_n(z) = \frac{\mathrm{cov}_z(n, C)}{\mathrm{var}_z(C)}, \qquad z \in Z,$$

where $\text{cov}_z(n, C)$ denotes the covariance between the rate of return on security n and the rate of growth of aggregate consumption in state z, and $\text{var}_z(C)$ denotes the variance in the rate of growth of aggregate consumption. Formalize these (conditional) covariance definitions and derive the following *Consumption–based Capital Asset Pricing Model*:

$$\mu_n(z) - A(z) = k(z)\beta_n(z)[\mu_C(z) - A(z)], \qquad z \in Z, \qquad n \in \{1, \dots, N\},$$

where A and k are functions to be determined. State your assumptions carefully. Identify the functions A and k.

EXERCISE 20.14 (Term Structure) A k–period pure *discount bond* is a security paying a dividend of one unit of consumption k periods in the future, and nothing at any other time. We wish to include in our model formulation of Paragraphs A and D pure discount bonds available in each period: one one–period bond, one two period bond, one three–period bond, and so on up to and including one K–period bond for some K. Note that the original model we have from this Section has securities that pay the same dividends each period as a function of the current state.

(A) Give two fundamentally different re–formulations of our model that allow us to formally include these pure discount bonds within an equilibrium and to use a version of (3) to price them. Do not include production. *Hint:* Take one formulation with bonds in zero net supply, allowing short sales, and one formulation with bonds in positive net supply.

(B) State a model for the term structure of interest rates. That is, obtain a formula for the price $\phi_k(z)$ in state z of a k–period bond, for any $k \in \{1, \dots, K\}$.

EXERCISE 20.15 In the framework of Paragraphs A through C, suppose one of the given N securities, say security number one, pays off only in odd periods, that is, in periods one, three, five, seven, and so on. How would one include such a security in the model and still be able to use a Stochastic Euler Equation to price it? Be formal, but brief.

EXERCISE 20.16 Prove Lemma 20I.

EXERCISE 20.17 Prove Proposition 20I.

EXERCISE 20.18 (Stock Market Equilibria and The Term Structure) An infinite horizon economy is made up of a single agent, a single commodity called consumption, and a single production technology. The agent has preferences over positive stochastic consumption processes $c = \{c_0, c_1, \dots\}$ given by the utility function

$$U(c) = E\left[\sum_{t=1}^{\infty} \rho^t \log(c_t)\right],$$

where $\rho \in (0,1)$. The productivity of capital is affected by a real–valued random shock process X defined by

$$X_{t+1} = A + BX_t + \epsilon_t; \qquad X_1 = x,$$

where A and B are scalars and where $\{\epsilon_1, \epsilon_2, \dots\}$ are joint normal independent random variables with zero mean and common variance $\sigma^2 > 0$. The technology begins with a stock $K_1 = \kappa > 0$ of consumption at time zero. The amount I_t of current stock not consumed is placed into production and yields a new stock of $I_t^{\gamma} e^{X(t)}$ in the following period, where $\gamma \in (0,1]$. The remainder, $K_t - I_t$, is available for current consumption c_t.

(A) (Central Planning Solution)   As the central planner for this economy, solve for the optimal consumption and production policy, that policy maximizing the agent's utility subject to feasibility. State the value function and the optimal stationary Markov control in closed form. Make minimal parameter assumptions. *Hint:* Try a value function of the form $V(\kappa, x) = a(x) + b \log(\kappa)$.

(B) (Stock Market Decentralization)   Set up a stock market economy with a single firm that owns the capital stock and sells some amount of it as dividends in each period, placing the remainder in the production technology explained above. All shares of the firm are owned initially by the agent, who is free to buy or sell shares at any time in exchange for consumption. Indicate a map from infinite horizon dividend streams to the firm's current share price under which the firm maximizes its current share price by producing according to the central planning solution. Provide an expression for the current value of the firm in equilibrium under which the agent optimally holds one share of the firm and consumes precisely the total dividends of the firm. Justify your solutions by a proof of equilibrium.

(C) (The Term Structure of Interest Rates)   Derive the term structure of interest rates in the form of an explicit expression for the equilibrium market value $\phi_n(x, \kappa)$ at any time t of an n–period discount bond (a security paying one unit of consumption at time $t + n$), given that $X_t = x$ and that

$K_t = \kappa$. You may need to use a well known expression for $E(e^Z)$, where Z is normally distributed with a given mean and variance. *Hint:*

$$\phi_n(x, \kappa) = e^{F(n,x,\kappa)}, \tag{16}$$

where

$$F(n, x, \kappa) = (1-\gamma^n)\log(\kappa) + n\log(\rho) - \log(\gamma\rho)\sum_{\tau=1}^{n}\gamma^{n-\tau+1} - m(n,x) + \frac{v(n)}{2},$$

with

$$m(n, x) = \sum_{\tau=1}^{n}\gamma^{n-\tau}\left(B^\tau x + \sum_{j=0}^{\tau-1}B^{\tau-j-1}A\right),$$

and

$$v(n) = \sum_{j=1}^{n}\left(\sum_{\tau=j}^{n}\gamma^{n-\tau}B^{\tau-j}\right)^2\sigma^2.$$

EXERCISE 20.19   State and prove the finite horizon analogue to Theorem 20D.

Notes

The results of Paragraphs A through E are easy extensions of Lucas (1978). The proof of Fact 4 of Paragraph D is based on Benveniste and Scheinkman (1979). Paragraphs F through H are an extension of Brock (1972, 1979, 1982). Our formulation, however, is quite different from that of Brock. For yet another formulation, see Kline (1986). The papers by Lucas, Brock, and Kline, as well as the complementary paper by Prescott and Mehra (1980), include further results. All of these papers should be consulted for additional references. Tauchen (1986) and Gagnon and Taylor (1986) give numerical methods for the solution models such as those of this section. Kandori (1985) extends to the general case (non–Markovian stochastics and general preference relations) certain aspects of this theory. Levine (1985) has related results.

Duffie, Geanakoplos, Mas–Colell, and McLennan (1988) have demonstrated stationary Markov equilibria for exchange economies with heterogeneous agents. For a monetary version of the exchange economy, see Lucas and Stokey (1987). The continuous–time theory paralleling the results here is summarized in Section 25. In particular, see Exercises 25.11 and 25.18. The Notes of Section 25 include other relevant sources. For an example of related results for an *overlapping generations model* of a Markov economy, see Spear, Srivastava, and Woodford (1986). [Cass and Yaari (1966) is a suitable point of introduction to the overlapping generations model of Samuelson (1958), which we do not cover here.] Donaldson, Johnson, and Mehra (1987) provides further characterization of the equilibrium term structure in the setting of this section. The term structure is taken up again in Section 25.

Chapter IV
CONTINUOUS–TIME ASSET PRICING

This chapter outlines the theory of asset pricing in continuous–time economies, more or less in parallel with the discrete–time treatment of Chapter III. The premier model for the generation of information in this setting is Brownian Motion. By applying Ito's Lemma, this model leads to a smooth and explicitly characterized transition in the expected value of smooth functions of an underlying state process. We review the Brownian Motion model in Section 21, with a brief summary of the Ito calculus. Principally, this covers stochastic differential equations, Ito's Lemma, the Feynman–Kac Formula, and Girsanov's Theorem, all in abbreviated form and without proof. These results are brought to bear immediately in Section 22, with a review of the Black–Scholes model for the arbitrage pricing of securities whose payoffs depend on the path taken by a given security price process. In Section 23 we again apply the Ito calculus, this time to the form of the Bellman Equation for stochastic control that applies when uncertainty is generated by Brownian Motion. Many of the results of Sections 21, 22, and 23 have natural analogues for a Poisson state variable process, but we will not have room for these parallels. In order to further develop intuition for portfolio and consumption choices in a Markov setting, we restrict ourselves in Section 24 to the case of independent and identically distributed returns to investment. Although this setting is restrictive, the results are remarkably specific. The equilibrium asset pricing theory of Section 25 has two main goals: the Consumption–Based Capital Asset Pricing Model and a characterization of interest rates. The equilibrium demonstrated in Section 25 is for a special case of the continuous–time stochastic economy of Section 16, taking time–additive expected utility, a single commodity, and uncertainty generated by Brownian Motion. The representative agent approach, as outlined in Paragraph L of the Introduction, is used to price securities.

21.   An Overview of the Ito Calculus

This section introduces several analytical tools from a body of knowledge known as the *Ito calculus*. These can be applied to the so–called "diffusion models" of asset price behavior. The focus of this theory is the stochastic (or "Ito") integral $\int \theta_t \, dB_t$, where B is a Brownian Motion. The central tool is Ito's Lemma, which reduces many stochastic problems to deterministic differential equations. We sample a bit of stochastic differential equations theory. Given a stochastic differential equation $dX_t = \mu(X_t) \, dt + \sigma(X_t) \, dB_t$, the function f defined by

$$f(x) = E\left[\int_0^T e^{-\rho t} u(X_t) \, dt + e^{-\rho T} v(X_T) \,\middle|\, X_0 = x \right]$$

is, under technical regularity conditions, equal to the solution to a partic- ular deterministic differential equation. This result is sometimes called the Feynman–Kac Formula. We learn how to change the drift $\mu(X_t)$ of an Ito process such as X by changing the underlying probability measure, using a collection of results known as Girsanov's Theorem.

A.   For the entire Section we fix $(\Omega, \mathcal{F}, F, P)$ to be a filtered probability space for the time set $T = [0, \infty)$, where $F = \{\mathcal{F}_t : t \geq 0\}$ is the standard filtration of a Standard Brownian Motion $B = (B^1, \ldots, B^N)$ in R^N.

An *Ito integral* is merely a stochastic integral with respect to Brownian Motion, as defined in Section 15. The most general Ito integral we will consider is of the form

$$\int \theta_t \, dB_t \equiv \sum_{n=1}^N \int \theta_t^n \, dB_t^n,$$

where $\theta = (\theta^1, \ldots, \theta^N)$ is an element of the vector space $\mathcal{L}$ of predictable processes satisfying $\int_0^t \theta_s \cdot \theta_s \, ds < \infty$ almost surely for all $t \geq 0$. Extensions of the Ito integral are cited in the Notes. We saw in Section 15 that, if θ^n is predictable and if

$$E\left(\left[\int_0^T \theta^n(t)^2 \, dt \right]^{1/2} \right) < \infty, \quad T \geq 0,$$

then $\int \theta_t^n \, dB_t^n$ is a martingale. We use this property repeatedly.

For our purposes, it is convenient to define an *Ito process* to be a stochastic process X of the form

$$X_t = x + \int_0^t a_s \, ds + \int_0^t \theta_s \, dB_s, \quad t \geq 0, \tag{1}$$

where x is a scalar "starting point", $\theta \in \mathcal{L}$, and $a = \{a_t : t \geq 0\}$ is an adapted process satisfying $\int_0^t |a_s| \, ds < \infty$ almost surely for all $t \geq 0$. We will also use (1) to represent an R^K-valued Ito process $X = (X^1, \ldots, X^K)$ with starting point $x \in R^K$, and with integrands a valued in R^K and θ valued in $M^{K,N}$ (the space of $K \times N$ matrices) satisfying the same conditions. One also sees the informal *stochastic differential* form for (1):

$$dX_t = a_t \, dt + \theta_t \, dB_t; \quad X_0 = x. \tag{2}$$

B. Let $C^r(R^K)$ denote the set of real–valued functions f on R^K that are r times continuously differentiable. For example, if $f \in C^2(R^K)$ then the *gradient*

$$\nabla f(x) = \left(\frac{\partial f(x)}{\partial x_1}, \ldots, \frac{\partial f(x)}{\partial x_K} \right)$$

and the *Hessian*

$$\nabla^2 f(x) = \left[\frac{\partial^2 f(x)}{\partial x_i x_j} \right]_{K \times K}$$

exist for all x, and define continuous functions on R^K. If $D = [D_{ij}]$ is a square matrix, let $\mathrm{tr}(D)$ denote the *trace* of D, defined by $\mathrm{tr}(D) = \sum_i D_{ii}$.

THEOREM (ITO'S LEMMA). *Suppose X is an R^K-valued Ito process of the form $X_T = x + \int_0^T a_t \, dt + \int_0^T \theta_t \, dB_t$. If $f \in C^2(R^K)$ then $\{\nabla f(X_t)\theta_t : t \geq 0\}$ is in $\mathcal{L}$, and for all $t \geq 0$,*

$$f(X_t) = f(x) + \int_0^t \mathcal{D}f(X_s) \, ds + \int_0^t \nabla f(X_s)\theta_s \, dB_s, \tag{3}$$

where

$$\mathcal{D}f(X_s) = \nabla f(X_s)a_s + \tfrac{1}{2}\mathrm{tr}\left(\theta_s^\top \nabla^2 f(X_s)\theta_s \right).$$

Proofs of Ito's Lemma, including extensions from Ito processes to arbitrary semimartingales, are cited in the Notes. Relation (3), *Ito's Formula*, is in highly compact notation. To get some sense of this formula, we suppose that B and X are one–dimensional processes. Then (3) is simply

$$f(X_t) = f(x) + \int_0^t \left[f'(X_s)a_s + \tfrac{1}{2}\theta_s^2 f''(X_s) \right] \, ds + \int_0^t f'(X_s)\theta_s \, dB_s. \tag{4}$$

Along with Ito's Lemma one usually reads heuristic justifications of the
term $\frac{1}{2}\theta_t^2 f''(X_t)$ as the limit of the second order terms of the Taylor series
expansions of $f(X_{t+\delta}) - f(X_t)$ as $\delta \downarrow 0$, using the fact that a Standard
Brownian Motion B has quadratic variation $\{[B_t] = t : t \geq 0\}$. While this
is the central idea of most proofs, there are many other details.

We can also apply Ito's Lemma to an Ito process X taking values in
a subset D of R^K. In that case we will denote by $C^r(D)$ the space of
real–valued functions on D with extensions to an open set $\widehat{D}$ containing
D that have r continuous derivatives on $\widehat{D}$. This is overly restrictive, but
eliminates certain complications. Ito's Formula (3) then applies to any
$f \in C^2(D)$.

Consider the R^{K+1}–valued Ito process $(X^1, \ldots, X^K, Y)$, where $X =
(X^1, \ldots, X^K)$ is an R^K–valued Ito process of the form (2), and $Y_t = t$ for
all t. In other words, Y is the "time process". If f is a $C^2(R^K \times [0, \infty))$
function, we define, for $(x, t) \in R^K \times [0, \infty)$,

$$f_x(x, t) = \left[\frac{\partial f(x, t)}{\partial x_1}, \ldots, \frac{\partial f(x, t)}{\partial x_K} \right],$$

$$f_t(x, t) = \frac{\partial f(x, t)}{\partial t}, \quad \text{and}$$

$$f_{xx}(x, t) = \left[\frac{\partial^2 f(x, t)}{\partial x_i x_j} \right]_{K \times K}.$$

For notational convenience, we also define

$$\mathcal{D}f(X_s, s) = f_x(X_s, s)a_s + f_t(X_s, s) + \tfrac{1}{2}\mathrm{tr}\left[\theta_s^\top f_{xx}(X_s, s)\theta_s \right], \quad s \in [0, \infty).$$

Manipulation of (3) then leaves the expression:

$$f(X_t, t) = f(x, 0) + \int_0^t \mathcal{D}f(X_s, s)\, ds + \int_0^t f_x(X_s, s)\theta_s\, dB_s, \quad t \geq 0, \quad (5)$$

to be compared with relation (3). The derivative $\partial^2 f(x, t)/\partial t^2$ does not
enter (5), and indeed the differentiability requirements for (5) can be weakened to $f \in C^{2,1}(R^K \times [0, \infty))$: the existence and continuity of f_x, f_t, and
f_{xx}. We can likewise apply (5) to any $f \in C^{2,1}(D \times [0, \infty))$, for a given
subset D of R^K and a D–valued process X, with the obvious extension of
our definition of $C^2(D \times [0, \infty))$).

C.   This brings us to the *stochastic differential equation*:

$$dX_t = \mu(X_t, t)\, dt + \sigma(X_t, t)\, dB_t; \quad X_0 = x, \quad (6)$$

where μ is an R^K-valued function on $R^K \times [0, \infty)$ and σ is an $M^{K,N}$-valued function on $R^K \times [0, \infty)$. Relation (6) is more rigorously written as the integral equation:

$$X_t = x + \int_0^t \mu(X_s, s)\, ds + \int_0^t \sigma(X_s, s)\, dB_s, \quad t \geq 0, \qquad (7)$$

which is merely relation (1) with $a_t = \mu(X_t, t)$ and $\theta_t = \sigma(X_t, t)$. What conditions on the *drift* μ and *diffusion* σ ensure that (7) is well defined? Is the resulting Ito process X Markov? We will supply sufficient conditions. First we extend the definition of the Euclidean norm $\| \cdot \|$ to the vector space $M^{K,N}$ of $K \times N$ matrices by writing $\| D \| \equiv [\mathrm{tr}(DD^{\mathsf T})]^{1/2}$. Let $f : R^K \times [0, \infty) \to M^{K,N}$. If there exists a scalar k such that

$$\| f(x, t) - f(y, t) \| \leq k \| x - y \| \qquad (8)$$

for all x and y in R^K and $t \geq 0$, we say that f satisfies a *Lipschitz condition* (in x). If there exists a scalar k such that

$$\| f(x, t) \| \leq k\,(1 + \| x \|) \qquad (9)$$

for all x in R^k and $t \geq 0$, we say that f satisfies a *growth condition* (in x).

PROPOSITION. *Suppose μ and σ are Borel measurable and satisfy Lipschitz* (8) *and growth* (9) *conditions. Then there exists a unique R^K-valued Ito process X satisfying*

$$X_t = x + \int_0^t \mu(X_s, s)\, ds + \int_0^t \sigma(X_s, s)\, dB_s, \quad t \geq 0. \qquad (10)$$

Furthermore, X is a continuous process and Markov with respect to $F = \{\mathcal{F}_t : t \geq 0\}$. Finally, the Ito integral $\int \sigma(X_t, t)\, dB_t$ is a martingale.

For those interested in "diffusions", which we do not define here, the hypotheses on μ and σ in this proposition ensure that the Ito process X is a diffusion process provided, in addition, that μ and σ are continuous. This fact and a proof of the proposition are cited in the Notes.

D. We now quote a simplified version of a result known in some circles as the Feynman–Kac Formula, a solution to a class of elliptical partial differential equations. We fix a finite time horizon $T \in (0, \infty)$ and state a regularity condition on the primitive functions μ, σ, u, g, and ρ involved in this formula.

HYPOTHESIS A. *The functions μ and σ defined in Paragraph C satisfy Lipschitz conditions* (8). *Real–valued functions u, g, and ρ on $R^K \times [0, T]$, for some scalar $T > 0$, also satisfy a Lipschitz condition. In $R^K \times [0, T]$, moreover, the functions μ, σ, u, g, ρ, μ_x, σ_x, u_x, g_x, ρ_x, μ_{xx}, σ_{xx}, u_{xx}, g_{xx}, and ρ_{xx} exist, are continuous, and satisfy a growth condition* (9).

Next we define a family $\{X^{xS} : x \in R^K, S \in [0, T]\}$ of Ito processes, with X^{xS} to be thought of as an Ito process starting at time S at the point x. Specifically, we define X_t^{xS} arbitrarily for $t < S$, and for $t \in [S, T]$ we let

$$X_t^{xS} = x + \int_S^t \mu(X_s^{xS}, s)\, ds + \int_S^t \sigma(X_s^{xS}, s)\, dB_s.$$

We next define $V : R^K \times [0, T] \to R$ by

$$V(x, S) = E\left[\int_S^T e^{-\phi(s)} u(X_s^{xS}, s)\, ds + e^{-\phi(T)} g(X_T^{xS}, T) \right], \qquad (11)$$

where the stochastic "discount" ϕ_t is defined by

$$\phi_t = \int_S^t \rho(X_s^{xS}, s)\, ds.$$

We note that ϕ_t is merely $r(t - S)$ when ρ is the constant scalar r, a familiar case.

PROPOSITION (FEYNMAN–KAC FORMULA). *Under Hypothesis A, V is well defined by* (11) *on $R^K \times [0, T]$, is $C^{2,1}(R^K \times [0, T])$, satisfies a growth condition* (9), *and solves the partial differential equation*

$$\mathcal{D}V(x, t) - \rho(x, t)V(x, t) + u(x, t) = 0, \quad (x, t) \in R^K \times [0, T], \qquad (12a)$$

and boundary condition

$$V(x, T) = g(x, T), \quad x \in R^K, \qquad (12b)$$

where

$$\mathcal{D}V(x, t) = V_t(x, t) + V_x(x, t)\mu(x, t) + \tfrac{1}{2}\mathrm{tr}\left[\sigma(x, t)^\top V_{xx}(x, t)\sigma(x, t) \right]. \quad (12c)$$

Moreover, V is the unique function with these properties.

In some guises the Feynman–Kac Formula (11) is also known as *Dynkin's Formula* or *Kolmogorov's Equation*. The Notes cite a different version of the theorem, allowing a random terminal date T and weakening the smoothness conditions of Hypothesis A. The proof of the above proposition cited in the Notes is an application of Ito's Lemma and some analytical details. We forego the latter, giving a sketch of the proof for the simple case:

$$V(x, S) = E\left[\int_S^T u(X_s)\, ds\right],$$

where $X_t = x + \int_S^t \mu(X_s)\, ds + \int_S^t \sigma(X_s)\, dB_s$, for $X_S = x$ and $t \geq S$. For any $\tau \in [S, \Gamma]$,

$$V(x, S) = E\left[\int_S^\tau u(X_s)\, ds\right] + E\left[\int_\tau^T u(X_s)\, ds\right].$$

We also know that

$$E\left[\int_\tau^T u(X_s)\, ds\right] = E\left[E\left[\int_\tau^T u(X_s)\, ds \,\Big|\, \mathcal{F}_\tau\right]\right]$$

$$= E\left[E\left[\int_\tau^T u(X_s)\, ds \,\Big|\, X_\tau\right]\right]$$

$$= E[V(X_\tau, \tau)].$$

The first equality follows from the law of iterated conditional expectations, relation (9.4), the second by the Markov property of X (Proposition 21C and relation (18.16)), and the last by technical details and the definitions of V and X. Thus

$$E[V(X_\tau, \tau)] - V(x, S) = -E\left[\int_S^\tau u(X_s)\, ds\right].$$

By Ito's Lemma, however,

$$V(X_\tau, \tau) - V(x, S) = \int_S^\tau \mathcal{D}V(X_s, s)\, ds + \int_S^\tau V_x(X_s, s)\sigma(X_s)\, dB_s.$$

On the basis of a technical argument, one can assume without loss of generality that $V_x\sigma$ is bounded. Then $\int V_x\sigma\, dB$ is a martingale by Proposition 21C, leaving

$$E\left[\int_S^\tau (\mathcal{D}V(X_s, s) + u(X_s))\, ds\right] = 0.$$

Since this restriction applies for all $\tau \geq S$, and since all of the functions involved are "smooth", we can allow τ to approach S and deduce that

$$\mathcal{D}V(x, s) + u(x) = 0.$$

Since x and $S \in (0, T)$ are arbitrary, we have sketched out the reasoning behind (12a). This is far from a proof, of course. Relation (12b) is merely the definition of V, taking $S = T$.

E.   A body of theory known as *Girsanov's Theorem* characterizes the behavior of semimartingales under a change of probability measure. We will only study the application to Ito processes with the time set $[0, T]$. For any $\theta = (\theta^1, \ldots, \theta^N)$ in $\mathcal{L}$, let $\xi(\theta)$ be the process defined by

$$\xi(\theta)_t = \exp\left[\int_0^t \theta_s \, dB_s - \frac{1}{2}\int_0^t \theta_s \cdot \theta_s \, ds\right], \quad t \in [0, T].$$

LEMMA. *For $\theta \in \mathcal{L}$, if $E\left[\exp\left(\frac{1}{2}\int_0^T \theta_s \cdot \theta_s \, ds\right)\right] < \infty$, then $\xi(\theta)$ is a positive martingale and $E[\xi(\theta)_T] = 1$.*

PROOF: We will prove the result assuming θ is bounded. The Notes cite a considerably lengthier proof of the general case. Let X be the Ito process:

$$X_t = \int_0^t \theta_s dB_s - \frac{1}{2}\int_0^t \theta_s \cdot \theta_s \, ds, \quad t \in [0, T].$$

Then $\xi(\theta)_t = e^{X_t}$, and by Ito's Lemma,

$$\xi(\theta)_t = 1 + \int_0^t \xi(\theta)_s \, \theta_s \, dB_s, \quad t \in [0, T]. \tag{13}$$

Since θ is bounded, it follows that

$$E\left[\left(\int_0^T \xi(\theta)_s^2 \, \theta_s \cdot \theta_s \, ds\right)^{1/2}\right] < \infty.$$

Then the stochastic integral $\int \xi(\theta)_t \theta_t \, dB_t$ is a martingale, implying from (13) that $\xi(\theta)$ is a martingale and that $E[\xi(\theta)_T] = 1$. ∎

Under the assumptions of this lemma, the random variable $\xi(\theta)_T$ is positive and has unit expectation. We can therefore define a probability measure Q^θ on $(\Omega, \mathcal{F})$ by

$$Q^\theta(A) = E\left[1_A \xi(\theta)_T\right], \quad A \in \mathcal{F},$$

meaning that Q^θ has Radon–Nikodym derivative $dQ^\theta/dP = \xi(\theta)_T$.

GIRSANOV'S THEOREM. *Suppose that* $\theta \in \mathcal{L}$ *satisfies*

$$E\left[\exp\left(\frac{1}{2}\int_0^T \theta_s \cdot \theta_s \, ds\right)\right] < \infty.$$

Then the R^N*-valued Ito process* $\widehat{B}$ *defined by*

$$\widehat{B}_t = B_t - \int_0^t \theta_s \, ds, \quad t \in [0, T],$$

is a Standard Brownian Motion in R^N *for the filtered probability space* $(\Omega, \mathcal{F}, F, Q^\theta)$, *restricted to the time set* $[0, T]$.

A proof of this fundamental result is cited in the Notes. Girsanov's Theorem basically allows one to change the drift of a given Ito Process by changing the probability measure. For example, suppose X is the R^N-valued Ito process on $(\Omega, \mathcal{F}, F, P)$ defined by some starting point $x \in R^N$ and the stochastic differential equation

$$dX_t = g(X_t, t)dt + \sigma(X_t, t)dB_t, \tag{14}$$

where the drift g and the diffusion σ are given functions with properties ensuring that X is well defined. For several types of applications we may wish to represent X as an Ito process with a new drift vector $f(x, t)$ replacing $g(x, t)$. This can be done by altering the given probability measure P, with the help of Girsanov's Theorem, as follows.

PROPOSITION. *Suppose* f, g, *and* σ *are Borel measurable and satisfy a Lipschitz condition* (8) *and a growth condition* (9). *Also suppose there is a scalar* k *such that* $\sigma(x, t)$ *is nonsingular and* $\| \sigma(x, t)^{-1} \| \le k$ *for all* $(x, t) \in R^N \times [0, T]$. *Then there exists a probability measure* Q *on* $(\Omega, \mathcal{F})$ *equivalent to* P *and a Standard Brownian Motion* $\widehat{B}$ *in* R^N *for* $(\Omega, \mathcal{F}, F, Q)$ *such that the Ito process* X *defined by* (14) *also obeys the stochastic differential equation:*

$$dX_t = f(X_t, t) \, dt + \sigma(X_t, t) \, d\widehat{B}_t.$$

Before proceeding with a proof, we might direct some attention to the definition of the stochastic integral $\int \sigma(X_t, t) \, d\widehat{B}_t$, which generally depends on the underlying probability measure chosen. There is no ambiguity here, however, since Proposition 15G ensures that this stochastic integral can be safely treated as the same semimartingale, whether defined on $(\Omega, \mathcal{F}, F, P)$

or $(\Omega, \mathcal{F}, F, Q)$. Of course, $\int \sigma(X_t, t) \, d\widehat{B}_t$ is a martingale on the latter filtered probability space by Proposition 21C, but not generally on the former. It should also be noted that the assumed bound on σ^{-1} can be replaced with other regularity conditions.

PROOF: Let θ be the process

$$\theta_t = \sigma(X_t, t)^{-1}[f(X_t, t) - g(X_t, t)], \quad t \in [0, T].$$

Let $Y_t = \int_0^t \theta_s \, ds$, $t \in [0, T]$. The conditions on σ, f, and g imply that θ satisfies the prerequisites for Girsanov's Theorem. Thus the Ito process $\widehat{B}$ defined by

$$\widehat{B}_t = B_t - Y_t, \quad t \in [0, T],$$

is a Standard Brownian Motion in R^N for $(\Omega, \mathcal{F}, F, Q)$, where Q is the probability measure Q^θ of Girsanov's Theorem. By the linearity of stochastic integration, relation (15.5), since $B = \widehat{B} + Y$, we have

$$\int \sigma(X_t, t) \, dB_t = \int \sigma(X_t, t) \, d\widehat{B}_t + \int \sigma(X_t, t) \, dY_t,$$

and thus

$$
\begin{aligned}
dX_t &= g(X_t, t) \, dt + \sigma(X_t, t) \, dB_t \\
&= g(X_t, t) \, dt + \sigma(X_t, t) \, d\widehat{B}_t + \sigma(X_t, t)\theta_t \, dt \\
&= \left(g(X_t, t) + \sigma(X_t, t)\sigma(X_t, t)^{-1}[f(X_t, t) - g(X_t, t)]\right) dt + \sigma(X_t, t) \, d\widehat{B}_t \\
&= f(X_t, t) \, dt + \sigma(X_t, t) \, d\widehat{B}_t.
\end{aligned}
$$

This is the desired result. ∎

EXERCISES

EXERCISE 21.1   Suppose Y is an R^2–valued Ito process of the form $\{Y_t = (t, X_t) : t \geq 0\}$ where X is a real–valued Ito process of the form $x + \int a_t \, dt + \int \theta_t \, dB_t$. Use Ito's Formula directly to show that, for any $f \in C^2(R^2)$,

$$f(t, X_t) = f(0, x) + \int_0^t \left[f_t(\tau, X_\tau) + f_x(\tau, X_\tau)a_\tau + \tfrac{1}{2}f_{xx}(\tau, X_\tau)\theta(\tau)^2 \right] d\tau$$

$$+ \int_0^t f_x(\tau, X_\tau)\theta(\tau) \, dB_\tau, \quad t \geq 0.$$

Write out this expression for $f(t, X_t)$ for the case $f(t, x) = e^{-\rho t} V(x)$, with ρ a positive scalar and V a twice continuously differentiable real–valued function on R. Finally, extend to the case in which X is an R^K–valued Ito process and $V \in C^2(R^K)$ to deduce that, for $t \geq 0$,

$$e^{-\rho t} V(X_t) = V(x) + \int_0^t e^{-\rho s} \nabla V(X_s) \theta_s \, dB_s$$

$$+ \int_0^t e^{-\rho s} \left[\nabla V(X_s) a_s + \tfrac{1}{2} \mathrm{tr}[\theta_s^\top \nabla^2 V(X_s) \theta_s] \quad \rho V(X_s) \right] \, ds.$$

EXERCISE 21.2   Use Ito's Lemma to derive relation (13).

EXERCISE 21.3   Consider the stochastic differential equation:

$$dX_t = \mu(X_t, t) \, dt + \sigma(X_t, t) \, dB_t; \qquad X_0 = 1,$$

where B is a Standard Brownian Motion and where the drift μ and diffusion σ are real–valued functions defined by $\mu(x, t) = ax$ and $\sigma(x, t) = bx$ for all $(x, t) \in R \times [0, \infty)$, for some scalars a and b. Show that, for any time $T \geq 0$, the random variable X_T is *log–normally distributed* with parameters $[[a - (b^2/2)]T, bT^{1/2}]$, or in other words, that $\log(X_T)$ is normally distributed with the stated mean and standard deviation. State X_T as a function of B_T. The process X is variously known as a *geometric Brownian motion, exponential Brownian motion*, or *log–normal diffusion*.

Notes

For extensions of the Ito integral $\int \theta_t \, dB_t$ to weaker measurability restrictions on θ, see Chung and Williams (1983), Kopp (1984), Durrett (1984), or Elliott (1982), to name but a few introductory mathematical treatments of stochastic integration. Lipster and Shiryayev (1977) is a more detailed source on Ito processes. Proofs of Ito's Lemma are given in each of the last–mentioned sources. Generalizations of Ito's Lemma to semimartingales may be found in Jacod (1979) or Dellacherie and Meyer (1982).

Standard but advanced sources for stochastic differential equations are Gihman and Skorohod (1972) and Ikeda and Watanabe (1981); however the treatments by Arnold (1974) and Friedman (1975) should be sufficient for most purposes, and Kallianpur (1980) has a brief summary. Oksendal (1985) is an easy introductory monograph. Freedman (1983a) and Williams (1979) are good background reading on diffusion processes. Stroock and Varadhan (1979) is an advanced treatise on diffusion processes; Stroock

(1987) is somewhat simpler. Krishnan (1984) has a "rough and ready" engineer's treatment of the Ito calculus and filtering theory, recommended for problem solving. Kallianpur (1980) is devoted to filtering.

A proof of Proposition 21C may be compiled from Section 14 of Elliott (1982), among many other sources. A definition of diffusion processes and a proof of the claim at the end of Paragraph 21C may be found in Kallianpur (1980), Chapter 5. The Feynman–Kac Formula, Proposition 21D, is proved by Dynkin (1965b) (Theorem 13.15) under different conditions, including a random terminal time and weaker smoothness conditions on the primitive functions. The version given as Proposition 21D is a simple case of Krylov (1980), Theorem 2.9.10. An extensive treatment of this topic is given by Freidlin (1985). Lemma 21E appears in Elliott (1982) as Theorem 13.36. The special form of Girsanov's Theorem shown in 21E is a consequence of Corollary 13.25 of Elliott (1982). More general forms may be found elsewhere in Chapter 13 of Elliott (1982), for example.

22. The Black–Scholes Model of Security Valuation

The Black–Scholes Option Pricing Formula and the Capital Asset Pricing Model offer simple closed form solutions to nontrivial practical problems in finance. Both have significantly affected the actual behavior of markets. The Black–Scholes model is a special case of the martingale security pricing model of Section 17, as we see at the end of this section. In explaining the Black–Scholes model, however, we will start with a simple example and gradually build in generality. We will in fact derive the Black–Scholes Formula in five different ways! These are: (1) by a limit from discrete–time as the length of a time interval shrinks to zero, using the central limit theorem; (2) by a direct solution to the partial differential equation derived from an absence of arbitrage; (3) by an indirect solution of this *PDE* using the Feynman–Kac formula; (4) by a limit of the underlying return processes from discrete–time using Donsker's Theorem; and (5) by a change of probability measure using Girsanov's Theorem. These methods have extensions well beyond the pricing of an option, but their extensions have different ranges of application, and individually offer different insights and methods. Some readers may benefit from a caution: The Black–Scholes model is not an equilibrium model. As opposed to the CAPM for example, the solution shown for derivative security prices in terms of other security prices does not depend on agents' preferences, except for the slight assumption that at least one agent is non–satiated. The Black–Scholes Formula is predicated on the notion that, whenever securities S and β can be traded

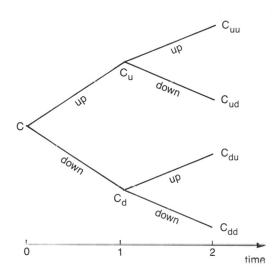

Figure 22.1   Contingent Values of a Security in a Binomial Tree

in such a manner as to exactly duplicate the dividends of security C, then C is redundant, and its market value is given in terms of the market values of S and β by an assumed absence of arbitrage. The market value of C must be the investment in S and β required to duplicate the dividends of C.

A.   Suppose that a given financial security, say a *stock*, has a total return of U on an *up* day, and a return of D on a *down* day. Another riskless security, or *bond*, has a return of R per day with certainty. For simplicity, we assume that $0 < D < R < U$. One can create a portfolio of stock and bond that duplicates the payoff of a third security, say a *crown*, with up–contingent value C_u and down–contingent value C_d. The equations for the required number of shares a of stock and b of bond are

$$aUS_0 + bR\beta_0 = C_u$$

$$aDS_0 + bR\beta_0 = C_d,$$

$$(1)$$

where S_0 and β_0 are the non–zero initial market values of the stock and bond, respectively. The solutions are

$$a = \frac{(C_u - C_d)}{(U - D)S_0}; \qquad b = \frac{(UC_d - DC_u)}{(U - D)R\beta_0}.$$

Of course, if the contingent payoffs C_u and C_d can be duplicated by purchasing a shares of stock and b of bond, then the initial market value C of the crown must be $C = aS_0 + b\beta_0$, for otherwise there would be arbitrage, as explained in Paragraph E of The Introduction. Using our solutions for a and b,

$$C = \frac{1}{R}[pC_u + (1-p)C_d],\tag{2}$$

where $p = (R-D)/(U-D)$. This formula can be treated as the discounted expected payoff of the security, with probabilities p of up and $(1-p)$ of down. Now suppose there is a second day of trade, with the same up and down–contingent returns on the stock and bond. Let C_{uu} denote the market value of the crown after two up days, C_{ud} after an up day followed by a down day, and so on, as illustrated in Figure 22.1. By the reasoning applied earlier,

$$C_u = \frac{1}{R}[pC_{uu} + (1-p)C_{ud}]\tag{3}$$

$$C_d = \frac{1}{R}[pC_{du} + (1-p)C_{dd}].\tag{4}$$

Substituting (3) and (4) into (2),

$$C = \frac{1}{R^2}[p^2 C_{uu} + p(1-p)C_{ud} + (1-p)pC_{du} + (1-p)^2 C_{dd}].\tag{5}$$

The analogy of pricing the crown at its discounted expected payoff is preserved, and the recursion can be extended indefinitely. After T periods, provided none of the securities pay intermediate dividends, we have

$$C = \frac{1}{R^T}E(C_T),\tag{6}$$

where C_T is the random market value of the crown T periods into the future, and E denotes expected value when treating successive days as independently up or down with probabilities p and $(1-p)$ respectively. To repeat, the probabilities p and $1-p$ are "artificial", and calculated from the given returns of the securities. There are 2^T possible states of the world at time T, and an equal number of contingent claims would be required for complete markets with a single round of trade. With trading allowed at all dates, however, two securities are enough for every possible claim to be replicated and priced. For example, let C_T denote the value of a call option on the stock at delivery date T with some exercise price K, or

$$C_T = (S_T - K)^+ \equiv \max(0, S_T - K).$$

Relation (6) yields

$$C = \frac{1}{R^T} \sum_{i=0}^{T} \left(\frac{T!}{i! \, (T-i)!} \right) p^i (1-p)^{T-i} \left(U^i D^{T-i} S_0 - K \right)^+. \qquad (7)$$

The formula evaluates $E(C_T)$ by calculating C_T given i up days out of T, then multiplies by the binomial formula for the probability of i up days, and finally sums over i. In some sense, continuous–time trading can be treated as the limit of discrete–time trading, as the number of trading intervals in a given period of time approaches infinity. Indeed, it will be shown (in Paragraph H) that the Black–Scholes Formula is the limit of relation (7) as the number of trading intervals per unit of time approaches infinity, applying the Central Limit Theorem.

D. Our goal now is to derive a continuous–time analogue to relation (7). Let B denote a Standard Brownian Motion that is a martingale with respect to a given filtered probability space $(\Omega, \mathcal{F}, F, P)$ for the time set $[0, \infty)$, where F satisfies the usual conditions. A given security, to be called a stock, has a price process S solving the stochastic differential equation

$$dS_t = S_t \mu \, dt + S_t \sigma \, dB_t; \qquad S_0 > 0, \qquad (8)$$

where μ and σ are strictly positive scalars. A second security, to be called a bond, has a price process $\beta = \{\beta_t : t \geq 0\}$ solving the differential equation

$$d\beta_t = \beta_t r \, dt, \qquad (9)$$

for some positive scalar $r < \mu$. We could say that the bond has a *continuously compounding interest rate* of r. Of course (9) is more conventionally written

$$\frac{d\beta(t)}{dt} = r\beta(t),$$

and has the unique solution $\beta_t = e^{rt}\beta_0$, $t \geq 0$. Both S and β can be formally treated as Ito processes. Let Θ denote the space of R^2–valued stochastic processes such that, for any (a, b) in Θ, the stochastic integrals $\int a_t \, dS_t$ and $\int b_t \, d\beta_t$ are well defined. Taking a as a process describing the number of shares of stock held, we recall from Section 15 that $\int_0^t a_\tau \, dS_\tau$ is the total gain realized by time t from trading stock. Aside from technical integrability requirements, in order to qualify as a member of Θ, the trading strategy (a, b) must be predictable. Roughly speaking, that is, the portfolio (a_t, b_t) of stock and bond held at any time t must depend only on information received up to time t, a reasonable restriction explained in more detail in Section 15. We will restrict ourselves to the time interval $[0, T]$, and assume for the present that no security pays dividends during this period.

A *self–financing trading strategy* is a trading strategy (a, b) in Θ with the property:

$$a_t S_t + b_t \beta_t = a_0 S_0 + b_0 \beta_0 + \int_0^t a_\tau \, dS_\tau + \int_0^t b_\tau \, d\beta_\tau, \quad t \in [0, T]. \quad (10)$$

The left hand side of (10) is the market value of the portfolio at time t; the right hand side is the sum of the initial portfolio value and the interim gain from trade.

An element x of $L^1(P)$, the space of random variables with a finite expectation, is a *redundant claim* if there exists a self–financing trading strategy $(a, b) \in \Theta$ such that $a_T S_T + b_T \beta_T = x$. The *arbitrage value* of x is in that case defined to be $a_0 S_0 + b_0 \beta_0$, and is easily shown to be uniquely determined. The stochastic process $\{a_t S_t + b_t \beta_t : t \in [0, T]\}$ is the *implicit price process* of x. By "redundant", we mean that the terminal value x can be produced by investing $a_0 S_0 + b_0 \beta_0$ at time zero in stock and bond, following the prescribed self–financing strategy (a, b) during $[0, T]$, and cashing in the proceeds $a_T S_T + b_T \beta_T$ equal to x at time T. (One should point out that the equality $x = a_T S_T + b_T S_T$ relates two vectors in $L^1(P)$, and as random variables this means only almost sure equality.) If another security market were set up to sell a redundant claim x payable at time T, then the initial market value of the new security at time zero must, barring "arbitrage", be $C = a_0 S_0 + b_0 \beta_0$. For suppose not, and a claim to x at time T can be purchased for $A \neq C$. Then if $A > C$, one could sell one share of the redundant claim for A, invest C in the self–financing strategy (a, b), and not be obligated to any future payments. The initial excess $A - C$ is an "arbitrage profit" that can be consumed at time zero or invested in the riskless security for later consumption. For arbitrarily larger profits, one can increase the scale of purchases and sales. If $A < C$, the opposite strategy yields arbitrage profits. As long as any agent in the economy, which we have not formally described, is non–satiated, such a situation cannot exist. Thus, as is said, "any redundant claim is priced by arbitrage". Of course, transactions costs destroy the argument, but we will continue to ignore this issue except to cite in the Notes work dealing with the Black–Scholes model and transactions costs.

THEOREM. *If $x \in L^1(P)$ is measurable with respect to the tribe generated by the stock price process, $\{S_t : t \in [0, T]\}$, then x is a redundant claim.*

Although the proof of this theorem is not deep, it is slightly complicated and we refer readers to the Notes for a source with the details. The theorem states roughly that if x is a random variable with finite expectation whose value is a (measurable) function of the path taken by the stock price process, then x is redundant: There is a self–financing strategy with the terminal value x. An example would be a call option on the stock with expiry at date T and exercise price K, having the terminal value $x = (S_T - K)^+$, which depends on the path taken by S only to the extent of the terminal value S_T of that path. It is one thing to know that claims depending on the stock price process are redundant and quite another to calculate their *arbitrage value*, the required investment in a corresponding self–financing strategy. That is the object of the remainder of this section. In carrying out this goal, we will verify the redundancy of the call option by solving for the self–financing strategy that replicates its terminal value.

C.   The implicit market value of a redundant security in the Black–Scholes model (8)–(9) can be determined by various analytical methods. The original approach is to state and solve a partial differential equation for the redundant security's market value using Ito's Lemma, as follows. Let S and β, the stock and bond price processes, be given by (8)–(9), and let $c = \{c_t : t \in [0, T]\}$ denote the implicit price process for a security, say a crown, with terminal value $c_T = g(S_T)$, where $g : R_+ \to R$ is a continuous function. We assume that $| g(S_T) |$ has finite expectation; a sufficient condition is a growth condition (21.9) on g. Our approach is to pretend that $c(t) = C(S_t, t)$ for all t in $[0, T]$, for some function $C \in C^{2,1}\big((0, \infty) \times [0, T]\big)$. That is, we assume that the market value of a claim to $y(S_T)$ is given at any time t by $C(S_t, t)$, for some function C sufficiently differentiable for an application of Ito's Lemma. On the basis of this assumption we will deduce an explicit solution for C. The solution is indeed sufficiently differentiable; this fact validates our analysis.

By Theorem 22B the crown is redundant, and can be replicated by some self–financing stock–bond trading strategy (a, b). That is, at any time t,

$$c(t) = C(S_t, t) = a_t S_t + b_t \beta_t = a_0 S_0 + b_0 \beta_0 + \int_0^t a_\tau \, dS_\tau + \int_0^t b_\tau \, d\beta_\tau. \quad (11)$$

The first equality is by assumption on C; the second is the fact that the value of the self–financing trading strategy (a, b) duplicates the value of the crown; the last equality is the definition of a self–financing strategy. By Ito's Lemma, at any time t in $[0, T]$,

$$C(S_t, t) = C(S_0, 0) + \int_0^t \mathcal{D}C(S_\tau, \tau) \, d\tau + \int_0^t C_x(S_\tau, \tau) S_\tau \sigma \, dB_\tau, \quad (12)$$

where $\mathcal{D}C$ is defined (as in Exercise 21.1) by

$$\mathcal{D}C(x,t) = C_x(x,t)\mu x + \tfrac{1}{2}C_{xx}(x,t)\sigma^2 x^2 + C_t(x,t),$$

with C_x and C_{xx} denoting the first and second partial derivatives of C with respect to the first (stock price) argument, and C_t denoting the partial derivative of C with respect to the second (time elapsed) argument. It is common, but unsuitable for our purposes, to write C instead as a function of the time remaining $T - t$, rather than the time elapsed t. We refer to Exercise 22.2 for the more conventional notation. Subtracting (11) from (12), using the definitions of dS_t and $d\beta_t$ from (8) and (9), we have

$$\int_0^t [\mathcal{D}C(S_\tau,\tau) - a_\tau \mu S_\tau - b_\tau r \beta_\tau]\, d\tau + \int_0^t [C_x(S_\tau,\tau)S_\tau \sigma - a_\tau S_\tau \sigma]\, dB_\tau = 0$$

(13)

for all t in $[0,T]$. We may treat (13) as an equation to be solved for a and b. Indeed, the two linear equations in (a_τ, b_τ) defined by equating the two integrands of (13) with zero determine a_τ and b_τ uniquely as:

$$a_\tau = C_x(S_\tau, \tau) \tag{14}$$

$$b_\tau = \frac{\mathcal{D}C(S_\tau, \tau) - C_x(S_\tau, \tau)\mu S_\tau}{r \beta_\tau}. \tag{15}$$

(If $r = 0$, a slightly more complicated argument made in Paragraph F shows that $b_\tau = [C(S_\tau, \tau) - C_x(S_\tau, \tau)S_\tau]/\beta_\tau$ is an appropriate solution for the bond holdings.) Since we must have $C(S_t, t) = a_t S_t + b_t \beta_t$ for any current time t and current stock price $S_t = x$, relations (14) and (15) yield the following partial differential equation (PDE) for C:

$$C(x,t) = xC_x(x,t) + \frac{\mathcal{D}C(x,t) - C_x(x,t)\mu x}{r},$$

for all $(x,t) \in (0,\infty) \times [0,T]$. Multiplying through by r and using the definition of $\mathcal{D}C$, we have the PDE

$$-rC(x,t) + C_t(x,t) + rxC_x(x,t) + \tfrac{1}{2}\sigma^2 x^2 C_{xx}(x,t) = 0, \tag{16}$$

for all $(x,t) \in (0,\infty) \times [0,T]$, with boundary conditions

$$C(x,T) = g(x), \quad x \geq 0, \tag{17}$$

$$C(0,t) = e^{-r(T-t)}g(0), \quad t \in [0,T]. \tag{18}$$

The *terminal boundary condition* (17) states that the terminal value of the crown is given by the function g. Boundary condition (18) is a simple consequence of the unique solution $S_t \equiv 0$ to the stochastic differential equation (8) for the stock price process given the initial price $S_0 = 0$.

D. To explicitly determine the market value of the crown it remains to solve (16) with the stated boundary conditions. Historically speaking, this PDE was first solved by a direct method involving the use of Fourier transforms, as outlined in Exercise 22.2. For example, if the crown is a European call option with exercise price $K \geq 0$, the terminal value function g is $x \mapsto (x - K)^+$. The solution to (16)–(17)–(18) for this case is shown in Exercise 22.2 to be

$$C(x,t) = x\Phi\left(\frac{\log(x/K) + (r + \frac{1}{2}\sigma^2)(T - t)}{\sigma\sqrt{T - t}}\right)$$

$$-Ke^{-r(T-t)}\Phi\left(\frac{\log(x/K) + (r - \frac{1}{2}\sigma^2)(T - t)}{\sigma\sqrt{T - t}}\right), \qquad (19)$$

where Φ is the Standard Normal cumulative distribution function:

$$\Phi(z) = \frac{1}{\sqrt{2\pi}} \int_{-\infty}^{z} e^{-t^2/2}\, dt, \quad z \in R.$$

Relation (19) is the Black–Scholes Option Pricing Formula.

E. A second method for solving (16)–(17)–(18) is the Feynman–Kac Formula. By Proposition 21D, provided g and its first two derivatives exist and satisfy a Lipschitz and a growth condition, we can state the solution to (16)–(17)–(18) by inspection as

$$C(x,t) = E\left[e^{-r(T-t)}g(X_{T-t})\right], \qquad (20)$$

where X is the solution to the stochastic differential equation

$$dX_t = rX_t\, dt + \sigma X_t\, dB_t; \quad X_0 = x. \qquad (21)$$

In other words, the value of the crown is its expected discounted payoff, replacing the stated stock price process S with a new "pseudo–price" process X having drift rX_t in place of μS_t. Indeed, the "instantaneous rate of return" μ on the stock is notably irrelevant for the value of any security whose payoff depends on the terminal market value of the stock. For a more explicit version of (20), we can apply Ito's Lemma to show that

$$X_t = \exp\left[(r - \frac{1}{2}\sigma^2)t + \sigma B_t\right]x, \quad t \geq 0. \qquad (22)$$

Noting that $B_t/\sqrt{t}$ has the Standard Normal density, relation (20) yields

$$C(S_0, 0) = \frac{e^{-rT}}{\sqrt{2\pi}} \int_{-\infty}^{+\infty} g\left(S_0\, e^{(r - \frac{1}{2}\sigma^2)T + \sqrt{T}\sigma z}\right) e^{-z^2/2}\, dz. \qquad (23)$$

If g is the function $x \mapsto (x - K)^+$, defining a call option with exercise price K, one can check that (23) and the Black–Scholes Formula (19) are equivalent. Of course, $x \mapsto (x - K)^+$ is not a differentiable function, but it can be well approximated by a differentiable function satisfying Hypothesis A of Paragraph 21D. That is, for any $\epsilon \in (0, \infty)$, let $g_\epsilon : (0, \infty) \to R$ be defined by

$$g_\epsilon(x) = \frac{x - K + \sqrt{(x - K)^2 + \epsilon}}{2},$$

a smooth approximation to $(x - K)^+$ for small $\epsilon > 0$. By allowing $\epsilon \to 0$, relation (19) then follows from (23) and a limiting argument cited in the Notes.

F. Paragraph E was hardly a test of the full power of the Feynman–Kac Formula as a solution to the market value of redundant securities in the Black–Scholes model. One may considerably expand the class of securities that can be explicitly evaluated, as follows. We take $K \geq 1$ "risky" securities whose vector price process $S = (S^1, \ldots, S^K)$ is the K–dimensional Ito process solving

$$dS_t = \mu(S_t, t)\, dt + \sigma(S_t, t)\, dB_t; \quad S_0 = x, \qquad (24)$$

where $x \in R^K$ is the vector of initial market values of the securities, $B = (B^1, \ldots, B^N)$ is a Standard Brownian Motion in R^N, and where the drift and diffusion functions μ and σ satisfy the conditions of Proposition 21C. Specifically, $\mu : R^K \times [0, \infty) \to R^K$ and $\sigma : R^K \times [0, \infty) \to M^{K,N}$ are Borel measurable and satisfy a Lipschitz (21.8) and a growth (21.9) condition, taking $M^{K,N}$ to denote the space of $K \times N$ matrices. We also assume that σ is continuous. Aside from these K risky securities, there is a bond whose price process β is defined by a continuous interest rate function $r : R^K \times R_+ \to R_+$ according to the stochastic differential equation

$$d\beta_t = r(S_t, t)\beta_t\, dt, \quad \beta_0 > 0. \qquad (25)$$

We also assume that r satisfies Lipschitz and growth conditions. Solving (25), we have $\beta_t = \beta_0 \exp\left(\int_0^t r(S_\tau, \tau)\, d\tau\right)$. Let $g : R^K \to R$ be a continuous function satisfying a Lipschitz (21.8) and a growth (21.9) condition. This function defines the market value $g(S_T)$ of a crown at time T. This completes the description of our primitives for the valuation problem. It remains to show that a claim to $g(S_T)$ at time T is redundant, to describe a self–financing trading strategy that replicates this payoff at time T, and to calculate the initial investment in this *replicating trading strategy*. This initial investment is the *arbitrage value* of a claim to $g(S_T)$.

For each $(x, t) \in R^K \times [0, T]$, let

$$C(x, t) = E \left[\exp \left(- \int_t^T r(X_\tau^{xt}, \tau) \, d\tau \right) g(X_T^{xt}) \right], \qquad (26)$$

where X^{xt} is an R^K–valued Ito process satisfying

$$X_\tau^{xt} = x + \int_t^\tau r(X_s^{xt}, s) X_s^{xt} \, ds + \int_t^\tau \sigma(X_s^{xt}, s) \, dB_s, \qquad \tau \in [t, T], \quad (27)$$

being defined arbitrarily for any time $\tau \in [0, t)$. According to the Feynman Kac Formula (Proposition 21D), provided the primitive functions r, σ, and g satisfy the regularity conditions corresponding to Hypothesis A of Paragraph 21D, the function C defined by (26) is $C^{2,1} \left(R^K \times [0, T) \right)$ and uniquely solves the PDE:

$$\mathcal{D}_X C(x, t) - r(x, t) C(x, t) = 0, \quad (x, t) \in R^K \times [0, T), \qquad (28)$$

with boundary condition $C(x, T) = g(x)$, $x \in R^K$, where $\mathcal{D}_X C$ is the usual function defined by Ito's Lemma, suppressing arguments, as

$$\mathcal{D}_X C = C_t + C_x rx + \tfrac{1}{2} \mathrm{tr}[\sigma^\top C_{xx} \sigma], \qquad (29)$$

taking the notational conventions set up in Paragraph 21B for the partial derivatives C_t, C_x, and C_{xx}. Let a be the R^K–valued process defined by

$$a_t = C_x(S_t, t), \quad t \in [0, T], \qquad (30)$$

and define the real–valued process b by

$$b_t = \frac{C(S_t, t) - C_x(S_t, t) S_t}{\beta_t}, \quad t \in [0, T]. \qquad (31)$$

The stochastic integrals $\int a_t \, dS_t$ and $\int b_t \, d\beta_t$ are well–defined, and we can take a and b as our risky security and bond trading strategies. By construction,

$$C(S_t, t) = a_t \cdot S_t + b_t \beta_t, \quad t \in [0, T]. \qquad (32)$$

This trading strategy (a, b) generates a total gain up to any time $t \in [0, T]$ of

$$\int_0^t a_\tau \, dS_\tau + \int_0^t b_\tau \, d\beta_\tau$$

$$= \int_0^t C_x(S_\tau, \tau) \mu(S_\tau, \tau) \, d\tau + \int_0^t C_x(S_\tau, \tau) \sigma(S_\tau, \tau) \, dB_\tau \quad (33)$$

$$+ \int_0^t \left(\frac{C(S_\tau, \tau) - C_x(S_\tau, \tau) S_\tau}{\beta_\tau} \right) r(S_\tau, \tau) \beta_\tau \, d\tau,$$

using our definitions of dS_t and $d\beta_t$. We define the function $\mathcal{D}_S C$ on $R^K \times [0, T)$ by

$$\mathcal{D}_S C(x, t) = C_t(x, t) + C_x(x, t)\mu(x, t) + \tfrac{1}{2}\mathrm{tr}\left[\sigma(x, t)^\top C_{xx}(x, t)\sigma(x, t)\right].$$

From (32) and (33),

$$\int_0^t a_\tau \, dS_\tau + \int_0^t b_\tau \, d\beta_\tau$$

$$= \int_0^t C_x(S_\tau, \tau)\sigma(S_\tau, \tau) \, dB_\tau$$

$$+ \int_0^t [r(S_\tau, \tau)C(S_\tau, \tau) - \mathcal{D}_X C(S_\tau, \tau) + \mathcal{D}_S C(S_\tau, \tau)] \, d\tau$$

$$= \int_0^t C_x(S_\tau, \tau)\sigma(S_\tau, \tau) \, dB_\tau + \int_0^t \mathcal{D}_S C(S_\tau, \tau) \, d\tau$$

$$= C(S_t, t) - C(S_0, 0)$$

$$= a_t \cdot S_t + b_t \beta_t - a_0 \cdot S_0 - b_0 \beta_0, \quad t \in [0, T]. \quad (34)$$

The penultimate equality of (34) is merely a consequence of Ito's Lemma; the previous equality is obtained from relation (28): $\mathcal{D}_X C - rC \equiv 0$. Relation (34) states that (a, b) is a self–financing trading strategy whose initial value is $C(S_0, 0)$ and whose value at time T is $g(S_T)$. It must then be that the initial value of the crown is

$$C(S_0, 0) = E\left[\exp\left(-\int_0^T r\left(X_t^{S_0 0}, t\right) \, dt\right) g\left(X_T^{S_0 0}\right)\right]. \quad (35)$$

This is merely the expected discounted value of the crown's terminal value, substituting the *pseudo–price process* $X^{S_0 0}$ from (27) for the given price process S. Again, the price drift μ is irrelevant.

Example.   Suppose r is a fixed scalar $\delta \geq 0$ and $\sigma(x,t) = [x]\,V$, where $[x]$ denotes the diagonal matrix whose k–th diagonal element is x_k for any $x \in R^K_{++}$, and where V is a $K \times N$ matrix. By eliminating redundant securities from the given K, we can assume without loss of generality that $VV^\top$ is non–singular. It follows from Ito's Lemma, taking X^{x0} defined by (27), that $Z \equiv \log(X^{x0}_T)$ is normally distributed in R^K with mean vector

$$m = \log(x) + \delta 1 T - \tfrac{1}{2} T v, \qquad (36)$$

where $v \in R^K$ has k–th element $v_k = V_k \cdot V_k$, with V_k denoting the k–th row of V. The covariance matrix of Z is $TVV^\top$. We then have $C(x,0) = e^{-\delta T} E[g(e^Z)]$, or using the formula for the density of Z given in Exercise 4.3,

$$C(x,0) = \int_{R^K} \frac{g(e^z)\,\exp[-(z-m)^\top(2TVV^\top)^{-1}(z-m)]}{2e^{\delta T}[\pi^K T \det(VV^\top)]^{1/2}}\,dz. \qquad (37)$$

This is an explicit solution, but involves a calculation that would typically be made numerically. Of course, for $K = 1$, relation (23) is a special case of (37). ♠

G.   In order to prove the claim at the end of Paragraph A we will appeal to the *Central Limit Theorem*, by which the probability distribution of a normalized sum of N independent random variables approaches the distribution of a normally distributed random variable, as N goes to infinity. First we need a notion of *convergence in distribution*.

Suppose Z is a metric space (endowed with its Borel tribe of measurable subsets) and $\{Y_1, Y_2, \ldots\}$ is a sequence of Z–valued random variables on some respective probability spaces $(\Omega_n, \mathcal{F}_n, P_n), n = 1, 2, \ldots$. These probability spaces could be the same space $(\Omega, \mathcal{F}, P)$. Then $\{Y_n\}$ *converges in distribution* to a Z–valued random variable Y if $E[f(Y_n)] \to E[f(Y)]$ for every bounded continuous real–valued function f on Z. We recall from Section 19 that this is equivalent to the convergence of the sequence $\{\sim Y_n\}$ of distributions to $\sim Y$, hence the name *convergence in distribution*. This is sometimes referred to as *weak convergence*, but that term can have other meanings as well. We state a simple version of the Central Limit Theorem.

CENTRAL LIMIT THEOREM. *Suppose $Y_1, Y_2, \ldots$ is a sequence of independent and identically distributed real–valued random variables on a probability space, each with expected value μ and variance $\sigma^2 > 0$. For each n, let $Z_n = Y_1 + \cdots + Y_n$. Then $\{(Z_n - n\mu)/(\sigma\sqrt{n})\}$ converges in distribution to a Standard Normal random variable.*

Readers are referred to the Notes for proofs of most of the results in this paragraph.

Example. (The De Moivre–Laplace Limit Theorem) Let $Y_1, Y_2, \ldots$ denote a sequence of *Bernoulli trials*, meaning that Y_1 is a random variable having outcomes 0 and 1 with respective probabilities $q \in (0,1)$ and $1-q$, and that $\{Y_n\}$ are independent and identically distributed (i.i.d.). We may think of $Z_n = Y_1 + \cdots + Y_n$ as the number of heads realized from n independent coin tosses with the same probability q of heads. The probability that $Z_n = k$, or k heads out of n, is given by the binomial formula

$$b(k; n, q) = \frac{n!}{k!(n-k)!} q^k (1-q)^{n-k}.$$

Each Y_n has expected value $\mu = q$ and variance $\sigma^2 = q(1-q)$. Recalling *Stirling's Formula*,

$$\lim_{n \to \infty} \frac{n!}{\sqrt{2\pi}\, n^{n+1/2}\, e^{-n}} = 1,$$

some analysis of series yields

$$\lim_{n \to \infty} \frac{b(k; n, q)}{(2\pi n \sigma^2)^{-1/2} \exp\left[\frac{-(k-n\mu)^2}{2n\sigma^2} \right]} = 1.$$

The denominator is precisely the density of a normally distributed random variable with mean μn and variance $n\sigma^2$, evaluated at the point k. We should therefore not be surprised at the conclusion of the Central Limit Theorem: $(Z_n - n\mu)/(\sigma\sqrt{n})$ converges in distribution to a Standard Normal random variable. ♠

Our work on the Black–Scholes model will depend on a Central Limit Theorem for sums of independent random variables without the same distribution, but satisfying the following condition. For each integer n, let $Y_1^n, Y_2^n, \ldots, Y_{k(n)}^n$ be independent real–valued random variables with finite non–zero variance on some probability space. If $k(n) \to \infty$, this defines a *triangular array of random variables*.

THE LINDEBERG CONDITION. *Suppose* $Y = \{Y_1^n, Y_2^n, \ldots, Y_{k(n)}^n : n \geq 1\}$ *is a triangular array of random variables of zero expected values. For each* n, *let* $s_n^2 = \text{var}(Y_1^n + \cdots + Y_{k(n)}^n)$. *Then* Y *satisfies the Lindeberg condition, by definition, if for any scalar* $\epsilon > 0$ *the triangular array* $\{U_1^n, U_2^n, \ldots, U_{k(n)}^n : n \geq 1\}$ *defined by*

$$U_k^n = Y_k^n, \quad |Y_k^n| \leq \epsilon s_n,$$

$$= 0, \quad |Y_k^n| > \epsilon s_n,$$

satisfies the condition:

$$\lim_{n \to \infty} \frac{\text{var}\left(U_1^n + \cdots + U_{k(n)}^n\right)}{s_n^2} = 1.$$

LINDEBERG'S CENTRAL LIMIT THEOREM. *Suppose* $\{Y_1^n, Y_2^n, \ldots, Y_{k(n)}^n :$ $n \geq 1\}$ *is a triangular array of random variables of zero expected values satisfying the Lindeberg Condition. For each positive integer* n, *let* $Z_n = Y_1^n + \cdots + Y_{k(n)}^n$ *and* $s_n^2 = \text{var}(Z_n)$. *Then* Z_n/s_n *converges in distribution to a Standard Normal random variable.*

COROLLARY. *Suppose* $Y_1, Y_2, \ldots$ *is a sequence of zero–mean independent random variables and there exists a scalar* K *such that* $|\,Y_k\,| \leq K$ *for all* k. *If* $s_n^2 \equiv \text{var}(Z_n) \to \infty$, *where* $Z_n = Y_1 + \cdots + Y_n$, *then* Z_n/s_n *converges in distribution to a Standard Normal random variable.*

PROOF: Since $s_n \to \infty$, for any $\epsilon > 0$ there exists an N such that $s_n > K/\epsilon$ for all $n \geq N$. The corresponding triangular array therefore satisfies the Lindeberg Condition. ∎

H. We now solve for the limit of the discrete–time binomial pricing model (6) as trading intervals become increasingly small. The terminal value of the discrete–time stock price of Paragraph A is $S_T = S_0 \prod_{t=1}^{T} G_t$, where $G_1, \ldots, G_T$ is the random sequence of up and down returns over the T periods. Equivalently, $S_T = S_0 e^{Y_1 + \cdots + Y_T}$, where $Y_t = \log(G_t)$. For example, if $T = 3$ and G_1, G_2, and G_3 have respective outcomes U, D, and D, then $S_T = S_0 e^{u+d+d}$, where $u = \log(U)$ and $d = \log(D)$. In Paragraph A we constructed the artificial probability $p = (R - D)/(U - D)$ of an up movement and treated $\{Y_t\}$ as a sequence of independent binomial trials, each having outcome u with probability p and outcome d with probability $(1 - p)$. We argued that the initial arbitrage–free value of the crown is

$$C = E\left[\frac{1}{R^T} g\left(S_0 e^{Y_1 + \cdots + Y_T}\right)\right].$$

Suppose there are k sub–periods per period, with returns R_k, U_k, and D_k for each sub–period replacing R, U, and D respectively. The same arguments imply that

$$C_k = E\left[\frac{1}{R_k^{Tk}} g\left(S_0 e^{Y_1^k + \cdots + Y_{Tk}^k}\right)\right], \tag{38}$$

where C_k is the initial value of the crown, and where $\{Y_t^k\}$ is a sequence of independent binomial trials, each having outcome $u_k = \log(U_k)$ with probability $p_k = (R_k - D_k)/(U_k - D_k)$ and outcome $d_k = \log(D_k)$ with probability $(1 - p_k)$. It remains to determine appropriate values of R_k, U_k, and D_k, and to evaluate $C^* = \lim_{k \to \infty} C_k$.

The sub–period riskless return R_k is unambiguously $e^{r/k}$, where $r = \log(R)$, for this yields the compounded riskless rate $(R_k)^k = R$ per period, as required. The choice of U_k and D_k requires some thought. With $k = 2$ for example, we would like the return patterns for one period under (U, D) and for two half–periods under (U_2, D_2) to be equivalent in some sense. The choices $U_k = \sqrt[k]{U}$ and $D_k = \sqrt[k]{D}$ are analyzed in an exercise, but seem unsatisfactory; the effect of two half–periods of returns $(\sqrt{U}, \sqrt{D})$ is qualitatively quite different from that of one period with returns of (U, D). Our alternative is to introduce probability explicitly into the model and to choose U_k and D_k so as to preserve the given mean μ and variance σ^2 of the rate of return per period. Suppose the original T period model has periods that are independently up and down with respective probabilities q and $(1 - q)$. The mean rate of return per period is then $\mu = qu + (1-q)d$. The variance of the rate of return per period is $\sigma^2 = q(1 - q)(u - d)^2$. In order to preserve the mean and variance of the rate of return per period, we set $U_k = \exp(\sigma/\sqrt{k} + \mu/k)$ and $D_k = \exp(-\sigma/\sqrt{k} + \mu/k)$, and take the probability of an up move to be $q = \frac{1}{2}$, regardless of the length of the sub–period. Then, indeed, the mean rate of return per period is

$$k \left[\frac{\log(U_k)}{2} + \frac{\log(D_k)}{2} \right] = \mu,$$

and the variance of the rate of return per period is

$$k \frac{1}{2} \cdot \frac{1}{2} \left[\log(U_k) - \log(D_k) \right]^2 = \sigma^2.$$

Once U_k and D_k are fixed, the "artificial" probability $p_k = (R_k - D_k)/(U_k - D_k)$ determines the arbitrage–free price C_k of the crown, and thus determines its limit C^* as $k \to \infty$.

An exercise calls for proof of the following application of Lindeberg's Central Limit Theorem.

PROPOSITION. *Let $\{Y_1^n, \ldots, Y_{k(n)}^n : n \geq 1\}$ be a triangular array of random variables such that the triangular array $\{Y_1^n - E(Y_1^n), \ldots, Y_{k(n)}^n - E(Y_{k(n)}^n) : n \geq 1\}$ satisfies the Lindeberg Condition. For each n, let $Z_n = Y_1^n + \cdots + Y_{k(n)}^n$. If $E(Z_n) \to \mu$ and $\mathrm{var}(Z_n) \to \sigma^2 \neq 0$, then Z_n converges in distribution to a Normally distributed random variable Z with mean μ and variance σ^2.*

For each $k \geq 1$, let $Z_k = Y_1^k + \cdots + Y_{Tk}^k$, where $Y_1^k, Y_2^k, \ldots$ are independent binomial random variables with probability p_k of outcome u_k and probability $1 - p_k$ of outcome d_k. We have

$$C_k = e^{-rT} E\left[g\left(S_0 e^{Z_k}\right)\right],$$

merely repeating (38) in a more convenient form, noting that $1/R_k^{Tk} = e^{-rT}$. It remains to apply the Central Limit Theorem to determine the limiting distribution of Z_k as the number k of sub–periods per period goes to infinity. An exercise shows that $\text{var}(Z_k) \to T\sigma^2$ and that $E(Z_k) \to (r - \frac{1}{2}\sigma^2)T$ as $k \to \infty$. Another exercise shows that the triangular array

$$\left\{Y_1^k - E\left(Y_1^k\right), \ldots, Y_{Tk}^k - E\left(Y_{Tk}^k\right) : k \geq 1\right\}$$

satisfies the Lindeberg Condition. Proposition 22H thus implies that Z_k converges in distribution to a normally distributed random variable Z with mean $(r - \frac{1}{2}\sigma^2)T$ and variance $T\sigma^2$. If the crown payoff function g is bounded and continuous, the definition of convergence in distribution then implies that

$$C_k = E\left|e^{-rT} g\left(S_0 e^{Z_k}\right)\right| \to C^* \equiv E\left[e^{-rT} g\left(S_0 e^Z\right)\right]. \tag{39}$$

This is precisely the valuation model stated by relation (23).

I. The limiting value (39) of a crown with payoff function g does not necessarily apply if g is unbounded; a further argument must be made. This caveat would apply, for example, to the unbounded call option payoff function $x \mapsto (x - K)^+$. In any case, however, we do have the convergence in distribution of $g\left(S_0 e^{Z_k}\right)$ to $g\left(S_0 e^Z\right)$, where Z is distributed as in relation (39), by the following result.

LEMMA. *Suppose $\{Z_n\}$ is a sequence of random variables valued in a metric space X converging in distribution to an X–valued random variable Z. If D is a metric space and $g : X \to D$ is continuous, then $g(Z_n)$ converges in distribution to $g(Z)$. Indeed, suppose g is instead merely measurable, and let $X^d \subset X$ denote the set of points at which g is not continuous. If $[\sim Z](X^d) = 0$, meaning the probability of a discontinuity is zero, then the same conclusion follows.*

The assumptions of the lemma can be weakened, as mentioned in the Notes, where a proof is cited. The following classical convergence theorem then extends our limiting valuation result (39) to payoff functions such as that of the call option. A sequence $\{U_n\}$ of real–valued random variables is *uniformly integrable* if

$$\lim_{k \to \infty} \left\{ \sup_n \; E\left[h_k\left(|\,U_n\,|\right)\right] \right\} = 0,$$

where h_k is the real–valued function given by:

$$h_k(t) = t, \quad t \geq k,$$
$$h_k(t) = 0, \quad t < k.$$

THEOREM. *Suppose $\{U_n\}$ is a sequence of real–valued random variables converging in distribution to U. If $\{U_n\}$ is uniformly integrable, then $E(U_n) \to E(U)$. Conversely, if $\{U_n\}$ and U are integrable and positive, then $E(U_n) \to E(U)$ implies that $\{U_n\}$ is uniformly integrable.*

A proof is cited in the Notes. An easy exercise shows that $\left\{g\left(S_0 e^{Z_k}\right)\right\}$ is uniformly integrable for $g(x) = (x - K)^+$. Then the limit C^* of relation (39) is given by relation (19), the Black–Scholes Formula. In other words, the limiting value of a call option as the size of trading intervals shrinks to zero, with appropriate adjustment of the returns U_k and D_k of the stock, is the Black–Scholes Option Pricing Formula, originally derived by rather advanced continuous–time mathematics. We have reached our goal, more carefully stated as follows.

PROPOSITION. *Suppose, for each integer $k \geq 1$, that $\{G_1^k, G_2^k, \ldots\}$ is a sequence of independent binomial trials $(U_k, D_k; p_k)$, where U_k, D_k, and p_k are the above specified functions of μ, σ, k, and r. Then, for any exercise price $K \in (0, \infty)$,*

$$\lim_{k \to \infty} \; E\left[e^{-rT}(S_0 G_0^k G_1^k \cdots G_{Tk}^k - K)^+\right] = C(S_0, 0),$$

where $C(S_0, 0)$ is the Black–Scholes Option Pricing Formula (19).

J.   The previous analysis does not fully clarify the role of Brownian Motion in the limiting Black–Scholes valuation model (39). We would like to show, for example, that the cumulative return process $X_n^k = Y_1^k + \cdots + Y_n^k$ is somehow related to Brownian Motion in the limit, as the number k of sub–periods per period goes to infinity. We will now sketch out the nature of Brownian Motion as the limit of discrete–time random walks such as X^k, as the number of k of sub–periods per period goes to infinity, a result known as *Donsker's Theorem*. This has implications going well beyond the option pricing formula, since the result applies to securities whose dividends depend on the path taken by the stock price process, and not merely its terminal value.

First, we let D denote the metric space of RCLL real–valued functions on $[0, T]$ under the *uniform metric* $(g, f) \mapsto \sup_{t \in [0,T]} |g(t) - f(t)|$, for functions g and f in D. This metric is illustrated in Figure 22.2. This is the *path space*, which is given the Borel tribe $\mathcal{D}$ generated by the uniform metric. A stochastic process X for returns can be treated as a D–valued random variable on a probability space $(\Omega, \mathcal{F}, P)$, taking $X(\omega) \in D$ as the path followed by X in state of the world $\omega \in \Omega$. Conventionally, D is given a more complicated topology cited in the Notes, but the current setup is sufficient for our needs.

Example. If $B = \{B_t : t \geq 0\}$ is a Standard Brownian Motion with respect to some filtered probability space, then the distribution of B restricted to $[0, T]$ is known as *Wiener measure* on the path space D. Since B is typically defined with continuous sample paths, we could also define Wiener measure on the smaller path space $C([0, T])$, given the same uniform metric topology, but that would be slightly less convenient for our purposes. The existence of Wiener measure on $(D, \mathcal{D})$ is a fact cited in the Notes. ♠

Let $\{Y_1, Y_2, \ldots\}$ denote a sequence of real–valued random variables on a probability space $(\Omega, \mathcal{F}, P)$. For any real number t, let $[t]$ denote the largest integer less than or equal to t; for examples, $[3.5] = 3$ and $[4] = 4$. For a given scalar $\sigma > 0$ and each positive integer n, let $Z_n = Y_1 + \cdots + Y_n$ and let $X^n : \Omega \times [0, T] \to R$ denote the stochastic process defined by

$$X^n(t) = \frac{1}{\sigma \sqrt{n}} Z_{[nt]}, \quad t \in [0, T]. \tag{40}$$

In other words, we take the discrete–time process $Z_1, Z_2, \ldots$ and "fill in the gaps" to form a continuous–time process X^n, normalizing by $\sigma \sqrt{n}$. Figure 22.3 illustrates the construction of typical sample paths for X^1, X^2, and X^3, given realized values of $Y_1, Y_2, \ldots$, for $T = 1$ and $\sigma = 1$. If the "jumps" $\{Y_i\}$ are independent with variance σ^2, then normalization by $\sigma \sqrt{n}$ gives "unit variance per unit time" movements to X^n for each n, which is one of the defining properties of Brownian Motion. A proof of the following classical convergence result is cited in the Notes.

THEOREM (DONSKER'S THEOREM). *Suppose $Y_1, Y_2, \ldots$ is a sequence of independent and identically distributed real–valued random variables with zero mean and variance $\sigma^2 > 0$. Then $\{X^n\}$ defined by (40) converges in distribution on the path space $(D, \mathcal{D})$ to Standard Brownian Motion.*

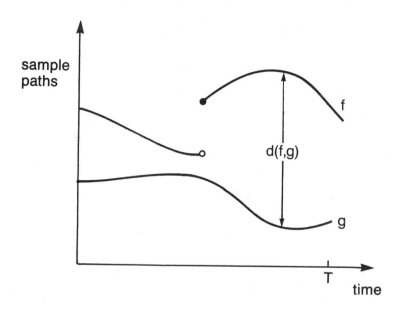

Figure 22.2   The Uniform Metric on RCLL Sample Paths

As stated, Donsker's Theorem does not quite cover the Black–Scholes model of rates of return $Y_1^k, \ldots, Y_{Tk}^k$, where, for each k, these random variables are independent and identically distributed binomial trials with outcomes $u_k = \sigma/\sqrt{k} + \mu/k$ and $d_k = -\sigma/\sqrt{k} + \mu/k$ under respective probabilities $p_k = (e^{r/k} - e^{d_k})/(e^{u_k} - e^{d_k})$ and $(1 - p_k)$. In order to cover this case, for each k, let $Z_n^k = Y_1^k + \cdots + Y_{kn}^k$, $n \le k$, and then let

$$X^k(t) = Z_{[t]}^k, \quad t \in [0, T]. \tag{41}$$

Then, by a variant of Donsker's Theorem cited in the Notes, we can safely record the desired sort of convergence result.

PROPOSITION. *The sequence $\{X^k\}$ of return processes defined by (41) converges in distribution on the path space $(D, \mathcal{D})$ to the Brownian Motion with drift:*

$$X(t) = \left(r - \tfrac{1}{2}\sigma^2\right)t + \sigma B_t, \quad t \in [0, T], \tag{42}$$

where B is a Standard Brownian Motion.

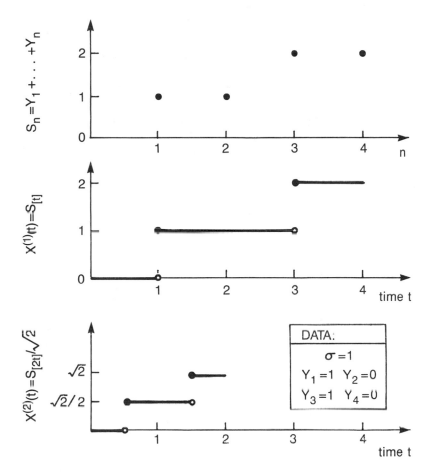

Figure 22.3   Construction of Normalized Sample Paths

We then have $E[h(X^k)] \rightarrow E[h(X)]$ for any bounded continuous real–valued function h on the path space D. In particular, if h is defined by

$$h(x) = e^{-rT} g\left(S_0 e^{x(T)}\right), \quad x \in D,$$

for some bounded and continuous $g : R \rightarrow R$, we again recover the crown valuation formula (23). More generally, we have a method of determining the limiting arbitrage value of a contingent claim whose dividends depend on the entire path of the stock price process, taking the limit as time intervals become smaller and smaller. (One can deduce, using the methods of Section 17, that the limit of the discrete–time arbitrage values is in fact the arbitrage value directly in continuous time.) To apply the last proposition, let $h : D \to R$ denote the function mapping the sample path of the cumulative return process X^k defined by (41) to the discounted present value of the dividend paid by a *path–dependent crown*. In discrete–time, we have already shown that the arbitrage value of this crown (with k sub–periods per period) is $E[h(X^k)]$ under the assumption that $Y_1^k, Y_2^k, \ldots$ is a sequence of binomial independent trials with outcomes u_k and d_k with respective probabilities p_k and $1 - p_k$, as defined above. By the last proposition, the limiting value is $\lim_{k \to \infty} E[h(X^k)] = E[h(X)]$, where X is defined by (42), provided h is continuous and bounded, or more generally, provided h is continuous and $\{h(X^k)\}$ is uniformly integrable. Indeed, by Lemma 22I, we can further relax to the case of uniform integrability and an assumption that the points of discontinuity of h have zero probability under the distribution of X.

Example 1.   For a path–dependent example, consider a crown that pays at time T the maximum value reached by the stock price process during $[0, T]$. Then we define h by

$$h(x) = e^{-rT} \max_{t \in [0,T]} S_0 e^{x(t)}, \quad x \in D,$$

which is certainly a continuous function on D given our uniform metric. A little additional work shows the uniform integrability of $\{h(X^k)\}$, given a well known expression for the distribution of $\max_{t \in [0,T]} B_t$. The explicit value of $E[h(X)]$ is known, and further explored in an exercise. ♠

Example 2.   A common problem is the evaluation of an option with the possibility of early exercise. Generally one can obtain a *liquidation time* for such a security, such as a put option, as a stopping time of the form $T(X) = \inf\{t \in [0, T] : S_t = f(t)\}$, where f is, say, a continuous function on $[0, T]$ and $S_t = S_0 e^{X_t}$. We think of $T(X)$ as the first time the stock price process reaches the minimum level required for liquidation, say for the early exercise of an option. Let $\tau(X) = \min\{T, T(X)\}$, also a stopping time, and consider a crown that pays $g(S_{\tau(X)})$ at the random time $\tau(X)$. Then our payoff function h is defined by

$$h(x) = \exp\left[-r\tau(x)\right] g\left(S_0 e^{x[\tau(x)]}\right), \quad x \in D.$$

Let us move to the infinite horizon time set $[0, \infty)$, and consider the case of $f(t) = F$, a constant. With $X_t = (r - \sigma^2/2)t + \sigma B_t$, we have

$$T(X) = T_F(X) \equiv \inf\left\{t \in [0, T] : B_t = \frac{\log(F/S_0) + (\sigma^2/2 - r)t}{\sigma}\right\}. \quad (43)$$

Using a standard formula cited in the Notes, the probability $P(T_F(X) > t)$ is equal to

$$\Phi\left(\frac{\log(F/S_0) - mt}{\sigma\sqrt{t}}\right) - \exp\left[\frac{2m\,\log(F/S_0)}{\sigma^2}\right]\Phi\left(\frac{-\log(F/S_0) - mt}{\sigma\sqrt{t}}\right),$$

where $m = (\sigma^2/2) - r$. Then, for example, we have a closed form solution for the market value of a bond paying the riskless amount b at the hitting time $T_F(X)$. From another well known expression for the *Laplace transform*, $E\left(\exp[-\lambda T_F(X)]\right)$, of $T_F(X)$, we calculate the price of this bond to be

$$E[b\,\exp(-rT_F(X))] = b\,\exp\left(\left[\frac{-\log(F/S_0)}{\sigma^2}\right][(m^2 + 2\sigma^2 r)^{1/2} - m]\right). \quad (44)$$

Many other securities can be evaluated using this approach. ♠

K. The final method we shall explore for the valuation of redundant securities in the Black–Scholes model applies the general martingale pricing model of Section 17 and Girsanov's Theorem of Section 21. We take the price process S solving the stochastic differential equation

$$dS_t = \mu(S_t, t)\,dt + \sigma(S_t, t)\,dB_t, \qquad t \in [0, T],$$

where B is a Standard Brownian Motion that is a martingale with respect to a given filtered probability space $(\Omega, \mathcal{F}, F, P)$, and where $\mu : R \times [0, T] \to R$ and $\sigma : R \times [0, T] \to R$ are Borel measurable and satisfy a Lipschitz (21.8) and a growth (21.9) condition. We also assume that $\sigma \geq k > 0$ for some scalar k. This latter assumption is easily relaxed to an assumption of strict positivity and continuity for σ. The generalization to a multidimensional stock price process S is avoided only for simplicity. We take the deterministic bond price process

$$\beta(t) = \exp\left(\int_0^t \rho(s)\,ds\right), \qquad t \in [0, T],$$

where $\rho : R \to R$ is positive and continuous. Here, $\rho(t)$ is the interest rate at time t. We first express market values relative to the bond as a numeraire, yielding the new bond price process $\widehat{\beta}(t) \equiv 1$ and the normalized risky security price process

$$\widehat{S}(t) = \frac{S(t)}{\beta(t)}, \quad t \in [0, T].$$

An application of Ito's Lemma shows that $\widehat{S}$ solves the stochastic differential equation

$$d\widehat{S}(t) = \widehat{\mu}(\widehat{S}, t)\, dt + \widehat{\sigma}(\widehat{S}_t, t)\, dB_t; \quad \widehat{S}_0 = S_0, \quad t \in [0, T], \qquad (45)$$

where, for each $(x, t) \in R \times [0, T]$,

$$\widehat{\mu}(x, t) = \frac{\mu[x\beta(t), t]}{\beta(t)} - \rho(t)x,$$

and

$$\widehat{\sigma}(x, t) = \frac{\sigma[x\beta(t), t]}{\beta(t)}.$$

Since $\widehat{\beta} \equiv 1$ and $E\left[|\widehat{S}_T|\right] < \infty$, the framework of Theorem 17E implies the existence of an equivalent martingale measure Q, a probability measure on $(\Omega, \mathcal{F})$ equivalent to P under which $\widehat{S}$ is a martingale with respect to $(\Omega, \mathcal{F}, F, Q)$. It follows, as in Section 17, that the initial market value of any redundant security claiming a random payoff $X \in L^1(P)$ at time T is $E^Q[X/\beta(T)]$. Let ξ be the martingale on $(\Omega, \mathcal{F}, F, P)$ defined by

$$\xi_t = E\left[\frac{dQ}{dP} \,\middle|\, \mathcal{F}_t\right], \quad t \in [0, T],$$

where $\frac{dQ}{dP}$ is the Radon–Nikodym derivative of Q with respect to P. As a consequence of Example 15F, assuming that F is generated by B, there exists some predictable process θ such that $\int \theta_t \, dB_t$ is well defined and satisfies:

$$\xi_t = 1 + \int_0^t \theta_s \, dB_s, \quad t \in [0, T].$$

Since Q and P are equivalent, ξ_t is strictly positive almost surely for all t, and ξ has continuous sample paths almost surely. Then φ, defined by

$$\varphi_t = \frac{\theta_t}{\xi_t}, \quad t \in [0, T],$$

satisfies $\int_0^T \varphi_t^2 \, dt < \infty$ almost surely, and $\int \varphi_t \, dB_t$ is thus well defined. By Ito's Lemma,

$$\log(\xi_t) = \int_0^t \varphi_s \, dB_s - \frac{1}{2} \int_0^t \varphi_s^2 \, ds, \quad t \in [0, T],$$

implying that

$$\frac{dQ}{dP} = \xi_T = \exp\left(\int_0^T \varphi_t \, dB_t - \frac{1}{2} \int_0^T \varphi_t^2 \, dt \right).$$

By Girsanov's Theorem of Paragraph 21E,

$$\widehat{B}_t = D_t - \int_0^t \psi_s \, ds, \quad t \in [0, T],$$

defines a Standard Brownian Motion $\widehat{B}$ on $(\Omega, \mathcal{F}, F, Q)$. From (45), since $dB_t = d\widehat{B}_t + \varphi_t \, dt$,

$$\widehat{S}_t = \widehat{S}_0 + \int_0^t \widehat{\mu}(\widehat{S}_s, s) \, ds + \int_0^t \widehat{\sigma}(\widehat{S}_s, s) \, dB_s$$

$$= \widehat{S}_0 + \int_0^t \left[\widehat{\mu}(\widehat{S}_s, s) + \widehat{\sigma}(\widehat{S}_s, s)\varphi_s \right] ds + \int_0^t \widehat{\sigma}(\widehat{S}_s, s) \, d\widehat{B}_s, \quad t \in [0, T].$$

Since $\widehat{S}$ and $\widehat{B}$ are martingales under Q, it follows that

$$Y_t = \widehat{S}_t - \widehat{S}_0 - \int_0^t \widehat{\sigma}(\widehat{S}_s, s) \, d\widehat{B}_s = \int_0^t \left[\widehat{\mu}(\widehat{S}_s, s) + \widehat{\sigma}(\widehat{S}_s, s)\varphi_s \right] ds, \quad t \in [0, T],$$

is also a martingale under Q with $Y_0 = 0$. But this can only be true if $Y_t = 0$ for all t, since any martingale with respect to $(\Omega, \mathcal{F}, F, Q)$ is of the form $\int \alpha_t \, d\widehat{B}_t$ plus a constant. Thus $\widehat{S}$ satisfies the stochastic differential equation $d\widehat{S}_t = \widehat{\sigma}(\widehat{S}_t, t)d\widehat{B}_t$ on $(\Omega, \mathcal{F}, F, Q)$.

To complete our recovery of the Black–Scholes model, suppose a redundant security is a crown, a claim to $g(S_T)$ at time T, where $g : R \to R$ is measurable and satisfies $E[|g(S_T)|] < \infty$. Then, from Section 17, the initial market value of this crown is

$$C = E^Q \left[\frac{g(S_T)}{\beta_T} \right] = E^Q \left[\frac{g\left(\widehat{S}_T \beta_T\right)}{\beta_T} \right].$$

By Ito's Lemma, $X_t = \widehat{S}_t\beta_t$ satisfies the stochastic differential equation

$$dX_t = \rho_t X_t\, dt + \sigma(X_t, t)\, d\widehat{B}_t; \quad X_0 = S_0. \tag{46}$$

We then have

$$C = E\left[\exp\left(-\int_0^T \rho(t)\, dt\right) g(X_T)\right], \tag{47}$$

which is a generalization of (20) and a special case of (35). For the original Black–Scholes model (8)–(9), we have $\rho(t) \equiv r$, for some scalar $r \geq 0$, and $\sigma(x, t) \equiv vx$, for some non–zero scalar v. Then Ito's Lemma and (46) imply that

$$X_T = S_0\, \exp\left((r - \tfrac{1}{2}v^2)T + v\widehat{B}_T\right),$$

leaving $C = E\left[e^{-rT}g(S_0 e^Z)\right]$, where Z is normally distributed with mean $(r - \tfrac{1}{2}v^2)T$ and variance $v^2 T$, which is relation (23). For $g(x) = (x - K)^+$, this is precisely the original Black–Scholes Formula (19).

EXERCISES

EXERCISE 22.1   Verify by calculation that the solution (19) for the price $C(S_t, t)$ of a call option with exercise price $K > 0$, time $T - t$ to expiry, and current stock price S indeed satisfies the partial differential equation

$$\tfrac{1}{2}C_{xx}x^2\sigma^2 + C_x xr - Cr + C_t = 0,$$

with boundary conditions $C(0, t) = 0$ and $C(x, T) = (x - K)^+$. Explain the former boundary condition.

EXERCISE 22.2   Use the following *Fourier transform method* to solve the PDE for the arbitrage–free value $\widehat{C}(x, \tau)$ of a call option with τ time to expiry and exercise price K. Note the special time convention here; we have $\widehat{C}(x, \tau) = C(x, T - \tau)$.

(A)   Linearize the PDE by substituting $V = \log(x)$. What are the new boundary conditions?

(B)   Let

$$\phi(\xi, \tau) = \frac{1}{\sqrt{2\pi}}\int_{-\infty}^{\infty} \widehat{C}(V, \tau)\, \exp(i\xi V)\, dV.$$

The function $\phi(\cdot,\tau)$ is known as the *Fourier transform* of $\widehat{C}(\cdot,\tau)$. Assuming that this integral is bounded and that all regularity conditions are satisfied, express $\widehat{C}_V$, $\widehat{C}_{VV}$, and $\widehat{C}_\tau$ in terms of derivatives of $\phi(\xi,\tau)$. Show that

$$ -\left[\tfrac{1}{2}(\xi^2 - i\xi)\sigma^2 + (1+i\xi)r\right]\phi = \phi_\tau. $$

(C)   Solve the ordinary differential equation above. Remember to include the initial term, $\phi(\xi,0)$.

(D)   The inverse Fourier transform recovers $\widehat{C}(V,\tau)$ as

$$ \widehat{C}(V,\tau) = \frac{1}{\sqrt{2\pi}} \int_{-\infty}^{\infty} \phi(\xi,\tau)\exp(-i\xi V)\,d\xi. $$

Noting that

$$ \phi(\xi,0) = \frac{1}{\sqrt{2\pi}} \int_{-\infty}^{\infty} \widehat{C}(V,0)\exp(i\xi V)\,dV, $$

show that $\widehat{C}(V,\tau)$ has the value

$$ \frac{1}{2\pi} \int_{-\infty}^{\infty}\int_{-\infty}^{\infty} \widehat{C}(W,0)\exp\left[f(\xi,W)\right]d\xi\,dW, $$

where

$$ f(\xi,W) = -\frac{\sigma^2}{2}\xi^2\tau + i\left(\frac{\sigma^2}{2} - r\right)\xi\tau - r\tau - i\xi(V-W). $$

Complete the integration with respect to ξ.

(E) To continue, we incorporate the initial condition, $\widehat{C}(W,0) = (e^W - K)^+$. Find the new limits of integration. Separate the expression into two integrals and simplify. *Hint:* Complete the squares in the exponents.

(F)   Replace V with the appropriate function of x. Simplify and obtain the Black–Scholes Formula:

$$ \widehat{C}(x,\tau) = x\Phi\left(\frac{\log(x/K)+(r+\tfrac{1}{2}\sigma^2)\tau}{\sigma\sqrt{\tau}}\right) $$
$$ - K\,e^{-r\tau}\Phi\left(\frac{\log(x/K)+(r-\tfrac{1}{2}\sigma^2)\tau}{\sigma\sqrt{\tau}}\right), $$

where Φ is the Standard Normal cumulative distribution function.

EXERCISE 22.3   Suppose a firm issues zero–coupon bonds worth $1 million and non-dividend paying common stock. On the maturity date, the firm must pay off the bonds if it can; otherwise, the bondholders can force bankruptcy declarations.

(A)   Show that the stockholders are essentially holding an option on the firm's value. What is the exercise price? Suppose that there is only one stockholder and one bondholder. Draw graphs of their payoffs as a function of the firm's value the slopes of the functions.

(B)   Suppose the firm now issues *subordinated debt* worth $500,000, that is, this debt is paid only after the original debt of $1 million is paid. The maturity date is the same. Draw graphs for the payoffs to the stockholder, original bondholder, and the junior bondholder. State their holdings in terms of options.

EXERCISE 22.4   Suppose that the Irish Cattle Company has 1000 shares of stock outstanding. To increase funds, it issues 500 warrants that can be exchanged for newly issued stock at price of $100. (*Warrants* are European call options issued by the company; new shares are issued when warrants are exercised.)

(A)   On the maturity date, what must be the value of a share of Irish Cattle in order for the warrants to be exercised? If the value of the firm is greater than this cut–off price, what is the payoff to the aggregate stockholders and aggregate warrant holders? Draw graphs of the payoffs for these two groups as a function of Irish Cattle value.

(B)   Would a warrant be worth the same as the corresponding European call option? Why or why not?

EXERCISE 22.5   *Convertible bonds*, like ordinary bonds, have precedence in payment over common stock. Convertible bonds, like warrants, allow for conversion into stock at a pre–specified conversion ratio at the discretion of the bondholder. Suppose a firm issues 100 convertible bonds. The firm also has 1500 shares of common stock outstanding. The bonds pay $1000 at maturity or can be exchanged for 25 shares of stock on that day.

(A)   At what stock value will the bonds be converted? Draw graphs of the payoffs for the aggregate stockholders and aggregate bondholders as functions of the firm's market value.

(B)   The payoff to a bondholder can be decomposed into a portfolio of calls. State the portfolio and its market value.

EXERCISE 22.6 Suppose $h \in C^2(R_+ \times [0,T])$ solves the partial differential equation

$$\tfrac{1}{2} h_{xx} x^2 \sigma^2 + h_x x r - h r + h_t = 0,$$

with boundary conditions $h(x,T) = g(x)$ and $h(0,t) = e^{-r(T-t)} g(0), t \in [0,T]$. Take the risky security and riskless bond of the Black–Scholes model (8)–(9) as given securities. Suppose a third security paying only terminal dividends $g(S_T)$ has initial market value $\alpha \neq h(S_0, 0)$. Construct a trading strategy that involves collecting one hundred dollars (the numeraire) at time zero and never paying or collecting other funds through time. Note that the arbitrage profit of one hundred dollars is arbitrary.

EXERCISE 22.7 Let $B = (B^1, B^2)$ denote a Standard Brownian Motion in R^2 that is a martingale with respect to the given filtered probability space. Suppose S^1 and S^2 are the price processes for two securities satisfying the stochastic differential equations

$$dS_t^k = [S_t^k \mu^k - D^k(S_t^k, t)] \, dt + S_t^k \sigma^k \, dB_t; \qquad S_0 = 1, \qquad k - 1, 2,$$

where μ^1 and μ^2 are positive scalar "expected rates of return", σ^1 and σ^2 are vectors in R^2 forming the respective rows of a 2 by 2 real nonsingular matrix σ, and D^1 and D^2 are bounded continuous real-valued functions on $R_+ \times [0,T]$ specifying the dividend rates of the two securities. There is a also a riskless bond whose value β compounds continuously at the riskless interest rate r, or $\beta_t = e^{rt}$. Consider a fourth security with dividends given by a bounded continuous function $\delta : R_+^2 \times [0,T] \to R$, where the dividend rate at time t is $\delta(S_t^1, S_t^2, t)$. The security pays a terminal dividend of $g(S_T^1, S_T^2)$, where g is a bounded continuous function on R_+^2.

(A) Derive a differential equation for the value of this security. Make minimal regularity assumptions and provide boundary conditions.

(B) Express the solution of the differential equation as the expectation of a closed form function of a "new" stock price process X.

EXERCISE 22.8 Evaluate the limit as $k \to \infty$ of the binomial pricing formula (7) for sub-periods of length $1/k$, taking the sub-period returns $R_k = \sqrt[k]{R}$ for the bond and $U_k = \sqrt[k]{U}$ and $D_k = \sqrt[k]{D}$ for the stock. State a new interest rate $\hat{r}$ under which the solution found is the "usual" Black–Scholes solution (19), replacing the given interest rate r with the artificial substitute $\hat{r}$. *Hint:* The solution is of the form $\hat{r} = r + \alpha \sigma^2$ for some scalar α to be found, where σ^2 is the limiting variance of one period returns on the stock under the probabilities $p_k = (R_k - D_k)/(U_k - D_k)$. Use l'Hôpital's Rule in evaluating the limit, and apply Proposition 22H. Clearly, the solution does not make good economic sense. Why ?

EXERCISE 22.9   Prove Proposition 22H.

EXERCISE 22.10   Show, as claimed in Paragraph H, that $\text{var}(Z_k) \to \sigma^2 T$ and that $E(Z_k) \to (r - \sigma^2/2)T$ as $k \to \infty$. *Hint:* Use l'Hôpital's Rule. Show that the underlying triangular array $\{Y_1^k - E(Y_1^k), \ldots, Y_{Tk}^k - E(Y_{Tk}^k) : k \geq 1\}$ satisfies the Lindeberg Condition.

EXERCISE 22.11   Show, as claimed in Paragraph I, that $\{g(S_0 e^{Z_k})\}$ is a uniformly integrable sequence in the case $g(x) = (x - K)^+$. *Hint:* Use the converse part of Theorem 22I.

EXERCISE 22.12   Let X denote a (μ, σ)–*Brownian Motion*, meaning that X solves the stochastic differential equation $dX_t = \mu \, dt + \sigma \, dB_t$; $X_0 = 0$. Let $M_t = \max_{\tau \in [0,t]} X_\tau$. It is known that the joint distribution of (X_t, M_t) is given by the cumulative distribution function, for $(x, m) \in R^2$,

$$F_t(x, m) \equiv P(\{X_t \leq x, M_t \leq m\})$$
$$= \Phi\left(\frac{x - \mu t}{\sigma \sqrt{t}}\right) - \exp(2\mu m / \sigma^2) \, \Phi\left(\frac{x - 2m - \mu t}{\sigma \sqrt{t}}\right). \tag{48}$$

Using this expression, formulate and solve the following arbitrage valuation problem. A stock and bond price process are given by (8)–(9). Take a crown to be an option to sell the stock at time T for the highest price it reached during the interval $[0, T]$.

(A)   Calculate the market value of the crown at time zero, barring arbitrage and transactions costs.

(B)   Calculate the market value of an option to buy the stock at the lowest price available during $[0, T]$.

EXERCISE 22.13   Let X be defined by (21) and $C(x, t)$ by (20). Show that $C(x, t)$ indeed satisfies (19) for $g(x) = (x - K)^+$.

EXERCISE 22.14   Prove Stirling's Formula.

EXERCISE 22.15   (An Extension of the Black–Scholes Model)   This section is mainly concerned with determining the prices of securities whose dividends depend on the market values of other available securities. In this exercise, we develop a model for pricing securities whose dividends depend on the state X of the economy, where X is a *Markov state variable process* valued in R^K, defined as the solution to the stochastic differential equation:

$$dX_t = \nu(X_t, t) \, dt + \eta(X_t, t) \, dB_t; \quad X_0 = x \in R^K, \tag{49}$$

where B is a Standard Brownian Motion in R^N and where the drift function $\nu : R^K \times [0, \infty) \to R^K$ and the diffusion function $\eta : R^K \times [0, \infty) \to M^{K,N}$ are Borel measurable and satisfy Lipschitz (21.8) and growth (21.9) conditions. This leaves X with the properties stated by Proposition 21C. Security markets consist of K securities paying real (consumption) dividends at rates specified by measurable functions $\delta_k : R^K \times [0, T] \to R$ for $1 \le k \le K$, such that $\int_0^T | \delta_k(X_t, t) | \, dt < \infty$ almost surely. The value of the k-th security is given in terms of the consumption numeraire by a strictly positive real–valued function $\mathcal{S}^k \in C^2(R^K \times [0, T])$. The scalar $\mathcal{S}^k(x, t)$ denotes the market value of the k-th security at time t if the state process X is in state x. By Ito's Lemma,

$$d\mathcal{S}^k(X_t, t) = \gamma_k(X_t, t)\,dt + \varphi_k(X_t, t)dB_t, \quad t \ge 0, \tag{50}$$

where the drift function γ_k and diffusion function φ_k are defined by

$$\gamma_k(x, t) = \mathcal{S}_x^k(x, t)\nu(x, t) + \mathcal{S}_t^k(x, t) + \tfrac{1}{2}\mathrm{tr}[\eta(x, t)^\top \mathcal{S}_{xx}^k(x, t)\eta(x, t)], \text{ and}$$

$$\varphi_k(x, t) = \mathcal{S}_x^k(x, t)\eta(x, t), \quad (x, t) \in R^k \times [0, T].$$

There is also a security whose market value is always equal to one, having the "interest rate" dividend process $\{r(X_t, t) : t \in [0, T]\}$, where $r : R^K \times [0, T] \to R_+$ is continuous.

(A) Provide assumptions implying that any other security is redundant and thus priced by arbitrage. *Hint:* One may proceed in the following manner. For a proposed security paying dividends at a rate given by a smooth bounded function $D : R^K \times [0, T] \to R$ and having terminal value zero, derive a partial differential equation in x and t for the market value $h : R^K \times [0, T] \to R$ of this security. Assume, of course, that h is sufficiently differentiable. An example candidate for a solution (that is definitely wrong) is the PDE

$$S(x, t)^\top \mu(x, t) + \tfrac{1}{2}\mathrm{tr}[\eta(x, t)^\top h_{xx}(x, t)\eta(x, t)] = 0, \quad (x, t) \in R^K \times (0, T).$$

Please leave the (x, t) arguments out of the solution. Provide the terminal boundary condition. Demonstrate that a solution to the proposed PDE is indeed the unique value of the security that precludes arbitrage.

(B) State assumptions on the primitive functions under which there is a solution h to the PDE chosen as a solution for Part (A). State an expression for the initial (time zero) arbitrage value of this security as an expectation of a functional of an Ito process.

EXERCISE 22.16 Derive relations (45) and (46).

EXERCISE 22.17 (Theoretical Futures Prices) This exercise will develop a general expression, and several specific closed form solutions, for the unique arbitrage–free futures price of futures contracts delivering assets paying stochastic dividends or requiring stochastic storage costs, provided the assets can be sold short. For additional material on the setting of this exercise, see Exercise 24.17.

For $t \in [0, T]$, let S_t denote the spot price of a given asset, and let F_t denote the futures price for delivery of this asset at T. We assume that both S and F are Ito processes. In principle, the purchase of one futures contract at t is a commitment to pay F_t for one unit of the asset at time T, or equivalently, a commitment to receive the net $S_T - F_t$ at T. In fact, a futures contract is resettled as the futures price moves. Gains or losses against a futures position are added to or subtracted from a margin account, which earns interest. For this problem, assume a constant interest rate of r. Let θ denote a (predictable) candidate futures position process, holding θ_t contracts at time t, such that $\int \theta_t \, dF_t$ is a well defined stochastic integral. Then, if X_t denotes the amount in the corresponding margin account at time t, we have the stochastic differential equation,

$$dX_t = r X_t \, dt + \theta_t \, dF_t,$$

the first term representing interest payments, the second representing resettlement gains from futures trading. Throughout, we assume that the asset can be held in positive or negative quantities. (In principle, it would be enough to know that the asset is held in amounts bounded away from zero, an important distinction for physical assets, which of course cannot be held negatively.) We also assume throughout that arbitrage is impossible.

(A) Suppose the underlying asset is stored costlessly from time t until time T, and that the asset pays no dividends. Show that $F_t = e^{r(T-t)} S_t$. This is known as the *theoretical forward price*.

(B) Suppose the underlying asset is stored at a deterministic cost rate of c_s at time s, for $t \leq s \leq T$ (where $c : [0, T] \to R$ is measurable and integrable). Show that

$$F_t = \int_t^T e^{r(T-s)} c_s \, ds + e^{r(T-t)} S_t.$$

This is known as the *cost–of–carry formula*.

(C)   Suppose that

$$dS_t = \widehat{\mu}(S_t, t)\, dt + \widehat{\sigma}(S_t, t)\, dB_t,$$

and that the asset pays dividends, net of storage costs, at the rate $\delta(S_t, t)$ at time t, where δ is a function satisfying regularity conditions to be considered. State an expression for the arbitrage–free futures price, which is commonly known as the *theoretical futures* price. Prove your formula under stated regularity conditions.

(D)   In the context of Part (C), let $\widehat{\mu}(S_t, t) = \mu S_t$, let $\widehat{\sigma}(S_t, t) = \sigma S_t$, and let $\delta(x, t) = \alpha x$, for some constants μ, σ, and α. Solve for the arbitrage–free futures–to–spot price ratio F_t/S_t in closed form. Solve for F_t/S_t with $\mu = 0.12$, $\sigma = 0.40$, $r = 0.07$, $T - t = 0.75$ years, and $\alpha = 0.03$. (These are typical values for the S&P 500 portfolio of stocks. Estimates of σ can be obtained by numerically inverting the Black–Scholes Option Pricing Formula; r can be estimated from short–term bond prices, and α from historical dividends.)

(E)   The *implied repo rate* is the interest rate r that equates the theoretical futures price obtained from the above calculations with the actual futures price F_t. Solve for the implied repo rate under the assumptions of part (D).

(F)   The theoretical futures price commonly reported in the financial industry is based on a constant deterministic dividend rate $\delta_s = \bar{\alpha} S_t$, $t \leq s \leq T$. Calculate the resulting arbitrage–free futures–to–spot price ratio F_t/S_t as a function of the constants r, $\bar{\alpha}$, μ, and σ and the time $T - t$ until delivery. (This can be compared with the formula obtained in Part (D) based on r, α, μ, σ, and $T - t$.) Assuming Part (D) describes the correct model, under which circumstances is this constant dividend model upward (or downward) biased at $\alpha = \bar{\alpha}$? Compare the implied repo rate implied by the two approaches in the same framework.

(G)   The *Value Line Average* is the *geometric mean*

$$V_t = \left(S_t^{(1)} S_t^{(2)} \cdots S_t^{(n)} \right)^{1/n}$$

of n different selected stocks. A futures contract delivers (by cash settlement) the Value Line Average V_T at the delivery date T. Under the assumption that $S_t = (S_t^{(1)}, \ldots S_t^{(n)})$ is an n–dimensional Ito process with stochastic differential $dS_t = \mu(S_t, t)\, dt + \sigma(S, t)\, dB_t$ and that there is continuous trading in all of the underlying stocks and a riskless bond, investigate this futures contract for a theoretical (arbitrage–free) futures price F_t. This part of the exercise is loosely stated in order to elicit creative responses. One should look for a general result, as well as a closed form solution under suitable parametric assumptions.

Notes

The binomial model of Paragraph A is a slight extension of that proposed in an early edition of Sharpe (1985). The redundancy theorem of Paragraph B is apparently due to Harrison (1982), Chapter 6, where the details and extensions may be found. The construction in Paragraph C is similar to one conceived by Merton (1977), who worked with rates of return. Our framework is more like that of Harrison (1982). The solution to the PDE (16) by Fourier transform methods outlined in Exercise 22.2 is from Merton (1973c). (This and the following three exercises were prepared by Susan Cheng.)

For a practical introduction to the Fourier transform, see Bracewell (1978). Cheng (1987) has a two–dimensional extension; Hemler (1987) has a general extension. Both Cheng and Hemler are interested in pricing the *quality delivery option* of the U.S. Treasury Bond futures contract. More recently, Carr (1987) has shown how to apply the Feynman–Kac Formula to this valuation problem.

The original argument of Black and Scholes (1973) is based on a "local no arbitrage" assumption, which we do not develop here. The solution to the general model of Paragraph F, using the Feynman–Kac Formula, is from Duffie (1986d), where extensions and numerical approximations are noted. Freidlin (1985) has more technical background on this method for solving elliptical PDE's. The limiting argument mentioned at the end of Paragraph E is also indicated in Duffie (1986d). This solution extends in application (only in this Brownian Motion setting) beyond that of Harrison and Kreps (1979), in that it allows stochastic interest rates and applies under weaker conditions on the security price process S, which need not "span" by continuous trading. The "risk–neutral" pricing concept applied here is that of Cox and Ross (1976). We have implicitly taken it that the options being priced are European options, in that they may be exercised only at expiry. Parkinson (1977) and Geske and Johnson (1984) have results on the pricing of American options, those allowing early exercise. For further details on options, see the book by Cox and Rubinstein (1985).

The Central Limit Theorems of Paragraphs G and H are all found with proofs in Billingsley (1968). Example 22G is from Feller (1971). Proposition 22H is a consequence of Theorem 5.5 of Billingsley (1968). The limiting binomial model of Paragraph H is based on Cox, Ross, and Rubinstein

(1979), although the calculations are somewhat different here. Lemma 22I is from Theorem 5.1 of Billingsley (1968). Paragraph J, an applicaton of Donsker's Theorem to the Black–Scholes model, is original. The pricing results here, however, can easily be derived using the martingale model of Harrison and Kreps (1979) shown in Section 17. One should see Margrabe (1978), Johnson (1985), as well as Goldman, Sosin, and Gatto (1979) for more explicit solutions to problems in the vein of Example 1 of Paragraph J, using different methods. We are mainly interested here in exploring the limiting relation between discrete and continuous time. This leads to a numerical Monte Carlo pricing approach, as explored by Boyle (1977) and Jones and Jacobs (1986).

The use of the uniform metric topology on the path space D is unusual. Typically Wiener measure is defined on the space $C([0, T])$ of continuous sample paths with the uniform metric topology, or on the space D of RCLL sample paths with the Skorohod topology. We have opted for D with the uniform metric topology because the continuous–sample path analogue of relation (40) is somewhat complicated, and because the Skorohod topology is also fairly complicated. The existence of Wiener measure on D with the uniform metric topology is a subtle issue, handled by Billingsley (1968), pp. 151–153. This discussion by Billingsley also allows us to state Donsker's Theorem in the form of Theorem 22J. For many applications, however, it is recommended that one work with the Skorohod topology on D, which allows, for example, an analogue to Donsker's Theorem for Poisson processes given by Billingsley (1968), p. 143, Problem 3. There are also many functions of interest whose continuity is more naturally examined in the context of the Skorohod metric. For extensions of the Black–Scholes model to the case of Poisson returns processes, see Merton (1976) and Cox and Ross (1976). We should also note that there is a metric for the Skorohod topology under which D is a Borel space, but that D is not separable given the uniform metric topology.

The convergence of $\{X^k\}$ defined by (41) to Brownian Motion with the stated drift and diffusion coefficients follows from Problem 7, p. 143, of Billingsley (1968), and another application of Theorem 5.5 of Billingsley (1968). The distributions of the maximum and of the first passage time of Brownian Motion applied in Examples 1 and 2 of Paragraph J and in the exercises are found in Harrison (1985). The martingale pricing model of Paragraph K is an extension of the example given by Harrison and Kreps (1979). The literature on applications of the Black–Scholes model is large, and no attempt to survey it here could be contemplated. The book by Cox and Rubinstein (1985) is superb on applications, with obvious emphasis on options markets, including institutional details. Leland (1985) treats the effect of transactions costs on the Black–Scholes model.

Recent applications of the Black–Scholes model to the arbitrage–free characterization of prices depending on the term structure of interest rates have been made by Ho and Lee (1986), in the discrete–time case, and to Heath, Jarrow, and Morton (1987), in the continuous–time case.

23. An Introduction to the Control of Ito Processes

We now turn our attention to the control of Ito processes. When the primitives are "smooth", Ito's Lemma, Bellman's Principle of Dynamic Programming, and the Markov property of Brownian Motion reduce the stochastic control problem to a deterministic problem: the Bellman Equation.

A.   We begin by sketching out the concept of continuous–time stochastic control, passing over technical details by assumption. Later we will state results more precisely. We proceed in the setting laid out in Paragraph 21A. In particular, $B = (B^1, \ldots, B^N)$ is a Standard Brownian Motion in R^N. Let $\mathcal{C}$ denote a set of predictable *control* processes taking values in some *action space* A, a measurable subset of a Euclidean space. Let

(a) Z be the *state space*, a measurable subset of R^K,

(b) μ be a measurable R^K–valued function on $A \times Z$,

(c) $\sigma : A \times Z \to M^{K,N}$ be measurable,

(d) u be a measurable real–valued function on $A \times Z$, the reward function, and

(e) ρ be a positive scalar *discount rate*.

The above are assumed to satisfy sufficient technical regularity conditions so as to have the property: For each starting point x in Z for the state and each control c in $\mathcal{C}$ there is a Z–valued Ito process, the *state process*, well–defined as:

$$X_t = x + \int_0^t \mu(c_s, X_s)\, ds + \int_0^t \sigma(c_s, X_s)\, dB_s, \qquad t \geq 0, \qquad (1)$$

such that the expectation

$$V^c(x) \equiv E_{cx}\left[\int_0^\infty e^{-\rho t} u(c_t, X_t)\, dt\right] \qquad (2)$$

exists. Here E_{cx} denotes expectation under the probability measure governing X for starting point x and control c. Alternatively, we could write "X^{xc}" for "X" to make the dependence of X on x and c explicit, but that would be cumbersome. We also assume, for each x in Z, that

$$V(x) \equiv \sup_{c \in C} \quad V^c(x) < \infty. \tag{3}$$

The *value function* V defined on Z by (3) is to be determined. We also wish to determine, if possible, a control $c^0 \in C$ such that $V(x) = V^{c^0}(x)$ for all x in Z. Then c^0 would be an *optimal control*. This is the *infinite horizon discounted stochastic control problem*: maximize (2) by choice of control c in C. Given an A-valued measurable function f on Z, a control of the form $c = \{f(X_t) : t \geq 0\}$ is a *stationary Markov control*; the current choice c_t depends only on the current state X_t. We do not restrict ourselves to Markov control; c_t may be chosen on the basis of all available information, including the entire sample path of X up to time t. The Markov property of Brownian Motion, however, typically allows one to conclude that no control is strictly better than an optimal Markov control. If c is the Markov control $\{f(X_t) : t \geq 0\} \in C$, then we may re-write (1) as

$$X_t = x + \int_0^t \hat{\mu}(X_s)\,ds + \int_0^t \hat{\sigma}(X_s)\,dB_s,$$

where $\hat{\mu}(x) = \mu[f(x), x]$ and $\hat{\sigma}(x) = \sigma[f(x), x]$. Proposition 21C, under its stated regularity conditions, then implies that X is a Markov process.

It is *Bellman's Principle of Optimality* that, under regularity conditions, for any x in Z and $t \geq 0$,

$$V(x) = \sup_{c \in C} \quad E_{cx}\left[\int_0^t e^{-\rho s} u(c_s, X_s)\,ds + e^{-\rho t} V(X_t)\right].$$

This follows by roughly the same reasoning applied in the discrete-time setting of Section 19. Bellman's Principle, and certain technical regularity conditions, will allow us to deduce the *Bellman Equation*. For a function W in $C^2(Z)$, consider the following version of the Bellman Equation:

$$\sup_{a \in A} \quad [\mathcal{D}^a W(x) - \rho W(x) + u(a, x)] = 0, \quad x \in Z, \tag{4}$$

where

$$\mathcal{D}^a W(x) = \nabla W(x)\mu(a, x) + \tfrac{1}{2}\mathrm{tr}\left[\sigma(a, x)^\top \nabla^2 W(x)\sigma(a, x)\right], \quad x \in Z.$$

Assuming that W indeed satisfies this Bellman Equation (4), our aim is to show that W is the value function V. With additional regularity assumptions, we first show that $W \geq V$, then the reverse. For a given x in Z and any $c = \{c_t : t \geq 0\}$ in $\mathcal{C}$, relation (4) implies that, for any $t \geq 0$,

$$e^{-\rho t} \left[\mathcal{D}^{c(t)} W(X_t) - \rho W(X_t) + u(c_t, X_t) \right] \leq 0. \tag{5}$$

Let $\beta_t = e^{-\rho t} \nabla W(X_t) \sigma(c_t, X_t)$, $t \geq 0$. By Ito's Lemma [in the form of Exercise 21.1 for $a_t = \mu(c_t, X_t)$ and $\theta_t = \sigma(c_t, X_t)$], for any $t \geq 0$,

$$e^{-\rho t} W(X_t) = W(x) + \int_0^t e^{-\rho s} \left[\mathcal{D}^{c(s)} W(X_s) - \rho W(X_s) \right] ds + \int_0^t \beta_s \, dB_s.$$

Relation (5) then implies that

$$W(x) \geq e^{-\rho t} W(X_t) + \int_0^t e^{-\rho s} u(c_s, X_s) \, ds - \int_0^t \beta_s \, dB_s, \quad t \geq 0. \tag{6}$$

We recall from Paragraph 21A that $\int \beta_t \, dB_t$ is a martingale provided that

$$E_{cx} \left[\left(\int_0^t \beta_s \cdot \beta_s \, ds \right)^{\frac{1}{2}} \right] < \infty, \quad t \geq 0,$$

which is the case under mild regularity conditions. In that case, we have $E\left[\int_0^t \beta_s \, dB_s \right] = 0$, and taking expectations through (6),

$$W(x) \geq E_{cx} \left[e^{-\rho t} W(X_t) \right] + E_{cx} \left[\int_0^t e^{-\rho s} u(c_s, X_s) \, ds \right], \quad t \geq 0. \tag{7}$$

Again with regularity conditions on the primitives, $E_{cx}[e^{-\rho t} W(X_t)] \to 0$ as $t \to \infty$, and we conclude that $W(x) \geq E_{cx}[\int_0^\infty e^{-\rho t} u(c_t, X_t) \, dt]$. Since c is arbitrary, $W(x) \geq V(x)$. Since x is arbitrary, $W \geq V$.

To show that $W \leq V$, we assume that the supremum in (4) is attained by some point in A denoted $f(x)$, for each x in Z, defining a A–valued function f on Z. We also assume that the process $c^0 = \{f(X_t) : t \geq 0\}$ is in $\mathcal{C}$, a valid control. These assumptions are not necessary to prove that $W = V$, but they suit this brief overview, for one then quickly shows as well that c^0 is an optimal control. Repeating relations (5), (6), and (7), now with equalities at $c = c^0$, we have

$$W(x) = E_{c^0 x} [e^{-\rho t} W(X_t)] + E_{c^0 x} \left[\int_0^t e^{-\rho s} u(c_s^0, X_s) \, ds \right], \quad t \geq 0.$$

We again let $t \to \infty$ and, under regularity conditions, the first term converges to zero, yielding $W(x) = V^{c^0}(x)$. Since $V^{c^0}(x) \leq V(x)$ by the definition of V, and because x is arbitrary, we know $W \leq V$. Having earlier shown that $W \geq V$, it follows that $W = V$ and that the stationary Markov control $\{f(X_t) : t \geq 0\}$ is optimal. This is only a sketch of the basic idea of the Bellman Equation in continuous–time, of course, and not a proof.

B. Regularity conditions supporting the analysis in Paragraph A are in three basic areas. One must ensure that the Ito process suggested by (1) actually exists for all starting points x in Z and controls c in C. This is an extension of the stochastic differential equations problem of Paragraph 21B. The second basic problem is the existence of a solution W to the Bellman Equation (4). The third basic regularity problem lies with existence of, and growth bounds on, the expectations of $W(X_T)$ and $\int_0^T \nabla W(X_t)\sigma(c_t, X_t)\, dB_t$ for all $T \geq 0$. This is again handled by smoothness assumptions on the primitives. There is a measure of vagueness that is unfortunately appropriate. It seems that each application calls for special assumptions and analytical tricks. In most cases, a solution is demonstrated by educated guesswork and verification. The continuous–time stochastic control machinery, still being unified and reinforced, is presently somewhat delicate. We cite a number of general references in the Notes.

C. We now state regularity conditions validating Bellman's Principle of Optimality and ensuring that any solution to the Bellman Equation is indeed the value function for the stochastic control problem. We move to a finite time horizon $[0, T]$, and include a terminal reward and a stochastic discount rate. We also allow the primitive functions to be time–dependent. The primitive functions μ, σ, u, and ρ of $(a, x, t) \in A \times R^K \times [0, T]$ are to satisfy

Assumption A:

(a) μ, σ, u, *and* ρ *are continuous,*

(b) μ, σ, u, *and* ρ *are continuous with respect to* x *uniformly over* $a \in A$ *for each* $t \geq 0$,

(c) $\mu(a, \cdot, \cdot)$ *and* $\sigma(a, \cdot, \cdot)$ *satisfy Lipschitz (21.8) and growth (21.9) conditions with the same scalar* k *for all* a *in* A,

(d) $u(a, \cdot, \cdot)$ *and* $\rho(a, \cdot, \cdot)$ *satisfy a growth condition (21.9), with the same scalar* k *for all* a *in* A, *and*

(e) $g : R^K \to R$ *is continuous and satisfies a growth condition (21.9).*

Under Assumption A, the following are well–defined for given x in R^K, c in $\mathcal{C}$, τ in $[0, T]$, and t in $[\tau, T]$:

$$X_t = x + \int_\tau^t \mu(c_s, X_s, s)\, ds + \int_\tau^t \sigma(c_s, X_s, s)\, dB_s, \tag{8}$$

$$\phi(t) = \int_\tau^t \rho(c_s, X_s, s)\, ds \tag{9}$$

$$V^c(x, \tau) = E_{cx} \left[\int_\tau^T e^{-\phi(s)} u(c_s, X_s, s)\, ds + e^{-\phi(T)} g(X_T) \right] \tag{10}$$

$$V(x, \tau) = \sup_{c \in \mathcal{C}} V^c(x, \tau). \tag{11}$$

These facts and a proof of the following theorem are cited in the Notes.

THEOREM (BELLMAN'S PRINCIPLE FOR STOCHASTIC CONTROL). *Under Assumption A, for any $(x, \tau) \in R^K \times [0, T]$ and any $t \in [\tau, T]$,*

$$V(x, \tau) = \sup_{c \in \mathcal{C}} \ E_{cx} \left[\int_\tau^t e^{-\phi(s)} u(c_s, X_s, s)\, ds + e^{-\phi(t)} V(X_t, t) \right].$$

This brings us again to the Bellman Equation, which states, under regularity conditions, that the value function is the unique function V in $C^{2,1}(R^K \times [0, T])$ satisfying, for any $(x, t) \in R^K \times [0, T]$,

$$\sup_{a \in A} \ [\mathcal{D}^a V(x, t) - \rho(a, x, t) V(x, t) + u(a, x, t)] = 0, \tag{12}$$

with boundary condition

$$V(x, T) = g(x), \quad x \in R^K, \tag{13}$$

where, for any a in A, x in R^K, and t in $[0, T]$,

$$\mathcal{D}^a V(x, t) = V_t(x, t) + V_x(x, t) \mu(a, x, t) + \tfrac{1}{2} \text{tr} \left[\sigma(a, x, t)^\top V_{xx}(x, t) \sigma(a, x, t) \right].$$

For historical reasons, the Bellman Equation in this form is sometimes referred to as the *Hamilton–Bellman–Jacobi Equation*.

The following growth condition on a real–valued function W on $R^K \times [0, T]$ is weaker than the growth condition defined by relation (21.9).

Growth Condition: There exist scalars k and $r \geq 0$ such that, for all $t \geq 0$,

$$| W(x, t) | \leq k(1 + | x |)^r, \quad x \in R^K. \tag{14}$$

We will cite a result relying on the following regularity condition.

Assumption B: *There exists on* $(\Omega, \mathcal{F}, F, P)$ *a Standard Brownian Motion* $\widehat{B}$ *in* R^N *that is independent of B.*

It may be noted that one can always redefine $(\Omega, \mathcal{F}, F, P)$ so that Assumption B is satisfied without changing the value function V or the set of optimal controls. This assumption is unnecessary if the diffusion matrix $\sigma(\cdot)$ satisfies regularity conditions, for example: $K = N$ and there is a scalar k such that $\sigma(a, x, t)$ is nonsingular with $\| \sigma(a, x, t)^{-1} \| \leq k$ for all (a, x, t).

PROPOSITION (BELLMAN'S EQUATION). *Suppose* $W \in C^{2,1}(R^K \times [0, T])$ *satisfies the growth condition* (14). *Under regularity Assumptions A and B, if W satisfies the Bellman Equation* (12) *and boundary condition* (13), *then* $W = V$, *the value function for problem* (8)–(9)–(10)–(11).

Again, a proof is cited in the Notes. We have stated that a "smooth" solution to the Bellman Equation must be the value function for the control problem. Conversely, it can also be shown that if the value function V is smooth, then V must satisfy the Bellman Equation. Proofs of these results are tortuous even under the given regularity conditions.

   The following corollary to the proposition above follows immediately from Ito's Lemma.

COROLLARY. *Under the assumptions of Proposition 23C, suppose f is a measurable A-valued function on* $R^K \times [0, T]$ *satisfying*

$$\mathcal{D}^{f(x,t)}V(x, t) - \rho[f(x, t), x, t]V(x, t) + u[f(x, t), x, t] = 0,$$

$$(x, t) \in R^K \times [0, T].$$

Then $c^0 = \{f(X_t, t) : t \geq 0\}$ *is an optimal control. That is,* $V^{c^0}(x, t) = V(x, t)$ *for all x in* R^K *and t in* $[0, T]$.

EXERCISES

EXERCISE 23.1   This exercise may be treated as a version of the Robinson Crusoe problem of Paragraph 19A in a continuous–time setting. The rate of growth of the capital stock is determined by a "random shock" process Y defined as the solution to the stochastic differential equation

$$dY_t = (aY_t - b)\, dt + k\sqrt{Y_t}\, dB_t, \quad Y_0 = y \in R,\ t \geq 0,$$

where a, b, and k are negative scalars with $-2b>k^2$, and B is a Standard Brownian Motion that is a martingale with respect to the given filtered probability space. A capital stock process K is defined by

$$K_t = \kappa + \int_0^t (K_s h Y_s - c_s)\, ds + \int_0^t K_s \epsilon \sqrt{Y_s}\, dB_s, \quad t \geq 0,$$

where h, κ, and ϵ are strictly positive scalars and c is an element of the space $\mathcal{C}$ of positive predictable consumption processes $c = \{c_t : t \geq 0\}$ satisfying $\int_0^T c_t\, dt < \infty$ almost surely for all $T \geq 0$. A given agent has the control problem

$$V(\kappa, y, 0) = \sup_{c \in \mathcal{C}} \ E\left[\int_0^T e^{-\rho t} \log(c_t)\, dt \right],$$

subject to $K_t \geq 0$ for all t in $[0, T]$, where T is a scalar time horizon.

(A) Show that the unique optimal consumption control is $\{\rho K_t/(1 - e^{-\rho(T-t)}) : t \geq 0\}$, and that the value function is of the form

$$V(\kappa, y, t) = A_1(t) \log(\kappa) + A_2(t)y + A_3(t), \quad (\kappa, y, t) \in R_+ \times R \times [0, T),$$

where A_1, A_2, and A_3 are (deterministic) real–valued functions of time. State the function A_1 and a differential equation for A_2 and A_3.

(B) Explicitly state the value function and the optimal consumption control for the infinite horizon case.

EXERCISE 23.2 (Continuous–Time Price Behavior and Portfolio Allocation) Consider a stock price process S satisfying the stochastic differential equation

$$dS_t = S_t \mu\, dt + S_t \sigma\, dB_t,$$

where μ and σ are strictly positive constants and B is a Standard Brownian Motion.

(A) State the mean, variance, and form of the probability distribution of $\log(S_T)$ for some time T in the future, conditional on the value of S_t for some current time $t < T$.

(B) Suppose there is also a riskless bond whose value is continuously compounding at the constant interest rate $r < \mu$ (as in the original Black–Scholes model). Suppose an agent invests one dollar in a portfolio at time zero, with fraction α in the stock and fraction $1 - \alpha$ in the bond, and that these fractions are maintained by continuously rebalancing the portfolio. Let W_t^α denote the market value of the portfolio at time t. State the mean, variance, and form of the probability distribution of $\log(W_T^\alpha)$, for a given time T.

(C) Suppose an agent has expected log utility for wealth at time T. Solve the problem of optimal choice of α from Part (B), assuming that α is fixed once and for all time. That is, solve the problem

$$\max_{\alpha \in R} \quad E[\log(W_T^\alpha)].$$

(D) Suppose that the fraction α_t invested in the stock at time t could be varied with time. Would the agent described in Part (C) wish to vary α_t from the solution α^* to Part (C)? State the optimal predictable policy $\{\alpha_t^* : t \in [0, T]\}$.

Notes

Modern and independently useful sources on the control of Ito Processes include Fleming and Rishel (1975), Gihman and Skorohod (1979), and Krylov (1980), the last of these being the most advanced. Theorem 23C is proved by Krylov (1980) (Theorem 3.3.6), as is Proposition 23C in a more general form (Theorem 5.3.14). These results are true as stated when the control space $\mathcal{C}$ is relaxed to include any progressively measurable A–valued process, where A is a Borel space. We have ignored this generalization merely for simplicity, as the term "progressively measurable" has not been defined here. Further regularity conditions for Bellman's Principle are given in Section 3.1 of Krylov (1980). Lions (1981, 1983) has an extension of some of Krylov's results to the infinite horizon discounted case. Chapter 16 of Elliott (1982) includes results on control with a classical Hamiltonian approach, making extensive use of Girsanov's Theorem. In this vein, one should also see the notes of Bensoussan (1983). The Notes to Section 19 should be consulted for discrete–time stochastic control. Gilbarg and Trudinger (1984) is a definitive source on elliptic partial differential equations, a class including the Feynman–Kac Formula for the Bellman Equation. Exercise 23.1 is due to Cox, Ingersoll, and Ross (1985a).

24. Consumption and Portfolio Choice with i.i.d. Returns

We are now in a position to solve the central problem facing agents in a
continuous–time stationary Markov economy: the choice of consumption
and portfolio strategies. Gains are assumed to be exponential Brownian
Motion, meaning that the rates of return on the available vector of securities
over disjoint time periods of equal length are independent with a fixed
multivariate normal distribution. For preferences, we assume utility for a
consumption process $c = \{c_t : t \geq 0\}$ to be of the form $E[\int_0^\infty e^{-\rho t} u(c_t)\, dt]$,
where u is concave and "smooth". Closed–form solutions are possible even
if u is not given a particular parametric form. The solutions are particularly
simple if u is of the hyperbolic absolute risk averse, or HARA, class. For
brevity, the ideas are sketched out in an infinite–horizon setting. The finite
horizon case is solved for HARA–class utilities in the exercises and cited
literature. Although this section does not directly address asset pricing,
the objective of Chapter IV, the theory of asset demands is clearly part of
the problem of equilibrium price determination.

A.   We adopt the Brownian model of information set out in Paragraph
21A. In particular, $B = (B^1, \dots, B^N)$ is a Standard Brownian Motion in
R^N. In a given economy there exist $K + 1$ securities with cumulative dividend processes $D = (D^0, D^1, \dots, D^K)$ and associated strictly positive Ito
price processes $S = (S^0, S^1, \dots, S^K)$ satisfying, for each $k \in \{0, 1, \dots, K\}$,

$$G_T^k \equiv S_T^k + D_T^k = S_0^k + D_0^k + \int_0^T S_t^k \mu_k\, dt + \int_0^T S_t^k \sigma_k\, dB_t, \quad T \geq 0, \quad (1)$$

for given scalars μ_k and vectors σ_k in R^N. We assume that $S_0^k > 0$ for each
security k. For example, for some scalar $\bar\mu_k$ and some $\bar\sigma_k \in R^N$, the price
process S^k could satisfy the stochastic differential equation

$$dS_t^k = S_t^k \bar\mu_k dt + S_t^k \bar\sigma_k\, dB_t, \tag{2}$$

and D^k would have the representation

$$dD_T^k = S_t^k(\mu_k - \bar\mu_k)\, dt + S_t^k(\sigma_k - \bar\sigma_k)\, dB_t. \tag{3}$$

Relation (1) defines the vector gain process $G = (G^0, G^1, \dots, G^K)$. The
space $L[G]$ is the set of security trading processes $\theta = (\theta^0, \theta^1, \dots, \theta^K)$ such
that the total gains from trade stochastic integral $\int \theta_t\, dG_t$ exists. The
scalars μ_k and $\|\sigma_k\|$ are known as the instantaneous expected rate of return
and the instantaneous standard deviation of the rate of return of the k-
th security, respectively, although these terms are notional and are purely

by analogy with the discrete–time theory. A suggestive notation for the total instantaneous return is "dG_t^k/S_t^{k}", the differential for gain divided by current price. Carrying through with this purely notational exercise, we have "$dG_t^k/S_t^k = \mu_k\,dt + \sigma_k dB_t$." Since Brownian Motion has i.i.d. increments over equal disjoint time intervals, we say this is a model of "i.i.d. returns". In fact, if we treat "dt" as 1 and "dB_t" as normally distributed in R^N with zero mean and identity covariance matrix, we recover the notional ("instantaneous") definitions of μ_k and $\|\sigma_k\|$.

The consumption set $\mathcal{C}$ for a given agent comprises those positive predictable processes $c = \{c_t : t \geq 0\}$ satisfying $E[\int_0^T c_t\,dt] < \infty$ almost surely for all $T \geq 0$. Consider the utility function

$$U(c) = E\left[\int_0^\infty e^{-\rho t} u(c_t)\,dt\right], \quad c \in \mathcal{C}, \tag{4}$$

(whenever the integral is well defined), where ρ is a strictly positive scalar and u is a given strictly concave increasing real–valued function on $(0, \infty)$. (We define $u(0)$ as $\lim_{q\downarrow 0} u(q)$, which may be finite or $-\infty$.) The agent in question has a preference relation on $\mathcal{C}$ represented by the utility functional U defined by (1). A consumption–trading strategy $(c, \theta) \in \mathcal{C} \times L[G]$ is *budget feasible* provided the associated *wealth process* X is positive, satisfying

$$X_T \equiv \theta_T \cdot S_T = x + \int_0^T \theta_t\,dG_t - \int_0^T c_t\,dt, \quad T \geq 0, \tag{5}$$

where $x \in (0, \infty)$ is the given initial wealth. A budget feasible plan (c, θ) is *optimal* provided there is no other budget feasible plan (c', θ') such that $U(c') > U(c)$. This is the agent's problem in the equilibrium setting of Section 16, adding initial wealth x to the formulation and extending the time horizon to infinity. Both of these changes can be incorporated within the equilibrium result of Section 16. We have assumed, however, that gains from trade G (expressed relative to the spot price for consumption), are of the form shown in relation (1), which is extremely special. A single agent example with this equilibrium price behavior is given in Exercise 25.7.

We can place the problem in a convenient stochastic control setting as follows. Let $\tau_{c,\theta}$ denote the stopping time $\inf\{t \geq 0 : X_t = 0\}$, the time at which the wealth process X reaches zero under a particular plan (c, θ). For $0 \leq t < \tau_{c,\theta}$, let

$$w_t^k = \frac{\theta_t^k S_t^k}{X_t}, \quad k = 0, 1, \ldots, K, \tag{6}$$

defining the vector process $w = (w^0, w^1, \ldots, w^K)$ of proportions of wealth invested in the securities up to time $\tau_{c,\theta}$. For $t \geq \tau_{c,\theta}$ and for each k, let $w_t^k = 1/(K+1)$ arbitrarily, since $X_t \equiv 0$ for $t \geq \tau_{c,\theta}$. Let $\tilde{\mu} = (\mu_0, \mu_1, \ldots, \mu_K) \in R^{K+1}$ and $\tilde{\sigma} = [\sigma_{kn}] \in M^{(K+1),N}$. Then relation (5) may be re–expressed as

$$X_T = x + \int_0^T X_t w_t^\top \tilde{\mu}\, dt + \int_0^T X_t w_t^\top \tilde{\sigma}\, dB_t - \int_0^T c_t\, dt, \quad T \geq 0, \quad (7)$$

with the constraints $\sum_{k=0}^K w^k \equiv 1$ and $\int_0^T w_t \cdot w_t\, dt < \infty$ almost surely for all $T \geq 0$. The former constraint is obvious, the latter ensures that the stochastic integral of (7) is well defined. Given $w_t, X_t > 0$, and S_t, one can reconstruct the implied portfolio θ_t uniquely, leaving a one–to–one correspondence between (c, w) strategies satisfying (7) and (c, θ) strategies satisfying (5).

B.   Things are simplified by supposing that one of the securities, say the security numbered zero, is "risk–free", or specifically that $\sigma_0 = 0$. Let $r = \mu_0$, distinguishing the *riskless rate of return*. Let $\mathcal{Z}$ denote the space of R^K–valued predictable processes $z = (z^1, \ldots, z^K)$ satisfying $\int_0^T z_t \cdot z_t\, dt < \infty$ almost surely for all $T \geq 0$. The stochastic control problem for choice of consumption and risky asset proportions is finally expressed as

$$V(x) = \sup_{(c,z) \in \mathcal{C} \times \mathcal{Z}} \left\{ V^{c,z}(x) \equiv E \left[\int_0^\infty e^{-\rho t} u(c_t)\, dt \right] \right\} \quad (8)$$

subject to

$$X_T = x + \int_0^T (X_t z_t^\top \lambda + rX_t - c_t)\, dt + \int_0^T X_t z_t^\top \sigma\, dB_t \geq 0, \quad T \geq 0, \quad (9)$$

where $\lambda \equiv (\mu_1 - r, \mu_2 - r, \ldots, \mu_K - r)$ is the vector of *instantaneous excess expected rates of return* and σ is the real $K \times N$ matrix whose k–th row is σ_k. Subject to regularity conditions, the problem is reduced to a solution $V \in C^2[(0,\infty)]$ to the Bellman Equation:

$$\sup_{(c,z) \in R_+ \times R^K} [\mathcal{D}^{c,z} V(x) - \rho V(x) + u(c)] = 0, \quad x \in (0, \infty), \quad (10)$$

where

$$\mathcal{D}^{c,z} V(x) = (xz^\top \lambda + rx - c)V'(x) + \tfrac{1}{2} x^2 z^\top \sigma \sigma^\top z V''(x).$$

HYPOTHESIS I. *The $K \times K$ matrix $\sigma\sigma^{\mathsf{T}}$ is nonsingular, and $\lambda \gg 0$.*

It should be pointed out that the problem can be solved even when $\sigma\sigma^{\mathsf{T}}$ is singular, under mild regularity conditions on μ, by choosing a basis set of securities. This is assigned as an exercise.

Provided the optimization problem defined by (10) has a solution (c^*, z^*) with $c^* > 0$, the first order necessary conditions for optimality are $V'(x) = u'(c^*)$ and

$$\lambda V'(x) + x\sigma\sigma^{\mathsf{T}} z^* V''(x) = 0. \tag{11}$$

In principle, we have the candidate solution $c^* = C(x) \equiv [u']^{-1}[V(x)]$, where $[u']^{-1}(\cdot)$ denotes the function inverting $u'(\cdot)$, and

$$z^* = Z(x) = -\frac{u'[C(x)]}{x\,u''[C(x)]C'(x)}(\sigma\sigma^{\mathsf{T}})^{-1}\lambda. \tag{12}$$

It remains to guess and verify the correct value function V.

As a preliminary step to the solution, let $\bar{\delta}$ and $\underline{\delta}$ denote the positive and negative roots, respectively, of the quadratic equation $\gamma\delta^2 - (r - \rho - \gamma)\delta - r = 0$, where

$$\gamma = \frac{1}{2}\lambda^{\mathsf{T}}(\sigma\sigma^{\mathsf{T}})^{-1}\lambda.$$

HYPOTHESIS II. *u is $C^3\big((0,\infty)\big)$, and satisfies $\int_0^\infty u'(q)^{-\underline{\delta}}\,dq < \infty$.*

Provided $\rho > r\alpha + (\gamma\alpha)/(1 - \alpha)$, Hypothesis II is satisfied by the HARA–class functions

$$u(c) = \frac{c^\alpha}{\alpha}, \quad \alpha < 1, \ \alpha \neq 0,$$

and also satisfied by letting $u(c) = \log(c)$.

PROPOSITION. *Suppose $u(0)$ is finite and Hypotheses I and II apply. If $\widehat{V}$ solves the Bellman Equation (10), then $\widehat{V} \geq V$, where V is the value function for the control problem (8)–(9).*

The proposition is demonstrated after the manner suggested in Paragraph 23A; a rigorous proof is cited in the Notes. We now construct a solution to the Bellman Equation. If such a solution $\widehat{V}$ can be shown to be the value of a particular control, then we are done, since this would imply that $\widehat{V}$ is indeed the value function V. Let h be the real–valued function on $[0,\infty)$ defined by

$$h(c) = \frac{c}{r} - \frac{1}{\gamma(\bar{\delta} - \underline{\delta})}\left[\frac{u'(c)^{\bar{\delta}}}{\bar{\delta}}\int_0^c u'(q)^{-\bar{\delta}}\,dq + \frac{u'(c)^{\underline{\delta}}}{\underline{\delta}}\int_c^\infty u'(q)^{-\underline{\delta}}\,dq\right]. \tag{13}$$

It can be verified that h is strictly increasing, so we are able to define its inverse by $C = h^{-1}$, meaning $C[h(c)] = c$ for all $c \in [0, \infty)$. From the assumed properties of u, C is $C^2[(0, \infty)]$. We take C as our candidate for the consumption policy as a function of wealth. Then the portfolio policy as a function of wealth is given by the R^K–valued function Z on $(0, \infty)$ defined by relation (12). Finally, we define $g : R_+ \to R$ by

$$g(c) = \frac{u(c)}{\rho} - \frac{1}{\gamma(\overline{\delta} - \underline{\delta})} \left[\frac{u'(c)^{1+\overline{\delta}}}{1 + \overline{\delta}} \int_0^c u'(q)^{\overline{\delta}} \, dq + \frac{u'(c)^{1+\underline{\delta}}}{1 + \underline{\delta}} \int_c^\infty u'(q)^{\underline{\delta}} \, dq \right].$$

HYPOTHESIS III. $\mid u(0) \mid < \infty$ and $u'(0) = \lim_{q \downarrow 0} u'(q) = \infty$.

An exercise in differentiation and algebra shows that $\widehat{V} = g \circ C$, the function defined by $\widehat{V}(x) = g[C(x)]$, solves the Bellman Equation (10), and that the supremum in (10) is attained at $[C(x), Z(x)]$, or

$$\mathcal{D}^{C(x), Z(x)} \widehat{V}(x) - \rho \widehat{V}(x) + u[C(x)] = 0, \quad x \in (0, \infty).$$

Thus $\widehat{V} \geq V$ by the last proposition. Let $c = \{C(X_t) : t \geq 0\}$ and $z = \{Z(X_t) : t \geq 0\}$. By an extension of the Feynman–Kac Formula to the time set $[0, \infty)$, it follows that $\widehat{V}(x) = V^{c,z}(x)$ for all $x > 0$. Thus $\widehat{V} \leq V$ from the definition of V, so $\widehat{V} = V$, applying the earlier established inequality. This implies that (c, z) is an optimal strategy. Of course, we are only claiming that all of this can be formally demonstrated. A proof of the following summary of our claims is cited in the Notes.

THEOREM. Under Hypotheses I, II, and III, $g \circ C$ is the value function V for the control problem defined by (8)–(9). An optimal strategy is given by the consumption plan $c = \{C(X_t) : t \geq 0\}$ and risky asset proportion strategy $z = \{Z(X_t) : t \geq 0\}$. The corresponding stopping time $\tau_{c,z}$ at which wealth reaches zero is infinite almost surely.

If Hypothesis III is not satisfied, the problem can still be solved in closed form. Wealth may in some cases reach zero with strictly positive probability, and $V(0)$ is defined as $(1/\rho)u(0) = \int_0^\infty e^{-\rho t} u(0) \, dt$. If $u(c) = c^\alpha / \alpha$, for $\alpha \neq 0$, for example, then Z has the constant value $(\sigma \sigma^\top)^{-1} \lambda / (1 - \alpha)$. In this case $C(x) = kx$, where

$$k = \frac{\rho - r\alpha}{1 - \alpha} - \frac{\alpha \gamma}{(1 - \alpha)^2}.$$

For other HARA–class functions, things are only slightly more complicated. There is also a simple solution without a riskless security. One can add endowments to the formulation as well as a random life span. These extensions are cited in the Notes.

EXERCISES

EXERCISE 24.1 Consider the deterministic control problem:

$$V(x, T) = \sup_{c \in C} \int_0^T e^{-\rho t} u(c_t)\, dt$$

subject to $\int_0^T c_t\, dt \leq x$, where C denotes the set of positive real–valued integrable functions on $[0, T]$, ρ is a positive scalar discount factor, $x \in (0, \infty)$ is initial scalar wealth, and u is the HARA–class function $u(q) = q^\alpha$ for some $\alpha \in (0, 1)$.

(A) Apply Bellman's Principle of Optimality to solve this problem explicitly. *Hint:* $V(x, t)$ is a HARA–class function of x.

(B) Report the solution for $\rho = 0$ by a direct application of Jensen's Inequality.

(C) Report the solution with $\rho > 0$ for the infinite horizon case: $T = \infty$.

EXERCISE 24.2 Solve the deterministic control problem

$$V(x) = \sup_{c \in C} \sum_{t=0}^{\infty} e^{-\rho t} u(c_t)$$

subject to $X_0 = x > 0$, $X_{t+1} = (X_t - c_t)(1 + r) \geq 0$, $t = 0, 1, \ldots$, where C denotes the space of positive sequences, ρ and r are positive scalars, and $u(q) = q^\alpha$ for $\alpha \in (0, 1)$. This is a version of the Robinson Crusoe problem of Section 19.

EXERCISE 24.3 Let C denote the set of deterministic consumption processes such that any c in C is positive real–valued and integrable (that is, $\int_0^\tau c_t\, dt < \infty$ for all $\tau \geq 0$). An agent has preferences over C represented by the utility functional

$$U(c) = \int_0^\infty e^{-\rho t} u(c_t)\, dt,$$

where $u(q) = q^\alpha$ for $\alpha \in (0, 1)$. The agent holds bonds paying interest continuously compounding at the rate $r \geq 0$ and money paying no interest.

Both securities are denominated in consumption terms. Only money is exchangeable for consumption; this is the so–called *Clower constraint*. The money stock process $m = \{m_t : t \geq 0\}$ thus evolves according to

$$m_t = m_0 + D_t - \int_0^t c_s \, ds \geq 0, \quad t \geq 0, \quad m_0 = x_m,$$

where D_t denotes the cumulative withdrawals from bonds to money up until time t and $x_m \geq 0$ denotes initial money stock. We assume withdrawals occur at fixed intervals of length $T > 0$, so that

$$m_{kT} = x_m + \sum_{i=0}^{k} d_i - \int_0^{kT} c_s \, ds \geq 0, \quad k = 0, 1, \ldots,$$

where d_i denotes withdrawals (or minus deposits) at the beginning of the i–th period of length T. The wealth in bonds at the beginning of period i is then

$$b_i = (b_{i-1} - d_{i-1})e^{rT}, \quad i = 1, 2, \ldots, \quad b_0 = x_b,$$

where x_b denotes the initial endowment of bonds. Give restrictions on α, ρ, and r under which there exists an optimal policy of withdrawals and consumption. Show that for $r > 0$, optimality implies that

$$\int_{(k-1)T}^{kT} c_t \, dt = d_{k-1} \geq 0, \quad k = 1, 2, 3, \ldots.$$

Show that the value function V for the control problem is of the form $V_T(x)$, where $x = x_m + x_b$ and $V_T(x)$ is a HARA–class function of x for all $T > 0$. Solve the problem explicitly for a given $T > 0$. Pay careful attention to withdrawals at time zero; they are of a special form. *Hint:* Use Exercise 24.1 as an intermediate step.

EXERCISE 24.4 In the context of Exercise 24.3, show that $V_T(x)$ is monotonically decreasing in T for $r > 0$, so that the "optimal" length of times between visits to the bank is zero. Now consider transactions costs as follows. One pays fixed plus proportional costs for all bond–to–money or money–to–bond transfers, or transaction costs $A \mid d_k \mid + F$ at the beginning of period k, for positive scalars A and F. One also pays a "small" fraction $\epsilon \geq 0$ of total value invested in bonds at each period, a "portfolio management fee". Thus, in one possible formulation, the values invested in money and bonds evolve according to

$$m_{kT} = m_0 + \sum_{i=0}^{k} (d_i - A \mid d_i \mid -F) - \int_0^{kT} c_s \, ds \geq 0, \quad k = 0, 1, \ldots,$$

where $m_0 = x_m$, and

$$b_k = (b_{k-1} - d_{k-1})(1 - \epsilon)e^{rT}, \quad k = 1, 2, \ldots, \quad b_0 = x_b.$$

Solve the problem of Exercise 24.3 again, assuming $x_m = 0, x_b > 0$, and $r > 0$. *Hint:* Look for withdrawal policies of the form $d_i = \lambda b_i + \gamma$, for fixed scalars λ and γ. Obtain an explicit expression for $V_T(x)$ and show that, in general, a non–zero optimal period length T exists for certain choices of the parameters.

EXERCISE 24.5 In the context of Exercise 24.4, suppose that the agent is able to choose the period T_i between the i-th and $(i+1)$-th visits to the bank rather than choosing fixed periods $T_i = T$, $i = 0, 1, \ldots$. Suppose the fixed transactions cost F is not zero and that an optimal solution exists.

(A)   Show that the optimal periods between visits to the bank are not, in general, constant. *Hint:* Use a proof by contradiction.

(B)   For $F = 0$, solve the problem and show that the optimal intervals between withdrawals are a constant. State an equation for this constant.

EXERCISE 24.6 Extend the analysis of Paragraph 19J to more than one security as follows. Let $r > 1$ denote the scalar–valued rate–of–return on a riskless security, and let $\Gamma = (\Gamma^1, \ldots, \Gamma^N)$ denote the vector of stationary rates of return on N risky assets. The vector rate–of–return process $\gamma = \{\gamma_0, \gamma_1, \gamma_2, \ldots\}$ is i.i.d. and for each time t, $\gamma_t = (\gamma_t^1, \ldots, \gamma_t^N)$ and $(\Gamma^1, \ldots, \Gamma^N)$ are equivalent in distribution. The agent wishes to maximize $E\left[\sum_{t=0}^{\infty} \rho^t u(c_t)\right]$, where ρ is a strictly positive scalar discount factor, and $u(q) = q^\alpha$ for $\alpha \in (0, 1)$. Assume the distribution of Γ is such that there exists a unique solution $z^* \in R^N$ to the one period portfolio problem:

$$\max_{z \in R^N} \quad E[u(\gamma(z))],$$

where

$$\gamma(z) = r + \sum_{n=1}^{N} (\Gamma_n - r)z_n,$$

such that $\gamma(z^*) \geq 0$ a.s. and $\rho E[\gamma(z^*)^\alpha] < 1$. Solve the multi–period problem explicitly from this point.

EXERCISE 24.7 Return to the setting of the previous exercise, substituting the utility function $u(q) = -e^{-\alpha q}$. Assume Γ has a multivariate log–normal distribution with parameters (μ, A), meaning that the R^N–valued random variable $\big(\log(\Gamma^1), \ldots, \log(\Gamma^N)\big)$ has a joint normal distribution with mean vector $\mu \in R^N$ and (nonsingular) covariance matrix A. Making regularity assumptions only on the parameters ρ, r, μ, A, and α, solve the problem explicitly.

EXERCISE 24.8 Suppose the continuous–time market setting of Paragraph A is characterized by a dividend process $D = (D^0, \ldots, D^K)$ and price process $S = (S^0, \ldots, S^K)$ satisfying (2) and (3).

(A) Determine the joint distribution of S_T for a given time $T > 0$. *Hint:* Write S_T as a function of B_T and T.

(B) Determine the distribution of X_T^k, the wealth held in security k at time T if one unit of wealth is invested in security k at time zero and all dividends are re–invested continually in security k.

(C) Determine the joint distribution of $X_T = (X_T^0, \ldots, X_T^K)$.

(D) Let $w \in R^{K+1}$, satisfying $\sum_{k=0}^K w_k = 1$, represent the fractions of a unit of wealth invested at time zero in each of the $K + 1$ securities. The securities are traded and the dividends are re–invested, without new additions or withdrawals from the portfolio, in such a manner that the fraction of wealth held in security k is always w_k. Write the resulting total wealth W_T held in the portfolio at time T as a function of B_T and determine its distribution.

EXERCISE 24.9 Extend the analysis in Exercise 24.3 to an uncertain setting as follows. There is a single risky security with price process

$$S_t = 1 + \int_0^t S_\tau \mu \, d\tau + \int_0^t S_\tau \sigma \, dB_\tau, \quad t \geq 0,$$

for given scalars μ and σ, where B is a Standard Brownian Motion. The corresponding cumulative dividend process D satisfies

$$D_t = \int_0^t S_\tau \nu \, d\tau + \int_0^t S_\tau \xi \, dB_\tau, \quad t \geq 0,$$

for scalars ν and ξ. There is also a riskless bond paying interest continuously at the fixed scalar rate $r > 0$. Consumption and investment decisions are made at fixed intervals of length $T > 0$. During the interval, all dividends are re–invested continually and there are no transactions between money and securities. Consumption decisions for the time interval

$[kT, (k+1)T)$ are made at time kT on the basis of current information. In other words, a consumption–investment strategy must be adapted to the filtration $G = \{\mathcal{G}_t : t \in [0, \infty)\}$, where $\mathcal{G}_t = \mathcal{F}_{kT}$ for $t \in [kT, (k+1)T)$ and for $k = 0, 1, 2, \ldots$, and where $F = \{\mathcal{F}_t : t \in [0, \infty)\}$ is the standard filtration of B. A superficial explanation of this formulation might be that an agent learns about the changes in value of the risky asset only when he or she visits the "bank" for withdrawals. A more sophisticated explanation is that information is received via the filtration F, but that each time the information is processed there are lump sum costs for reaching a decision. Continuous–time control would then involve infinite informational costs. The agent thus chooses to solve the problem at intervals of length T, and act as though he or she receives information via G. The consumption space $\mathcal{C}$ comprises those positive G–adapted consumption processes c satisfying $E\left[\int_0^\tau c_t^2\, dt\right] < \infty$ almost surely for all $\tau > 0$. Let

$$U(c) = E\left(\int_0^\infty e^{-\rho t} u(c_t)\, dt\right),$$

where ρ is a strictly positive scalar and $u(q) = q^\alpha$ for $\alpha \in (0,1)$. The problem is then

$$V(x) = \sup_{c,d} \; U(c)$$

subject to

$$X_{k+1} = (X_k - d_k)\gamma_{k+1}, \quad X_0 = x > 0,$$

$$\int_{kT}^{(k+1)T} c_t\, dt = d_k, \quad d_k \le X_k, \; k = 0, 1, 2, \ldots,$$

where x is initial scalar wealth, X_k is wealth at time kT, d_k is withdrawals from investment securities (stock and bond) to money at time kT, and γ_{k+1} is the value at time $(k+1)T$ of a unit of wealth invested in stocks and bonds in the chosen proportions at time kT, with interim stock dividends continually re–invested in stocks and interim bond interest continually re–invested in bonds. (We are ignoring withdrawals of money for investment purposes since bonds clearly dominate money as an investment vehicle.)

(A) Give explicit solutions for optimal d and c, and a closed form expression for $V(x)$ involving only the given scalar parameters.

(B) Show that V is decreasing in T.

EXERCISE 24.10 In the framework of Exercise 24.9, we will now allow the agent to choose the length of time T_k between the k–th and $(k+1)$–th withdrawals on the basis of information available at time $\tau_k = \sum_{i=0}^{k} T_i$. In other words, the filtration $H = \{\mathcal{H}_t : t \in [0, \infty)\}$ is also controlled, and $\mathcal{H}_t = \mathcal{F}_{\tau_k}$ for $t \in [\tau_k, \tau_{k+1})$. There are transactions costs on total money withdrawals of the form $\gamma \mid d_k \mid +\beta$, and a fraction $\epsilon \geq 0$ of total invested wealth is charged as a management fee at the beginning of each period, as in Exercise 24.4.

(A)   Suppose the fixed transaction cost β is not zero. Prove that if an optimal policy $\{(T_k, d_k), c, k = 0, 1, \ldots, \}$ of inter–withdrawal times T_k, withdrawals d_k, and a consumption process c exists, then T_k depends non-trivially on X_k, the current level of wealth. (The controls must be H–adapted.)

(B)   If an optimal policy exists and $\beta = 0$, show that the optimal periods $\{T_k\}$ between withdrawals are optimally a fixed scalar T independent of wealth. *Hint:* Write out the Bellman Equations for d_0 and T_0 completely. For the latter, apply Ito's Lemma.

(C)   In the case $\alpha = \frac{1}{2}$, derive an equation for the fixed fraction λ of risky wealth X_k withdrawn at time τ_k. Write an expression for the constant inter–withdrawal period T.

EXERCISE 24.11   (Extensions of The Basic Control Problem)

(A)   Solve the continuous–time portfolio–consumption problem presented in Paragraphs 24A and 24B under the assumptions:
(a) $u(q) = q^\alpha$ for $\alpha \in (0, 1)$,
(b) $\sigma\sigma^\top$ is nonsingular,
(c) $\lambda \gg 0$, and
(d) $\rho > r\alpha + \gamma\alpha/(1 - \alpha)$, where γ is as stated before relation (11).

That is, state and prove the closed form solution for the value function V, the optimal consumption control, c, and the optimal portfolio control z. Make additional regularity assumptions on the parameters as needed. *Hint:* The solution is perfectly analogous to the discrete–time case. Show that the stated controls are the unique optimal controls. *Hint:* One should prove that a solution $\widehat{V}$ to the Bellman equation satisfies $E[e^{-\rho t}\widehat{V}(X_t)] \to 0$ as $t \to \infty$ for any feasible policy, in order to prove optimality.

(B)   Solve the same problem without a riskless security, making regularity assumptions as found necessary.

(C)   Solve the same problem with a finite time horizon $[0, T]$.

(D)   Solve Part (A), even for singular $\sigma\sigma^\top$, first stating an appropriate regularity condition on μ. *Hint:* There is no uniqueness result for optimal portfolio control.

(E)   Solve Parts (A), (B), and (C), for the case $u(q) = \log(q)$. *Hint:* With the logarithmic reward, one must be especially careful in the infinite horizon case to show that the solution to the Bellman Equation is in fact the value function for the problem.

EXERCISE 24.12   (Futures Hedging in Continuous Time)   Let B denote a Standard Brownian Motion in R^N that is a martingale with respect to a given agent's filtered probability space. The agent has the objective of maximizing $E[u(W_T)]$, where W_T denotes wealth at some future time T and $u : R \to R$ is increasing and strictly concave. The wealth W_T is the sum of a fixed portfolio of assets and the terminal value of the margin account of a futures trading strategy, as elaborated below. This problem, to be spelled out below, is one of characterizing optimal futures hedging. The first component of wealth is the spot market value of a fixed portfolio $p \in R^M$ of M different assets whose market values $S^1,\ldots,S^M$ vary through time according to the respective stochastic differential equations

$$dS_t^m = \mu_m(t)\,dt + \sigma_m(t)\,dB_t; \quad t \geq 0; \quad S_0^m = 1,$$

where, for each m, $\mu_m : [0,\infty) \to R$ and $\sigma_m : [0,\infty) \to R^N$ are continuous functions. There are futures contracts for K assets with delivery at some date $\tau > T$, having price processes satisfying the stochastic differential equations:

$$dF_t^k = m_k(t)\,dt + v_k(t)\,dB_t; \quad t \geq 0, \quad 1 \leq k \leq K,$$

where m_k and v_k have the same properties as μ_m and σ_m. For simplicity, assume that there is a constant continuously compounding interest rate r for borrowing or lending. As usual, one takes a futures position by merely committing oneself to mark a margin account to market. Conceptually, that is, if one holds a long (positive) position of ten futures contracts on a particular asset and the price of the futures contract goes up by a dollar, then one forfeits ten dollars to the short side of the contract out of one's margin account. The margin account earns interest at the riskless rate (or, if the margin account balance is negative, one loses interest at the riskless rate). We ignore margin calls or borrowing limits. The second component of the agent's wealth at time T is of course the value of the margin account at that time.

(A)   Carefully formulate the stochastic process X for the dollar value of the margin account of the agent, depending of course on the K–dimensional process θ describing the agent's futures position. *Hint:* Show that $dX_t = r X_t\, dt + \theta_t\, dF_t$.

(B)   Set up the agent's dynamic hedging problem for choice of futures position θ in the framework of continuous–time stochastic control. State the Bellman equation and first order conditions. Derive an explicit expression for θ_t involving the (unknown) value function. Make regularity assumptions such as differentiability and non–singularity. *Hint:* Let $W_t = p \cdot S_t + X_t$, $t \in [0, T]$, define the state process.

(C)   Solve for the optimal policy θ_t in the case $m_t \equiv 0$; no expected returns to futures trading.

(D)   Solve the problem explicitly for the case $u(w) = -e^{-\gamma w}$ where $\gamma > 0$ is a scalar risk aversion coefficient.

EXERCISE 24.13   A risky security pays no dividends and has a price process S satisfying the stochastic differential equation

$$dS_t = \mu S_t\, dt + \sigma S_t\, dB_t; \qquad S_0 > 0,$$

where μ and σ are strictly positive scalars. A riskless security has value one at all times and pays dividends at the constant rate $r \in [0, \mu)$. Using the stochastic control methodology, solve the following series of problems.

(A)   For some initial level of wealth w, minimize the expected time to reach a given level of wealth $W > w$, without intermediate consumption. The decision, of course, is the fraction of current wealth, say z_t, to invest in the risky asset at each time t. *Hint:* z_t is a constant.

(B)   The *continuously compounded rate of return on investment* between any two times t and T is the random variable $\mathcal{R}(t, T)$ defined by

$$W(t) \exp[\mathcal{R}(t, T)(T - t)] = W(T),$$

where $W(\tau)$ is the market value of the portfolio held at any time τ. Solve the problem of maximizing the expected continuously compounded return, $E[\mathcal{R}(0, T)]$, without intermediate consumption.

(C)   Maximize $E[\log[W(T)]]$, without intermediate consumption.

(D)   Maximize $E[\int_0^\infty e^{-\rho t} \log(c_t)\, dt]$, where c_t is the rate at which consumption is depleting wealth at time t. Consumption must be positive (of course), and is constrained to leave current wealth positive at all times. *Hint:* The feedback control for the optimal fraction z_t of wealth invested in the risky asset is the same in each case!

EXERCISE 24.14 Show that the function $g \circ C$ defined in Paragraph B indeed solves the Bellman Equation for this control problem.

EXERCISE 24.15 This exercise has the objective of developing intuition for the relationship between different "infinitesimal random variables", in particular, the rates of return of securities, modeled here by $\mathcal{R}$, and increments in a state–variable process, modeled by X. In a static market setting, suppose $B = (B^1, \ldots, B^N)$ is a vector of independent joint standard normal random variables on a given probability space. Let $X = \nu + \eta B$, where η is a $K \times N$ matrix, defining X as a K–dimensional joint normal random variable with mean $\nu \in R^K$. Let $\mathcal{R} = \mu + \sigma B$, where σ is an $M \times N$ real matrix, similarly defining an M–dimensional joint normal random variable with mean $\mu \in R^M$.

(A) Find the covariance matrix of the $(M \mid K)$ dimensional random variable $(\mathcal{R}, X)$.

(B) Assume $\sigma\sigma^\top$ is non–singular. "Regress" X on $\mathcal{R}$. That is, obtain coefficients $\alpha \in R^K$ and β, a $K \times M$ matrix, such that $X - \alpha - \beta\mathcal{R}$ has a covariance matrix with minimum trace subject to $E(X) = E(\alpha + \beta\mathcal{R})$. *Hint:* Use Part (A) of the question and apply the usual first order conditions for optimality, noting that the partial derivative of the trace of the product $ADA^\top$ of matrices with respect to A is the matrix $D^\top A^\top + DA^\top$, where D is $M \times M$ and A is $K \times M$.

(C) Show that $E(X \mid \mathcal{R}) = \alpha + \beta\mathcal{R}$.

(D) Suppose $\mathcal{R}$ denotes the vector of rates of return on M securities. Obtain an expression for the variance of the rate of return on a portfolio of risky securities $z \in R^M$, where $1 - z_1 - z_2 - \cdots - z_M$ is invested at a riskless rate of return given by the scalar r.

(E) Suppose $u(W) = -e^{-\gamma W}, W \in R$, for a scalar $\gamma > 0$. Solve the portfolio problem:

$$\max_{z \in R^M} \quad E\big[u\big(W_0[z^\top \mathcal{R} + (1 - z_1 - z_2 - \cdots - z_M)r]\big)\big],$$

where W_0 is a scalar representing initial wealth.

EXERCISE 24.16 In some cases it is convenient for technical reasons to have the dimension N of the Brownian Motion B in relation (9) equal to the dimension K of the risky asset price process. When $K \leq N$ and σ is full rank, show this to be the case without loss of generality for problems such as (8)–(9), as follows. Define the square root $A^{1/2}$ of a square matrix A, whenever possible, to be the square matrix of same dimensions defined by $A^{1/2}A^{1/2} = A$. Show that it suffices that A is symmetric positive definite, and that the inverse of $A^{1/2}$, denoted $A^{-1/2}$, is also well–defined. Show that $\widehat{B}_t = (\sigma\sigma^\top)^{-1/2}\sigma B_t$ makes for a well defined Standard Brownian Motion $\widehat{B}$ in R^K, not R^N. Let $\widehat{\sigma} = (\sigma\sigma^\top)^{1/2}$. Then show that the problem (8)–(9) is identical once $\widehat{B}$ and $\widehat{\sigma}$ replace B and σ, respectively. (An easy extension of this idea works also, under mild conditions, when σ is stochastic.)

EXERCISE 24.17 (Portfolio Insurance)   For this exercise, we assume riskless borrowing at the continuously compounding interest rate r, no transactions costs, and no arbitrage possibilities. Let S_t denote the market value of a given portfolio of securities at time t. *Portfolio insurance* is the adoption of a security trading strategy at time t that produces, at a given date T, the payoff of the stock portfolio S_T, plus the payoff P_T of a European put option on the portfolio with expiry date T (and some exercise price K), net of the amount due on a riskless loan that finances the initial cost P_t of the put option. That is, portfolio insurance requires an initial payment of S_t at time t, and produces the payoff $W_T = S_T + P_T - e^{r(T-t)}P_t$ at time T. (Since a put option conveys the right, but not the obligation, to sell the underlying asset at the exercise price K, we know that $P_T = (K - S_T)^+$.)   The key element of this exercise is a characterization of preferences consistent with the optimality of portfolio insurance, beginning in Part (D). As such, the exercise fits into the topic of Section 24. The methods of Section 22, however, are more appropriate for this problem. Moreover, the pricing theory of Exercise 22.17 for continuously resettled contracts is also extended here.

(A) Suppose S satisfies the stochastic differential equation

$$dS_t = \widehat{\mu}(S_t,t)\,dt + \widehat{\sigma}(S_t,t)\,dB_t,$$

for suitable $\widehat{\mu}$, $\widehat{\sigma}$, and B. Suppose there is a futures contract that delivers the portfolio at a date $\tau \geq T$. The futures price at date t is denoted F_t. Suppose that F is also an Ito process. Futures contracts are resettled frequently. Here, we assume (as in Exercise 22.17) that the futures contract resettles continually, with profits or losses invested or borrowed risklessly in a margin account. If θ denotes a predictable futures position strategy, the current value X_t of the corresponding margin account therefore satisfies the stochastic differential equation

$$dX_t = rX_t\,dt + \theta_t\,dF_t,$$

assuming that θ is appropriately integrable with respect to F. Assume conditions under which the cost–of–carry formula applies to provide an arbitrage–free characterization of the futures price process, as worked out in Exercise 22.17. State restrictions on $\hat{\mu}$ and $\hat{\sigma}$ under which there exists a futures strategy θ^I that, in combination with the portfolio commitment, produces the portfolio insurance payoff W_T.

(B)   Assuming that $\hat{\mu}(S_t, t) = \mu S_t$ and $\hat{\sigma}(S_t, t) = \sigma S_t$ for given constants μ and σ, explicitly state the futures strategy θ^I for portfolio insurance.

(C)   Suppose the portfolio of stocks pays dividends at the rate αS_t at any time t, where $\alpha > 0$ is a constant. Under the assumptions of Part (B), state a futures strategy and a strategy for borrowing or lending risklessly that produces the portfolio insurance payoff previously described.

(D)   Some people believe that there is a natural clientele for portfolio insurance. In this part, we examine the class of preferences consistent with the optimality of portfolio insurance. Consider the problem, at time zero,

$$\max_{\theta \in \Theta} E[u(S_T + X_T^\theta)], \tag{14}$$

where Θ is the space of square–integrable predictable futures strategies, X^θ is the corresponding margin account process, and $u : R_+ \to R$ is concave and differentiable. Under the assumptions of part (B), state an ordinary differential equation for the function u restricted to the interval $(K - e^{rT} P_0, \infty)$, as a necessary condition for optimality of the portfolio insurance strategy θ^I. (As usual, u is unique up to an affine transformation.) *Hint:* This problem may be difficult unless one reduces the problem to the general form:

$$\max_x \int u[x(z)] f(z) \, dz \quad \text{subject to} \quad e^{-rT} \int x(z) g(z) \, dz \le S_0, \tag{15}$$

where z parameterizes possible values of $\log(S_T)$ and f and g are different density functions for this random variable. Since the optimal strategy θ^I generates the portfolio insurance payoff W_T, which is a "nice" function of the terminal price S_T, we know that θ^I is also optimal among the smaller class of futures strategies that payoff nice functions of S_T. But this is the same as optimizing over any (well–behaved) function $x(\cdot)$ of the log of the terminal asset price, subject to some budget constraint that can be written as in (15). Why? The first order conditions for (15), evaluated at the solution to the optimization problem (that is, the portfolio insurance payoff), generate the desired differential equation. For a complete response, one should ensure that pointwise "differentiation under the integral sign" leads to the correct infinite–dimensional first order conditions for (15), as described by the Saddle Point Theorem of Section 8. For the purposes of this exercise, however, this characterization of optimality may be assumed.

(E)   Under the assumptions of part (D), state the Arrow–Pratt measure of absolute risk aversion, $-u''(q)/u'(q)$, of the function u evaluated at any point $q > K - e^{rT}P_0$. Is u risk averse in this range?

(F)   State a class of preference orders over distributions of wealth at date T consistent with the optimality of portfolio insurance in this settting. (This Part is somewhat challenging).

(G)   A *futures option* is an option that pays off $(K - F_T)^+$ (in the case of a put) at the expiry date T, for a given exercise price K. Under the assumptions of Part (B), state a formula for this particular put option price. Please note that the futures delivery date τ is not necessarily the date T.

(H)   In actuality, the futures option described in Part (G) does not pay off $(K - F_T)^+$ at date T, but rather is resettled in the manner of a futures contract. That is, if φ_t denotes the futures option price at time t, there is a margin account in which a futures option holding strategy θ is marked to market by crediting the corresponding margin account X according to the stochastic differential equation:

$$dX_t = rX_t \, dt + \theta_t \, d\varphi_t.$$

Derive a futures option pricing formula in a general form and, under the parametric assumptions of Part (B), in a closed form.

Notes

The use of Brownian Motion to model the behavior of security prices dates back to Bachelier (1900). In fact, this may be the first work on a mathematical model of Brownian Motion! Hotelling (1931) formulated optimal consumption policies in a deterministic dynamic setting. Early results for the stochastic control of investment are due to Phelps (1962). Mirrlees (1974), in a paper appearing originally in 1965, may have been the first to apply the Ito calculus to this problem. Levhari and Srinivasan (1969) has a solution for a discrete–time case. Multiple risky assets were introduced by Samuelson (1969) in discrete–time, and Merton (1969) in continuous–time. Merton (1971, 1973b) extended his earlier results. Hakansson (1970) extends the discrete–time results.

The solutions in Paragraph *B* for a general utility function are due to Karatzas, Lehoczky, Sethi, and Shreve (1986). This paper, Richard (1975), and Merton (1971) include the extensions mentioned at the end of Paragraph B. See Sethi and Taksar (1986) for corrections to some of Merton's results. See also Lehoczky, Sethi, and Shreve (1983). Aase (1984) reports other problem solutions. For an advanced treatment with a non–stationary HARA–class utility, see Jacka (1984). Karatzas (1987) surveys the application of stochastic control to financial decisions.

For recent work on optimal portfolio and consumption choice using an abstract martingale approach, an alternative to traditional Markov stochastic control, see Cox (1983), Pliska (1982), Huang (1984), Back (1986), Back and Pliska (1986a, 1986b), Pagès (1987), Karatzas, Lehoczky, and Shreve (1986), Lehoczky, Sethi, and Shreve (1985), and Cox and Huang (1985, 1986). Richardson (1987) applies this approach in a mean–variance preference setting. Exercise 24.17, on the optimality of portfolio insurance, may also be viewed as an application of this martingale approach

Foldes (1979) studies the continuous–time consumption–investment problem without using the stochastic integral. This follows his discrete–time paper, Foldes (1978). For other discrete–time approaches, see Boyd (1985) and several articles in the book edited by Los and Los (1974).

Some of the exercises are original. Proofs of some of the exercises involving transactions costs may be found in Duffie and Sun (1986). For further results involving transactions costs, see Constantinides (1986) and, especially, Davis and Norman (1987). The exercise on dynamic hedging with futures is from Duffie and Jackson (1986a). The exercise involving equivalent forms of "log–maximal" behavior is from notes prepared by John Cox. The books by Malliaris (1982) and Ingersoll (1987) include additional material on the topics of this section.

25. Continuous–Time Equilibrium Asset Pricing

This section characterizes the equilibrium behavior of interest rates and expected rates of returns on securities in a simple continuous–time economy. The model's primitives comprise agents' preferences, endowments, and exogenously specified securities. Everything is based on the demonstration of equilibria with *representative agent pricing*, by which we mean that the equilibrium price functional is the gradient of the utility functional of a (fictitious) single agent, evaluated at the aggregate level of consumption. Under technical regularity conditions, this is equivalent to the efficiency of the equilibrium consumption allocation. With the discrete–time model of Section 20, for example, the consumption allocation is automatically efficient since there is but a single agent. Ignoring technicalities momentarily, the agent's utility functional in Section 20 is of the form $U(c) = E[\sum_{t=1}^{\infty} \rho^t u(c_t)]$, where u is differentiable, for any consumption process $c = \{c_1, c_2, \ldots\}$. The corresponding gradient at the aggregate consumption process $e = \{e_1, e_2, \ldots\}$ is the linear functional $\nabla U(e)$ assigning the market value

$$\nabla U(e) \cdot \delta = E\left[\sum_{t=1}^{\infty} \rho^t u'(e_t) \delta_t\right]$$

to any consumption dividend process $\delta = \{\delta_1, \delta_2, \ldots\}$. Taking current (time t) consumption as the numeraire, this tells us that the ex dividend price S_t of an asset claiming the dividend process δ has the representation

$$S_t = \frac{1}{u'(e_t)} E\left[\sum_{\tau=t+1}^{\infty} \rho^{\tau-t} u'(e_\tau) \delta_\tau \;\middle|\; \mathcal{F}_t\right], \tag{1}$$

where $\mathcal{F}_t$ denotes the tribe of events corresponding to information at time t. Since we do not restrict ourselves to a single agent model in this section, the efficiency of an equilibrium allocation requires the effect of complete markets. For this, we will assume that the given securities are sufficient for *dynamic spanning*, by which we mean that any possible new security is redundant given the presently available securities. To this end, with uncertainty stemming from a K–dimensional Brownian Motion, a minimum of $K + 1$ securities are needed, given unrestricted continual trading. (Not any $K + 1$ securities, however, will suffice.) Transactions costs are not yet easily handled in this theory, and would lead to different conclusions. The resulting equilibrium asset pricing model, in parallel with (1), is of the form

$$S_t = \frac{1}{u'(e_t)} E\left[\int_t^T e^{-\rho(\tau-t)} u'(e_\tau) \delta_\tau \, d\tau \;\middle|\; \mathcal{F}_t\right], \tag{2}$$

with the notation left for now to the insights of the reader. From (2), it is short work to obtain the behavior of interest rates as well as the *Consumption–Based Capital Asset Pricing Model*, the two main objectives of this section.

A. We work on a finite time interval $[0, T]$, a probability space $(\Omega, \mathcal{F}, P)$ on which is defined a Standard Brownian Motion B in R^N, and the standard filtration $F = \{\mathcal{F}_t : t \in [0, T]\}$ of B. All probabilistic statements are made, dropping "almost surely", relative to the filtered probability space

$(\Omega, \mathcal{F}, F, P)$, our basic model for uncertainty. The choice space of *consumption processes* is the vector space L including any predictable process c such that $E \left(\int_0^T c_t^2 \, dt \right) < \infty$. Informally, if $c \in L$ is a consumption process, then at any time t, the current consumption rate c_t is based only on information available up to that time. Similarly, a spot consumption price process is an element p of L, with p_t denoting the unit price of consumption of the single commodity at a given time t. This specializes the general model of Section 16 in two significant ways: First, there is only a single consumption commodity; second, uncertainty stems from Brownian Motion, rather than an abstract filtration.

Each of the I agents in this (pure exchange) economy is represented by a pair (U^i, e^i), where U^i is a utility function on the (usual) positive cone L_+ of consumption processes and $e^i \in L_+$ is an *endowment process*, for $i \in \{1, \ldots, I\}$. The remaining primitives are financial securities in zero net supply paying dividends in units of account. We initially designate one of these as a numeraire, and for simplicity take this numeraire to be a pure discount bond redeemable at the terminal date T for one unit of account. The *cumulative dividends* of this numeraire are thus described by the process D^0 defined by $D_t^0 = 0$, $t < T$, and $D_T^0 = 1$. (We eventually normalize to "real" prices, that is, convert to current consumption as the current numeraire.) The remaining securities, say K in number, are represented by cumulative dividend processes $D^1, \ldots, D^K$, where, for each security k, D^k is an adapted process with continuous sample paths, and D_t^k has finite variance for all t. (The restriction to continuous sample paths is relaxed in a paper cited in the Notes.) The entire *continuous–time economy* is thus described by a collection

$$\mathcal{A} = \big((\Omega, \mathcal{F}, F, P), (U^i, e^i), D \big), \quad i \in \{1, \ldots, I\},$$

where $D = (D^0, \ldots, D^K)$ is the $(K+1)$–dimensional cumulative dividend process.

B. Agents take as given a spot consumption price process $p \in L$ and a $(K+1)$–dimensional adapted security price process $S = (S^0, \ldots, S^K)$ such that the *gain process* $G = (S + D)$ is an Ito process, which therefore has a stochastic differential representation

$$dG_t = \nu_t \, dt + \sigma_t \, dB_t,$$

where ν is an $(K+1)$–dimensional predictable process and σ is an $(K+1) \times N$–matrix valued predictable process. This allows one to define cumulative gains from trade for any predictable portfolio process $\theta = (\theta^0, \ldots, \theta^K)$

satisfying technical regularity conditions. For regularity, we demand that
a portfolio process θ is *square–integrable*, meaning that

$$E \left(\int_0^T \theta_t^\top \sigma_t \sigma_t^\top \theta_t \, dt \right) < \infty,$$

and that $\int_0^T | \theta_t \cdot \nu_t | \, dt$ is finite almost surely. These regularity condi-
tions defining a *portfolio process* imply that the gain–from–trade integral
$\int \theta_t \, dG_t = \sum_{k=0}^K \int \theta_t^k \, dG_t^k$ is well–defined, and further (by the definition
of stochastic integration), that $\int \theta_t \, dG_t$ is a martingale whenever G is a
martingale. Let Θ denote the vector space of all portfolio processes.

A *budget–feasible plan* for agent i is a pair $(c, \theta) \in L_+ \times \Theta$ such that,
for any time t,

$$\theta_t \cdot S_t = \int_0^t \theta_s \, dG_s + \int_0^t p_s \cdot (e_s^i - c_s) \, ds, \tag{3}$$

and such that $\theta_T \cdot S_T = 0$. Relation (3) is merely the accounting restriction
that current portfolio wealth must be generated only from trading gains and
net consumption sales. The restriction $\theta_T \cdot S_T = 0$ is the essential budget
constraint. A budget feasible plan (c, θ) for agent i is *optimal* for agent
i if there is no budget feasible plan (c', θ') such that $U^i(c') > U^i(c)$. An
equilibrium for an economy $\mathcal{A}$ is a collection $((S, p), (c^1, \theta^1), \dots, (c^I, \theta^I))$
such that, given the security price process S and the consumption spot
price process p, for each agent i the plan (c^i, θ^i) is optimal, and such that
markets clear: $\sum_i c^i - e^i = 0$ and $\sum_i \theta^i = 0$. Although Section 16 shows
conditions on an economy sufficient for the existence of such an equilibrium,
these conditions are not sufficient for the asset pricing models of interest
here.

C. We lay out the following regularity conditions on an economy $\mathcal{A}$.

(a) *For each agent i, U^i is represented via a smooth function $u_i : R_+ \times [0, T] \to R$ as*

$$U^i(c) = E \left[\int_0^T u_i(c_t, t) \, dt \right],$$

*where, for each t in $[0,T]$, the function $u_i(\cdot, t) : R_+ \to R$ is strictly
concave, increasing, with a first derivative on $(0, \infty)$ denoted $u_{ic}(\cdot, t)$
satisfying $\lim_{k \downarrow 0} u_{ic}(k, t) = +\infty$.*

By *smooth*, we mean that there is some constant $\bar{\epsilon}$ such that, for any
$\epsilon \in (0, \bar{\epsilon})$, the restriction of u_i to $(\epsilon, \bar{e} + \epsilon) \times [0, T]$ is C^∞ and has a bounded

second derivative $u_{icc}(q,t) = \partial^2 u_i(q,t)/\partial q^2$ with respect to consumption, where $\bar{e}$ is the essential supremum of the aggregate consumption process (which might be $+\infty$). (A C^∞ function is one with an extension to an open set having continuous derivatives of any order.) Based on work cited in the Notes, this can be relaxed. A frequently used example satisfying condition (a) is the function $u(q,t) = e^{-\rho t} q^\alpha$, for some $\rho > 0$ and $\alpha \in (0,1)$.

(b) *The aggregate endowment process* $e = \sum_{i=1}^I e^i$ *is an Ito process, bounded away from zero, where the stochastic differential represen-tation,* $de_t = \mu_e(t)\,dt + \sigma_e(t)\,dB_t$, *has* $E\left(\int_0^T \sigma_e(t) \cdot \sigma_e(t)\,dt\right) < \infty$.

(c) *The martingales* $M^1, \ldots, M^K$ *defined by*

$$M_t^k = E[D_T^k \mid \mathcal{F}_t], \quad t \in [0,T], \tag{4}$$

form a martingale generator.

Condition (c) means that any martingale Y can be represented in the form

$$Y_t = Y_0 + \sum_{k=1}^K \int_0^t \varphi_s^k\,dM_s^k, \quad t \in [0,T],$$

for predictable processes $\varphi^1, \ldots, \varphi^K$ stochastically integrable with respect to M^1, M^K. For (c) it is sufficient, for example, that $(M^1, \ldots, M^N)$ has a stochastic differential $\beta_t\,dB_t$, where the matrix process β_t^{-1} exists and is uniformly bounded. For instance, one could let $D^k = B^k$, $1 \leq k \leq N$. Weaker conditions would in fact suffice, as indicated in the Notes, allowing the "log–normal" case $D_t^k = \exp(B_t^k)$, $1 \leq k \leq N$, and variations thereof.

D. Armed with the strong conditions listed in the previous paragraph, we are prepared to claim the existence of an equilibrium also satisfying strong conditions. One should keep in mind here that the numeraire for our main result is the pure discount bond, D^0, not current consumption. We will later convert to the consumption numeraire.

THEOREM. *Under conditions* (a), (b), *and* (c) *of Paragraph C, there exists an equilibrium* $((S,p),(c^i,\theta^i))$ *for the given economy* $\mathcal{A}$ *with the following two properties. First, at any time* t,

$$S_t = E[D_T - D_t \mid \mathcal{F}_t]. \tag{5}$$

Second, there exists a (representative agent) utility function $\bar{u} : R_+ \times [0,T] \to R$ *satisfying regularity condition* (a) *such that, at any time* t, $p_t = \bar{u}_c(e_t, t)$.

PROOF: We outline the proof in three steps, each of which involves extensive arguments drawn from other work.

Step A (The Static Pure Exchange Equilibrium)   Let $\mathcal{E}$ denote the static
pure exchange economy $(\succeq_i, e^i)$, $i \in \{1, \ldots, I\}$, where $\succeq_i$ is the preference
relation on L_+ represented by U^i. By a result cited in the Notes, $\mathcal{E}$ has
a (static) equilibrium $(c^1, \ldots, c^I; \pi)$, whose price functional $\pi : L \to R$ is
represented by some bounded $p \in L_+$ in the form:

$$\pi \cdot x = E\left[\int_0^T p_t x_t \, dt\right], \quad x \in L. \tag{6}$$

Furthermore, c^i is bounded away from zero for any agent i with $e^i \neq 0$.

Step B (Dynamic Trading Implementation)   As in Section 16, the static
equilibrium $((c^i), \pi)$ for $\mathcal{E}$ can be implemented by security trading strategies
$(\theta^1, \ldots, \theta^I)$ to form a stochastic equilibrium $((S, p), (c^i, \theta^i))$. To outline the
basic parts of this implementation procedure, pick any agent i and let Y
be the martingale defined by

$$Y_t = E\left(\int_0^T p_s(c_s^i - e_s^i)\, ds \,\middle|\, \mathcal{F}_t\right).$$

With S defined by (5), the gain process $G = S + D$ is a martingale generator
by condition (c). By the definition of a martingale generator, there exist
predictable processes $\varphi^1, \ldots, \varphi^K$ such that

$$Y_t = Y_0 + \sum_{k=1}^{K} \int_0^t \varphi_s^k \, dG_s^k, \quad t \in [0, T]. \tag{7}$$

Let φ^0 be the predictable process defined by

$$\varphi_t^0 = Y_t - \int_0^t p_s(c_s^i - e_s^i)\, ds - \sum_{k=1}^{K} \varphi_t^k S_t^k. \tag{8}$$

An exercise shows that the trading strategy $\theta^i = (\varphi^0, \varphi^1, \ldots, \varphi^K)$ defined
by (7) and (8) forms a budget feasible plan (θ^i, c^i) for agent i. A simple
proof by contradiction suffices to show that (θ^i, c^i) is moreover optimal
for agent i. We can choose such a plan for each of the I agents. Now,
suppose we replace the trading strategy θ^I so chosen for agent number I
with the new trading strategy $\hat\theta^I = -\sum_{i=1}^{I-1} \theta^i$. This implies clearing in the

security markets. Consumption market clearing in the given equilibrium for the static economy $\mathcal{E}$ (as well as the linearity of integration) then implies that $(\widehat{\theta}^I, c^I)$ is budget feasible for agent I. Since (θ^I, c^I) is optimal for I, it follows that $(\widehat{\theta}^I, c^I)$ is also optimal for I. Thus we have shown the existence of an equilibrium in the stochastic economy $\mathcal{A}$.

Step C (Representative Agent Pricing)   As the final step, we recall the representative agent construction of Exercise 8.13. Details of this construction in our setting here are given in a paper cited in the Notes. We merely sketch out the arguments, assigning the details as an exercise in an analogous finite-dimensional setting. By the Saddle Point Theorem, there exist strictly positive constants $\lambda_1, \ldots, \lambda_m$ such that the aggregate consumption process e solves the *representative agent problem*

$$\max_{x \in L_+} \quad \overline{U}(x) \quad \text{subject to} \quad \pi \cdot x \leq \pi \cdot e, \tag{9}$$

where $\overline{U} : L_+ \to R$ is defined by

$$\overline{U}(x) = \sup_{x^1, \ldots, x^I} \sum_{i=1}^{I} \lambda_i U^i(x^i) \quad \text{subject to} \quad \sum_{i=1}^{I} x^i \leq x. \tag{10}$$

(The constant λ_i is the reciprocal of the Lagrange multiplier for the budget constraint of agent i in the static equilibrium for $\mathcal{E}$.) Problem (9) is equivalent to the problem

$$\max_{x \in L_+} \quad E\left[\int_0^T \overline{u}(x_t, t)\, dt\right] \quad \text{subject to} \quad E\left[\int_0^T p_t(x_t - e_t)\, dt\right] \leq 0, \tag{11}$$

where $\overline{u} : R_+ \times [0, T] \to R$ is defined, at each t in $[0, T]$, by

$$\overline{u}(q, t) = \sup_{q_1, \ldots, q_I} \sum_{i=1}^{I} \lambda_i u_i(q_i, t) \quad \text{subject to} \quad \sum_{i=1}^{I} q_i \leq q. \tag{12}$$

It follows that $\overline{u}$ is a strictly concave increasing utility function. As shown in an exercise, the implicit function theorem implies that $\overline{u}$ is smooth. Since e solves (11), there exists a Lagrange multiplier $\gamma > 0$ for (11) such that $\overline{u}_c(e_t, t) = \gamma p_t$ almost everywhere. Without loss of generality, $\gamma = 1$. ∎

E.   Our next task is to convert the "nominal" (bond numeraire) asset pricing formula (5) to a "real" (consumption numeraire) asset pricing formula. For simplicity, we restrict attention here to a security paying real dividends

according to a consumption dividend rate process $\delta \in L$. This corresponds
to the nominal cumulative dividend process D defined by $D_t = \int_0^t p_s \delta_s \, ds$.
By Theorem 25D, the nominal price process S of this security in equilibrium
is given by

$$S_t = E\left[\int_t^T p_s \delta_s \, ds \,\bigg|\, \mathcal{F}_t\right], \quad t \in [0, T]. \tag{13}$$

From the representative agent pricing part of Theorem 25D, the real price
process defined by $\widehat{S}_t = S_t/p_t$ therefore satisfies the pricing equation

$$\widehat{S}_t = \frac{1}{\bar{u}_c(e_t, t)} E\left[\int_t^T \bar{u}_c(e_s, s)\delta_s \, ds \,\bigg|\, \mathcal{F}_t\right]. \tag{14}$$

This pricing formula extends in the obvious way to the case of state
dependent utility as well, but that generalization does not lead to the
pricing models that follow. Essentially all of our remaining results stem
from relation (14), the natural analogue to the discrete–time pricing equation (1).

F. There are several ways to define the equilibrium interest rate process,
any of which should mean the process specifying interest rates on riskless
"short term" borrowing. In continuous–time, a convenient definition of the
real equilibrium interest rate is the stochastic process $r = \{r_t : t \in [0, T]\}$
which is the real dividend rate demanded by a security whose real price is
always unity. Thus, r is by definition the *real rate of interest* for a given
equilibrium $\big((S, p), (x^i, \theta^i)\big)$ if and only if, for any times t and $\tau \geq t$,

$$p_t = E\left[\int_t^\tau p_s r_s \, ds + p_\tau \,\bigg|\, \mathcal{F}_t\right]. \tag{15}$$

We should point out that, because of the dynamic spanning condition (c), it
is indeed possible to borrow at the equilibrium interest rate, either because
there actually exists a security with a constant price paying dividends at a
rate of r_t times its price (but this is not formally within our model), or by
forming a suitable trading strategy.

Since the conditions of Theorem 25D imply that $p_t = \bar{u}_c(e_t, t)$, Ito's
Lemma shows that p is itself an Ito process in equilibrium, and can be
represented by some predictable process μ_p in the stochastic differential
form

$$dp_t = \mu_p(t) \, dt + \bar{u}_{cc}(e_t, t)\sigma_e(t) \, dB_t, \tag{16}$$

where $\bar{u}_{cc}(\cdot, t)$ denotes the second derivative of $\bar{u}(\cdot, t)$. (We could also write
out an explicit expression for $\mu_p(t)$.) Since $p_t = \bar{u}_c(e_t, t)$, the process

$\{-\mu_p(t)/p_t : t \in [0,T]\}$ is called *minus the rate of growth of marginal representative utility for aggregate consumption.* We have the following characterization of equilibrium interest rates.

PROPOSITION. *Under conditions* (a), (b), *and* (c), *there exists an equilibrium for the economy* $\mathcal{A}$ *in which the real interest rate process* r *satisfies* $r_t = -\mu_p(t)/p_t$ *(which is minus the growth rate of marginal representative utility for aggregate consumption).*

PROOF: This follows from the fact that $\overline{u}_{cc}(e_t, t)$ is a bounded process, implying that the process $\int \overline{u}_{cc}(e_t, t)\sigma_e(t)\, dB_t$ is a martingale, leaving (15) from (16) for $r_t = -\mu_p(t)/p_t$. $\blacksquare$

In Paragraph II, we study this characterization of interest rates in a special example.

G. We now characterize the equilibrium excess expected rate of return on any security with a real dividend rate process $\delta \in L$. Based on the pricing equation (13), we leave it as an exercise to show that the equilibrium nominal price process S of such a security is an Ito process with the stochastic differential form

$$dS_t = -\delta_t \overline{u}_c(e_t, t)\, dt + \overline{\sigma}(t)\, dB_t, \tag{17}$$

where $\overline{\sigma}$ is an R^N-valued predictable process. The corresponding real price process $\widehat{S}$ defined by $\widehat{S}_t = S_t/p_t$ is also an Ito process (by Ito's Lemma), and has a stochastic differential representation of the form

$$d\widehat{S}_t = \widehat{\mu}(t)\, dt + \widehat{\sigma}(t)\, dB_t, \tag{18}$$

for some predictable process $\widehat{\mu}$ and some R^N-valued predictable process $\widehat{\sigma}$. Also by Ito's Lemma,

$$dS_t = \left[p_t\widehat{\mu}(t) + \widehat{S}_t\mu_p(t) + \widehat{\sigma}(t)^\top \overline{u}_{cc}(e_t, t)\sigma_e(t)\right] dt + \overline{\sigma}(t)\, dB_t, \tag{19}$$

using (17). Combining (17) and (19),

$$\delta_t + \widehat{\mu}(t) + \frac{1}{p_t}\widehat{S}_t\mu_p(t) + \frac{1}{p_t}\widehat{\sigma}(t)^\top \overline{u}_{cc}(e_t, t)\sigma_e(t) = 0. \tag{20}$$

We then have the *Consumption–Based Capital Asset Pricing Model*, or CCAPM,

$$\widehat{\mu}(t) + \delta_t - r_t\widehat{S}_t = \frac{-\overline{u}_{cc}(e_t, t)}{\overline{u}_c(e_t, t)}\widehat{\sigma}(t)^\top \sigma_e(t). \tag{21}$$

A bit of additional work yields a more familiar version of the CCAPM in terms of asset returns. For $\widehat{S}_t \neq 0$, we can define the *total real rate of expected return* on the given security at time t as

$$\mathcal{R}_t = \frac{\widehat{\mu}(t) + \delta(t)}{\widehat{S}(t)},$$

the expected real rate of capital plus dividend gain divided by the current market value. Letting $\sigma_S(t) = \widehat{\sigma}(t)/\widehat{S}(t)$ and $\mu_S(t) = \widehat{\mu}(t)/\widehat{S}_t$, it is sometimes common to represent $\widehat{S}_t$ in the form

$$d\widehat{S}_t = \widehat{S}_t \mu_S(t)\, dt + \widehat{S}_t \sigma_S(t)\, dB_t. \tag{22}$$

Via a purely heuristic interpretation, it is typical to view $\sigma_S(t)^\top \sigma_S(t)$ as the *instantaneous variance* of the return of the given security at time t, and to view $\sigma_S(t)^\top \sigma_e(t)$ as the *instantaneous covariance* between the return on the security and increments of aggregate consumption at time t. We then have the more familiar CCAPM relation

$$(\mathcal{R}_t - r_t) = \frac{-\overline{u}_{cc}(e_t, t)}{\overline{u}_c(e_t, t)}\, \sigma_S(t)^\top \sigma_e(t). \tag{23}$$

The representative agent's Arrow–Pratt absolute risk aversion measure, $-\overline{u}_{cc}(e_t, t)/\overline{u}_c(e_t, t)$, is the constant of proportionality between *excess expected rate of return*, on the left of (23), and instantaneous covariance of return with "consumption increments", on the right. One can also write a traditional "beta" version of the CCAPM in terms of excess expected returns on a portfolio of securities "perfectly correlated with consumption", in the following sense. Because of the dynamic spanning condition (c), we can assume without loss of generality that there is a security satisfying relation (23) with $\widehat{\sigma}(t) = \sigma_e(t)$ and $\sigma_S(t) = \sigma^*(t) \equiv \widehat{\sigma}(t)/\widehat{S}_t$. Denoting the total real rate of excess expected return of this security by $\mathcal{R}_t^e$, relation (23) implies that

$$\beta_S(t) = \frac{\sigma_S(t)^\top \sigma^*(t)}{\sigma^*(t)^\top \sigma^*(t)}.$$

Now, for an arbitrary security, the definition

$$\beta_S(t) = \frac{\sigma_S(t)^\top \sigma_e(t)}{\sigma_e(t)^\top \sigma_e(t)},$$

leads to the following *beta version of the CCAPM* (23), for an arbitrary security:

$$\mathcal{R}_t - r_t = \beta_S(t)(\mathcal{R}_t^e - r_t). \tag{23'}$$

Relation (23) is actually a stronger result than (23′), since (23′) is true even if the constant of proportionality in (23) were to be something other than the represenative agent's Arrow–Pratt risk aversion measure. Using the approach of stochastic control in a Markov setting, Exercise 25.13 provides an alternative derivation of the CCAPM.

We summarize with the following statement of the CCAPM.

PROPOSITION (CCAPM). *Under conditions* (a), (b), *and* (c), *there exists an equilibrium in which the real return on any security paying a real dividend rate process* $\delta \in L$ *satisfies relation* (21). *When the market value* $\widehat{S}_t$ *of the security is not zero, the real excess expected rate of return* $\mathcal{R}_t$ *satisfies the equivalent relation* (23), *as well as the traditional beta version of the CCAPM, relation* (23′).

We can easily extend the definition of a risky security to allow for lump sum dividends $d_1, \ldots, d_n$, where d_j is a random variable paid at some (possibly random) stopping time $T(j)$, for $j \subset \{1, \ldots, n\}$. This leaves a cumulative dividend process D of the form:

$$D_t = \int_0^t \delta_s \, ds + \sum_{\{j : T(j) \le t\}} d_j, \tag{24}$$

for some dividend rate process $\delta \in L$. Relation (5) prices such a security in equilibrium by arguments from a paper cited in the Notes, where further extensions are allowed. The CCAPM relations (21) and (23) also apply to such a security in equilibrium for any time t not equal to the time of a lump sum dividend payment. The calculations are identical.

H. In order to illustrate the *term structure of interest rates*, we will work out a single–agent example. Technological "shocks" are given by a process Y defined as the solution to the stochastic differential equation

$$dY_t = (aY_t - b) \, dt + k\sqrt{Y_t} \, dB_t; \quad Y_0 = y,$$

where a, b, and k are negative with $-2b > k^2$, and where B is a Standard Brownian Motion. A single firm produces consumption dividends from capital stock according to the stochastic integral equation:

$$K_t = K_0 + \int_0^t [K_s h Y_s - \delta_s] \, ds + \int_0^t K_s \epsilon \sqrt{Y_s} \, dB_s, \tag{25}$$

where h, K_0, and ϵ are strictly positive scalars with $h > \epsilon^2$, and where δ is the real dividend process defined by

$$\delta_t = \rho K_t / [1 - e^{-\rho(T-t)}], \tag{26}$$

with ρ denoting another strictly positive scalar. Relation (25) describes the current capital stock of the firm, K_t, as the sum of its initial value K_0 and the cumulative production to date, $\int_0^t K_s h Y_s \, ds + \int_0^t K_s \epsilon \sqrt{Y_s} \, dB_s$, net of cumulative dividends $\int_0^t \delta_s \, ds$. Let L_{++} denote the subset of L_+ whose elements are strictly positive almost everywhere. There is a single agent with the utility function $U : L_{++} \rightarrow R$ defined by

$$U(c) = E \left[\int_0^T e^{-\rho t} \log(c_t) \, dt \right], \qquad (27)$$

where $\rho > 0$ is the scalar "discount rate". The agent is not endowed directly with consumption, but rather is endowed with one share of the firm. (The results of the model would be the same if the agent is instead endowed directly with the consumption process δ in a pure exchange setting.) We have given the firm no production decision; it merely holds the capital stock K_t and pays dividends as specified by δ. We might have allowed the firm to choose a dividend process δ endogenously. We would then need to specify the goals of the firm as at the end of Section 20. A natural decentralization result can be obtained by setting up a market for the firm's shares, specifying a market valuation functional for the firm, and assigning the firm the objective of maximizing its market value. For the example here, the result is obtained in Exercise 25.16. In a non–market economy, however, wherein the single agent controls the firm and has no other access to consumption, Exercise 23.1 tells us that the agent would choose precisely the dividend function δ specified by (26). If the firm's share is the only risky security sold, and if its (real) price process $\widehat{S}$ is defined by $\widehat{S}_t = K_t$, the current capital stock, then indeed an equilibrium follows. That is, by the solution to Exercise 23.1, given $(\widehat{S}, \delta)$, the agent optimally chooses the consumption process $c = \delta$ and trading strategy $\theta_t \equiv 1$. This is also confirmed in Exercise 25.16.

A slight adjustment of the proof of Proposition 25F (to account for failure of the technical regularity conditions of the Proposition) shows that the equilibrium real interest rate process r is given as usual by $r_t = -\mu_p(t)/p_t$, where $p_t = u_c(\delta_t, t)$ for $u(q, t) = e^{-\rho t} \log(q)$. It follows that

$$r_t = (h - \epsilon^2) Y_t, \quad t \in [0, T], \qquad (28)$$

with the required intermediate calculations left as an exercise. By Ito's Lemma, r solves the stochastic differential equation

$$dr_t = [a r_t + b(\epsilon^2 - h)] \, dt + k \sqrt{(h - \epsilon^2) r_t} \, dB_t, \quad t \in [0, T]. \qquad (29)$$

For $a < 0$, the solution to (29) is known as a *continuous–time first or-der autoregressive process*. The interest rate process r has negative drift whenever

$$r_t \geq \frac{b}{a}(h - \epsilon^2), \tag{30}$$

and positive drift otherwise. As $t \to \infty$, the expectation of r_t converges to $(h - \epsilon^2)b/a$. Relation (29) leads to an explicit calculation of the probability distribution of future equilibrium interest rates in this single–agent economy, as cited in the Notes. Certain parameter restrictions ensure that r is positive–valued given a positive starting point.

In this setting, the *term structure* is the family of bond prices $\{f_{t,s} : 0 \leq t \leq s \leq T\}$, with $f_{t,s}$ denoting the real (consumption numeraire) price at time t of an $(s - t)$ period *real discount riskless bond*, a security that pays the nominal cumulative dividend process D defined by $D_\tau = 0$, $\tau < s$ and $D_\tau = p_s$, $\tau \geq s$. In other words, $f_{t,s}$ is the price at time t of a bond promising one unit of consumption at time s. With the extension of our pricing formula (5) to securities of the form given by relation (24), an exercise shows that

$$f_{t,s} = \frac{E(p_s \mid \mathcal{F}_t)}{p_t} = e^{-\rho(s-t)} \delta_t E\left(\frac{1}{\delta_s} \middle| \mathcal{F}_t\right). \tag{31}$$

A further exercise shows that $f_{t,s} = F(r_t, t, s)$, where F is of the form

$$F(r, t, s) = Q_1(t, s) \exp[Q_2(t, s)r], \quad t \leq s, \tag{32}$$

for (deterministic) real–valued functions Q_1 and Q_2 to be found explicitly as an exercise.

EXERCISES

EXERCISE 25.1 Show that the trading strategy φ defined by relations (7) and (8) is such that (φ, c^i) is budget feasible for agent i. Show that (φ, c^i) is optimal for i. *Hint:* For optimality, use a proof by contradiction and the properties of the static equilibrium.

EXERCISE 25.2 In the proof of Theorem 25D, show that $(\widehat{\theta}^I, c^I)$ is budget feasible for agent I. Show that $(\widehat{\theta}^I, c^I)$ optimal for I.

EXERCISE 25.3 Among other applications, the *implicit function theorem* assures that a function Z is smooth when defined by

$$Z(x) \in \arg \max_{z \in R^n} V(x, z), x \in R^m,$$

for some "smooth" real–valued function V on $R^m \times R^n$, at least under regularity conditions.

IMPLICIT FUNCTION THEOREM. *Suppose $f : R^m \times R^n \to R^m \times R^n$ is a C^k function, for some integer $k \geq 1$, such that the Jacobian matrix $\nabla f(a, b)$ of f evaluated at $(a, b) \in R^m \times R^n$ is nonsingular. If $f(a, b) = 0$, then there exists a ball $B_a \subset R^m$ centered at a, a ball $B_b \subset R^n$ centered at b, and a C^k function $Z : B_a \to B_b$, such that $f[x, Z(x)] = 0$ for all x in B_a. Furthermore, B_a can be chosen so that $y = Z(x)$ is the unique solution to $f(x, y) = 0$ for all x in B_a.*

Show that the representative agent function $\bar{u}$ defined by relation (12) is C^k for any integer k. *Hint:* Define the Lagrangian and consider the system of equations defined by the first order conditions. Show that, for any k, the amount of consumption q_i allocated to agent i is a C^k function of the total amount of consumption available, q.

EXERCISE 25.4   Confirm that relation (16) follows as stated in Paragraph 25F. Write out an explicit expression for $\mu_p(t)$ as defined in (16).

EXERCISE 25.5   Supply the calculations left out of the proof shown for Proposition 25F.

EXERCISE 25.6   Supply the calculations leading to relations (19), (20), (21), and (23).

EXERCISE 25.7   This is an alternative to the Cox–Ingersoll–Ross model of the term structure found in Paragraph 25H. In the Cox–Ingersoll–Ross model, the equilibrium interest rate has an attractive mean–reverting property. Here we derive a less attractive term structure because of a cruder model for adjustment of the capital stock. Although one must make some minor technical assumptions, there is only one natural closed form solution.

The capital stock K solves the stochastic integral equation

$$K_t = K_0 + \int_0^t (hK_s - \delta_s)\, ds + \int_0^t \epsilon K_s\, dB_s, \quad t \geq 0, \tag{33}$$

where ϵ is a strictly positive scalar, B is a Standard Brownian Motion that is a martingale with respect to the given filtered probability space, and $\delta = \{\delta_t : t \geq 0\}$ is a positive predictable dividend process. In other words, the single firm in question depletes its capital stock K_t at the rate δ_t. We take an infinite horizon setting and assume that the firm depletes its stock so as to maximize the single consumer's infinite horizon discounted expected utility for consumption of dividends:

$$U(\delta) = E\left[\int_0^\infty e^{-\rho t} u(\delta_t)\, dt\right],$$

where $\rho > 0$ is a scalar discount factor and u is the power function $q \mapsto q^{\alpha}$, for some $\alpha \in (0, 1)$.

(A)   Solve the firm's dividend control problem.

The consumer ignores what the firm is trying to do, and merely takes note that the firm's common share sells for $\mathcal{S}(K_t)$, $t \geq 0$, where $\mathcal{S}$ is a C^2 strictly increasing function, and that each share pays the dividend process δ that the firm determines. (The firm and the consumer have the same information filtration; this can be generalized.) The consumer is free to purchase any number of these shares (or to short sell them), and is also able to borrow or lend (that is, to buy or sell a security whose value is identically one and whose dividend rate is $r(K_t)$, for some function r of the current capital stock). These are the only two securities available. The consumer has one share of the firm's stock and none of the "bond" as an initial endowment. Let W_t denote the consumer's total wealth at any time t in stock and bond. The consumer must choose at any time t the fraction z_t of wealth to hold in the firm's share (with the remainder held in the bond) and must also decide at what rate to consume. (Consumption is the numeraire.)

(B)   Briefly formulate the consumer's portfolio–consumption control problem. Derive the Bellman equation and first order conditions, assuming differentiability and interior optima.

Choose a pricing function $\mathcal{S}$ and an interest rate function r at which the consumer optimally holds none of the bond and one share of the firm. In other words:

(C)   State an equilibrium security price process and interest rate process, both as functions of the current capital stock K_t.

(D)   Calculate the initial equilibrium market value of a zero net supply bond paying one unit of wealth at a given time $\tau > 0$. Supply also the equilibrium market value of a *consol*, a pure income bond paying consumption perpetually at a fixed rate of one unit of consumption per unit of time.

(E)   State a differential equation for the equilibrium market value of a security paying dividends at a rate given by a bounded C^2 function d (with bounded derivative) of the current capital stock. Include a boundary condition.

(F)   Solve (A)–(E) again for a finite horizon $T > \tau$.

EXERCISE 25.8   Show that the equilibrium real interest rate process r in the example of Paragraph 25H is indeed given by $r_t = -\mu_p(t)/p_t$, where $p_t = u_c(\delta_t, t)$. In other words, extend the proof of Proposition 25F to this special case.

EXERCISE 25.9   Based on the previous exercise, verify relations (28) and (29).

EXERCISE 25.10   (The Cox–Ingersoll–Ross Term Structure)

(A) Verify relation (31) as the definition of the term structure in the single agent example of Paragraph 25H.

(B)   Verify the form of relation (32) for the term structure.

(C)   Supply the definitions of the functions Q_1 and Q_2 in relation (32).

EXERCISE 25.11   Consider the following continuous–time analogue to the Markov single–agent asset pricing model of Section 20. Let B be a Standard Brownian Motion in R^N adapted, let $\{\mathcal{F}_t : t \geq 0\}$ be its standard filtration, and let X denote a K–dimensional Ito process solving the stochastic differential equation

$$dX_t = \nu(X_t)\, dt + \eta(X_t)\, dB_t; \quad X_0 = x \in R^K, \tag{34}$$

where $\nu : R^K \to R^K$ and $\eta : R^K \to M^{K,N}$ are sufficiently well–behaved for existence. There are K securities in total supply of one each, paying dividends according to a measurable function $d : R^K \to R^K_+$. That is, security n pays dividends at the rate $d(X_t)_n$ at time t. The single agent chooses a predictable positive real–valued consumption process $c = \{c_t : t \geq 0\}$ and a predictable R^K–valued security portfolio process $\theta = \{\theta_t : t \geq 0\}$, where c_t represents the rate of consumption of the single numeraire good at time t, and θ_t represents the portfolio of securities held at time t. The market value of the securities is given by an R^K–valued Ito process S, with $S(t)_n$ denoting the market value of the n–th security at time t. The wealth process $W^{c\theta}$ of an agent initially endowed with all of the securities and adopting the consumption–portfolio strategy (c, θ) is thus given by

$$W^{c\theta}_T = \mathbf{1}^\top S_0 + \int_0^T \left[\theta_t^\top d(X_t) - c_t\right]\, dt + \int_0^T \theta_t\, dS_t, \quad T \geq 0,$$

where $\mathbf{1} = (1, 1, \ldots, 1) \in R^K$. The agent has a strictly concave increasing reward function $u : R_+ \to R$ and a utility for a consumption process c of

$$U(c) = E\left[\int_0^\infty e^{-\rho t} u(c_t)\, dt\right],$$

where $\rho \in (0, \infty)$. An equilibrium for this economy is a security price process S such that the problem

$$\max_{c, \theta} U(c) \quad \text{subject to} \quad W_t^{c\theta} \geq 0, \quad t \in [0, \infty),$$

has a solution (c, θ) with $c_t = \mathbf{1}^\top d(X_t)$ and $\theta_t = \mathbf{1}$ for all $t \in [0, \infty)$.

(A) Suppose the security price process is $S_t = \mathcal{S}(X_t)$ for all t, for some twice continuously differentiable function $\mathcal{S} : R^K \to R^K$. Provide the Bellman Equation for the agent's stochastic control problem.

(B) Based on your understanding of the relationship of this model with the discrete-time Markov analogue, give an expression for the term structure of interest rates. That is, provide an expression for the market value at time t of a T–period pure discount bond, which is a zero net supply contract to pay one unit of the consumption numeraire at time $t + T$. No proof or explanation is required here. The expression should involve only the primitives of the model, ν, η, d, u, ρ, the initial state $x \in R^K$, and future states, $X_t, t \geq 0$.

(C) Show an equation for the market value of any security as a necessary condition for an equilibrium, under stated regularity conditions, using the following infinite horizon version of the Feynman–Kac Formula. (We drop the argument $x \in R^K$ from all functions for simplicity.) We do not supply the "Strong Regularity Conditions" referred to in the result; there is a range of possible assumptions that are cumbersome and purely of mathematical interest.

A VERSION OF THE FEYNMAN–KAC FORMULA. *Suppose* $g : R^K \to R$ *and* $h : R^K \to R$ *are measurable, and that the quadruple* (ν, η, h, g) *satisfies the Strong Regularity Conditions. Then* $F \in C^2(R^K)$ *satisfies the partial differential equation* $\mathcal{D}F - hF + g = 0$ *if and only if*

$$F(x) = E\left[\int_0^\infty \exp\left[-\int_0^t h(X_s)\, ds\right] g(X_t)\, dt\right], \quad x \in R^K,$$

where $\mathcal{D}F = \nabla F \nu + \frac{1}{2}\mathrm{tr}(\eta^\top \nabla^2 F \eta)$.

(D)   Consider the special case:

$$u(a) = \frac{a^{(\alpha+1)} - 1}{\alpha + 1}, \quad \alpha \in (-1, 0),$$

$$\nu(x) = Ax, \qquad A \in M^{K,K},$$

$$\eta(x) = D, \qquad D \in M^{K,N}$$

$$1^\top d(x) = e^{b^\top x}, \quad b \in R^K.$$

Make special note of the fact that the diffusion function η takes the value of the fixed matrix D, independent of x, while $\nu(x)$ depends (linearly) on x. First derive the following conditional moments, which will be useful in subsequent calculations. Show that

$$E[X_t | \mathcal{F}_s] = M_{t-s} X_s,$$

where $M_\tau = e^{\tau A}$, and that

$$\text{cov}(X_t | \mathcal{F}_s) \equiv E\big[(X_t - M_{t-s} X_s)(X_t - M_{t-s} X_s)^\top \mid \mathcal{F}_s\big] = \Sigma(t - s),$$

where

$$\Sigma(\tau) = \int_0^\tau e^{tA} DD^\top \left(e^{tA}\right)^\top dt.$$

Hint: The exponential e^{tA}, for a square matrix A, is defined by

$$e^{tA} = I + At + \frac{A^2 t^2}{2!} + \cdots + \frac{A^n t^n}{n!} + \cdots.$$

The only property of e^{tA} useful for this problem is the following. Suppose $y : R_+ \to R^K$ is a function of time solving the ordinary differential equation

$$\frac{dy(t)}{dt} = Ay(t); \quad y(0) = x \in R^K, \quad A \in M^{K,K}.$$

It follows that, for any time t, $y(t) = e^{At}x$. It may also be useful to know that an R^K–valued random variable Z has a mean vector m and a covariance matrix Q if and only if, for any $b \in R^K$, we have $E(b^\top Z) = b^\top E(Z)$ and $\text{var}(b^\top Z) = b^\top Q b$. *Remark:* If the case $K \geq 1$ proves too difficult, try the case $K = 1$; partial credit will be given.

(E)   For the special case given by part (D), solve for the term structure of interest rates. That is, provide a closed form expression for the market value of a T–period pure discount bond at time t. Simplify to the greatest possible extent.

(F)   For the special case given by part (D), solve for the current equilibrium interest rate process $r = \{r_t : t \geq 0\}$ in this economy. For partial credit, take the special case $K = 1$.

(G)   For this last part, a further extension of the Black–Scholes model, we do not take the parametric assumptions of Part (D). Suppose the interest rate process is given by $r_t = \gamma(X_t)$ for all t, where $\gamma : R^K \to R$, and that the security price process is given by $S_t = S(X_t)$ for all t, for some twice continuously differentiable function $S : R^K \to R^K$. Give a partial differential equation for the arbitrage–value of an additional security defined by a dividend process $\{\delta(X_t) : t \geq 0\}$, where $\delta : R^K \to R$ is measurable. In particular, state regularity conditions implying redundancy of this additional security. Finally, give a solution to the PDE you suggest, in the form of an expectation, and provide the corresponding regularity conditions.

EXERCISE 25.12   (Asset Pricing via Bellman's Equation)   We adopt the Markov framework of Exercise 22.15. The state variable process X and securities' properties are precisely as defined in that exercise. Here we loosely pass over many technical conditions in order to view the asset pricing models in a traditional setting of Bellman's Equation. We generalize a given agent's utility functional to the state–dependent form:

$$U(c) = E\left[\int_0^T u(c_t, X_t, t)\, dt\right] < \infty,$$

where $u : R_+ \times R^K \times [0, T] \to R$ is a Borel measurable function such that $u(a, \cdot, \cdot) : R^K \times [0, T] \to R$ satisfies a Lipschitz (21.8) and a growth (21.9) condition, with the same constant k for all $a \geq 0$. We assume that $u(\cdot, x, t)$ is strictly increasing, strictly concave, and differentiable for all (x, t). We define the real–valued instantaneous expected rate of return μ_k for the k–th security by

$$\mu_k(x, t) = \frac{\gamma_k(x, t) + \delta_k(x, t)}{S^k(x, t)}, \quad (x, t) \in R^K \times [0, T].$$

Defining the R^N–valued function σ_k on $R^K \times [0, T]$ by $\sigma_k = \varphi_k / S^k$, we can then express the gain process G^k, defined by

$$G_t^k = S^k(X_t, t) + \int_0^t \delta_k(X_s, s)\, ds, \quad t \in [0, T], \tag{35}$$

in the form

$$G_t^k = \mathcal{S}^k(X_0,0) + \int_0^t \mathcal{S}^k(X_s,s)\mu_k(X_s,s)\,ds + \int_0^t \mathcal{S}^k(X_s,s)\sigma_k(X_s,s)\,dB_s.$$

This is in direct parallel with the i.i.d. model given by relation (24.9). Following the procedure outlined in Paragraph 24A, one can translate an agent's choice of consumption process c in L_+ and trading strategy θ in Θ into a control (c,z), where $c \in L_+$ and $z = (z_1,\ldots,z_K)$ is an R^K–valued predictable process representing the fractions of wealth held in the K risky securities. Let $\mathcal{Z}$ denote the space of such portfolio fractions satisfying $\int_0^T z_t \cdot z_t\,dt < \infty$ almost surely.

Let $\sigma(x,t)$ denote the $K \times N$ matrix whose (k,j)–element is the j–th element of $\sigma_k(x,t)$, for all (x,t) in $R^K \times [0,T]$. It is safe to think of $\sigma\sigma^\top$ as the instantaneous covariance of the rates of return of the securities, and then to treat $z^\top \sigma\sigma^\top z$ as the instantaneous variance of the return to a portfolio $z \in R^K$. Let

$$\lambda(x,t) = [\mu_1(x,t) - r(x,t),\ldots,\mu_K(x,t) - r(x,t)]$$

denote the vector of *excess expected rates of return* of the K securities in state $x \in R^K$ at time t. The *wealth process* W determined by given (c,z) in $L_+ \times \mathcal{Z}$ is defined by

$$W_t = w + \int_0^t [W_s z_s^\top \lambda(X_s,s) + W_s r(X_s,s) - c_s]\,ds + \int_0^t W_s z_s^\top \sigma(X_s,s)\,dB_s,$$

where $w \geq 0$ is a given scalar for initial wealth. The agent's value function is given, for $(x,w,t) \in R^K \times R_+ \times [0,T]$, as

$$V(x,w,t) = \sup_{(c,z)\in L_+ \times \mathcal{Z}} E\left[\int_t^T u(c_s,X_s,s)\,ds\right],$$

subject to $X_t = x$, $W_t = w$, and $W_s \geq 0$ for all $s \geq t$. The *adjoined state process* (X,W) for this problem has a (c_t,z_t)–control–dependent drift given by

$$[\nu(x,t),\ wz_t^\top \lambda(x,t) + wr(x,t) - c_t] \in R^{K+1},$$

in state x with wealth w at time $t \in [0,T]$, and a control dependent $M^{(K+1),N}$–valued diffusion function b on $R^K \times R^K \times R_+ \times [0,T]$ given by

$$b(z_t) = \begin{pmatrix} \eta(x,t) \\ wz_t^\top \sigma(x,t) \end{pmatrix},$$

where only the dependence of b on z_t is shown explicitly, the arguments (w, x, t) being suppressed. We assume that the value function V for this control problem is sufficiently differentiable, and allow V'' to denote the matrix of second order partial derivatives of V not involving t, or in block form,

$$V'' = \begin{pmatrix} V_{xx} & V_{xw} \\ V_{wx} & V_{ww} \end{pmatrix}_{(K+1)\times(K+1)},$$

where

$$V_{wx}(x, w, t) = V_{xw}(x, w, t)^{\top} = \left[\frac{\partial^2 V(x, w, t)}{\partial w \partial x_1}, \dots, \frac{\partial V(x, w, t)}{\partial w \partial x_K} \right]_{1\times K},$$

$$V_{xx}(x, w, t) = \left[\frac{\partial^2 V(x, w, t)}{\partial x_i \partial x_j} \right]_{K \times K} \quad \text{and}$$

$$V_{ww}(x, w, t) = \frac{\partial^2 V(x, w, t)}{\partial w^2}.$$

One can deduce from Proposition 23C regularity conditions under which the value function V must also satisfy the Bellman Equation: for all $(x, w, t) \in R^K \times R_+ \times [0, T]$,

$$\sup_{(c_t, z_t) \in R_+ \times R^K} \left\{ \mathcal{D}^{c_t, z_t} V(x, w, t) \mid u(c_t, x, t) \right\} - 0, \tag{36}$$

and an obvious boundary condition, where, dropping the (x, w, t) arguments whenever convenient,

$$\mathcal{D}^{c_t, z_t} V \equiv V_t + V_x \nu + V_w(wz_t^{\top} \lambda + wr - c_t) + \tfrac{1}{2}\mathrm{tr}\left[b(z_t)^{\top} V'' b(z_t) \right].$$

The regularity conditions imposed in Proposition 23C are sufficiently severe and numerous that we must treat the Bellman Equation (36) as an "ideal" characterization of control, rather than a routine necessary condition. We assume that the supremum demanded in relation (36) is achieved by some $(c_t, z_t) \in \mathrm{int}(R_+ \times R^K)$.

(A) Verify the following first order conditions for (36):

$$u_c = V_w \tag{37}$$

$$V_{ww}\sigma\sigma^{\top}z_t w + V_w\lambda + \sigma\eta^{\top}V_{xw} = 0. \tag{38}$$

Let us now explicitly account for I different agents merely by adding superscript i for agent i to our notation in an obvious way. We presume, for each agent i, that V_{ww}^i is a strictly negative–valued function, which may be interpreted as strictly concave indirect utility for wealth, a symptom of risk aversion. We also assume that V_w^i is strictly positive–valued, with the obvious interpretation of monotonicity. We continue to suppress from the notation the arguments of functions whenever convenient. Relation (38) then implies that

$$\frac{-V_w^i}{V_{ww}^i}\lambda = \sigma\sigma^\top z_t^i w^i + \sigma\eta^\top \frac{V_{xw}^i}{V_{ww}^i}.$$

It is convenient to devote the first I coordinates of the state process X to the equilibrium wealth levels of the I agents. That is, from this point we take it that $X_i(t) = W^i(t)$. (Agent i takes the process X_i as given, however.) The *market indirect risk tolerance* is the real–valued function $\widehat{\tau}$ defined by

$$\widehat{\tau}(x,t) = \sum_{i=1}^I \frac{-V_w^i(x,x_i,t)}{V_{ww}^i(x,x_i,t)}, \quad (x,t) \in R^K \times [0,T]. \tag{39}$$

We also define the R^K–valued function H by

$$H(x,t) = \sum_{i=1}^I \frac{V_{xw}^i(x,x_i,t)}{V_{ww}^i(x,x_i,t)}, \quad (x,t) \in R^K \times [0,T]. \tag{40}$$

(B)   Show that
$$\lambda = \sigma\sigma^\top \frac{\mathcal{S}}{\widehat{\tau}} + \sigma\eta^\top \frac{H}{\widehat{\tau}}. \tag{41}$$

We assume the securities are held in total supply of one each. The *market portfolio* is then the R^K–valued function M defined by $M(x,t) = \mathcal{S}(x,t)/[\mathbf{1}^\top \mathcal{S}(x,t)]$, representing the fractions of total wealth held in the various securities at time t and in state x. The *instantaneous expected rate of return on the market* is the real–valued function μ_M defined by $\mu_M(x,t) = M(x,t)^\top \mu(x,t)$. The *instantaneous standard deviation of the market rate of return* is the real–valued function σ_M defined by $\sigma_M = (M^\top \sigma\sigma^\top M)^{1/2}$. We assume that σ_M is everywhere non–zero.

(C)   Show that
$$\frac{\widehat{\tau}}{\mathbf{1}^\top \mathcal{S}}(\mu_M - r) = \sigma_M^2 + M^\top \sigma\eta^\top \frac{H}{\mathbf{1}^\top \mathcal{S}}. \tag{42}$$

(D) Assuming that the dimension N of the underlying Brownian Motion is one, or that $H \equiv 0$, show that $\lambda = \beta_M(\mu_M - r)$ where β_M is the *market beta* function $\sigma\sigma^\top M/\sigma_M^2$, the familiar Capital Asset Pricing Model in a continuous–time setting. In general, however, one cannot eliminate or identify H, and the following Part (E) shows that the CAPM for one–dimensional Brownian Motion is tautological.

(E) Let $\pi \in R^K$ be any portfolio (with $\pi_1 + \cdots + \pi_K = 1$) of non–zero market value. Defining μ_π and β_π analogously to the corresponding definitions for the market portfolio, show that $\lambda = \beta_\pi(\mu_\pi - r)$ provided the underlying Brownian Motion is one–dimensional.

    Of course, there is always a *single–beta asset pricing model*, at least if $\sigma\sigma^\top$ is nonsingular. Let $\xi = S + (\sigma\sigma^\top)^{-1}\sigma\eta^\top H$ and let $\Xi = \xi/\sum_{k=1}^K \xi^k$, with the obvious domain and range, assuming that $\sum_{n=1}^K \xi^k \neq 0$. We let $\mu_\Xi - \sum_{n=1}^K \Xi_k\mu_k$ denote the real–valued *expected return on portfolio* Ξ, and define $\beta_\Xi \equiv (\sigma\sigma^\top)\Xi/(\Xi^\top\sigma\sigma^\top\Xi)$ as the R^K valued *beta function* for the N securities relative to portfolio Ξ.

(F) Derive the *single–beta model*: $\lambda = \beta_\Xi(\mu_\Xi - r)$.

    We are still unable to identify H, and our single–beta model is therefore not a testable restriction on expected rates of return, in contrast to the Capital Asset Pricing Model, which specifies the market portfolio M for the unknown portfolio Ξ. We note, however, that every "mean–variance efficient" portfolio is a linear combination of investments at the market interest rate r and in the single portfolio Ξ. Specifically, suppose that $\pi^* \in R^K$ solves

$$\max_{\pi \in R^K} \quad \pi^\top \mu(x,t) + (1 - \pi_1 - \cdots - \pi_K)r(x,t)$$

subject to

$$\pi^\top \sigma(x,t)\sigma(x,t)^\top \pi \leq \bar{v},$$

where the scalar $\bar{v} > 0$ is some fixed level of "variance".

(G) Show that, if $\lambda \geq 0$, then $\pi^* = \alpha\,\Xi(x,t)$ for some scalar α. Thus, if agents hold only mean–variance efficient portfolios, then agent i holds a risky portfolio $\alpha_i\,\Xi$, implying in equilibrium that

$$S = \sum_{i=1}^I \alpha_i\,\Xi w_i = \bar{\alpha}\,\Xi,$$

for some scalar $\bar{\alpha}$, which means of course that $\Xi = M$. Agents will not, in general, hold only mean–variance efficient portfolios. Agents will be willing to deviate from mean–variance efficient portfolios in order to hedge against movements in the state–variable process. For this reason, H in relation (41) has been referred to as a *hedging term*.

EXERCISE 25.13 (CCAPM)   We continue where Part (A) of the previous exercise left off. We need yet stronger regularity assumptions about the nature of an assumed equilibrium. First we suppose that the supremum demanded by (36) is achieved by interior $(c_t, z_t) \in R_+ \times R^K$, where $c_t = C(x, w, t)$ for some C^2 function $C : R^K \times R_+ \times [0, T] \to R_+$. The first order conditions (37) and (38) then imply, by the chain rule for differentiation, that

$$u_{cx} + u_{cc}C_x = V_{wx} \tag{43}$$

and that

$$u_{cc}C_w = V_{ww}, \tag{44}$$

where subscripts indicate partial differentiation with respect to the indicated arguments, assuming the required derivatives exist. The *risk tolerance* of u is the function τ defined by $\tau = -u_c/u_{cc}$.

(A)   Provided $u_{cx} \equiv 0$, for example if u does not depend on the state x at all, show that

$$\tau\lambda = C_w \sigma\sigma^\top zw + \sigma\eta^\top C_x^\top. \tag{45}$$

Ito's Lemma implies that $dC(X_t, W_t, t) = \mu_c(t)\, dt + \sigma_c(t)\, dB_t$, $t \in [0, T]$, for processes μ_c and σ_c, as indicated by Theorem 21B. Omitting some arguments,

$$\sigma_c(t) = C_x\eta + C_w W_t z_t^\top \sigma, \quad t \in [0, T]. \tag{46}$$

(B)   Show that

$$\tau(X_t, W_t, t)\lambda(X_t, W_t, t) = \sigma(X_t, t)\sigma_c(t)^\top, \quad t \in [0, T]. \tag{47}$$

Interpreting $\sigma(X_t, t)\sigma_c(t)^\top$ as the "instantaneous" covariances at time t between the rates of return of the K securities and the agent's consumption rate, we see that the agent optimally equates these covariances with a multiple of the expected excess rates of return of the securities. Let C^i denote the consumption feedback function for agent i under the above assumptions, and let σ_c^i denote the corresponding process defined by (46). Aggregate consumption in equilibrium is then $e_t = C(X_t, t) = \sum_{i=1}^{I} C^i(X_t, W_t^i, t)$, $t \in [0, T]$. Let $\tilde\tau = \sum_{i=1}^{I} \tau_i$ denote the *market direct risk tolerance*.

(C)   Show that $\tilde\tau\lambda = \sigma\sigma_e^\top$, where $\sigma_e \equiv C_x\eta = \sum_{i=1}^{I} \sigma_c^i$.

This can be viewed as a version of the *Consumption–Based Capital Asset Pricing Model*, predicting that the ratio λ_n/λ_k of the equilibrium expected excess rates of return of two securities is given by the ratio of the "covariances" of their rates of return with aggregate consumption. A more familiar relationship is obtained by presuming that $\sigma\sigma^\top$ is nonsingular and by defining the portfolio function $\pi = (\sigma\sigma^\top)^{-1}\sigma\sigma_e^\top/k$, where k is a real-valued function normalizing the sum of the entries of π to unity. Then the expected rate of return on this portfolio is $\mu_\pi = \pi^\top\mu$.

(D)   Show that $\lambda = \beta_\pi(\mu_\pi - r)$, where $\beta_\pi = \sigma\sigma^\top\pi/(\pi^\top\sigma\sigma^\top\pi)$ is the R^K–valued beta of the securities relative to π.

The portfolio process π may be treated as that portfolio "most highly correlated" with movements in aggregate consumption. In order to confirm this view, we adopt the static framework of Exercise 24.15, including the definitions given there to X and $\mathcal{R}$. Suppose e_x is a row vector in R^K and that the real–valued random variable $c = A + e_x X$ is an "aggregate consumption increment", for some scalar A.

(E)   Show that $\hat\pi = (\sigma\sigma^\top)^{-1}\sigma\eta^\top e_x^\top$ solves the problem:

$$\min_{\pi\in R^N}\quad \text{var}(\pi^\top\mathcal{R} - e) \qquad \text{subject to}\quad \text{var}(\pi^\top\mathcal{R}) = \text{var}(\hat\pi^\top\mathcal{R}).$$

EXERCISE 25.14   (Static CAPM by Representative Agent Pricing)   For comparison with our continuous–time results, consider a static pure exchange model, with agents defined by endowments $e^1,\dots,e^I$ in the space L of random variables with finite variance on a given probability space, and by von Neumann Morgenstern utility functions $u_1,\dots,u_I$ on R. There are also $K + 1$ securities in zero supply with linearly independent payoffs $D = (D^0,\dots,D^K)$, each in L, where D^0 is a non–zero constant. Without loss of of generality, $D^0 \equiv 1$. An equilibrium is a vector $S = (S^0,\dots,S^K)$ of security prices and portfolios $\theta^1,\dots,\theta^I$ in R^{K+1} summing to zero and solving, for respective i, the problem

$$\max_{\theta\in R^{K+1}}\quad E[u_i(e^i + \theta\cdot D)] \quad \text{subject to}\quad \theta\cdot S = 0.$$

We suppose throughout that, for all i, u_i is quadratic.

(A)   Demonstrate an equilibrium by constructing agents' security demands as functions of security prices, and then solving for market clearing security prices.

(B)   Suppose that $e^i \in \text{span}(D^0,\dots,D^K)$ for each agent i. Show that, for sufficiently small risk aversion coefficients, the equilibrium allocation is uniquely defined and fully Pareto efficient. *Hint:* Based on the equilibrium demonstrated in Part (A), postulate a (complete markets) static equilibrium for the economy defined by the same preferences, the same endowments, and the consumption space $L^2(P)$. The equilibrium price functional, $p : L \to R$, can be guessed quite easily on the basis of Part (D). One can then apply the efficiency properties of complete markets equilibria.

(C)   Based on Part (B), demonstrate strictly positive weights $\lambda_1, \ldots, \lambda_I$ such that the function $\bar{u} : R \to R$ defined by

$$\bar{u}(c) = \max_{c_1 + \cdots + c_I \leq c} \sum_{i=1}^{I} \lambda_i u_i(c_i)$$

provides equilibrium security prices by the representative agent formula $S = E[\bar{u}'(e)D]$, where $e = e^1 + \cdots + e^I$ is aggregate consumption. *Hint:* A review of Paragraph L of The Introduction may be useful.

(D)   Show that $\bar{u}$ is also quadratic, and that for some numbers A and B,

$$S^k = A\,E(D^k) + B\,\mathrm{cov}(e, D^k)$$

for any security k.

(E)   Suppose, for a given security k, that S^0, $\mathrm{var}(e)$, and S^k are non–zero. Show that

$$E(\mathcal{R}^k) - r = \beta_k[E(\mathcal{R}^e) - r], \tag{48}$$

where $\mathcal{R}^k = D^k/S^k, \beta_k = \mathrm{cov}(e, \mathcal{R}^k)/\mathrm{var}(e)$, $r = 1/S^0$, and $\mathcal{R}^e = e/\theta \cdot S$ for some portfolio θ such that $e = \theta \cdot D$. This is the Capital Asset Pricing Model (CAPM). We could equally well view the endowment e^i of agent i as the payoff $M^i \cdot D$ of a portfolio $M^i \in R^{K+1}$ of securities held instead in positive total supply $M = \sum_i M^i$. The portfolio M is the market portfolio, and since $M \cdot D = e$, the CAPM shown in (48) is the original (Sharpe–Lintner, market–portfolio–based) CAPM. Of course, with further rounds of trade, the payoff of the market portfolio M is $M \cdot (D + \widehat{S}) = e + M \cdot \widehat{S}$, where $\widehat{S}$ is the ex dividend security price vector. The market–based CAPM is no longer correct unless $(M \cdot \widehat{S} - e)$ and e are perfectly correlated.

(F)   Completely solve an example of a two period (quadratic) model with at least two different agents, extending the above one period model, in which the CCAPM characterizes equilibrium asset prices, but with the property that the market–portfolio beta model is not correct at the initial round of trading.

EXERCISE 25.15 (A Finite–Dimensional Capital Asset Pricing Theory)
Let $(\Omega, \mathcal{F}, P)$ denote a probability space, with Ω a finite set, and let $\mathcal{T} = \{1, 2, \ldots, T\}$ be a finite time set. Let $F = \{\mathcal{F}_1, \mathcal{F}_2, \ldots, \mathcal{F}_T\}$ be a filtration of sub–tribes of $\mathcal{F}$ and let L denote the space of adapted real–valued processes for $(\Omega, \mathcal{F}, F, P)$. Let $\mathcal{E} = (\succeq_i, e^i)$, $i \in \{1, \ldots, I\}$ denote a pure exchange economy for the choice space L, where $\succeq_i$ is a preference relation on L_+ represented by a strictly concave increasing utility function $U_i : L_+ \to R$. Let $(c^1, \ldots, c^I, \pi)$ denote an equilibrium for $\mathcal{E}$.

(A) Show that there exist strictly positive scalars $\lambda_1, \lambda_2, \ldots, \lambda_I$ such that, for all i, c^i solves the problem

$$\max_{x \in L_+} \quad \lambda_i U_i(x) - \pi \cdot (x - e^i).$$

If U_i is differentiable and $c^i \in L_{++} = \text{int}(L_+)$, show that $\pi = \lambda_i \nabla U_i(c^i)$. *Hint:* See Section 8.

(B) Show that the scalars $\lambda_1, \ldots, \lambda_I$ of Part (A) can be chosen so that the allocation $(c^1, \ldots, c^I)$ solves the problem

$$\max_{x^1, \ldots, x^I} \quad \sum_i \lambda_i U_i(x^i) \quad \text{subject to} \quad \sum_i x^i \le e = \sum_i e^i.$$

(C) Again using $\lambda_1, \ldots, \lambda_I$ from Parts (A) and (B), define the utility function $U : L_+ \to R$ by

$$U(x) = \max_{x^1, \ldots, x^I} \quad \sum_i \lambda_i U_i(x^i) \quad \text{subject to} \quad \sum_i x^i \le x.$$

Show that U is strictly concave and increasing. Show that the aggregate endowment e solves the problem

$$\max_{c \in L_+} \quad U(c) \quad \text{subject to} \quad \pi \cdot c \le \pi \cdot e.$$

(D) Suppose, for each agent i and for some integer $n > 1$, that U_i is C^n (n times continuously differentiable) and that $c^i \in L_{++}$. Show the existence of a ball B_e centered at e in the (Euclidean) space L and unique C^{n-1} functions $C_1, \ldots, C_I$, where $C_i : B_e \to L_+$, such that $U(x) = \sum_i \lambda_i U_i[C_i(x)]$ for all x in B_e. That is, C_i assigns an efficient allocation to agent i as a function of the available aggregate endowment. *Hint:* Use the Implicit Function Theorem, as stated for instance in Exercise 25.3.

(E)   Under the conditions of Part (D), show that the restriction of U to B_e is C^{n-1} and that $\pi = \lambda \nabla U(e)$ for some strictly positive scalar λ. Show that π/λ is also an equilibrium price functional, so that $\pi = \nabla U(e)$ may be assumed.

(F)   For any linear functional $\widehat{\pi} : L \to R$, show the existence of some $\widehat{p} \in L$ such that we have the representation $\widehat{\pi} \cdot c = E\left[\sum_t \widehat{p}_t c_t\right]$ for any $c \in L$. *Hint:* Show that L is a Hilbert space under the inner product

$$(a \mid b) = E\left[\sum_{t=1}^{T} a_t b_t\right].$$

As stated in Section 6, for any continuous linear functional $\widehat{\pi}$ on a Hilbert space L with inner product $(\cdot \mid \cdot)$, there is a unique vector $\widehat{p}$ in L such that $\widehat{\pi} \cdot c = (\widehat{p} \mid c)$ for any $c \in L$.

(G)   Suppose that, for each agent i, there exists a function $u_i : R_+ \times T \to R$ such that $U_i(c) = E\left[\sum_t u_i(c_t, t)\right]$. Construct a strictly concave increasing function $u : R_+ \times T \to R$ such that $U(c) = E\left[\sum_t u(c_t, t)\right]$.

(H)   Under the conditions of Parts (D) and (G), show that, for each t, the derivative $u_c(q, t) = [\partial u(q, t)]/\partial q$ exists at any point q in $\{e_t(\omega) : \omega \in \Omega\}$. Show that the representation $p \in L$ of π from Parts (E) and (F) is given by $p_t = \lambda u_c(e_t, t)$ for all t.

(I)   Define securities $D = (D^0, \ldots, D^N)$, a stochastic economy $\mathcal{A}$, and a stochastic equilibrium analogously to the continuous–time model used in Section 25. Define, in terms of properties of the filtration F, the minimum number of securities $N(F)$ required to "implement" the static equilibrium $\left((c^i), \pi\right)$ for $\mathcal{E}$ as a stochastic equilibrium $\left(S, p, (\theta^i, c^i)\right)$ for $\mathcal{A}$, in analogy to the proof of Theorem 25D. *Hint:* See Sections 12 and 14.

(J)   For the stochastic equilibrium defined in Part (I) and under the conditions of Parts (D) and (G), show that, in the numeraire of current consumption, the equilibrium ex dividend price process $\widehat{S}$ of a security promising real (consumption) dividends $\delta \in L$ satisfies

$$\widehat{S}_t = \frac{1}{u_c(e_t, t)} E\left[\sum_{s=t+1}^{T} u_c(e_s, s)\delta_s \,\bigg|\, \mathcal{F}_t\right],$$

where u_c is defined in Part (G).

(K)   Prove that the minimum number $N(F)$ of securities, from Part (I), is in fact a sufficient number.

(L) Suppose, for each time t and agent i, that the function $u_i(\cdot,t) : R_+ \to R$ discussed in Part (G) is quadratic at any $q < \max(\{e_t(\omega) : \omega \in \Omega\})$, and that $c^i \in L_{++}$. Show that $u(\cdot,t)$, defined in Part (G), has the same quadratic property.

(M) Under the conditions of Part (L), prove a version of the CCAPM. For $T = 2$, prove a version of the (market portfolio–based) Capital Asset Pricing Model.

(N) Extend Parts (A) through (M) to a production economy. That is, let $\mathcal{E}$ be a production economy $((\succeq_i, e^i); (Y_j); (\theta_{ij}))$, and make natural extensions of each of the above results for the case of production. *Hint:* Where differentiability is required, assume $Y_j = \{y \in L : g_j(y) \leq 0\}$ for some differentiable function $g_j \cdot I_t \to R$.

EXERCISE 25.16 (Stochastic Production Decentralization) This exercise is to verify that the Cox–Ingersoll–Ross model of the term structure can indeed be decentralized as a stock market economy, as suggested in Paragraph 25H. The objective is to construct a stochastic equilibrium $((S,p), \delta, (c, \theta))$, such that

(a) δ is the optimal real output rate process of a firm controlling the capital stock production process and maximizing its share price,

(b) S, the (nominal) stock price process of the firm that is taken as given by the agent, is equal to the (nominal) share price process generated as the value function of the firm's optimization problem, and

(c) $(c_t, \theta_t) = (\delta_t, 1)$ solves the agent's optimal consumption and trading strategy problem, given (S, δ) as the nominal price process and real dividend rate process of the firm.

(A) Formally define a stochastic equilibrium consistent with the loose description just given. In particular, state precisely the agent's problem and the firm's problem.

(B) Show that the real dividend rate $\delta_t = \rho K_t / [1 - e^{-\rho(T-t)}]$ and (real) stock price process K_t are consistent with equilibrium, in terms of first order conditions for optimality in the appropriate Bellman Equations for both the firm and the agent. *Hint:* Be careful about real versus nominal values.

EXERCISE 25.17 Demonstrate scalars $\lambda_1, \ldots, \lambda_I$ satisfying the representative agent pricing scheme (9)–(10)–(11)–(12), and $p_t = \bar{u}_c(e_t, t)$ for all t. *Hint:* The Saddle Point Theorem of Section 8 may be useful.

Notes

The seminal continuous–time asset pricing model is due to Merton (1973a). In the case of one and only one "state variable" that is also the equilibrium interest rate, Merton is able to eliminate the "portfolio" H in relation (25) and obtain a "multi–beta" asset pricing model, wherein all assets' excess expected rates of return are given in terms of their "betas" with respect to the market portfolio and the equilibrium interest rate.

The body of Section 25 is built around Duffie and Zame (1987), which includes the infinite–dimensional existence proof for a static economy, referred to in Step A of the proof of Theorem 25D. Araujo and Monteiro (1986) independently gave an existence theorem that could also be adapted to Step A of this proof. Araujo and Monteiro (1987) shows a corresponding result of generic non–existence of equilibria, in a certain sense. Duffie and Zame (1987) is designed to provide primitive conditions on a multi–agent economy that support the "Consumption–Based Capital Asset Pricing Model" of Breeden (1979) as well as the single–agent interest rate models of Cox, Ingersoll, and Ross (1985a, 1985b). Cox, Ingersoll, and Ross (1985b) and a "synthesis paper" by Breeden (1986) include further results. The versions of this theory outlined in Section 25 do not rely on a Markovian state variable assumption. For the breakdown of the CCAPM with transactions costs, see Grossman and Laroque (1987). For empirical tests, see Breeden, Gibbons, and Litzenberger (1986).

The CAPM of Chamberlain (1985) has preference assumptions that are notably weaker than expected concave utility. A simple sufficient condition for an informational assumption made by Chamberlain is that the underlying Brownian Motion is one–dimensional. In general, Chamberlain assumes that the representative agent marginal utility variable is a measurable function of a one–dimensional Brownian Motion.

Lehoczky and Shreve (1986) have a closed–form solution of the equilibrium model of Theorem 25D for a case in which the utility functions of agents are the same and given by a time additive power function. The representative agent pricing notion used in this section, especially in Step C of the proof of Theorem 25D, is from Constantinides (1982) (for the finite–dimensional case) and Huang (1987) (for the continuous–time case). One should see Mas–Colell (1985, 1986b) for further discussion of this topic.

Proposition 25F is an extension of the corresponding single–agent Markov model of Cox, Ingersoll, and Ross (1985b). Paragraph 25H is a simplification of the term structure example given in Cox, Ingersoll, and Ross (1985a). The corresponding discrete–time model is given by Gibbons and Sun (1986), and tested by Gibbons and Ramaswamy (1986). For the term structure model extended to the case of incomplete observation of the state process, see Dothan and Feldman (1986) as well as Gennotte (1984).

The extension of Theorem 25D to cover securities of the form suggested by relation (24) is given by Duffie (1986c). Exercise 25.11 is based, in part, on Hansen and Singleton (1986).

BIBLIOGRAPHY

Aase, K. (1984). "Optimum Portfolio Diversification in a General Continuous Time Model," *Stochastic Processes and their Application.* **18**, pp. 81–98.

Abel, A. (1986). "Stock Prices under Time–Varying Dividend Risk: An Exact Solution in an Infinite–Horizon General Equilibrium Model," Unpublished. Wharton School, University of Pennsylvania.

Aghion, P. and P. Bolton (1986). "An 'Incomplete Contracts' Approach to Bankruptcy and the Optimal Financial Structure of the Firm," Unpublished. Departnent of Economics, Harvard University.

Aliprantis, C., D. Brown, and O. Burkinshaw (1987). "Edgeworth Equilibria in Production Economies," *Econometrica.* **55**, pp. 1109–1138.

Allen, F. and D. Gale (1987). "Optimal Security Design," Unpublished. Department of Economics, University of Pittsburgh.

Araujo, A. (1984). "Demand Functions with Infinitely Many Goods: Non–existence Results," Unpublished. Instituto de Matemática Pura e Aplicada, Rio de Janeiro.

Araujo, A. and P. Monteiro (1985). "On Walrasian Equilibria in Sequence Economies," Unpublished. Instituto de Matemática Pura e Aplicada, Rio de Janeiro.

Araujo, A. and P. Monteiro (1986). "Existence without Uniform Conditions," Unpublished. Instituto de Matemática Pura e Aplicada, Rio de Janeiro.

Araujo, A. and P. Monteiro (1987). "Generic Non–Existence of Equilibria in Finance Models," Unpublished. Instituto de Matemática Pura e Aplicada, Rio de Janeiro.

Arnold, L. (1974). *Stochastic Differential Equations: Theory and Applications.* New York: Wiley.

Arrow, K. (1951). "An Extension of the Basic Theorems of Classical Welfare Economics." **In** J. Neyman, *Proceedings of the Second Berkeley Symposium on Mathematical Statistics and Probability.* Berkeley: University of California Press, pp. 507–532.

Arrow, K. (1953). "Le rôle des valeurs boursières pour la repartition la meillure des risques," *Econometrie.* Colloq. Internat. Centre National de la Recherche Scientifique, **40** (Paris, 1952), pp. 41–47; discussion, pp. 47–48, C.N.R.S. Paris, 1953. English Translation. *Review of Economic Studies* **31** (1964), pp. 91–96.

Arrow, K. (1970). *Essays in the Theory of Risk Bearing.* London: North–Holland.

Arrow, K. (1983). *Collected Papers of Kenneth J. Arrow, Volume 2: General Equilibrium.* Cambridge, Massachusetts: Belknap Press of Harvard University Press.

Arrow, K. and G. Debreu (1954). "Existence of an Equilibrium for a Competitive Economy," *Econometrica.* **22**, pp. 265–290.

Arrow, K. and F. Hahn (1971). *General Competitive Analysis.* San Francisco, California: Holden–Day.

Aumann, R. (1966). "Existence of Competitive Equilibrium in Markets with a Continuum of Traders," *Econometrica.* **32**, pp. 39–50.

Avondo–Bodino, G. (1962). *Economic Applications of the Theory of Graphs.* New York: Gordon and Breach.

Bachelier, L. (1900). "Théorie de la Speculation," *Annales Scientifiques de l'Ecole Normale Supérieure.* troisième serie **17**, pp. 21–88, Translation: *The Random Character of Stock Market Prices,* ed. Paul Cootner, Cambridge, MA: MIT Press.

Back, K. (1986). "Securities Market Equilibrium Without Bankruptcy: Contingent Claim Valuation and The Martingale Property," Research Paper 683. Center For Mathematical Studies in Economics and Management Science, Northwestern University.

Back, K. and S. Pliska (1986a). "Discrete versus Continuous Trading in Securities Markets with Net Worth Constraints," Working Paper 700. Center for Mathematical Studies in Economics and Management Science, Northwestern University.

Back, K. and S. Pliska (1986b). "The Shadow Price of Information in Continuous Time Decision Problems," Working Paper 690. Center for Mathematical Studies in Economics and Management Science, Northwestern University.

Balasko, Y. (1986). "Foundations of the Theory of General Equilibrium," Working Paper 86–22. Center for Analytic Research in Economics and the Social Sciences, University of Pennsylvania.

Balasko, Y. and D. Cass (1985). "Regular Demand with Several, General Budget Constraints," Working Paper 85–20. Center for Analytic Research in Economics and the Social Sciences, University of Pennsylvania.

Balasko, Y. and D. Cass (1986). "The Structure of Financial Equilibrium: I. Exogenous Yields and Unrestricted Participation," Working Paper 85–23R. Center for Analytic Research in Economics and the Social Sciences, University of Pennsylvania.

Balasko, Y., D. Cass, and P. Siconolfi (1987). "The Structure of Financial Equilibrium with Exogenous Yields: II. Restricted Participation," Working Paper 87–16. Center for Analytic Research in Economics and the Social Sciences, University of Pennsylania.

Balcer, Y. and K. Judd (1985). "Optimal Consumption Plans and Portfolio Management with Duration–Dependent Returns," Working Paper 662. Center for Mathematical Studies in Economics and Management Science, Northwestern University.

Bartle, R. (1976). *The Elements of Real Analysis (Second Edition).* New York: Wiley.

Bellman, R. (1957). *Dynamic Programming.* Princeton, New Jersey: Princeton University Press.

Bensoussan, A. (1983). "Lectures on Stochastic Control." In S. Mitter and A. Moro, *Nonlinear Filtering and Stochastic Control,* Lecture Notes in Mathematics Number 972. New York: Springer–Verlag.

Benveniste, L. and J. Scheinkman (1979). "On the Differentiability of the Value Function in Dynamic Models of Economics," *Econometrica.* **47**, pp. 727–732.

Berge, C. (1966). *Espaces Topologiques—Fonctions Multivoques (Deuxième Edition).* Paris: Dunod.

Bertsekas, D. (1974). "Necessary and Sufficient Conditions for Existence of an Optimal Portfolio," *Journal of Economic Theory.* **8**, pp. 235–247.

Bertsekas, D. (1976). *Dynamic Programming and Stochastic Control.* New York: Academic Press.

Bertsekas, D. and S. Shreve (1978). *Stochastic Optimal Control, The Discrete Time Case.* New York: Academic Press.

Bester, H. (1982). "On Shareholder Unanimity in the Mean–Variance Model," *Economics Letters.* **10**, pp. 363–367.

Bewley, T. (1972). "Existence of Equilibria in Economies with Infinitely Many Commodities," *Journal of Economic Theory.* **4**, pp. 514–540.

Bhattacharya, G. (1987). "Notes on Optimality of Rational Expectations Equilibria with Incomplete Markets," *Journal of Economic Theory.* **42**, pp. 191–208.

Bick, A. (1986). "On Viable Diffusion Price Processes," Unpublished. Graduate School of Business, New York University.

Billingsley, P. (1968). *Convergence of Probability Measures.* New York: Wiley.

Billingsley, P. (1986). *Probability and Measure (Second Edition).* New York: Wiley.

Black, F. (1972). "Capital Market Equilibrium with Restricted Borrowing," *Journal of Business.* **45**, pp. 444–454.

Black, F. and M. Scholes (1973). "The Pricing of Options and Corporate Liabilities," *Journal of Political Economy.* **81**, pp. 637–654.

Blackwell, D. (1965). "Discounted Dynamic Programming," *Annals of Mathematical Statistics.* **36**, pp. 226–235.

Blume, L., D. Easley, and M. O'Hara (1982). "Characterization of Optimal Plans for Stochastic Dynamic Programs," *Journal of Economic Theory.* **28**, pp. 221–234.

Bourgin, R. (1983). *Geometric Aspects of Convex Sets with the Radon–Nikodym Property, Lecture Notes in Mathematics Number 993.* New York: Springer–Verlag.

Boyd, J. (1985). "Symmetries, Dynamic Equilibria, and The Value Function," Unpublished. Indiana University.

Boyle, P. (1977). "Options: A Monte Carlo Approach," *Journal of Financial Economics.* **4**, pp. 323–338.

Bracewell, R. (1978). *The Fourier Transform and its Applications (Second Edition).* New York: McGraw-Hill.

Brealey, R. and S. Myers (1984). *Principles of Corporate Finance (Second Edition).* New York: McGraw-Hill.

Breeden, D. (1979). "An Intertemporal Asset Pricing Model with Stochastic Consumption and Investment Opportunities," *Journal of Financial Economics.* **7**, pp. 265-296.

Breeden, D. (1986). "Consumption, Production, Inflation and Interest Rates," *Journal of Financial Economics.* **16**, pp. 3–39.

Breeden, D., M. Gibbons, and R. Litzenberger (1986). "Empirical Tests of the Consumption–Oriented CAPM," Research Paper 879. Graduate School of Business, Stanford University.

Breeden, D. and R. Litzenberger (1978). "Prices of State–Contingent Claims Implicit in Option Prices," *Journal of Business.* **51**, pp. 621–651.

Brennan, M. and E. Schwartz (1977). "The Valuation of American Put Options," *Journal of Finance.* **32**, pp. 449–462.

Brennan, M. and E. Schwartz (1979). "A Continuous Time Approach to the Pricing of Bonds," *Journal of Banking and Finance.* **3**, pp. 133–155.

Brock, W. (1972). "Optimal Economic Growth and Uncertainty: The Discounted Case," *Journal of Economic Theory.* **4**, pp. 479–513.

Brock, W. (1979). "An Integration of Stochastic Growth Theory and The Theory of Finance, Part I: The Growth Model." **In** J. Green and J. Scheinkman, *General Equilibrium, Growth, and Trade.* New York: Academic Press, pp. 165–192.

Brock, W. (1982). "Asset Prices in a Production Economy." **In** J. McCall, *The Economics of Information and Uncertainty.* Chicago: University of Chicago Press, pp. 1–46.

Brown, D. (1987). "Aggregation and Efficiency in Sequentially Complete Markets with Random Lifetimes and Nonmarketable Income," Unpublished. Indiana University.

Brown, D. and M. Gibbons (1985). "A Simple Econometric Approach for Utility–Based Asset Pricing Models," *Journal of Finance.* **40**, pp. 359–381.

Burke, J. (1986). "Existence of Equilibrium for Incomplete Market Economies with Production and Stock Trading," Unpublished. Department of Economics, Texas A & M University.

Campbell, J. (1984). "Bond and Stock Returns in a Simple Exchange Model," Unpublished. Department of Economics, Princeton University.

Campbell, J. (1986). "A Defense of Traditional Hypotheses about the Term Structure of Interest Rates," *Journal of Finance.* **41**, pp. 183–193.

Carr, P. (1987). "Treasury Bond Futures and the Quality Option," Unpublished. Graduate School of Management, University of California, Los Angeles.

Cass, D. (1984). "Competitive Equilibria in Incomplete Financial Markets," Working Paper 84–09. Center for Analytic Research in Economics and the Social Sciences, University of Pennsylvania.

Cass, D. (1985). "On The 'Number' of Equilibrium Allocations with Incomplete Financial Markets," Working Paper 85–16. Center for Analytic Research in Economics and the Social Sciences, University of Pennsylvania.

Cass, D. and Y. Yaari (1966). "A Re–Examination of the Pure Consumption Loans Model," *Journal of Political Economy.* **74**, pp. 353–367.

Chae, S. (1985). "Existence of Equilibria in Incomplete Markets," Unpublished. Rice University, forthcoming in *Journal of Economic Theory*.

Chamberlain, G. (1983a). "A Characterization of the Distributions that Imply Mean–Variance Utility Functions," *Journal of Economic Theory*. **29**, pp. 185–201.

Chamberlain, G. (1983b). "Funds, Factors, and Diversification in Arbitrage Pricing Models," *Econometrica*. **51**, pp. 1305–1323.

Chamberlain, G. (1985). "Asset Pricing in Multiperiod Securities Markets," Unpublished. Department of Economics, University of Wisconsin, Madison.

Chamberlain, G. and M. Rothschild (1983). "Arbitrage, Factor Structure, and Mean–Variance Analysis on Large Asset Markets," *Econometrica*. **51**, pp. 1281–1304.

Cheng, S. (1987). "Pricing Models for Multiple–Currency Option Bonds," Unpublished. Graduate School of Business, Stanford University.

Chorin, A. (1971). "Hermite Expansions in Monte–Carlo Computation," *Journal of Computational Physics*. **8**, pp. 172–182

Chorin, A. (1973). "Accurate Evaluation of Wiener Integrals," *Mathematics of Computation*. **27**, pp. 1–15.

Chow, Y. and H. Teicher (1978). *Probability Theory: Independence Interchangeability Martingales*. New York: Springer–Verlag.

Christensen, P. (1987). "An Intuitive Approach to the Harrison and Kreps Concept of Arbitrage Pricing for Continuous Time Diffusions," Unpublished. Department of Management, Odense University, Denmark.

Chung, K.L. (1974). *A Course in Probability Theory (Second Edition)*. New York: Academic Press.

Chung, K.L. and R. Williams (1983). *An Introduction to Stochastic Integration*. Boston: Birkhäuser

Clarke, F. (1983). *Optimization and Nonsmooth Analysis*. New York: Wiley.

Connor, G. (1984). "A Unified Beta Pricing Theory," *Journal of Economic Theory*. **34**, pp. 13–31.

Constantinides, G. (1982). "Intertemporal Asset Pricing with Heterogenous Consumers and Without Demand Aggregation," *Journal of Business*. **55**, pp. 253–267.

Constantinides, G. (1986). "Capital Market Equilibrium with Transactions Costs," *Journal of Political Economy*. **94**, pp. 842–862.

Cox, J. (1983). "Optimal Consumption and Portfolio Rules when Assets Follow a Diffusion Process," Working Paper 658. Graduate School of Business, Stanford University.

Cox, J. and C. Huang (1985). "A Variational Problem Arising in Financial Economics with an Application to a Portfolio Turnpike Theorem," Unpublished. Sloan School of Management, Massachusetts Institute of Technology.

Cox, J. and C. Huang (1986). "Optimal Consumption and Portfolio Policies when Asset Prices Follow a Diffusion Process," Unpublished. Sloan School of Management, Massachusetts Institute of Technology.

Cox, J., J. Ingersoll, and S. Ross (1981). "A Re–examination of Traditional Hypotheses about the Term Structure of Interest Rates," *Journal of Finance*. **36**, pp. 769–799.

Cox, J., J. Ingersoll, and S. Ross (1985a). "A Theory of the Term Structure of Interest Rates," *Econometrica.* **53**, pp. 385–408.

Cox, J., J. Ingersoll, and S. Ross (1985b). "An Intertemporal General Equilibrium Model of Asset Prices," *Econometrica.* **53**, pp. 363–384.

Cox, J. and S. Ross (1976). "The Valuation of Options for Alternative Stochastic Processes," *Journal of Financial Economics.* **3**, pp. 145–166.

Cox, J., S. Ross, and M. Rubinstein (1979). "Option Pricing: A Simplified Approach," *Journal of Financial Economics.* **7**, pp. 229–263.

Cox, J. and M. Rubinstein (1985). *Options Markets.* Englewood Cliffs, New Jersey: Prentice–Hall.

Davis, M. and A. Norman (1987). "Portfolio Selection with Transaction Costs," Imperial College, University of London.

Day, M. (1973). *Normed Linear Spaces (Third Edition).* New York: Springer–Verlag.

Debreu, G. (1953). "Une Economie de l'Incertain," Unpublished. Electricité de France.

Debreu, G. (1954). "Representation of a Preference Ordering By a Numerical Function." **In** R. Thrall, *Decision Processes.* New York: Wiley, Chapter 11, pp. 159–165.

Debreu, G. (1959). *Theory of Value.* Cowles Foundation Monograph 17, New Haven Connecticut: Yale University Press.

Debreu, G. (1962). "New Concepts and Techniques For Equilibrium Analysis," *International Economic Review.* **3**, pp. 257–273.

Debreu, G. (1970). "Economies with a Finite Set of Equilibria," *Econometrica.* **38**, pp. 387–392.

Debreu, G. (1972). "Smooth Preferences," *Econometrica.* **40**, pp. 603–615.

Debreu, G. (1976). "Smooth Preferences, A Corrigendum," *Econometrica.* **44**, pp. 831–832.

Debreu, G. (1982). "Existence of Competitive Equilibrium." **In** K. Arrow and M. Intriligator, *Handbook of Mathematical Economics, Volume II.* Amsterdam: North–Holland, pp. 697–743.

Debreu, G. (1983). *Mathematical Economics.* Cambridge: Cambridge University Press.

Dekel, E. (1986). "An Axiomatic Characterization of Preferences Under Uncertainty: Weakening the Independence Axiom," *Journal of Economic Theory.* **40**, pp. 304–318.

Dekel, E. (1987). "Asset Demands Without the Independence Axiom," Unpublished. Department of Economics, University of California, Berkeley.

Dellacherie, C. and P. Meyer (1978). *Probabilities and Potential.* New York: North–Holland.

Dellacherie, C. and P. Meyer (1982). *Probabilities and Potential B: Theory of Martingales.* New York: North–Holland.

DeMarzo, P. (1986). "An Extension of the Modigliani–Miller Theorem to Stochastic Economies with Incomplete Markets," Technical Report 498. Institute for Mathematical Studies in the Social Sciences, forthcoming in *Journal of Economic Theory.*

DeMarzo, P. (1987). "Majority Rule and Corporate Control: The Rule of the Dominant Shareholder," Unpublished. Department of Economics, Stanford University.

Detemple, J. and L. Selden (1986). "A General Equilibrium Analysis of Option and Stock Market Interactions," Unpublished. Graduate School of Business, Columbia University.

Dhrymes, P. (1978). *Mathematics for Econometricians*. New York: Springer–Verlag.

Diamond, P. (1967). "The Role of a Stock Market in a General Equilibrium Model with Technological Uncertainty," *American Economic Review*. **57**, pp. 759–776.

Dixit, A. (1976). *Optimization in Economic Theory*. Oxford: Oxford University Press.

Donaldson, J., T. Johnson, and R. Mehra (1987). "The Behavior of the Term Structure of Interest Rates in a Real Business Cycle Model," Unpublished. Graduate School of Business, Columbia University.

Donaldson, J. and R. Mehra (1984). "Comparative Dynamics of an Equilibrium Intertemporal Asset Pricing Model," *Review of Economic Studies*. **51**, pp. 491–508.

Dothan, M. and D. Feldman (1986). "Equilibrium Interest Rates and Multiperiod Bonds in a Partially Observable Economy," Unpublished. Vanderbilt University.

Dreyfus, J.-F. (1984). "On the Modelling of Stock Market Economies: Definition, Existence and Optimality of Competitive Equilibria," Working Paper 84 17. Center for Analytic Research in Economics and the Social Sciences, University of Pennsylvania.

Drèze, J. (1974). "Investment under Private Ownership: Optimality, Equilibrium and Stability." In J. Drèze, *Allocation Under Uncertainty: Equilibrium and Optimality*. New York: Wiley, pp. 129–165.

Duffie, D. (1985a). "Predictable Representation of Martingale Spaces and Changes of Probability Measure," *Séminaire de Probabilités*. **XIX**, Lecture Notes in Mathematics Number 1123, ed. J. Azema and M. Yor, New York: Springer–Verlag, pp. 278–284.

Duffie, D. (1985b). "Price Operators: Extensions, Potentials, and the Markov Valuation of Securities," Research Paper 813. Graduate School of Business, Stanford University.

Duffie, D. (1986a). "Competitive Equilibria in General Choice Spaces," *Journal of Mathematical Economics*. **14**, pp. 1–23.

Duffie, D. (1986b). "On The Term Structure of Interest Rates," Research Paper 916. Graduate School of Business, Stanford University.

Duffie, D. (1986c). "Stochastic Equilibria: Existence, Spanning Number, and The 'No Expected Financial Gain From Trade' Hypothesis," *Econometrica*. **54**, pp. 1161–1184.

Duffie, D. (1986d). "An Extension of the Black–Scholes Model of Redundant Security Valuation," Unpublished. Mathematical Sciences Research Institute, Berkeley California, forthcoming in *Journal of Economic Theory*.

Duffie, D. (1987). "Stochastic Equilibria with Incomplete Financial Markets," *Journal of Economic Theory*. **41**, pp. 405–416.

Duffie, D. and M. Garman (1985). "Intertemporal Arbitrage and the Markov Valuation of Securities," Working Paper 975. Graduate School of Business, Stanford University.

Duffie, D., J. Geanakoplos, A. Mas–Colell, and A. McLennan (1988). "Stationary Markov Equilibria," Unpublished. Graduate School of Business, Stanford University.

Duffie, D. and C. Huang (1985). "Implementing Arrow–Debreu Equilibria by Continuous Trading of Few Long–Lived Securities," *Econometrica.* **53**, pp. 1337–1356.

Duffie, D. and C. Huang (1986a). "Multiperiod Security Markets With Differential Information: Martingales and Resolution Times," *Journal of Mathematical Economics.* **15**, pp. 283–303.

Duffie, D. and C. Huang (1986b). "Stochastic Production–Exchange Equilibria," Research Paper 974. Graduate School of Business, Stanford University.

Duffie, D. and M. Jackson (1986a). "Optimal Hedging and Equilibrium in a Dynamic Futures Market," Research Paper 814. Graduate School of Business, Stanford University.

Duffie, D. and M. Jackson (1986b). "Optimal Innovation of Futures Contracts," Research Paper 917. Graduate School of Business, Stanford University.

Duffie, D. and W. Shafer (1985). "Equilibrium in Incomplete Markets I: A Basic Model of Generic Existence," *Journal of Mathematical Economics.* **14**, pp. 285–300.

Duffie, D. and W. Shafer (1986a). "Equilibrium in Incomplete Markets II: Generic Existence in Stochastic Economies," *Journal of Mathematical Economics.* **15**, pp. 199–216.

Duffie, D. and W. Shafer (1986b). "Equilibrium and the Role of the Firm in Incomplete Markets," Research Paper 915. Graduate School of Business, Stanford University.

Duffie, D. and H. Sonnenschein (1988). "Arrow and General Equilibrium Theory," Research Paper 976. Graduate School of Business, Stanford University, forthcoming in *Journal of Economic Literature.*

Duffie, D. and T. Sun (1986). "Transactions Costs and Portfolio Choice in a Discrete–Continuous Time Setting," Research Paper 921. Graduate School of Business, Stanford University.

Duffie, D. and W. Zame (1987). "The Consumption–Based Capital Asset Pricing Model," Research Paper 922. Graduate School of Business, Stanford University.

Durrett, R. (1984). *Brownian Motion and Martingales in Analysis.* Belmont, California: Wadsworth Publishing Company.

Dynkin, E. (1965a). *Markov Processes, Volume I.* Berlin: Springer–Verlag.

Dynkin, E. (1965b). *Markov Processes, Volume II.* Berlin: Springer–Verlag.

Dynkin, E. and A. Yushkevich (1979). *Controlled Markov Processes.* Berlin, New York: Springer–Verlag.

Ekern, S. and R. Wilson (1974). "On The Theory of the Firm in an Economy with Incomplete Markets," *Bell Journal of Economics and Management Science.* **5**, pp. 171–180.

Elliott, R. (1982). *Stochastic Calculus and Applications.* New York: Springer–Verlag.

Epstein, L. and S. Zin (1987). "Substitution, Risk Aversion and the Temporal Behavior of Consumption and Asset Returns I: A Theoretical Framework," Working Paper 8715. Department of Economics, University of Toronto.

Fama, E. (1976). *Foundations of Finance.* New York: Basic Books.

Fama, E. (1978). "The Effects of a Firm's Investment and Financing Decisions on the Welfare of its Security Holders," *American Economic Review.* **68**, pp. 272–284.

Fama, E. and M. Miller (1972). *The Theory of Finance.* New York: Holt, Rinehart and Winston.

Fan, K. (1952). "Fixed–Point and Minimax Theorems in Locally Convex Topological Linear Spaces," *Proceedings of the National Academy of Sciences.* **38**, pp. 121–126.

Feldman, M. and C. Gilles (1985). "An Expository Note on Individual Risk without Aggregate Uncertainty," *Journal of Economic Theory.* **35**, pp. 26–32.

Feller, W. (1968). *An Introduction to Probability Theory and Its Applications, Vol. I (Third Edition).* New York: Wiley.

Feller, W. (1971). *An Introduction to Probability Theory and Its Applications, Vol. II (Second Edition).* New York: Wiley.

Fenchel, W. (1953). "Convex Cones, Sets, and Functions," Lecture Notes. Department of Mathematics, Princeton University.

Fishburn, P. (1970). *Utility Theory for Decision Making.* New York: Wiley.

Fishburn, P. (1982). *The Foundations of Expected Utility.* Dordrecht: Reidel.

Fleming, W. and R. Rishel (1975). *Deterministic and Stochastic Optimal Control.* Berlin: Springer–Verlag.

Foldes, L. (1978). "Martingale Conditions for Optimal Saving—Discrete Time," *Journal of Mathematical Economics.* **5**, pp. 83–96.

Foldes, L. (1979). "Optimal Saving and Risk in Continuous Time," *Review of Economic Studies.* **46**, pp. 39–65.

Föllmer, H. and Dieter Sondermann (1986). "Hedging of Non–Redundant Contingent Claims." In A. Mas-Colell and W. Hildenbrand, *Contributions to Mathematical Economics.* Amsterdam: North–Holland, pp. 205–223.

Freedman, D. (1983a). *Brownian Motion and Diffusion.* New York: Springer–Verlag.

Freedman, D. (1983b). *Markov Chains.* New York: Springer–Verlag.

Freidlin, M. (1985). *Functional Integration and Partial Differential Equations.* Princeton, New Jersey: Princeton University Press.

Friedman, A. (1975). *Stochastic Differential Equations and Applications, Vol. I.* New York: Academic Press.

Friesen, P. (1974). "A Reinterpretation of the Equilibrium Theory of Arrow and Debreu in Terms of Financial Markets," Technical Report 126. Institute for Mathematical Studies in the Social Sciences, Stanford University.

Gagnon, J. and J. Taylor (1986). "Solving and Estimating Stochastic Equilibrium Models with the Extended Path Method," Unpublished. Department of Economics, Stanford University.

Gale, David (1960). *The Theory of Linear Economic Models.* New York: McGraw-Hill.

Gale, Douglas (1986). "Bargaining and Competition," *Econometrica.* **54**, pp. 785–818.

Geanakoplos, J., M. Magill, M. Quinzii, and J. Dreze (1987). "Generic Inefficiency of Stock Market Equilibrium When Markets are Incomplete," Working Paper M8735. Department of Economics, University of Southern California.

Geanakoplos, J. and A. Mas–Colell (1985). "Real Indeterminacy with Financial Assets," Unpublished. Cowles Foundation, Yale University.

Geanakoplos, J. and H. Polemarchakis (1986). "Existence, Regularity, and Constrained Suboptimality of Competitive Allocations when the Asset Market is Incomplete." In W. Heller and D. Starrett, *Essays in Honor of Kenneth J. Arrow, Volume III*. Cambridge: Cambridge University Press, pp. 65–96.

Geanakoplos, J. and W. Shafer (1987). "Solving Systems of Simultaneous Equations in Economics," Unpublished. Department of Economics, University of Southern California.

Gennotte, G. (1984). "Continuous–Time Production Economies Under Incomplete Information I: A Separation Theorem," Working Paper 1612–84. Sloan School, Massachusetts Institute of Technology.

Geske, R. (1979). "The Valuation of Compound Options," *Journal of Financial Economics*. **7**, pp. 63–81.

Geske, R. and H. Johnson (1984). "The American Put Option Valued Analytically," *Journal of Finance*. **39**, pp. 1511–1524.

Gevers, L. (1974). "Competitive Equilibrium of the Stock Exchange and Pareto Efficiency." In J. Drèze, *Allocation under Uncertainty: Equilibrium and Optimality*. New York: Wiley, pp. 167–191.

Gibbons, M. and K. Ramaswamy (1986). "The Term Structure of Interest Rates: Empirical Evidence," Unpublished. Graduate School of Business, Stanford University.

Gibbons, M. and T. Sun (1986). "The Term Structure of Interest Rates: A Simple Exposition of the Cox, Ingersoll, and Ross Model," Unpublished. Graduate School of Business, Stanford University.

Gihman, I. and A. Skorohod (1972). *Stochastic Differential Equations*. Berlin: Springer-Verlag.

Gihman, I. and A. Skorohod (1979). *Controlled Stochastic Processes*. Berlin: Springer–Verlag.

Gilbarg, D. and S. Trudinger (1984). *Elliptic Partial Differential Equations of the Second Order (Second Edition)*. New York: Springer–Verlag.

Glicksberg, I. (1952). "A Further Generalization of the Kakutani Fixed Point Theorem, With Application to Nash Equilibrium Points," *Proceedings of the American Mathematics Society*. **3**, pp. 170–174.

Goldman, B., H. Sosin, and M. Gatto (1979). "Path Dependent Options: 'Buy at the Low, Sell at the High'," *Journal of Finance*. **34**, pp. 1111–1127.

Grauer, F. and R. Litzenberger (1979). "The Pricing of Commodity Futures Contracts, Nominal Bonds, and Other Risky Assets under Commodity Price Uncertainty," *Journal of Finance*. **44**, pp. 69–84.

Green, R. and S. Spear (1987). "Equilibria with Incomplete Markets and Overlapping Generations," Unpublished. Graduate School of Industrial Administration, Carnegie–Mellon University.

Grossman, S. and O. Hart (1979). "A Theory of Competitive Equilibrium in Stock Market Economies," *Econometrica*. **47**, pp. 293–330.

Grossman, S. and O. Hart (1987). "One Share/One Vote and the Market for Corporate Control," Unpublished. Department of Economics, Princeton University.

Grossman, S. and G. Laroque (1987). "Asset Pricing and Optimal Portfolio Choice in the Presence of Illiquid Durable Consumption Goods," Unpublished. Department of Economics, Princeton University.

Grossman, S. and J. Stiglitz (1976). "On Stockholder Unanimity in Making Production and Financial Decisions," Technical Report No. 224. Institute for Mathematical Studies in the Social Sciences, Stanford University.

Guesnerie, R. and J.-Y. Jaffray (1974). "Optimality of Equilibrium of Plans, Prices, and Price Expectations." In J. Drèze, *Allocation Under Uncertainty: Equilibrium and Optimality*. New York: Wiley, pp. 70–86.

Hakansson, N. (1970). "Optimal Investment and Consumption Strategies under Risk for a Class of Utility Functions," *Econometrica*. **38**, pp. 587–607.

Haller, H. (1984). "Competition in a Stock Market with Small Firms," Unpublished. University of Mannheim, West Germany.

Halmos, P. (1982) *A Hilbert Space Problem Book (Second Edition)*. New York: Springer–Verlag.

Hansen, L. and S. Richard (1987). "The Role of Conditioning Information in Deducing Testable Restrictions Implied by Dynamic Asset Pricing Models," *Econometrica*. **55**, pp. 587–614.

Hansen, L. and K. Singleton (1982). "Generalized Instrumental Variables Estimation of Nonlinear Rational Expectations Models," *Econometrica*. **50**, pp. 1269–1286.

Hansen, L. and K. Singleton (1983). "Stochastic Consumption, Risk Aversion, and the Temporal Behavior of Asset Returns," *Journal of Political Economy*. **91**, pp. 249–265.

Hansen, L. and K. Singleton (1986) "Efficient Estimation of Linear Asset Pricing Models with Moving Average Errors," Unpublished. Department of Economics, University of Chicago.

Harris, M. (1987). *Dynamic Economic Analysis*. New York: Oxford University Press.

Harris, M. and A. Raviv (1987). "Corporate Governance: Voting Rights and Majority Rules," Working Paper 33. Kellogg School, Northwestern University.

Harrison, J.M. (1982). "Stochastic Calculus and its Applications," Lecture Notes, Graduate School of Business, Stanford University.

Harrison, J.M. (1985). *Brownian Motion and Stochastic Flow Systems*. New York: Wiley.

Harrison, J.M. and D. Kreps (1979). "Martingales and Arbitrage in Multiperiod Securities Markets," *Journal of Economic Theory*. **20**, pp. 381–408.

Harrison, J.M. and S. Pliska (1981). "Martingales and Stochastic Integrals in the Theory of Continuous Trading," *Stochastic Processes and Their Applications*. **11**, pp. 215–260.

Harrison, J.M. and S. Pliska (1983). "A Stochastic Calculus Model of Continuous Trading: Complete Markets," *Stochastic Processes and their Applications*. **15**, pp. 313–316.

Hart, O. (1974). "On The Existence of Equilibria in a Securities Market Model," *Journal of Economic Theory*. **9**, pp. 293–311.

Hart, O. (1975). "On The Optimality of Equilibrium When the Market Structure is Incomplete," *Journal of Economic Theory.* **11**, pp. 418–443.

Hart, O. (1977). "Takeover Bids and Stock Market Equilibrium," *Journal of Economic Theory.* **9**, pp. 53–83.

Hart, O. (1979a). "Monopolistic Competition in a Large Economy with Differentiated Commodities," *Review of Economic Studies.* **46**, pp. 1–30.

Hart, O. (1979b). "On Shareholder Unanimity in Large Stock Market Economies," *Econometrica.* **47**, pp. 1057–1082.

Hart, O. (1987). "Capital Structure as a Control Mechanism in Corporations," Research Paper 441. Department of Economics, Massachusetts Institute of Technology.

Hartigan, J. (1983). *Bayes Theory.* New York: Springer–Verlag.

Heath, D., R. Jarrow, and A. Morton (1987). "Bond Pricing and the Term Structure of Interest Rates: A New Methodology," Unpublished. Cornell University.

Hellwig, M. (1981). "Bankruptcy, Limited Liability, and the Modigliani–Miller Theorem," *American Economic Review.* **71**, pp. 155–170.

Hemler, M. (1987). "The Quality Delivery Option in Treasury Bond Futures Contracts," Unpublished. Graduate School of Business, University of Chicago.

Hestenes, M. (1975). *Optimization Theory: The Finite Dimensional Case.* New York: Wiley.

Hildenbrand, W. (1974). *Core and Equilibria of a Large Economy.* Princeton, New Jersey: Princeton University Press.

Hildenbrand, W. and P. Kirman (1976). *Introduction to Equilibrium Analysis.* Amsterdam: North–Holland Elsevier.

Himmelberg, C., T. Parthasarathy, and F.S. Van Vleck (1976). "Optimal Plans for Dynamic Programming Problems," *Mathematics of Operations Research.* **1**, pp. 390–394.

Ho, T. and S. Lee (1986). "Term Structure Movements and Pricing Interest Rate Contingent Claims," *Journal of Finance.* **41**, pp. 1011–1029.

Holmes, R. (1975). *Geometric Functional Analysis and Its Applications.* New York: Springer–Verlag.

Hotelling, H. (1931). "The Economics of Exhaustible Resources," *Journal of Political Economy.* **39**, pp. 137–175.

Howard, R. (1960). *Dynamic Programming and Markov Processes.* Cambridge, Massachusetts: MIT Press.

Huang, C. (1985a). "Information Structures and Viable Price Systems," *Journal of Mathematical Economics.* **14**, pp. 215–240.

Huang, C. (1985b). "Information Structure and Equilibrium Asset Prices," *Journal of Economic Theory.* **31**, pp. 33–71.

Huang, C. (1987). "An Intertemporal General Equilibrium Asset Pricing Model: The Case of Diffusion Information," *Econometrica.* **55**, pp. 117–142.

Huang, C. and R. Litzenberger (1988). *Foundations for Financial Economics.* (forthcoming) Amsterdam: North–Holland.

Huberman, G. (1982). "A Simple Approach to Arbitrge Pricing Theory," *Journal of Economic Theory.* **28**, pp. 183–191.

Hunt, G. (1966). *Martingales et Processus de Markov*. Paris: Dunod.

Husseini, S., J.-M. Lasry, and M. Magill (1986). "Existence of Equilibrium with Incomplete Markets," Unpublished. Department of Economics, University of Southern California, forthcoming in *Journal of Mathematical Economics*.

Ikeda, N. and S. Watanabe (1981). *Stochastic Differential Equations and Diffusion Processes*. Amsterdam: North-Holland.

Ingersoll, J. (1977). "A Contingent-Claims Valuation of Convertible Securities," *Journal of Financial Economics*. 4, pp. 289–322.

Ingersoll, J. (1987). *Theory of Financial Decision Making*. Totowa, New Jersey: Rowman and Littlefield.

Jacka, S. (1984). "Optimal Consumption of an Investment," *Stochastics*. 13, pp. 45–60.

Jacod, J. (1977). "A General Theorem of Representation for Martingales," *Proceedings of the Symposia in Pure Mathematics*. 31, pp. 37–53.

Jacod, J. (1979). *Calcul Stochastique et Problèmes de Martingales, Lecture Notes in Mathematics No. 714*. Berlin: Springer–Verlag.

Jänich, K. (1984). *Topology*. New York: Springer–Verlag.

Jarrow, R. (1988). *Finance Theory*. Englewood Cliffs, New Jersey: Prentice–Hall.

Jarrow, R. and R. Green (1985). "Spanning and Completeness in Markets with Contingent Claims," Unpublished. Cornell University.

Jensen, M. and W. Meckling (1976). "Theory of the Firm: Managerial Behavior, Agency Costs and Ownership Structure," *Journal of Financial Economics*. 3, pp. 305–360.

Jewitt, I. (1987). "Risk Aversion and the Choice Between Risky Prospects: The Preservation of Comparative Statics Results," *Review of Economic Studies*. 54, pp. 73–85.

Johnson, H. (1985). "Options on The Maximum or the Minimum of Several Assets," Unpublished. University of California, Davis.

Jones, R. and R. Jacobs (1986). "History Dependent Financial Claims: Monte Carlo Valuation," Unpublished. Simon Fraser University.

Kakutani, S. (1941). "A Generalization of Brouwer's Fixed-Point Theorem," *Duke Mathematical Journal*. 8, pp. 451–459.

Kallianpur, G. (1980). *Stochastic Filtering Theory*. New York: Springer–Verlag.

Kandori, M. (1985). "Equivalent Equilibria," Unpublished. Institute for Mathematical Studies in the Social Sciences, Technical Report No. 511, forthcoming in *International Economic Review*.

Karatzas, I. (1987). "Applications of Stochastic Calculus in Financial Economics," Unpublished. Graduate School of Business, Columbia University.

Karatzas, I., J. Lehoczky, S. Sethi, and S. Shreve (1986). "Explicit Solution of a General Consumption/Investment Problem," *Mathematics of Operations Research*. 11, pp. 261–294.

Karatzas, I., J. Lehoczky, and S. Shreve (1986). "Optimal Portfolio and Consumption Decisions for a 'Small Investor' on a Finite Horizon," Technical Report 383. Department of Statistics, Carnegie–Mellon University.

Klein, E. and A. C. Thompson (1984). *Theory of Correspondences—Including Applications to Mathematical Economics.* New York: Wiley.

Kline, D. (1986). "Stock Market Decentralization of a Markov Production Economy," Unpublished. Engineering–Economic Systems Department, Stanford University.

Koopmans, T. (1972). "Representation of Preference Orderings Over Time." In C. McGuire and R. Radner, editors, *Decision and Organization.* Amsterdam: North–Holland.

Kopp, P. (1984). *Martingales and Stochastic Integrals.* Cambridge: Cambridge University Press.

Kozek, A. and Z. Suchanecki (1980). "Multifunctions of Faces for Conditional Expectations of Selectors and Jensen's Inequality," *Journal of Multivariate Analysis.* **10**, pp. 579–598.

Krasa, S. (1987). "Existence of Competitive Equilibria for Option Markets," Research Paper Number 977. Graduate School of Business, Stanford University.

Kraus, A. and R. Litzenberger (1975). "Market Equilibrium in a Multiperiod State Preference Model with Logarithmic Utility," *Journal of Finance.* **30**, pp. 1213–1227.

Kreps, D. (1979). "Three Essays on Capital Markets," Technical Report 298. Institute for Mathematical Studies in The Social Sciences, Stanford University.

Kreps, D. (1981a). "Arbitrage and Equilibrium in Economies with Infinitely Many Commodities," *Journal of Mathematical Economics.* **8**, pp. 15–35.

Kreps, D. (1981b). "Single Person Decision Theory," Lecture Notes. Graduate School of Business, Stanford University.

Kreps, D. (1982). "Multiperiod Securities and the Efficient Allocation of Risk: A Comment on the Black–Scholes Option Pricing Model." In J. McCall, *The Economics of Uncertainty and Information.* Chicago: University of Chicago Press, pp. 203–232.

Krishnan, V. (1984). *Nonlinear Filtering and Smoothing: An Introduction to Martingales, Stochastic Integrals and Estimation.* New York: Wiley.

Krylov, N. (1980). *Controlled Diffusion Processes.* New York: Springer–Verlag.

Kuhn, H. and A. Tucker (1951). "Nonlinear Programming." In J. Neyman, *Second Berkeley Symposium on Mathematical Statisitics and Probability.* Berkeley: University of California Press.

Lang, S. (1969). *Analysis II.* Reading, Massachusetts: Addison–Wesley.

Lehoczky, J. P. and S. Shreve (1986). "Explicit Equilibrium Solutions for a Multi–Agent Consumption/Investment Problem," Technical Report 384. Department of Statistics, Carnegie–Mellon University.

Lehoczky, J. and S. Sethi (1981). "A Comparison of the Ito and Stratonovich Formulation of Problems in Finance," *Journal of Economic Dynamics and Optimal Control.* **3**, pp. 343–356.

Lehoczky, J., S. Sethi, and S. Shreve (1983). "Optimal Consumption and Investment Policies Allowing Consumption Constraints and Bankruptcy," *Mathematics of Operations Research.* **8**, pp. 613–636.

Lehoczky, J., S. Sethi, and S. Shreve (1985). "A Martingale Formulation for Optimal Consumption/Investment Decision Making." **In** G. Feichtinger, *Optimal Control and Economic Analysis 2.* Amsterdam: North–Holland.

Leland, H. (1973). "Capital Asset Markets, Production, and Optimality: A Synthesis," Technical Report 115. Institute for Mathematical Studies in the Social Sciences, Stanford University.

Leland, H. (1974). "Production Theory and The Stock Market," *Bell Journal of Economics and Management Science.* **5**, pp. 125–144.

Leland, H. (1978). "Information, Management Choice, and Stockholder Unanimity," *Review of Economic Studies.* **45**, pp. 527–534.

Leland, H. (1985). "Option Pricing and Replication with Transactions Costs," *Journal of Finance.* **40**, pp. 1283–1301.

Levhari, D. and T. Srinivasan (1969). "Optimal Savings Under Uncertainty," *Review of Economic Studies.* **59**, pp. 153–165.

Levine, D. (1985). "Infinite Horizon Equilibria with Incomplete Markets," Working Paper 418. Economics Department, University of California, Los Angeles.

Lintner, J. (1965). "The Valuation of Risky Assets and the Selection of Risky Investment in Stock Portfolios and Capital Budgets," *Review of Economics and Statistics.* **47**, pp. 13–37.

Lions, P.L. (1981). "Control of Diffusion Processes in R^N," *Communications in Pure and Applied Mathematics.* **34**, pp. 121–147.

Lions, P.L. (1983). "Optimal Control of Diffusion Processes," Unpublished. Université de Paris IX, Dauphine.

Liptser, R. and A. Shiryayev (1977). *Statistics of Random Processes I: General Theory.* New York: Springer–Verlag.

Los, J. and M. Los (1974). *Mathematical Models in Economics.* Amsterdam: North–Holland.

Lucas, R. (1978). "Asset Prices in an Exchange Economy," *Econometrica.* **16**, pp. 1429–1445.

Lucas, R. and E. Prescott (1971). "Investment Under Uncertainty," *Econometrica.* **39**, pp. 659–681.

Lucas, R. and N. Stokey (1987). "Money and Interest in a Cash–in–Advance Economy," *Econometrica.* **55**, pp. 491–514.

Luenberger, D. (1969). *Optimization by Vector Space Methods.* New York: Wiley.

Luenberger, D. (1979). *Introduction to Dynamic Systems.* New York: Wiley.

Luenberger, D. (1984). *Introduction to Linear and Nonlinear Programming (Second Edition).* Reading, Massachusetts: Addison–Wesley.

Machina, M. (1982). "'Expected Utility' Analysis Without the Independence Axiom," *Econometrica.* **50**, pp. 277–323.

Magill, M.J.P. and W. Shafer (1984). "Allocation of Aggregate and Individual Risks Through Futures and Insurance Markets," Unpublished. Department of Economics, University of Southern California.

Magill, M.J.P. and W. Shafer (1985). "Equilibrium and Efficiency in a Canonical Asset Trading Model," Working Paper M8530. Department of Economics, University of Southern California.

Makowski, L. (1983). "Competitve Stock Markets," *Review of Economic Studies.* **50**, pp. 305–330.

Malliaris, A. (1982). *Stochastic Methods in Economics and Finance.* Amsterdam: North–Holland.

Margrabe, W. (1978). "The Value of an Option to Exchange One Asset for Another," *Journal of Finance.* **33**, pp. 177–186.

Marimon, R. (1987). "Kreps' 'Three Essays on Capial Markets' Almost Ten Years Later," Unpublished. Department of Economics, University of Minnesota, forthcoming: *Revista Espanola de Economia.*

Mas–Colell, A. (1985). *The Theory of General Economic Equilibrium—A Differentiable Approach.* Cambridge: Cambridge University Press.

Mas–Colell, A. (1986a). "The Price Equilibrium Existence Problem in Topological Vector Lattices," *Econometrica.* **54**, pp. 1039-1054.

Mas–Colell, A. (1986b). "Valuation Equilibrium and Pareto Optimum Revisited." **In** W. Hildenbrand and A. Mas–Colell, *Contributions to Mathematical Economics.* Amsterdam: North–Holland, pp. 317–332.

Mas–Colell, A. (1987). "An Observation on Geanakoplos and Polemarchakis," Unpublished. Department of Economics, Harvard University.

Mas–Colell, A. and S. Richard (1987). "A New Approach to the Existence of Equilibria in Vector Lattices," Unpublished. Department of Economics, Harvard University.

McKenzie, L. (1954). "On Equilibrium in Graham's Model of World Trade and Other Competitive Systems," *Econometrica.* **22**, pp. 147–161.

McLennan, A. and H. Sonnenschein (1986). "Sequential Bargaining, Simple Markets, and Perfect Competition," Unpublished. Department of Economics, Cornell University.

McManus, D. (1984). "Incomplete Markets: Generic Existence of Equilibrium and Optimality Properties in an Economy with Futures Markets," Unpublished. Department of Economics, University of Pennsylvania.

Mehra, R. (1985). "On The Existence and Representation of Equilibrium in an Economy with Growth and Nonstationary Consumption," Unpublished. Graduate School of Business, Columbia University.

Memin, J. (1980). "Espaces de Semimartingales et Changement de Probabilités," *Zeitschrift für Wahrscheinlichkeitstheorie.* **52**, pp. 9-39.

Merton, R. (1969). "Lifetime Portfolio Selection under Uncertainty: The Continuous Time Case," *Review of Economics and Statistics.* **51**, pp. 247–257.

Merton, R. (1971). "Optimum Consumption and Portfolio Rules in a Continuous Time Model," *Journal of Economic Theory.* **3**, pp. 373–413.

Merton, R. (1973a). "An Intertemporal Capital Asset Pricing Model," *Econometrica.* **41**, pp. 867–888.

Merton, R. (1973b). "Erratum," *Journal of Economic Theory.* **6**, pp. 213–214.

Merton, R. (1973c). "The Theory of Rational Option Pricing," *Bell Journal of Economics and Management Science.* **4**, pp. 141–183.

Merton, R. (1974). "On The Pricing of Corporate Debt: The Risk Structure of Interest Rates," *Journal of Finance.* **29**, pp. 449–470.

Merton, R. (1976). "Option Pricing when the Underlying Stock Returns are Discontinuous," *Journal of Financial Economics.* **5**, pp. 125–144.

Merton, R. (1977). "On the Pricing of Contingent Claims and the Modigliani–Miller Theorem," *Journal of Financial Economics.* **5**, pp. 241–250.

Merton, R. (1982). "On the Microeconomic Theory of Investment under Uncertainty." In K. Arrow and M. Intriligator, *Handbook of Mathematical Economics, Vol. II.* Amsterdam: North–Holland Publishing Company, pp. 601–669.

Merton, R. (1987). "Capital Market Theory and the Pricing of Financial Securities," Working Paper 1818–86. Sloan School of Management, Massachusetts Institute of Technology.

Merton, R. and M. Subrahmanyam (1974). "The Optimality of a Competitive Stock Market," *Bell Journal of Economics and Management Science.* **5**, pp. 145–170.

Meyer, P.-A. (1966). *Probability and Potentials.* Waltham, Massachusetts: Blaisdell.

Meyer, P.-A. (1967). *Processus de Markov.* Lecture Notes in Mathematics Number 26, Berlin: Springer Verlag.

Milne, F. and H. Shefrin (1986). "Information and Securities: A Note on Pareto Dominance and the Second Best," Australian National University.

Mirrlees, J. (1974). "Optimal Accumulation Under Uncertainty: the Case of Stationary Returns to Investment." In J. Drèze, *Allocation Under Uncertainty: Equilibrium and Optimality.* New York: Wiley, pp. 36–50.

Modigliani, F. and M. Miller (1958). "The Cost of Capital, Corporation Finance, and the Theory of Investment," *American Economic Review.* **48**, pp. 261–297.

Mossin, J. (1973). *Theory of Financial Markets.* Englewood Cliffs, New Jersey: Prentice–Hall.

Mulière, P. and M. Scarsini (1987). "A Note on Stochastic Dominance and Inequality Measures," Unpublished. Statistics Department, Stanford University, forthcoming in *Journal of Economic Theory.*

Müller, S. (1983). "On a Characterization of Complete Securities Markets," Research Paper 141. Department of Economics, University of Bonn.

Müller, S. (1984). "On the Valuation of Contingent Claims in Arbitrage Pricing Models," Research Paper 142. Department of Economics, University of Bonn.

Müller, S. (1985). *Arbitrage Pricing of Contingent Claims.* Lecture Notes in Economics and Mathematical Systems, Vol. 254, New York: Springer–Verlag.

Myers, S. (1984). "The Capital Structure Puzzle," *Journal of Finance.* **39**, pp. 575–592.

Myers, S. and N. Majluf (1984). "Corporate Financing and Investment Decisions when Firms Have Information that Investors do not Have," *Journal of Financial Economics.* **13**, pp. 187–221.

Myers, S. and R. Ruback (1987). "Discounting Rules for Risky Assets," Working Paper 1853–87. Sloan School, Massachusetts Institute of Technology.

Nachman, D. (1985). "Arbitrage Operations and Market Expansion," Unpublished. College of Management, Georgia Institute of Technology.

Nermuth, M. (1985). "General Equilibrium with Futures Trading," Working Paper 8502. Department of Economics, University of Vienna.

Nermuth, M. (1987). "Futures Markets, Information Structures, and the Allocation of Resources," *European Economic Review.* **31**, pp. 226–234.

Neumann, J. von (1937). "Über ein ökonomisches Gleichungssystem und eine Verallgemeinerung des Brouwerschen Fixpunktsatzes," *Ergebnisse eines mathematischen Kolloquiums.* **8**, pp. 73–78. English Translation: *Review of Economic Studies.* **13**, pp. 1–9.

Neumann, J. von and O. Morgenstern (1947). *Theory of Games and Economic Behavior (Second Edition).* Princeton, New Jersey: Princeton University Press.

Nielsen, L. (1985). "Preference Structure and Equilibrium in The Classical Capital Asset Pricing Model," Unpublished. Department of Finance, University of Texas at Austin.

Nielsen, L. (1986). "Mutual Fund Separation, Factor Structure and Robustness," Unpublished. Department of Finance, University of Texas at Austin.

Nielsen, L. (1987). "Equilibrium in CAPM Without a Riskless Asset," Working Paper 87/88–2–3. Department of Finance, University of Texas at Austin.

O'Nan, M. (1976). *Linear Algebra (Second Edition).* New York: Harcourt Brace Jovanovich.

Ohashi, K. (1987). "On Security Prices at the Terminal Date in a Continuous Time Trading with Dividends Model," Unpublished. Hitosubashi University.

Oksendal, B. (1985). *Stochastic Differential Equations.* Berlin: Springer–Verlag.

Pagès, H. (1987). "Optimal Consumption and Portfolio Policies when Markets are Incomplete," Unpublished. Department of Economics, Massachusetts Institute of Technology.

Parkinson, M. (1977). "Option Pricing: The American Put," *Journal of Business.* **50**, pp. 21–36.

Parthasarathy, K. (1967). *Probability Measures on Metric Spaces.* New York: Academic Press.

Perlman, M. (1974). "Jensen's Inequality for a Convex Vector–Valued Function on an Infinite–Dimensional Space," *Journal of Multivariate Analysis.* **4**, pp. 52–65.

Phelps, E. (1962). "The Accumulation of Risky Capital: A Sequential Utility Analysis," *Econometrica.* **30**, pp. 729–745.

Pliska, S. (1982). "A Stochastic Calculus Model of Continuous Trading: Return Processes and Investment Plans," Research Paper 517. Center for Mathematical Studies in Economics and Management Science, Northwestern University.

Pliska, S. (1986). "A Stochastic Calculus Model of Continuous Trading: Optimal Portfolios," *Mathematics of Operations Research.* **11**, pp. 371–382.

Polemarchakis, H. (1986). "Portfolio Choice, Exchange Rates and Indeterminacy," Unpublished. Graduate School of Business, Columbia University.

Polemarchakis, H. and B. Ku (1986). "Options and Equilibrium," Unpublished. Graduate School of Business, Columbia University.

Prescott, E. and R. Mehra (1980). "Recursive Competitive Equilibrium: The Case of Homogeneous Households," *Econometrica.* **48**, pp. 1365–1379.

Prisman, E. (1985). "Valuation of Risky Assets in Arbitrage Free Economies with Frictions," Unpublished. University of Arizona.

Radner, R. (1967). "Equilibre des Marchés a Terme et au Comptant en Cas d'Incertitude," *Cahiers d'Econométrie*. **4**, pp. 35–52.

Radner, R. (1972). "Existence of Equilibrium of Plans, Prices and Price Expectations in a Sequence of Markets," *Econometrica*. **40**, pp. 289–303.

Radner, R. (1974). "A Note on Unanimity of Stockholders' Preferences Among Alternative Production Plans: A Reformulation of the Ekern–Wilson Model," *The Bell Journal of Economics and Management Science*. **5**, pp. 181–186.

Raikov, D. (1965). *Vector Spaces*. Groningen, The Netherlands: P. Noordhoff Ltd.

Reed, M. and B. Simon (1980). *Methods of Modern Mathematical Physics, Volume I: Functional Analysis (Revised and Enlarged Edition)*. New York: Academic Press.

Reisman, H. (1986). "Option Pricing for Stocks with a Generalized Log–Normal Price Distribution," Unpublished. Department of Finance, University of Minnesota.

Repullo, R. (1986). "On The Generic Existence of Radner Equilibria when there are as Many Securities as States of Nature," *Economics Letters*. **21**, pp. 101–105.

Revuz, D. (1975). *Markov Chains*. Amsterdam: North–Holland.

Richard, S. (1975). "Optimal Consumption, Portfolio, and Life Insurance Rules for an Uncertain Lived Individual in a Continuous Time Model," *Journal of Financial Economics*. **2**, pp. 187–203.

Richard, S. (1978). "An Arbitrage Model of the Term Structure of Interest Rates," *Journal of Financial Economics*. **6**, pp. 33–57.

Richard, S. (1979). "A Generalized Capital Asset Pricing Model." In E. Elton and M. Gruber, *Portfolio Theory, 25 Years After, TIMS Studies in The Management Sciences 11*. The Institute of Management Sciences, pp. 215–232.

Richard, S. (1985). "Prices in Banach Lattices with Convex Preferences," Unpublished. Graduate School of Industrial Administration, Carnegie–Mellon University.

Richard, S. (1986). "Competitive Equilibria in Riesz Spaces," Unpublished. Graduate School of Industrial Administration, Carnegie–Mellon University.

Richard, S. (1987). "A New Approach to Production Equilibria in Vector Lattices," Unpublished. Graduate School of Industrial Administration, Carnegie–Mellon University.

Richard, S. and W. Zame (1986). "Proper Preferences and Quasi–Concave Utility Functions," *Journal of Mathematical Economics*. **15**, pp. 231–247.

Richardson, H. (1987). "A Minimum Variance Result in Continuous Trading Portfolio Optimization," Unpublished. U.S. Naval Academy, Center for Naval Analysis.

Robertson, A.P. and W.J. Robertson (1973). *Topological Vector Spaces (Second Edition)*. Cambridge: Cambridge University Press.

Rockafellar, R.T. (1970). *Convex Analysis*. Princeton, New Jersey: Princeton University Press.

Ross, S.A. (1976a). "The Arbitrage Theory of Capital Asset Pricing," *Journal of Economic Theory*. **13**, pp. 341–360.

Ross, S.A. (1976b). "Options and Efficiency," *Quarterly Journal of Economics*. **90**, pp. 75–89.

Ross, S.A. (1978). "A Simple Approach to the Valuation of Risky Streams," *Journal of Business*. **51**, pp. 453–475.

Ross, S.A. (1987). "Arbitrage and Martingales with Taxation," *Journal of Political Economy.* **95**, pp. 371–393.

Ross, S.M. (1980). *Introduction to Probability Models (Second Edition).* New York: Academic Press.

Ross, S.M. (1983). *Introduction to Stochastic Dynamic Programming.* New York: Academic Press.

Rothschild, M. (1986). "Asset Pricing Theories." **In** W. Heller and D. Starrett, *Uncertainty, Information and Communication—Essays in Honor of Kenneth J. Arrow, Volume III.* Cambridge: Cambridge University Press, pp. 97–128.

Rothschild, M. and J. Stiglitz (1970). "Increasing Risk: I. A Definition," *Journal of Economic Theory.* **2**, pp. 225–243.

Rothschild, M. and J. Stiglitz (1971). "Increasing Risk II: Its Economic Consequences," *Journal of Economic Theory.* **3**, pp. 66–84.

Rothschild, M. and J. Stiglitz (1972). "Addendum to 'Increasing Risk: I. A Definition'," *Journal of Economic Theory.* **5**, pp. 306.

Royden, H. (1968). *Real Analysis (Second Edition).* New York: Macmillan.

Rubinstein, M. (1974a). "A Discrete–Time Synthesis of Financial Theory," Working Paper 20. School of Business, University of California, Berkeley.

Rubinstein, M. (1974b). "An Aggregation Theorm for Securities Markets," *Journal of Financial Economics.* **1**, pp. 225–244.

Rubinstein, M. (1976). "The Valuation of Uncertain Income Streams and The Pricing of Options," *Bell Journal of Economics.* **7**, pp. 407–425.

Rudin, W. (1973). *Functional Analysis.* New York: McGraw–Hill.

Samuelson, P. (1958). "An Exact Consumption Loan Model of Interest with or without the Social Contrivance of Money," *Journal of Political Economy.* **66**, pp. 467–482.

Samuelson, P. (1969). "Lifetime Portfolio Selection by Dynamic Stochastic Programming," *Review of Economics and Statistics.* **51**, pp. 239–246.

Sargent, T. (1985). "Dynamic Macroeconomic Theory," Lecture Notes. Department of Economics, University of Minnesota.

Satterthwaite, M. (1981). "On the Scope of the Stockholder Unanimity Theorems," *International Economic Review.* **22**, pp. 119–133.

Scarsini, M. (1986). "Comparison of Random Cash Flows," *IMA Journal of Mathematics in Management.* **1**, pp. 25–32.

Schaefer, H. (1971). *Topological Vector Spaces.* New York: Springer–Verlag.

Schaefer, H. (1974). *Banach Lattices and Positive Operators.* Berlin: Springer–Verlag.

Schäl, M. (1975). "Conditions for Optimality in Dynamic Programming and for the Limit of n–Stage Optimal Policies to be Optimal," *Zeitschrift Wahrscheinlichkeitstheorie.* **32**, pp. 179–196.

Scheinkman, J. and L. Weiss (1984). "Borrowing Constraints and Aggregate Economic Activity," Technical Report 445. Institute for Mathematical Studies in the Social Sciences, Stanford University.

Sethi, S., N. Derzko, and J. Lehoczky (1982). "Mathematical Analysis of the Miller–Modigliani Theory," *Operations Research Letters.* **1**, pp. 148-152.

Sethi, S., N. Derzko, and J. Lehoczky (1984). "General Solution of the Stochastic Price–Dividend Integral Equation: A Theory of Financial Valuation," *SIAM Journal of Mathematical Analysis.* **15**, pp. 1100–1113.

Sethi, S. and M. Taksar (1986). "A Note on Merton's 'Optimum Consumption and Portfolio Rules in a Continuous–Time Model'," Unpublished. University of Toronto, forthcoming in *Journal of Economic Theory.*

Shafer, W. (1984). "Representation of Preorders on Normed Spaces," Unpublished. Department of Economics, University of Southern California.

Shafer, W. and H. Sonnenschein (1975). "Equilibrium in Abstract Economies Without Ordered Preferences," *Journal of Mathematical Economics.* **2**, pp. 345–348.

Shah, S. and A. Thakor (1987). "Optimal Capital Structure and Project Financing," *Journal of Economic Theory.* **42**, pp. 209–243.

Sharpe, W. (1964). "Capital Asset Prices: A Theory of Market Equilibrium Under Conditions of Risk," *Journal of Finance.* **19**, pp. 425–442.

Sharpe, W. (1981). "Factor Models, The Arbitrage Pricing Theory and Capital Asset Pricing Models," Unpublished. Graduate School of Business, Stanford University.

Sharpe, W. (1985). *Investments (Third Edition).* Englewood Cliffs, New Jersey: Prentice–Hall.

Shefrin, H. (1981). "Transaction Costs, Uncertainty and Generally Inactive Futures Markets," *Review of Economic Studies.* **48**, pp. 131–137.

Shreve, S. and D. Bertsekas (1979). "Universally Measurable Policies in Dynamic Programming," *Mathematics of Operations Research.* **4**, pp. 15–30.

Siconolfi, P. (1986). "Equilibrium with Restricted Participation on Incomplete Financial Markets," Working Paper 86–03R. Center for Analytic Research in Economics and the Social Sciences, University of Pennsylvania.

Singleton, K. (1987). "Specification and Estimation of Intertemporal Asset Pricing Models," Research Paper 964. Graduate School of Business, Stanford University.

Smart, D. (1980). *Fixed Point Theorems.* Cambridge University Press.

Spear, S., S. Srivastava, and M. Woodford (1986). "On the Structure of Equilibrium in Stochastic Overlapping Generations Models," Unpublished. Carnegie–Mellon University.

Stapleton, R. and M. Subrahmanyam (1978). "A Multiperiod Equilibrium Asset Pricing Model," *Econometrica.* **46**, pp. 1077–1093.

Stiglitz, J. (1972). "On the Optimality of the Stock Market Allocation of Investment," *Quarterly Journal of Economics.* **86**, pp. 25–60.

Stiglitz, J. (1974). "On The Irrelevence of Corporate Financial Policy," *American Economic Review.* **64**, pp. 851–866.

Stiglitz, J. (1982). "The Inefficiency of the Stock Market Equilibrium," *Review of Economic Studies.* **49**, pp. 241–261.

Stricker, C. (1984). "Integral Representation in the Theory of Continuous Trading," *Stochastics.* **13**, pp. 249–265.

Stroock, D. (1987). *Lectures on Stochastic Analysis: Diffusion Theory.* Cambridge: Cambridge University Press.

Stroock, D. and S.R.S. Varadhan (1979). *Multidimensional Diffusion Processes*. New York: Springer–Verlag.

Sun, T. (1986). "Martingale Representation of the Security Markets," Unpublished. Graduate School of Business, Stanford University.

Sundaresan, S. (1985). "Intertemporally Dependent Preferences in the Theories of Consumption, Portfolio Choice and Equilibrium Asset Pricing," Unpublished. Graduate School of Business, Columbia University.

Tauchen, G. (1986). "Quadrature–Based Methods for Obtaining Approximate Solutions to the Integral Equations of Nonlinear Rational Expectations Models," Unpublished. Economics Department, Duke University.

Ting, O.T. and K.W. Yip (1975). "A Generalized Jensen's Inequality," *Pacific Journal of Mathematics*. **58**, pp. 255–259.

Varian, H. (1984). *Microeconomic Analysis (Second Edition)*. New York: Norton.

Wald, A. (1936). "Über eine Gleichungssysteme der Mathematischen Ökonomie," *Zeitschrift für Nationalökonomie*. **7**, pp. 637–670. English Translation: *Econometrica*, **19**, (1951), pp. 368–403.

Wald, A. (1950). *Statistical Decision Functions*. New York: Wiley.

Walras, L. (1874–1877). *Eléments d'économie politique pure (Fourth Edition)*. Lausanne: L. Corbaz, English Translation of the definitive edition by W. Jaffé (1954), *Elements of Pure Economics*, London: Allen and Unwin.

Werner, J. (1985a). "Arbitrage and the Existence of Competitive Equilibrium," Research Paper A–2. Department of Economics, University of Bonn, forthcoming in *Econometrica*.

Werner, J. (1985b). "Equilibrium in Economies with Incomplete Financial Markets," *Journal of Economic Theory*. **36**, pp. 110–119.

Werner, J. (1986). "Asset Prices and Real Indeterminacy in Equilibrium with Financial Markets," Unpublished. Department of Economics, University of Bonn.

Werner, J. (1987). "Structure of Financial Markets and Real Indeterminacy of Equilibria," Working Paper B–80. Department of Economics, University of Bonn.

Wiesmeth, H. (1987). "Complete Markets," Unpublished. Department of Economics, University of Bonn.

Williams, D. (1979). *Diffusions, Markov Processes and Martingales, Vol. 1*. New York: Wiley.

Yannelis, N. and W. Zame (1986). "Equilibria in Banach Lattices Without Ordered Preferences," *Journal of Mathematical Economics*. **15**, pp. 85–110.

Younes, Y. (1986). "Competitive Equilibrium for Incomplete Market Structures," Unpublished. Centre d' Etudes Prospectives d'Economie Mathématique Appliquées à la Planification, Paris, France.

Zame, W. (1987). "Equilibria in Production Economies with an Infinite–Dimensional Commodity Space," *Econometrica*. **55**, pp. 1075–1108.

AUTHOR INDEX

A

Aase, A., 291
Aghion, P., 130
Allen, F., 130
Araujo, A., 101, 320
Arnold, L., 231
Arrow, K., 25, 49, 50, 93, 116, 130, 154, 168
Aumann, R., 49
Avondo-Bodino, G., 116

B

Bachelier, L., 290
Back, K., 291
Balasko, Y., 117
Bartle, R., 55, 147
Bellman, R., 201
Benveniste, L., 219
Berge, C., 201
Bertsekas, D., 182, 201
Bewley, T., 49
Billingsley, P., 264, 265
Black, F., 26, 101, 154
Blackwell, D., 201
Blume, L., 201
Bolton, P., 130
Bourgin, R., 89
Boyd, J., 291
Boyle, P., 265
Bracewell, R., 264
Breeden, D., 130, 320
Brock, W., 219
Brown, D., 117
Burke, J., 129

C

Carr, P., 264
Cass, D., 116, 117, 220
Chae, S., 117
Chamberlain, G., 26, 101, 320
Cheng, S., 264
Chow, Y., 55
Chung, K., 55, 138, 147, 231
Clarke, F., 81
Connor, G., 90, 101
Constantinides, G., 291, 320
Cox, J., 26, 264, 265, 273, 291, 320

D

Davis, M., 291
Day, M., 35, 67, 74
Debreu, G., 39, 49, 50, 116, 117
Dekel, E., 60
Dellacherie, C., 138, 147, 231
DeMarzo, P., 129
Diamond, P., 129
Donaldson, J., 220
Dothan, M., 321
Drèze, J., 129, 130
Durrett, R., 138, 147, 231
Dynkin, E., 201, 232

E

Easley, D., 201
Ekern, S., 129
Elliott, R., 231, 232, 273
Epstein, L., 155

345

SYMBOL GLOSSARY

349

R^N, 29

$X \cap Y$, xviii

$X = \{X_t : t \in \mathcal{T}\}$, 131

$x \mapsto f(x)$, xviii

$x \succ y$, 35

$x > 0$, 71

$x \geq 0$, 71

$x \gg 0$, 71

$x \perp y$, 64

$x \sim y$, 35

$x \succeq y$, 35

x^+, 53

x^-, 53

$x^\top y$, 32

$x^{-1}(A)$, 51

$x_n \to x$, 31

$[p; \alpha]$, 47

$[S]$, 141

$\#\xi$, 104

$\{x_n\}$, 31

ΔX_t, 135

$\Delta \theta(\xi)$, 107

$\mathcal{D}$, 226

$\mathcal{I}$, 39

$\mathcal{J}$, 39

$\mathcal{P}$, 140

$\mathcal{T}$, 130

$\mathrm{cov}(x, y)$, 63

$\mathrm{rank}(\cdot)$, 110

$\mathrm{span}(A)$, 67

$\mathrm{var}(x)$, 63

$\mathrm{core}(X)$, 37

$\mathrm{icr}(Z)$, 46

$\mathrm{int}(X)$, 30

$\mathrm{tr}(D)$, 223

$\int \sigma(X_t, t)\, dB_t$, 225

$\int \theta\, dS$, 139, 143

$\int_0^t \theta_\tau^2\, d[S]_\tau$,

$\int_B x\, dP$, 55

$\int_\Omega x\, dP$, 53

$_P\!\int \theta\, dS$, 146

$\Longleftrightarrow$, xviii

$\Longrightarrow$, xviii

$\lim_{\alpha \downarrow \beta} f(\alpha)$, xviii

$\nabla u_i(x)$, 5

$\|\cdot\|$, 29

$\|\cdot\|_\infty$, 62

$\|\cdot\|_*$, 34

$\|\cdot\|_q$, 61

$\|\cdot\|_S$, 142

$\|\cdot\|_{\mathcal{M}^2}$, 142

$\partial f(x)$, 79

$\prod_{n=1}^N X_n$, 33

$\psi \,\square\, x$, 106

$\sigma(\mathcal{A})$, 52

$\sim Y$, 204

$\spadesuit$, xix

$\succ$, 35

$\succeq$, 35

$\gg$, 71

$\mathcal{E}_{az}(f)$, 188

$\mathcal{L}$, 61

$\mathcal{L}(\cdot, \lambda_0)$, 76

$\mathcal{P}(B)$, 172

$\overline{X}$, 30

SUBJECT INDEX

351